Urban Policy in Latin America

This book evaluates the impact of 20 years of urban policies in six Latin American countries: Argentina, Brazil, Chile, Colombia, Ecuador and Mexico. It argues that evaluating the fulfillment of past commitments is essential for framing and meeting the new commitments that were made in Habitat III over the next 20 years.

Taken as a whole, the book provides a critical assessment of the economic, social and environmental consequences of urban interventions during Habitat II. The country-level chapters have been written by recognized experts in urban issues, with firsthand knowledge of the Habitat process and deep familiarity with the problems, statistics, actors and political contexts of their nations. The latter part of the volume considers wider topics such as the Habitat Commitment Index, the New Urban Agenda and the regional- and global-scale lessons that can be extracted from this group of countries.

Urban Policy in Latin America will be of interest to advanced students, researchers and policymakers across development economics, urban studies and Latin American studies.

Michael Cohen is Director of the doctoral program in Public and Urban Policy, Professor of International Affairs and was Founding Director of the Graduate Program in International Affairs from The New School University in New York. He is also Co-director of the Observatory on Latin America (OLA). He has written extensively on development policy, urban development, Africa and Argentina. He has participated actively in international urban policy debates since the Habitat I Conference in 1976.

María Carrizosa is Coordinator of the Observatory of Latin America and a PhD candidate in Public and Urban Policy at The New School. She teaches graduate and undergraduate courses in public and private universities in New York. She is an architect and philosopher, with an MS in International Affairs and has postgraduate studies in Geography. Her doctoral research analyzes labor informality from a spatial lens.

Margarita Gutman has a PhD in Architecture from the University of Buenos Aires (UBA). She is a Professor of Urban Studies and International Affairs and co-director of the Observatory on Latin American (OLA) at The New School in New York. She is Profesora Consulta and member of the Doctoral Commission at the School of Architecture, Design and Urbanism, UBA. She is author, co-author or editor of 19 books on urban history, urban anticipations, political mobilization, architectural history, urban policy and neoliberal transitions, among other topics.

T0382805

Routledge Studies in Development Economics

For more information about this series, please visit: www.routledge.com/series/SE0266

Urban Policy in Latin America

Towards the Sustainable Development Goals?

**Edited by Michael Cohen,
María Carrizosa and Margarita Gutman**

LONDON AND NEW YORK

First published 2020
by Routledge
2 Park Square, Milton Park, Abingdon, Oxon OX14 4RN

and by Routledge
605 Third Avenue, New York, NY 10017

First issued in paperback 2021

Routledge is an imprint of the Taylor & Francis Group, an informa business

British Library Cataloguing-in-Publication Data
A catalogue record for this book is available from the British Library

Library of Congress Cataloging-in-Publication Data
A catalog record for this book has been requested

ISBN 13: 978-0-367-78496-6 (pbk)
ISBN 13: 978-0-367-13699-4 (hbk)

Typeset in Bembo
by Apex CoVantage, LLC

Contents

Illustrations

Maps

Tables

Contributors

Fernando Carrión is an academic at the Latin American School of Social Sciences FLACSO – Ecuador. He is also President of the Organization of Historical Centers in Latin America and the Caribbean (OLACCHI). Fernando has been a council member of the Metropolitan District of Quito, Director of FLACSO-Ecuador, international consultant, and columnist for the newspaper *Diario Hoy*. His areas of expertise are historical centers, security in cities, urban policy, local development, development policies and urban planning.

María Carrizosa is Coordinator of the Observatory of Latin America and a PhD candidate in Public and Urban Policy at The New School. She is adjunct professor at The New School and at the City University of New York. She is an architect and philosopher, with an MS in International Affairs and has postgraduate studies in Geography. María has 15 years of professional experience, including positions in the public sector; international organizations; and nongovernmental organizations (NGOs) in Colombia, Mexico, Kazakhstan, Uganda and the United States. Her experience as a consultant includes projects with the World Bank, IFC, UNDP, the Spanish Agency for International Cooperation (AECID) and the Latin American Development Bank (CAF). Her doctoral research analyzes labor informality from a spatial lens.

Andrea Catenazzi is an architect specializing in planning and management of urban policies from the University of Buenos Aires (UBA). She has a PhD in Geography and Urban Development from the University of the Sorbonne, Paris 3. She was an Associate Professor and Coordinator of the Urbanism Area of the Conurbano Institute (ICO) at the National University of General Sarmiento (UNGS). Currently, she is a postgraduate professor in politics and urban planning at national universities, including UNGS, UBA, Mar del Plata National University, La Plata National University and Tres de Febrero National University. She coordinates interdisciplinary teams of planning with special emphasis on the territorial analysis of public policies. She participates internationally in different management and academic spaces in areas related to urban research and education (UNESCO, IDB, EPFL). She is the author of several book chapters and articles in specialized journals.

Michael Cohen is Director of the doctoral program in Public and Urban Policy, Professor of International Affairs, Founding Director of the Graduate Program in International Affairs, Director of the Doctoral Program in Public and Urban Policy, as well as Co-director of the Observatory on Latin American (OLA) at The New School University in New York. He worked at the World Bank between 1972 and 1999, where he was responsible for formulating most of the bank's urban policy. He worked in 55 countries and was Head of the Urban Development Division. He has written extensively on development policy, urban development, Africa and Argentina, including two books: *Argentina's Economic Growth and Recovery* and the volume edition, *The Global Economic Crisis in Latin America: Impacts and Responses*. He was a member of the National Academy of Sciences of the United States in the panels of Infrastructure and Urban Demographic Dynamics. He has participated actively in international urban policy debates since the Habitat I Conference in 1976.

Michelle DePass holds a bachelor's degree from Tufts University, a Juris Doctor from Fordham Law School, an honorary doctorate from Fordham University and a Master of Public Administration from Baruch College, where she was a National Urban Fellow. Michelle was an early leader in the environmental justice movement and has had a career in governmental, academic, philanthropic and nonprofit arenas. She served in the Obama administration as assistant administrator of the U.S. Environmental Protection Agency, as a program officer at the Ford Foundation. From 2013 to 2018, DePass was dean of the Milano School of International Affairs, Management and Urban Policy and Tishman Professor of Environmental Policy and Management at the New School. Currently, she is the president and chief executive officer of Meyer Memorial Trust.

Edesio Fernandes is a lawyer from the Federal University of Minas, an urban planner with a master's degree in law and a PhD from the University of Warwick. Edesio is a lecturer and associate professor of the DPU at the University of London, the Institute of Urban Development IHS of the Netherlands and the Lincoln Land Institute in Cambridge, New York University, as well as three universities in Brazil. He is the founder and coordinator of IRGLUS, the International Research Group on Law and Urban Space, associated with UN-Habitat. His subjects of major interest are urban land, urban and environmental law, urban planning, governance and metropolitan administration, regularization, the Right to the City movement and human and constitutional rights.

Margarita Gutman holds a doctorate and is an architect from the University of Buenos Aires. She is Professor of Urban Studies and International Affairs, and Co Director of the Observatory on Latin America (OLA) at The New School. She is also Profesora Consulta and member of the Doctoral Commission of the School of Architecture, Design, and Urban Planning at the University of Buenos Aires (FADU-UBA). From 2004 to 2009, she has been Full Professor and holder of a Chair (Cátedra) of History of

Architecture and Cities at FADU-UBA. She is author, co-author or editor of 19 books on urban history, urban anticipations, political mobilization, architectural history, urban policy, and neoliberal transitions, among other topics. She was a Scholar at The Getty Research Institute and at the Woodrow Wilson International Center, Fellow at the International Center for Advanced Studies of New York University, and Senior Fellow at the Vera List Center for Art and Politics, The New School.

Martha Susana Jaimes is a PhD candidate in the Public and Urban Policy program at The New School in New York and an economist and Master of Economics at the Universidad de Los Andes in Bogotá, Colombia. She was a fellow at the Latin American Observatory of The New School and was a researcher at the Global Urban Futures Project, and is currently a researcher at the Schwartz Center for Economic Policy Analysis of The New School. Martha has served as an advisor to the Secretary of Economic Development for CONFIS and as deputy director of Strategic Studies within the same entity. Previously, she worked as research assistant at CEDE of the Faculty of Economics of the Universidad de Los Andes. Her teaching experience includes courses in the area of history of economic thought, economic history and macroeconomics at universities such as Los Andes, Jorge Tadeo Lozano, and the New York University (NYU).

Agustín Manuel Mango is an architect with experience in habitat issues and urban policies. He is a PhD student in Geography and Cartography at University of Buenos Aires (UBA). Mango is assistant professor at UBA's Architecture School and holds a Fellowship from the Argentinian National Scientific and Technical Research Council (CONICET). He has worked at the Buenos Aires Legislature following the Commission for Urban Planning, Housing, Public Works and Transport and as a cartographer at the Chaco provincial government.

Jorge Enrique Torres Ramírez is an Economist specialized in Latin American Land Markets and Policies and in Social Economy. Since 1974 he has been linked to CENAC, the Center for Construction and Urban and Regional Development Studies in Colombia, which he has directed for over 20 years. Jorge is a researcher, advisor and consultant, with vast experience in territorial planning, urban development, urban indicators, housing deficit, poverty, housing and habitat quality assessment, real estate markets, among others. He has been a consultant for the Inter-American Development Bank, the United Nations Development Program, UN-Habitat, USAID, GTZ and many national and local government agencies in Colombia and in other countries.

Eduardo Reese is an architect specializing in urban and regional planning. He is the Director of the Economic and Social Rights Area of CELS, the Center for Legal and Social Studies in Buenos Aires, and a teacher of the Territorial Development Workshop at the National University of General

Sarmiento (UNGS). He is also a graduate-level professor at the Universities of Buenos Aires, La Plata, Mar del Plata and Córdoba, and coordinates the professional development course on "Land Management in Large Urban Projects" of the Lincoln Institute of Land Policy. Eduardo has been a technical advisor to the master plans of more than 20 cities in Argentina, Deputy Administrator of the Housing Institute, Secretary of Socioeconomic Policies of the Ministry of Human Development of the Province of Buenos Aires, Counselor at the Urban Planning Council of the city of Buenos Aires and Secretary of Planning of the city of Avellaneda.

Alfredo Rodríguez is an urban planner with a degree in City Planning from Yale. He has been working at SUR Professional Consultants since 1978. He is currently a member of the National Council for Urban Development for the government of Chile. Alfredo is the author of dozens of books and articles on urban policy, social housing and gender violence in cities.

Paula Rodríguez holds a PhD in Social Sciences from the University of Buenos Aires. She works at SUR Professional Consultants. She is a co-editor and author of books and articles on urban space production and urban policy.

Lena Simet is a teaching fellow at the New School University in New York and a doctoral candidate in Public and Urban Policy. Lena is the lead researcher and coordinator of the Global Urban Futures Project at the New School, as part of which she steered the design of the Habitat Commitment Index, a quantitative tool used to assess country performance in fulfilling international urban-related goals. Lena taught as an Adjunct Professor at the City University of New York, and has worked in different capacities in Argentina, Kazakhstan, Mexico and Uganda on urban projects with the CAF, UNDP and GIZ. Lena has written chapters and articles on housing and urban issues, published by Cambridge University Press, Rowman & Littlefield, the *Housing Studies Journal* and *Environment and Urbanization*.

Alexandra Velasco is an ecologist by profession and holds a master's in infrastructure planning from the University of Stuttgart. She is a specialist in sustainable mobility, traffic engineering and transportation planning. She was co-founder of *Ciclopaseo* in Quito in 2003 and an activist for the rights of pedestrians and cyclists. She has worked in the municipality of Quito as coordinator of non-motorized transport and in the Ministry of Sports as National Director of Recreation. She is an author and co-author of several articles, research studies and consultancies related to mobility, traffic studies and transport with a human scale. She is currently working with a German cooperation agency in the preparation of the Sustainable Intermediate Cities program.

Mary Watson is the Executive Dean of the Schools of Public Engagement. In this capacity, she leads the founding division of The New School with the aim of advancing its innovative approaches to action oriented, engaged learning in the world. She is co-founder of The New School's university-wide Social Innovation Initiative and Impact Entrepreneurship Initiative, which includes The New School Collaboratory, a Rockefeller Foundation-funded initiative on university community partnerships. Watson is also the recipient of The New School's Distinguished University Teaching Award. Watson is a leader in university networks advancing change in higher education, including the Critical Edge Alliance and the Ashoka Changemaker campus initiative. She earned her PhD in organization studies from Vanderbilt University.

Alicia Ziccardi is a researcher at the Institute of Social Research and Director of the Program of Studies on the City (PUEC) at the Universidad Nacional Autónoma de Mexico (UNAM). She is a member of the National System of Researchers and the Mexican Academy of Sciences, and professor of the Postgraduate Programs in Urbanism and Political and Social Sciences of the UNAM. Ziccardi is the coordinator of URBARED and the CONACYT Thematic Network on Historical Centers of Mexican Cities. She is also a member of the Economic and Social Council of Mexico City and the author and coordinator of numerous books, chapters and articles on urban poverty, social exclusion, urban and housing policies, citizen participation, governance and local development.

Acknowledgments

This book has been prepared in two steps. A Spanish version was written and published during 2016 for the Habitat III Conference. We wish to thank the authors of the six country chapters of this book for agreeing to "travel with us" from Habitat II to Habitat III by focusing on a critical evaluation of the progress in each of their countries: Eduardo Reese, Andrea Catenazzi, Fernando Carrión, Edesio Fernandes, Alfredo Rodríguez, Paula Rodríguez, Jorge Enrique Torres Ramírez, Alexandra Velasco and Alicia Ziccardi. We are grateful to their teams and the institutions they represent: the National University of General Sarmiento and the Center for Economic, Social and Cultural Rights (CELS) of Argentina; the Department Planning Unit (DPU) of University College London (UCL) in England; the South Corporation of Social and Education Studies (SUR) of Chile; the Center of Studies of the Construction and the Urban and Regional Development (CENAC) of Colombia; the Latin American Faculty of Social Sciences (FLACSO) of Ecuador; and the University Program of Studies on the City (PUEC-UNAM) of Mexico.

In particular, we appreciate the significant support during 2015–2017 from the Ford Foundation, which enabled the development of the Global Urban Futures Project and its collaboration with the New School's Observatory on Latin America (OLA). The substantive contributions and institutional orientations of Don Chen and Ana Marie Arilagos were crucial in establishing this partnership in the preparations for Habitat III.

We warmly thank Michelle DePass, then Dean of the Milano School of International Affairs, Management and Urban Policy, who provided leadership in the launch of this initiative and the continuing support of Mary Watson, Executive Dean of the New School for Public Engagement.

We are grateful for the support of the CAF – the Development Bank of Latin America – for its support of the discussion of this book during its preparation in Buenos Aires in July 2016. In particular, we thank José Carrera, then Vice-President of Social Development; Hely Olivares, Executive of the Vice-Presidency of Social Development; and Pablo López, Senior Executive in Argentina.

We wish to thank the faculty of Architecture, Design and Urbanism of the University of Buenos Aires (FADU-UBA) for collaborating in a public conference in July 2016, "Latin American Urban Dialogues: From Habitat II to Habitat III" on the book. We thank its leadership, including Luis Bruno, then Dean; Ariel Misuraca, Secretary-General; Marcelo Lorelli, Secretary of Communication and Student Policies; Ariel Pradelli, Operating Secretary; and Guillermo Cabrera, Secretary of Academic Affairs.

We would like to thank Lena Simet, coordinator of the Global Urban Futures Project, who led the work of the Habitat Commitment Index (HCI), and the many graduate students whose collaborative work on the HCI created a productive atmosphere for undertaking an evaluation of the results of Habitat II. Ileana Versace of the International Programs Department of the UBA FADU and coordinator of the OLA in Buenos Aires also supported this process. We thank Marcelo Corti, our colleague and editor of *Café de las Ciudades*, for so effectively managing the Spanish publication of the first version of this book. We are extremely pleased to have been able to renew our academic and professional connections through this publication.

The second step in this project has been through collaboration with Routledge in preparing the publication of this English version. We are grateful to Natalie Tomlinson for managing the project and particularly the external review of this book that identified many helpful suggestions from knowledgeable reviewers.

We would also like to acknowledge the support of translators Fernando Bercovich and Ines Elvira Rocha.

Finally, we believe that this book represents collective thinking about two decades of dense political and economic change in Latin America and how those changes affected the development and implementation of public policies in cities. We are grateful to all those who contributed to this collective thinking. The assessments presented in this book represent their respective individual authors. It has been our privilege to work with an exceptional group of Latin American urban experts.

Prologue to the English edition

We live in a world where cities are ever increasing in their influence on global development. Despite extensive urban research since the 1970s, our understanding of the mechanisms involved in successfully advancing a global urban agenda is still murky at best. We have witnessed the grand gestures of the United Nations Millennium Development Goals, Sustainable Development Goals, and New Urban Agenda, among others, and examined the extent to which the goals have been achieved. Yet without a clear articulation of how change is brought about at the local level, we have been left with methodological debates about measuring progress absent the more essential understanding of process. To create the momentum required to build global sustainable urban economies, knowing the global "if" is simply not enough; we need to interrogate the local "how."

This book develops new protocols for evidencing the progress and underlying processes in urban economic advancement. Through a close examination of the United Nations Habitat II (1996) and Habitat III (2006) commitments, the authors assess the progress made over the decade between them in six rapidly urbanizing Latin American countries: Argentina, Brazil, Chile, Colombia, Ecuador, and Mexico. A contribution of this volume, a portion of which was previously available in Spanish, is the development of the Habitat Commitment Index (HCI). Based on a methodology established by Sakiko Fukuda-Parr, professor of international affairs at The New School, to evaluate global compliance with social and economic rights, the HCI measures progress on the commitments established in Habitat II according to country capabilities.

Led by my colleagues at the Observatory on Latin America (OLA) at The New School in New York City and in collaboration with scholars from Argentina, Brazil, Chile, Colombia, Ecuador, England, and Mexico, this volume is a labor of research and love. Unfettered by blind commitment to goals and emboldened by a critical lens into the processes they wish to explore, the current volume advances what is known about the Habitat commitments' progress at the city and national level. Further, it engages us in a larger debate about the commitments approach as a whole, providing insights into government and other institutional practices that enact policymaking and other processes.

Beginning in 1919 and continuing to the present day, The New School has embodied strong commitments to advancing social progress by upending conventional wisdom about the world's most pressing challenges. Like the authors of this volume, we know that commitments are not enough, and The New School has put promises into concrete action for nearly a century. It is my pleasure to offer you the insights of this volume. The authors advance and challenge the prevailing wisdom of urban development progress, and through rigorous analysis and imaginative conceptualization, their approach provides a path toward a more just and sustainable urban world. I invite you to be inspired by their work.

Mary Watson
Executive Dean, Schools of Public Engagement,
The New School

Prologue to the Spanish edition

This book has been produced by the Global Urban Futures Project supported by the Ford Foundation and the Observatory on Latin America (OLA) of the Milano School of International Affairs, Management, and Urban Policy of The New School, a university in New York. Its objective is to assess the progress made by six major Latin American countries: Argentina, Brazil, Chile, Colombia, Ecuador, and Mexico, in addressing the challenges of rapid urban growth over the past two decades. This assessment has been undertaken within the historical framework of the commitments made by national governments during the Habitat II Conference held in Istanbul in 1996. That framework included many general commitments by states about urban governance, policy, housing, infrastructure, environment, urban form, and the productivity of urban economies in contributing to national economic growth.

The experience of policy reform and institutional development in these countries is a significant reference point in considering how the 2030 Sustainable Development Goals adopted by all national governments at the United Nations in September 2015 will be implemented. Twelve of the seventeen goals will have to be achieved in cities in the 2015–2030 period. This calls for strengthened urban policy and planning within a broader multi-sector approach in which these problems are addressed in order to achieve the goals of sustainable development and social justice. These goals are universal and relevant to all countries, whether industrialized or developing. The stakes for countries and the world as a whole are very great, whether one is considering the threat of climate change, growing inequality, or the need for inclusive economic growth.

The book includes country chapters, a cross-cutting analysis of country experiences, a summary of the results of a quantitative study of the fulfillment of the Habitat II commitments in the Habitat Commitment Index, and a forward-looking concluding chapter that focuses on the need for a new urban practice, particularly one that is more focused on assuring that social exclusion is reduced as nations and cities work to meet these urban challenges.

In addition to our gratitude to the Ford Foundation, I would like to thank the Corporación Andina de Fomento and the Julien Studley Foundation for their support for this project. In addition, we are grateful for the collaboration

with civil society organizations in Africa, Asia, and Latin America whom we
have partnered with and who have provided their indigenous knowledge to
this inquiry. We are also proud of our Policy, International Affairs, and Environmental graduate student team that worked on this project, and particularly
Lena Simet, the Coordinator of the Global Urban Futures Project, and María
Carrizosa, Coordinator of the Observatory on Latin America.

Michelle DePass
Dean of the Milano School of International Affairs,
Management, and Urban Policy, The New School (2013–2018)

1   Introduction

*Michael Cohen, Margarita Gutman, and
María Carrizosa*

Setting the context

The urbanization of Latin America has been an integral and dynamic part of its development from the pre-Columbian period and the Spanish and later Portuguese colonization of the region starting in the 16th century. The creation of urban settlements, their growth, and the many linkages between them and to rural areas have been powerful forces in the transformation of the region, generating unique production mechanisms, economic wealth and income, cultural expansion, new physical and spatial forms, and political and institutional forms of authority (Engerman and Sokoloff, 2005). This 500-year process continues, as individual countries, regions, and urban areas of all sizes continue to evolve, building on their own specific histories while also responding to rapidly changing external pressures generated, in part, from globalization.

Accompanying these processes have been highly visible physical and spatial changes in Latin American urban areas, with the growth of modern central cities and, at the same time, vast informal settlements. These physical forms are undeniable indicators of high degrees of inequality in incomes, wealth, economic opportunities, and, above all, quality of life. A person's location is the most powerful determinant of their well-being (World Bank, 2009). Accelerating demographic growth during the first half of the 20th century intensified these patterns, with the resulting expansion of urban settlements into cities and mega-cities such as Sao Paulo, Buenos Aires, or Mexico City. Growth of secondary cities has also continued, with the vast majority of Latin Americans now living in what previously were small towns. Also, incipient rural centers grow into small cities in an unplanned manner, a largely understudied phenomena of informal territorial urbanization.

In the post–World War II period, rapid urban growth led to the proliferation of informal settlements: the *barriadas* of Lima, the *villas* of Buenos Aires, *barrios pirata* in Bogotá, and the *favelas* of Rio de Janeiro and Sao Paulo. These settlements were and are frequently perceived by municipal governments as being beyond their effective control. Together with international development institutions, from the 1970s to the present, national and municipal governments have consistently developed programs to provide low-cost housing and to improve the housing conditions and infrastructure services of residents of these settlements.[1]

This focus on housing and infrastructure was shared by academic researchers studying individual settlements and cities, and provided a rich tapestry of information and insights about these areas ((Hardoy and Tobar, 1969), (Ward, 1998), (Gilbert, 2001), and others). A body of knowledge on the specificities of Latin American urbanization emerged. Going back to the 1950s, the literature on Latin American informal settlements is extensive and has generated whole new vocabularies about poverty and inequality ((Portes, 1979), (Camargo and Hurtado, 2012), (Cravino, 2006), and (Clemente, 2014)). Of course, this includes the widely applied notion of "marginality" of low-income urban households that was later debunked (Perlman, 1976). Since the 1980s, there has been an important diversification of Latin American urban studies, building on work on informal settlements to include research on crime and violence (Hazen and Rodgers, 2014), gender ((Moser, 2009) and (Falú, 2009)), environment (Hardoy et al., 2001), transport (Prudhomme et al., 2004), water supply and sanitation (Hardoy et al., 2005), and housing finance (Stein and Vance, 2008), as well as the process of decentralization of responsibility from national to local governments (Campbell, 2003). Growing awareness of climate change and natural disasters has also led to many recent studies of these phenomena in Latin American urban areas (Hardoy et al., 2011). New terms continue to be added and continue to surface to explain the nature of these communities, including social exclusion, assets, vulnerability, risk management ((Cardona et al., 2004), (Cardona et al., 2017)), and creativity (Oroza, 2016).

These efforts in Latin American cities have also been accompanied by increasing global recognition about the importance of cities in the economic and social progress of countries ((Cohen, 1991), (Henderson, 1991), (Spence et al., 2008), (OECD, 2006)). The field of comparative urban policy has developed significantly since the 1970s, as the importance of national- and local-level policies and actions is appreciated and understood as a critical factor in the quality of urban life ((Ward et al., 2016), (OECD, 2017)). The Latin American literature is increasingly compared to studies in other regions, showing that there are some significant similarities and differences between regions, while still asserting the particularity of specific cities. For instance, there has been growing interest of India and South Africa to learn the experience of Brazil. But this exchange has been hindered by language, with only a very small proportion of the rich Latin American urban literature translated into other languages.

One interesting area of comparative studies is research on the evolution of local government structures, processes, and capabilities in an effort to understand how local governments can play a more effective role in improving the efficiency and equity of urban areas (Bahl and Bird, 2018). An important focus of this research has been the understanding that subnational governments heavily depend on national governments and what is now understood as "national urban policies". The widely observed financial and technical weaknesses of local governments are recognized as a global phenomenon. First, this led to a call for greater decentralization of national authority and resources to local government, then to an emphasis on "capacity-building" of local public institutions, and, later, in an era of privatization of public services in many countries, it led to a growing recognition of the role of civil society and the private sector in the provision of urban infrastructure and urban management mechanisms.

This evolving body of knowledge in Latin America was consistent with the adoption in almost all Latin American countries of the macro-economic principles and instruments known as the Washington Consensus of the 1990s. Approaches to urban policy fit within the broader macro-economic framework of liberalization of trade and the financial sector, privatization of public services, deregulation of domestic economic activity, and emphasis on private property rights. While the adoption of these policies, supplemented with monetary policies, in the early 1990s calmed down the high inflation in Argentina and Bolivia and temporarily helped to manage macro-economic crises in Mexico, Brazil, and Argentina, these impacts proved to be short-lived, in large part due to unforeseen consequences that included growing unemployment, poverty, and inequality, as well as the deindustrialization of Latin American countries in the face of global competition ((French-Davis, 2005), (Cohen, 2012)).

In response to these policies, Latin America experienced a "democratic fiesta" between 2002 and 2005, in which 250 million voters in elections in 10 countries – Argentina, Bolivia, Brazil, Chile, Ecuador, El Salvador, Nicaragua, Paraguay, Uruguay, and Venezuela – rejected the policies of the Washington Consensus and brought in new progressive governments to address growing poverty and inequality, particularly in urban areas (Navia, 2006). While this so-called "turn to the left" was widely understood as reflecting region-wide and national perceptions of the need to reverse Washington Consensus policies, it also reflected the perception that urban conditions had worsened considerably across the region, with growing crime and social exclusion.

The objectives of this book

In this context, this book presents a qualitative evaluation of the impact of 20 years of public policies aimed at solving urban problems in six Latin American countries: Argentina, Brazil, Chile, Colombia, Ecuador, and Mexico. It aims to contribute to a small but relevant academic and policy literature that analyzes the impact and scope of urban interventions. The book argues that an evaluation of the fulfillment of past international commitments by national governments is necessary, and even essential, to understand the likelihood of the achievement of the new commitments for 2016–2036 adopted first as the Sustainable Development Goals (SDGs) in late 2015 and then as the New Urban Agenda at the Habitat III conference. A rigorous assessment of the level of compliance with the prior agreements reached at the Habitat II conference in Istanbul in

1996, supported by a clear enumeration and identification of unfulfilled goals, is a critical input for achieving the new goals. This enumeration needed to include a locally informed interpretation of the processes of compliance. Without such an analysis, the commitments made in 2015–2016 in New York and Quito have an uncertain future.

This qualitative evaluation is complemented by a global quantitative evaluation of improvements in urban well-being from 1996 to 2016, using available quantitative data of 15 indicators from 169 countries. This evaluation is presented in two chapters, one by Martha Susana Jaimes, a Colombian economist, who analyzes the findings of this evaluation for Latin America through the Habitat Commitment Index, an analytic tool invented in the New School in 2015–2016. A second chapter, by Lena Simet, a German urban policy specialist, focuses on the analysis of city-level improvements and identifies the lack of comparable data as a formidable obstacle to monitoring and evaluating city-level achievements. Simet considers this problem in light of the post–Habitat III efforts to build support for implementation of the New Urban Agenda and the SDGs.

The six evaluations that form the core of this book provide a critical, historical, contextualized perspective of urban policy implementation in Latin America from 1996 to 2016. They are an important complement to official national reports prepared by the national governments for the Habitat III conference held in Quito, Ecuador, in October 2016, as well as a useful precedent in the light of the efforts towards the SDGs' agenda, in particular, that of Goal 11, on sustainable cities. In all cases, the authors of country-specific chapters are local experts with more than 30 years of experience in urban issues, who have first-hand experience of the Habitat II process, and are familiar with the problems, statistics, actors, and political swings of their respective countries. All of them are experienced analysts or activists, highly recognized in their country of origin and also across the region. Their chapters are thus grounded in solid empirical evidence and go beyond merely bureaucratic understandings. While each chapter responds to a set of common themes, such as governance and urban and environmental policies, sustainability and environmental management, reduction of the housing deficit, physical upgrading of cities, productivity and urban economy, poverty reduction, and urban forms adopted, all of them have different formats that correspond to the unique issues that each context and each author's voice pose.

This set of evaluations is a unique contribution to the study of urban policy both in a global context and in Latin America. Growing interest in cities and urban policies over the last several decades has not been accompanied by a consistent historical analysis of the impact of policies and programs carried out by governments in response to the numerous challenges generated by demographic and spatial urban growth. Although hundreds of studies on low-income neighborhoods and communities have been conducted around the world, relatively little effort has been devoted to studying the impact and scope of public policies, programs, and projects.

In some cities, formal evaluations have been carried out on specific projects, but in most cases, evaluation is focused on the direct project outputs, such as the number of dwellings built or meters of built infrastructure, rather than on impact, that is, on the social, economic, physical, and environmental outcomes of urban interventions. While there is extensive experience in project implementation, global efforts to understand its results or consequences have remained very scarce.[2]

This observation may be surprising and even disturbing, but it is nevertheless true. It is notable that despite the increasing visibility of the urban phenomenon, including the proliferation of informal settlements, growing environmental deterioration, and increased participation of cities in global and national gross domestic product (GDP), as well as the already recognized impact of climate change on cities, the consequences of policies and programs for both developing and industrialized countries are yet to be scrutinized. A 2000 study of a set of urban projects financed internationally in more than 11,000 urban areas in developing countries concluded that the consequences of this portfolio of efforts were largely unknown (Cohen, 2000).

The 20 years between the Habitat II and Habitat III conferences offer a significant time period to assess country efforts to address urban problems. Important questions could be posed, such as: What were the factors that affected the performance of the countries? What is the relative weight of the internal urban factors, such as the type of government or the rate of population growth, against external factors such as global economic crises, when determining effective impacts at national and urban levels? What are the results of past commitments? Do they have a visible impact on current local urban conditions? Moreover, what is the meaning of an international commitment in relation to local conditions? Are these commitments mandatory for national or for local governments? If so, which institutions have a legal obligation to fulfill them?

While these issues are historically interesting in relation to the processes of United Nations' conferences, they should also be considered within a larger analytical framework by examining the impacts of public policies and collective actions on urban areas and their citizens. Unfortunately, such studies are very scarce, and there are, in fact, very few examples in Latin America.

Organization of the book

The book is organized in four parts: an introductory section, which includes an overview comparative chapter on urban policy in developing countries; six country case studies; two chapters on the quantitative evaluation of urban performance in Latin America and the challenges of monitoring the implementation of the urban goal of the SDGs and the New Urban Agenda; and two final chapters, one a cross-cutting analysis of the experiences of the six countries, and the other a forward-looking conclusion about the importance of transforming urban practice to better achieve urban policy goals.

The studies of Mexico and Chile in this book draw attention to housing policies in those countries that were deemed successful but which have nevertheless weakened urban policy. Mexico and Chile had great success in this period curbing the quantitative housing deficit. Without underestimating the importance of this achievement, a judicious study of this phenomenon is fundamental, because a housing policy that reduces the quantitative deficit at the expense of the qualitative deficit is not desirable. This is well illustrated in both cases by Professor Alicia Ziccardi and Alfredo Rodriguez, both long-time respected researchers and analysts of urban conditions in their countries. A policy of "*mucha vivienda y poca ciudad*" is unbalanced and brings new problems to cities and their inhabitants, such as excessive spatial growth without adequate provision of urban transport, infrastructure services, or social facilities. Projects in both of these countries quickly faced environmental and physical deterioration, as well as increasing insecurity.

The Mexico chapter prepared by Alicia Ziccardi and her team in the University Program of Studies on the City (PUEC) of the National Autonomous University of Mexico (UNAM) offers an informed view to understand in detail the case of Mexico. It begins by establishing the general political and economic context in four presidential six-year terms: the government of Ernesto Zedillo (1994–2000), Vicente Fox (2000–2006), Felipe Calderón (2006–2012), and Enrique Peña Nieto (2012–2018). It then provides an overall assessment of urban policy developments over the period, supported by a statistical database and analysis of the urban legal framework. This approach makes it possible to establish that public policies have weakened in their impact, that urban strategies prioritized neoliberal and private-sector approaches to housing provision, that the participatory bodies have limits to their effectiveness, and that a sectorial vision focused on housing undermined the integrity of territorial policies as a whole. Ultimately, the net impacts of these policies were numerous negative effects in the quality of life of citizens.

The chapter on Chile was written by Alfredo Rodríguez and Paula Rodríguez of SUR, the Southern Corporation for Social and Education Studies, a Chilean nongovernmental organization (NGO). The authors review the significant progress made in Chile over this period in terms of poverty reduction, per capita income growth, social housing construction (more than 1.5 million units built, curbing the quantitative deficit), and almost full coverage of urban infrastructure, among others. However, the authors contend that the Habitat II commitments were not met in Chile. They explain that these commitments were not binding, but rather were based on universal rights without any reference to specific action plans, budgets, or implementation mechanisms to ensure their effective compliance. It is striking that in the Mexican and Chilean cases, the critiques made by these authors is based on an assessment of the large-scale efforts and results on the ground.

The studies of Brazil and Colombia demonstrate that while following the Habitat II conference in 1996, both these countries had seemingly ideal regulatory environments with notable legislative breakthroughs; however, these policy processes were not followed up by effective implementation. Both Brazil and Colombia have played a role of regional – and even global – leadership in the normative realm of urban policy following global conferences. Their approaches included constitutional reforms intended to institutionalize certain global agendas within their territories. For example, these have included recognizing the "social function of property" and the regulation of territorial planning at the municipal level that incorporates redistributive instruments for urban land management. However, the case studies show that legislative reforms do not necessarily ensure effective implementation across the country as a whole. Normative policies by themselves are not strong enough to transform urban practices and conditions. Implementation processes have a long maturation period, and they often fail due to inadequate financial resources or technical capacity, or for other reasons related to local politics.

The Brazilian chapter, by Edesio Fernandes, a well-known Brazilian urban expert, lawyer, and professor at University College, London, is unique in its audacious and somber tone, undoubtedly affected by the political upheavals occurring in Brazil while this work was being written. The Brazilian perspective enriched the cross-sectional analysis and contributed fundamental elements in the construction of the collective conclusions of this book. Two of its strategic contributions stand out. First, its judgment about "artificial decentralization" resonates with similar views in Mexico, Colombia, and Ecuador. In Brazil in 2016, 5,550 municipalities had autonomy in their territorial and administrative planning. However, Fernandes argues that decentralization has not been synonymous with democratization, because this autonomy is weak.

Another notable insight relates to the problems faced by professional practice in the implementation of the urban agenda. Fernandes notes that the lack of efficiency of urban planning is not only related to the absence of regulation or resources, but it is also due to its excessively formal and unnecessarily obscure language, which produces a dissociation between planning and urban management. Even more disturbing is the observation that "urban planners and administrators have not understood the dynamics of speculative exclusion from which they themselves originate".

Jorge Enrique Torres Ramírez, author of the chapter on Colombia and a long-time urban analyst, identifies similarities with other countries in issues such as the dominance of housing policy over urban policy, noted in Mexico and Chile, or the paradox of decentralization in the Brazilian case. Since the 1990s Colombia has recognized the social and ecological function of property in its constitution and in the planning law and requires municipalities to issue territorial plans. Twenty years later, virtually all of the municipalities have such plans. However, a review of these plans reveals profound technical shortcomings in these instruments, as well as a minimum use of redistributive tools for land-value capture. For instance, 86 percent of municipalities are fiscally unsustainable, which explains in part the difficulties in implementation.

The role of internal armed conflict in Colombia's urbanization process, the atypical progressive densification of major cities, the prevalence of tenants in the real estate market, and the absence of the "houses without people" phenomenon found in other Latin American countries are all distinctive features in the Colombian case. The chapter highlights the following contradiction: National resources are concentrated almost exclusively in the construction of new housing, ignoring the scale of the qualitative deficit in the built environment. In this sense, Torres presents information that suggests the existence of a new window of opportunity in Colombia for housing and neighborhood upgrading within new environmental policies of mitigation and adaptation to climate change.

The chapters on Argentina and Ecuador focus heavily on the challenges of social inclusion. In both cases, it is interesting to note that an important share of the period under analysis has been in the hands of progressive governments that had the opportunity to implement ambitious social policies. The evidence and reflections presented on these two country case studies show that, along with notable advances in poverty reduction, the development of a primary infrastructure, and even the (modest) reduction of the housing deficit, there has been a continued deregulation in urban land markets coupled with a lack of integration of sector policies, which has prevented effective completion of the commitments established in Habitat II. In both chapters the authors identify chronological periods of policy change. In the case of Argentina, these are three cycles: two neoliberal phases, from 1991 to 2002, separated by the administrations of Nestor Kirchner and Cristina Fernandez de Kirchner (2003–2015), and from 2015 to the present under the presidency of Maurico Macri. In the Ecuadorian case, the 2007 dollarization undertaken by President Rafael Correa has marked different periods in the country's urban history.

The Argentine chapter, written by professors and activists Eduardo Reese and Andrea Catenazzi, focuses on four questions: 1) What commitments did the Habitat II document establish? 2) What were the actions defined in the national agenda? 3) What were the key public issues in that period? 4) What were the significant actions by civil society? This approach allows a balanced reading of the issues and highlights the role of different constituencies, including their responsibilities, possibilities, and achievements. The authors' assessment looks at accomplishments while also identifying the "pending challenges" for Argentina. Reese and Catenazzi prioritize two urgent tasks that the national urban agenda must address. First, the regulation of land markets, which requires more than the issuance of rules and regulations to achieve effective implementation. The second pending issue is the "territorial integration of sector policies". Undoubtedly, these tasks are relevant beyond Argentina and even Latin America, and they reflect a fundamental shift in the conception and implementation of a new urban agenda and practice. The authors argue that the aim is not only to "spatialize" social and economic policies but also to articulate more efficiently the actions of the public administration in the territory. The objective, then, is to move towards another paradigm of public action, urban practice, and the role of urban institutions, which in turn requires a new type of education in public policy and urban planning for future professionals.

The authors of the Ecuador chapter, Fernando Carrión, a well-known urban planner, author, and professor at FLACSO-Ecuador, and Alexandra Velasco sharply criticize the 20-year gap between these urban summits and the fact that the adoption of agendas and commitments is disconnected from their actual fulfillment. They wonder if the time has come for local governments to be the main actors in this process, because without giving a voice and vote to the cities, which are responsible for implementing the subscribed agenda, what is at stake is an "unacceptable ventriloquism". In detailing the specificities of the Ecuadorian case, the authors point out, for example, that the traditional Ecuadorian binodal urban structure with Quito and Guayaquil has given way to a greater fragmentation over the last 20 years. Urban growth rates have declined, intermediate cities have gained preponderance, and globalization is increasingly determining urban issues. Rural–urban migration and urban land invasions by squatters were key determinants of urbanization in the past, but today, Carrión and Velasco argue that international migration, drug trafficking, and remittances – both economic and cultural – are the driving forces behind current patterns of urban development. They suggest that the economic crisis caused by the end of the oil boom, the fall of Chinese demand, and the strong appreciation of the dollar are obscuring the future of Rafael Correa's "Citizen Revolution". Thus, the effective realization of the "socialism of the twenty-first century" is today facing instability and an uncertain future.

The third part of this book includes two chapters that summarize the findings of a quantitative assessment of performance of Latin American countries in achieving global urban goals, as developed by the work team of the Global Urban Futures Project, which consists of 20 faculty and students from different programs of The New School. The first chapter, written by the Colombian economist Martha Susana Jaimes, describes the performance of these Latin American countries in a composite index, called the Habitat Commitment Index (HCI), developed by the Global Urban Futures Project at the New School. The HCI index is based on the methodology established by Sakiko Fukuda-Parr, Professor of International Affairs at The New School, to evaluate global compliance with social and economic rights. The methodology was adapted to measure the urban compliance of each country with the commitments established in Habitat II, according to their capabilities.

The second chapter in the third part, written by the German urban economist Lena Simet, presents the findings of the HCI 2.0 project, an effort to assemble and evaluate city-level data about urban performance. This work is considered in the context of the global monitoring effort underway to track the achievement of the SDGs and the New Urban Agenda. It focuses on the obstacles of actually doing analysis at the city level.

The final chapters of the book focus first on a cross-cutting analysis by María Carrizosa, a Colombian architect and philosopher, of the six countries in terms of their performance between 1996 and 2016, and second a forwarding-looking conclusion by Michael Cohen and Margarita Gutman about the importance of transforming urban practice to better achieve urban policy goals.

* * *

Together, these chapters offer a contribution to the growing literature on the view from communities, particularly the urban poor, in so far as they demonstrate the failure of normative urban policy at the country and city levels, even when supported by international processes. It should not be surprising that the view from the bottom and from the excluded is so consistent across countries and cities, even if the form and modes of communication differ (Roy, 2011). More than 20 years ago, Jorge Wilheim, the late Brazilian architect and urban planner and former Deputy Secretary-General of the Habitat II Conference, wrote: "The time has come to think locally in order to learn how to act globally. This is as true as the reverse" (Wilheim, 1997). Two decades later, this is still true.

Notes

1 These programs were supported in Argentina, Brazil, Chile, Colombia, Ecuador, El Salvador, Guatemala, Honduras, Mexico, Nicaragua, Peru, and Venezuela.
2 While some publications such as Irazabal (2009), Bouillon, (2012), Ward et al (2014), Bredenoord et al (2014), Ward (2015), Angotti (2017), Boano and Vergara (2017), and others focus on specific cases or subsectors within the urban agenda, fewer efforts are directed to the evaluation of the Habitat II agenda (1996–2016).

Bibliography

Bahl, R. and Bird, R., (2018), *Fiscal Decentralization and Local Finance in Developing Countries: Development from Below*, Elgar, Northampton, MA.

Camargo, A. and Hurtado, A., (2012), "Informalidad del siglo XXI: Características de la oferta informal de suelo y vivienda en Bogotá durante la primera década del siglo XXI", *Territorios*, 27, pp. 71–103.

Campbell, T., (2003), *The Quiet Revolution: Decentralization and the Rise of Political Participation in Latin American Cities*, University of Pittsburgh Press, Pittsburgh.

Cardona, O. D., et al., (2004), "A Disaster Risk Management Performance Index", *Nat Hazards*, 41, Springer.

Cardona, O. D., et al., (2017), "Integration of Probabilistic and Multi-Hazard Risk Assessment within Urban Development Planning and Emergency Preparedness and Response: Application to Manizales, Colombia", *International Journal Disaster Risk Sciences*, 2017:8, pp. 270–283.

Clemente, A., (ed.), (2014), *Territorios Urbanos y Pobreza Persistente*, Editorial Espacio, Buenos Aires.

Cohen, M. A., (1991), *Urban Policy and Economic Development: An Agenda for the 1990s*, World Bank, Washington.

Cohen, M. A., (2000), "Urban Assistance and the Material World", *Environment and Urbanization*, 13:1, pp. 37–60.

Cohen, M. A., (2012), *Argentina Economic Growth and Recovery*, Routledge, New York.

Cravino, M. C., (2006), "Las Villas de la Ciudad. Mercado e informalidad urbana", In *Instituto del Conurbano – Universidad Nacional de General Sarmiento*, Los Polvorines, San Miguel.

Davila, J. and Brand, P., (2012), "Movilidad urbana y pobreza", In *Development Planning Unit*, UCL/Universidad Nacional de Colombia, Medellín.

Engerman, S. and Sokoloff, K., (2005), "Colonialism, Inequality, and Long Paths of Development", Working Paper# 11057, National Bureau of Economic Research, Cambridge, MA.

Falú, A., (ed.), (2009), "Women in the City on Violence and Rights", In *Chile: Women and Habitat Network of Latin America*, Editions Sur, Santiago.

Ffrench-Davis, R., (2005), *Reformas para America Latina después del Fundamentalismo Neoliberal*, Siglo 21 and UNECLAC, Buenos Aires.

Gilbert, A., (2001), *The Megacity in Latin America*, United Nations University Press, Tokyo; among Many Others.

Hardoy, A., Hardoy, J., Pandiella, G., and Urquiza, G., (2005), "Governance for Water and Sanitation Services in Low-Income Settlements: Experiences with Partnership-Based Management in Moreno, Buenos Aires", *Environment and Urbanization*, 17:1, April, pp. 183–200.

Hardoy, J. E., Mitlin, D., and Satterthwaite, D., (2001), *Environmental Problems in an Urbanizing World*, Earthscan, London.

Hardoy, J. E., Pandiella, G., and Velásquez, L. E., (2011), "Local Disaster Risk Reduction in Latin American Urban Areas", *Environment and Urbanization*, 23:2, pp. 401–413.

Hardoy, J. E. and Tobar, C., (1969), *Urbanización en America Latina*, Universidad de Buenos Aires Editorial del Instituto.

Hazen, J. M. and Rodgers, D. (eds.), (2014), *Global Gangs: Street Violence across the World*, University of Minnesota Press, Minneapolis.

Henderson, J. V., (1991), *Urban Development: Theory, Fact, and Illusion*, OUP Catalogue, Oxford University Press, Oxford.

Moser, C., (2009), *Ordinary People, Extraordinary Lives: Assets and Poverty Reduction in Guayaquil, 1978–2004*, Brookings Institution, Washington.

Navia, P., (2006), "La elección presidencial de 2005 en Chile", Revista Iberoamericana de Análisis Político, Año 3/Número 4/5, Fondo de Cultura Económica, Buenos Aires, November.

OECD, (2006), *Competitive Cities in the Global Economy*, OECD Territorial Reviews, Paris; Vernon Henderson, J., (1991), *Urbanization: Theory, Fact, and Illusion*, Oxford University Press, Oxford and New York.

OECD, (2017), *National Urban Policy in OECD Countries*, OECD Publishing, Paris.

Oroza, E., (2016), *Architecture of Necessity*. Available at: http://architectureofnecessity.com/architecture-of-necessity-by-ernesto-oroza/

Perlman, J., (1976), *The Myth of Marginality*, University of California Press, Berkeley.

Portes, A., (1979), "Housing Policy, Urban Poverty, and the State: The Favelas of Rio de Janeiro, 1972–1976", *Latin American Research Review*, 14:2, pp. 3–24.

Prudhomme, R., Huntzinger, H., and Kopp, P., (2004), *Stronger Municipalities for Stronger Cities in Argentina*, Inter-American Bank for Development. Available at: https://publications.iadb.org/en/publication/11699/stronger-municipalities-stronger-cities-argentina

Roy, A., (2011), "Slumdog Cities: Rethinking Subaltern Urbanism", *International Journal of Urban and Regional Research*, 35:2, pp. 223–238.

Spence, M., Annez, P., and Buckley, R., (2008), *Urbanization and Economic Growth*, Growth Commission, Washington, DC.

Stein, A. and Vance, I., (2008), "The Role of Housing Finance in Addressing the Needs of the Urban Poor: Lessons from Central America", *Environment and Urbanization*, 20:1, April, pp. 13–30.

Ward, P., (1998), *Mexico City*, John Wiley and Sons, New York and Chichester.

Ward, P., Jiménez, E., Di Virgilio, M., and Camargo, A., (2016), *Políticas de Vivienda en Ciudades Latinoamericanas*, Universidad de Rosario, Bogotá; OECD, (2017), *Conference on National Urban Policies*, Paris.

Wilheim, J., (1997), "The Transition Period to the Next Millennium", In Uner, K. (ed.), *Cities Fit for People*, United Nations, New York, pp. 122–128.

World Bank, (2009), *World Development Report 2009: Reshaping Economic Geography*, World Bank, Washington.

2 The evolution of urban policy in developing countries

A comparative and historical perspective

Michael Cohen

The concept of urban policy in developing countries has evolved considerably since the end of the colonial period in the 1950s. Although this evolution has been captured in academic literatures on the policy process, on urban planning, and on the many dilemmas of urban social policy, including race relations, school desegregation, and environmental quality, to name a few, this chapter will examine the evolution of the concept of urban policy in the realm of urban governance and urban development in developing countries. This evolution "in the real world" is noteworthy, because it demonstrates an ever-broadening understanding of the multiple arenas in which urban policies operate and affect people's lives.

Indeed, urban policy has become increasingly enriched as a notion, because it now includes issues such as employment, sustainable livelihoods for urban households, climate change mitigation and adaptation, community participation, gender violence, and public accountability, among others. These issues are currently perceived as cutting-edge concerns of municipal engagement, yet they sit on a historical foundation of architecture, land use planning, infrastructure design, and social policy going back to ancient civilizations, whether the Aztecs, the Mayans, or early Mesopotamia.

Early 20th-century discussion of urban policy was initially rooted in the forms of colonial local public administration of Africa and South Asia, for example, with debates about the virtues of British "indirect rule" versus the French "direct rule." These debates largely centered on the degree of local autonomy to be granted to local jurisdictions and the formal roles of local residents in local administration. An extensive literature on these issues was published in colonial and later national journals of public administration ((Marris, 1967), (Burkhead and Miner, 1971)). This literature had very little to say about the nature of urban areas themselves, but rather focused almost entirely on administration.

This administrative focus expanded in the 1960s with growing concerns about housing and public infrastructure, particularly with the rising expectations of now self-governing cities and towns following independence ((Cohen, 1974), (Stren, 1975)). Independence brought increased rural-to-urban migration and growing urban populations. This shift of emphasis was mirrored by the emerging awareness of housing-focused urban assistance programs in international institutions such as the United Nations and the World Bank, as well as by bilateral agencies such as the Commonwealth Development Corporation and the French Agency for Territorial Development. In the 1970s several dozen major low-cost housing projects were launched in countries as diverse as Senegal, India, Jamaica, El Salvador, and the Philippines. Many of these were sites and services projects, providing urban land and infrastructure to low-income households, who were then expected to build their own houses (Cohen, 1982). This burst of activity was followed by so-called second-generation projects of the 1980s in which this housing focus was considerably broadened to include the strengthening of the financial and technical capabilities of local governments. In simple terms, the aid agencies had discovered that municipalities were needed to provide basic urban services such as water supply, sanitation, and garbage collection to housing project areas. Working with national housing ministries did not guarantee the provision of urban services.

This shift was also significant because it put the countries of Africa and Asia on the same institutional level as Latin American countries in which municipal governments were well-established and important actors in the provision of urban services in cities such as Mexico City, Santiago, or Bogota. The subject of "urban management" then emerged in the 1980s to include not only the direct provision of infrastructure services and housing but also a wide spectrum of other municipal services that were also part of urban policy (as reflected in the publications of the UN Habitat Urban Management program between 1986 and 1999). This included urban public health, education, urban transport, environmental sanitation, public space, and public security. Although many of these subjects were under the responsibility of national-sector ministries, for example, particularly for health or education, it was nonetheless recognized that providing these services within urban areas was also a part of what was understood as "urban policy."

The focus on urban management also coincided with a growing emphasis in European countries on the notion of "subsidiarity," that decision-making authority should be located as close to real problems on the ground. This concept was consistent with the notion that authority and resources needed to be "decentralized" away from national governments to local authorities ((Campbell, 2003), (Dillinger and Webb, 1999)). In fact, the speed and effectiveness of decentralization reforms were often affected by the colonial institutional histories of local government. The francophone African countries were ready to "decentralize" authority, but still wished to retain the all-powerful central control of ministries of interior or local government that approved annual budgets, organizational changes, and personnel policies. In contrast, municipal officials in former British colonies had long been more empowered from the decades of indirect rule and had over time acquired many of the technical skills to manage infrastructure investment, operation, and maintenance.

Officials in the larger cities of Latin American countries, such as Bogota, Buenos Aires, or Sao Paulo had also built up strong capabilities to formulate and manage urban policies. Secondary urban centers in many countries continued to face a deficit in terms of technical skills. Indeed, in Brazil, the national government had created the National Institute of Municipal Administration (IBAM) in 1952 to train local government officials from throughout the country.

In the 1990s, the meaning of urban policy broadened considerably with the inclusion of urban environmental policy as an arena for municipal action. Officials who were learning about infrastructure planning and maintenance now had to learn about environmental hazards, risks, and strategies in urban areas and how their actions in other policy areas could help manage environmental challenges. Global consciousness of environmental threats was raised after the 1992 Rio Summit on the Environment, and this was conveyed to cities as well through the notion of the "brown agenda," not just the "green agenda" affecting future generations, but dirty water and air in cities, which could make residents ill.

This broadening of the urban policy agenda for local governments was increasingly challenged in the early 1990s with calls for the privatization of public services. The impact of the Margaret Thatcher and Ronald Reagan administrations' policies towards privatization was enhanced in Latin America through the policies of the Washington Consensus (Murillo, 2009). Argentina, for example, under President Carlos Menem, nationalized more than 20 public services in 1991–1992, far more than Thatcher had done in over a decade. The argument for privatization was that public agencies were inefficient, slow, and costly, weighing heavily on national fiscal deficits. If privatization worked for some services such as telecommunications, it was less clear that it could work successfully in the water sector. Indeed, in Bolivia, water tariff increases spurred "water wars" in Cochabamba. In Argentina, the government of Nestor Kirchner broke the contract with the French concessionaires, Suez, on the grounds that water revenues were being repatriated to French stockholders rather than investing in the extension of water supply to communities without service.

The privatization of public services dramatically complicated the notion of urban policy in Latin American cities, because it was coupled with a general condemnation of the public-sector provision as inefficient and unnecessarily costly. The issue of planning per se was undermined, following the belief that the role of the state needed to be curtailed in order to achieve development objectives. This political orientation led to the reduction of public-sector capacity in many fields, including areas such as environmental regulation and regional planning. The meaning of urban policy itself as a coordinating framework for public-sector policies and regulations in many other sectors affecting urban areas was diluted and, in many cities, simply neglected.

In its place came strategic planning that focused frequently on mega-urban projects that were expected to have transformative effects on urban areas. Municipal officials from Barcelona, fresh from the success of the 1992 Olympics, realized that they could "sell" the notion of strategic planning to cities and towns in Latin America. Strenuous efforts were made to sell "the Barcelona approach" to local governments, including in the lead-up to the 2014 World Cup and the 2016 Olympics in Rio de Janeiro. Projects such as Puerto Madero in Buenos Aires were private–public partnerships. Major urban rehabilitation strategies such as in Medellin, Colombia, were also undertaken, combining public- and private-sector resources and visions to substantially improve the quality of life in Medellin (Municipality of Medellín, 2014).

If the direct private provision of urban services proved to be a temporary phenomenon in many cities, another form of private-sector involvement in urban policy emerged forcefully with the deregulation of housing and land markets. Developers were able to assemble large areas of peripheral urban land and frequently to use public-sector financing to construct low-cost housing projects.

This was a new way for the private sector to manage the housing market. Well-known examples include the post-apartheid plan in South Africa, where the national government financed the construction of at least 1 million housing units in projects built by private-sector companies. The profit-driven logic of the private sector led developers to purchase inexpensive land on the periphery of urban areas, which meant that the projects generated significant profits for the developers, but the residents ended up living in locations that were too far from employment opportunities. This scenario was repeated in Chile, where Alfredo Rodriguez and colleagues illustrated how the Chilean government provided subsidies, nominally for the poor, but actually for construction companies that built poor-quality housing in distant locations (Rodríguez et al., 2015).

This phenomenon was well illustrated in Mexico City, where by 2016 there were 5 million empty housing units, too far from employment and lacking in urban amenities. As Alicia Ziccardi writes in the chapter on Mexico, there was "*mucha vivienda, poca ciudad.*" Similar patterns were found in Argentina, Brazil, India, and Thailand. A particularly shocking example is China, where in 2016, it was estimated by the state electricity authority that they had 62 million customers with a zero monthly electricity bill, suggesting that these units were vacant.

These examples raise questions about the meaning of urban policy itself. Who is making urban policy in the neoliberal era? Has policy itself no longer come to be a product of the public sector, but rather a de facto consequence of private-sector behavior? Is the "public interest" still a relevant concept? Or, more operationally, have evolving notions of urban policy given rise to new forms of urban practice?

The shifting relationship between the definition of context and the choice of urban policy instruments

One of the most interesting changes in urban practice in the post–World War II period has been the shifting perception and use of appropriate urban policy instruments. These changes have reflected some of the dynamics of urban growth in both rich and poor countries, including in both the reconstruction of Europe after World War II and the decolonization of countries in Africa and Asia. *Context has influenced instruments, but so, too, have instruments reinforced definitions of contexts.*

Rather than proceed through an orderly chronological explanation of these changes to make this point, the process is well illustrated by a fast-forward view of the recent consequences of globalization for urban practice in the last two decades. Rather than focus on the *barrio* or *quartier*, much attention now is devoted to the linkages of urban spaces to the broader global economy. Seminal analytic work such as *The Global City* by Saskia Sassen and many others extended the urban vision towards a larger scale and higher degrees of complexity (Sassen, 1990). It is now widely accepted that economic, political, technological, and media processes at the global level have direct, immediate impacts in cities. The speed and quality of communication have increased the speed and quality of understanding.

From this perspective, it is worthwhile to consider the various instruments of urban policy in terms of what instruments were intended to do and how those objectives, both implicitly and explicitly, addressed the issue of context. The instruments considered in this chapter include master plans, projects, strategic investment plans, urban policies and regulations, contracts, and, more recently, in the face of the 2008–2011 global economic crisis, stimulus packages, which might be considered national economic policies but which have many direct, significant impacts on urban well-being. In addition, each of these instruments has been used by the multilateral and bilateral agencies providing urban assistance in developing countries.

Master plans

The use of master plans in the 20th century reflected the perception that urban areas could be ordered, planned, and managed by the organization of their *spaces*. These plans were largely spatial plans, reflected in their multicolor presentations in which different colors represented different uses. They were essentially two-dimensional plans, and although they sought to be dynamic representations of urban growth and change, they in fact were more frequently static. They explicitly asked professionals and the citizenry alike to fit their aspirations and their desired physical forms into the plan. *The plan was the context.* Whatever lay "outside the plan" was indeed outside. In many urban areas, what was outside the plan was, by definition, also illegal and thereby subject to demolition by public authorities. This approach goes back to many different historical contexts, whether Haussmann's Paris, Robert Moses's interventions in New York, or the many efforts of different governments from 1890 to 1930 to "civilize Rio" through displacement (Meade, 1997). Looking back, it is clear that this aspect of displacement is one of the major characteristics of both historical and contemporary master plan approaches.

By the mid-1970s, there were strong criticisms of the master plan approach, particularly in developing countries and in Latin American cities, due to its inability to capture the dynamics and startling pace of urban growth. Master plans were regarded as expensive exercises, long in preparation, and frequently out of date by the time they were completed. And, as noted earlier, they were not instruments of inclusion, but rather approaches to legitimize displacement.

Projects

Within the physical framework of the master plan were *sites* that were identified for specific projects. These sites had well-drawn boundaries and linkages to other parts of the plan. *Projects were intended to embody the physical objectives of the plan in built urban forms, whether housing, infrastructure, or social services.* Projects were, by definition, narrowly circumscribed and often ignored what was on the perimeter and/or periphery of the site. A French observer of World Bank practices in Dakar once noted that the World Bank was interested in "sites" but not "land," an important distinction. This included the dynamic pressures of the land market: who was able to have access to land and at what price and how sites contributed to the broader urban form of cities. The context of the project was deliberately excluded in maps in which neighboring areas were often colored white, as if nothing was there or, if there was something, it had no material bearing on what was included inside the project.

Over time projects were also criticized as overly focused interventions in urban areas, usually lacking sufficient attention to the wider geographical, environmental, and institutional contexts. By the early 1980s, it was clear from a sample of some 60 World Bank–assisted projects that these interventions were "projectizing" the city, dividing rather than integrating, and creating differences in living standards and norms that could become sources of economic, social, and political conflict (Cohen, 1983). This same narrow approach is evident in the dozens of slum upgrading projects financed by the Inter-American Development Bank in Latin American countries, particularly in Brazil, Chile, and Mexico, where the focus has been on infrastructure and benefits *within* communities, with little or no attention to their potential wider economic, social, and environmental impacts outside communities. This is most apparent in the lack of attention to employment that might be generated from these projects in the surrounding urban areas (Cohen and Hershey, 2008).

Strategic investment plans

A third urban instrument that emerged in the 1970s was the strategic investment plan, in which a series of projects were linked together as instruments intended to address a broader set of urban issues than individual projects bounded in individual sites. In some sense, these strategic investment plans were the first step towards recognizing that the city was a "space of flows," as described by Manuel Castells (Castells, 1989), which implied that the projects were intended to help in directing, channeling, and managing these flows to assure that basic needs were met but that other urban objectives could also be achieved. The latter included objectives like increasing the efficiency of the urban transportation system or developing areas of the city in an "integrated" manner that included both housing and residential infrastructure, along with so-called productive investments such as industrial parks or factories. The strategic investment plans actually acknowledged that the urban area was larger than a project area, that some spaces had higher priority than others, and that "strategy" meant making choices in space. Choosing therefore implied both positive and negative space, both of which were part of context.

This approach ran into trouble during the macro-economic difficulties of the 1980s – both in Africa with structural adjustment and in Latin America with its debt crisis. In both places this heavily skewed public-sector strategy was also criticized by the changing political views of the time towards a greater role for the private sector. This critique of public institutions was in part also an excuse for not being able to provide the needed public investment resources to carry out strategic planning.

Policies and regulations

A fourth instrument was the use of policy and regulations *to guide urban behavior* and not only to allocate investment funds, as was often the case in projects and strategic investment plans. Policies shifted attention *towards desired outcomes* – what was needed – by assuming that actors would follow rules of behavior in design, construction, and use. The challenge therefore was to determine which rules might encourage behavior in specific directions and what were the so-called "enabling conditions" required for desired outcomes to be achieved. The case studies in this book provide extensive evidence on the plethora of urban policies and regulations adopted by Latin American governments and their relatively marginal impact on behavior in many Latin American urban areas.

The challenge for policy instruments in many cities was the lack of institutional capacity to actually implement and enforce policy. Just as the local building codes had little effective control over the spread of squatter settlements in many cities in developing countries, grand policy pronouncements had little impact in many cities. In Cote d'Ivoire in 1969, the then Minister of Urbanisme Michel Goly Kouassi had declared: "Construct big, beautiful, and forever," but this approach did not stop the spread of bidonvilles in peripheral areas of Abidjan (Cohen, 1974). It also did not stop the spread of favelas in Rio de Janeiro or the barriadas in Lima.

Market-oriented policies

A fifth type of instrument, market-oriented policy, was an important variant of policy itself. The difference lay in the assertion that market-oriented policies were intended to affect not only individual actors but also the *whole pattern of behaviors of all actors, individually and in the aggregate. Context in this sense meant not only spaces, sites, and flows but also all the interactions between actors, which helped to determine supply, demand, and price* (Mayo and Angel, 1993). These policies presumed to affect everything within a specified geographical area. Yet they did not presume that their outcomes would necessarily order spaces, sites, and flows in any particular shape or location, except to assert that these relations would somehow maximize individual welfare, and in so doing, also maximize collective welfare. This assertion – that the pursuit of individual benefit would maximize social benefit – was in fact more of a hypothesis than a fact and indeed has been repeatedly disproven in many contexts.

One of the great failures of market-oriented policies was the assumption that both buyers and sellers had perfect and equal information, and therefore the outcome of sales would reflect optimum prices. In reality, numerous cumulative asymmetries exist in these relationships, particularly so in poor communities in poor countries (Stiglitz, 2002). What these policies did achieve was to reinforce income and wealth differences within the urban population and in many cities actually worsen the urban income distribution. The extreme version of this outcome is seen in metropolitan Buenos Aires, with its more than 600 gated communities housing about 500,000 people and which occupy more than 1.6 times the area of downtown Buenos Aires with 3.5 million people (Gutman and Hardoy, 2007).

Contracts

A sixth type of urban instrument was the contract, normally between an urban public institution and a set of private providers of service. The use of contracts was widespread in France and was adopted in the AGETYPES projects in the 1980s and 1990s, whereby public institutions entered into contracts with private companies promising to provide heretofore public services. Contracts focused on the issue of *agency* within the city and how responsibility for "public" services could be transferred to "private" agents within a given context. In this sense, "context" is in fact institutional context related to jurisdiction.

This approach assumed that private companies could operate and maintain urban services better than public institutions could. This assertion was also a hypothesis. In some cities in the United States, such as Phoenix, public workers actually won back the privatized contract in terms of price and quality of work. Similar results have occurred in cities in Latin America.

Stimulus packages

A seventh type of instrument is the notion of a stimulus package that has been a frequently used response to global economic crises and downturns (Cohen, 2012). In 2008 the crisis originated in the United States' subprime mortgage market and affected all countries in the global economy through the channels of finance, demand for commodities, and prices of commodities. Similar disruptions in the global economy over the last decade has meant that global contraction led to the contraction of local urban economies as well, with immediate consequences for investment, savings, employment, and secondary impacts through reduced revenues reflecting reduced economic activity, and tertiary impacts through reduced public expenditures.

The core instruments of stimulus packages were public expenditures that were intended in a pure Keynesian fashion *to stimulate demand for goods and services by putting more money into circulation and into the hands of consumers.* The speed of public expenditures was to be reflected in the speed of creating new demand and hence economic recovery.

The most interesting aspect of the application of stimulus packages as responses to the economic crisis, given the fact that urban areas account for more than 80 percent of global gross domestic product (GDP) and more than 60 percent of all GDP in all developing countries, is that *"stimulated demand" is not defined in relation to either urban spaces, urban sites, or urban flows.* The stimulus packages that were adopted in most countries were nonspatial and nonphysical, yet they were expected to stimulate economic behaviors that mostly occur in cities by financing a set of physical investments. As packages of these investments, they seem to have been designed without regard for negative externalities such as environmental impact or positive externalities such as bundling of infrastructure services. In a sense, these macro-economic approaches have been designed without regard to 50 years of professional learning about the social, environmental, political, and cultural dimensions of urban infrastructure and the built environment more generally.

In July 2009, *The New York Times* reported that significant proportions of spending in the United States had actually gone to rural infrastructure, a destination that had little to do with short-term stimulus of economic multipliers. This outcome reminds us of the story of the man looking for his eyeglasses under the streetlight even though he knows that he has lost them in a darkened corner. When asked why he is looking under the light, he replies, "That's where the light is." This outcome demonstrates an absence of concern or awareness of context.

Another interesting example was the transfers of funds in 2009–2010 from the Chinese central government to provinces and cities, particularly in the interior of China, in order to create employment and stimulate demand. In many cases, local municipalities did not have the capacity to spend the increased funds, so the funds either remained unused or were used to pay off municipal debts. In both cases, this result demonstrated that the eagerness to allocate public monies has ignored capacity constraints.

Refocusing urban policy instruments to the context

The brief descriptions of the evolution and use of urban policy instruments suggest the need for more attention to context. If, in the case of stimulus packages, there was an urgent need to stimulate demand, increase employment, and reduce urban poverty, three foci seem appropriate:

- Focus on achieving specific positive impacts in cities, rather than including rural areas at the same time. Cities have denser populations and economic activities, and hence more powerful multipliers.
- Focus on expenditures in cities with higher numbers of people in slums (i.e. the sites of highest vulnerability).
- Focus on cities with high shares of employment in the informal sector, where multipliers work quickly and reach the poor.

The relevance of urban policy instruments to the real world

Some observers of internationally supported urban assistance projects remarked in the 1970s that some projects seemed to want the context to more closely resemble the projects rather than the projects more closely relating to the real world. This criticism seems appropriate again today in the world of national efforts to affect cities through national economic policies, market-oriented investment strategies, and often high-profile private-sector investments in large residential developments or shopping centers. Many of these instruments have been perceived as effective catalysts of new economic and social behavior, without considering the contexts in which they would operate.

A lesson from the implementation of some national urban policies has been that their application in local contexts often is "anti-poor" and ineffective in strengthening local urban institutions at the city level to perform essential urban management functions. The cases of Brazil, Chile, and Mexico, presented in later chapters, demonstrate that many national urban policies have proven to be dominated by the desire to increase housing production, usually by private developers, without sufficient attention paid to the damaging urban consequences that these policies and projects generate.

This disappointing record of urban policy in many Latin American countries underlines the need for more historical evaluation of policies and the application of these lessons to the design of new initiatives. This book is intended to contribute to that objective.

Bibliography

Burkhead, J. and Miner, J., (1971), *Public Expenditure*, Aldine and Atherton, New Brunswick.

Campbell, T., (2003), *The Quiet Revolution: Decentralization and the Rise of Political Participation in Latin American Cities*, University of Pittsburg Press, Pittsburg.

Castells, M., (1989), *The Informational City: Information Technology, Economic Restructuring, and the Urban Regional Process*, Blackwell, Cambridge, MA.

Cohen, M. A., (1974), *Urban Policy and Political Conflict in Africa: A Study of the Ivory Coast*, University of Chicago Press, Chicago.

Cohen, M. A., (1982), *Learning by Doing: Urban Development Lending 1972–1982*, World Bank, Washington.

Cohen, M. A., (1983), *Learning by Doing: World Bank Lending for Urban Development, 1972–1982*, World Bank, Washington.

Cohen, M. A., (2012), "La ciudad en el contexto de la crisis mundial: entender los efectos y reforzar la eficacia de los paquetes de estimulo", In Belil, M., Borja, J., and Corti, M., (eds.), *Ciudades, una ecuación imposible*, Icaria, Barcelona, pp. 35–58.

Cohen, M. A. and Hershey, P., (2008), "Inter-American Development Bank Urban Upgrading and Employment Generation: A Conceptual Approach and Methodology for Selecting and Conducting Case Studies", Working Paper, The New School University, New York.

Dillinger, W. and Webb, S., (1999), "Decentralization and Fiscal Management in Colombia", World Bank Policy Research Working Paper No. 2122.

Gutman, M. and Hardoy, J. E., (2007), *Buenos Aires 1536–2006, Historia de la region metropolitana*, Ediciones Infinito, Buenos Aires.

Marris, P., (1967), *Family and Social Change in an African City*, Routledge, London; Miner, H., (ed.), (1967), *The City in Modern Africa*, Frederick A. Praeger, New York.

Mayo, S. and Angel, S., (1993), *Housing: Enabling Markets to Work*, World Bank, Washington.

Meade, T. A., (1997), *'Civilizing' Rio: Reform and Resistance in a Brazilian City, 1889–1930*, University Park, Pennsylvania State University Press, Pennsylvania.

Municipality of Medellín, (2014), *Laboratorio Medellín: Catálogo de diez prácticas vivas*, UN Habitat-Inter-American Development Bank, Municipality of Medellín, Medellín.

Murillo, M. V., (2009), *Political Competition, Partisanship, and Policy Making in Latin American Public Utilities*, Cambridge University Press, Cambridge.

Rodríguez, A., Rodríguez, P., and Sugranyes, A., (2015), *Con Subsidio, Sin Derecho: la situacion del derecho a una vivienda adecuada en Chile*, Ediciones SUR, Santiago.

Sassen, S., (1990), *The Global City*, Princeton University Press, Princeton.

Stiglitz, J. E., (2002), "Information and the Change in the Paradigm in Economics", *American Economic Review*, 92:3, pp. 460–501.

Stren, R. E., (1975), *Urban Inequality and Housing Policy in Tanzania: The Problem of Squatting*, Research Series: Institute of International Studies, University of California, Berkeley, No. 24.

3 Mexico: from Habitat II to Habitat III

Assessment of the commitments undertaken

*Alicia Ziccardi**

Introduction

This chapter assesses the fulfillment of commitments made by the government of Mexico at the Second United Nations Conference on Human Settlements (Habitat II). To this end, six major themes were identified – governance and urban development, environment, housing and urban infrastructure, urban economy and productivity, urban poverty, inequality and social exclusion, and urban morphology – to analyze the advances, setbacks, and challenges faced by Latin American cities before the development of a New Urban Agenda in Quito, Ecuador, during the Third United Nations Conference on Human Settlements that took place in 2016.

Since Habitat II, Mexico continued to experience an intense urbanization process. In 1995, 58.4 million Mexicans – of a total of 91.2 million – lived in one of the localities of the National Urban System (NUS).[1] By 2010 they were 81.2 million of a total of 112.3 million, that is – according to data from the last national census – 7 of every 10 Mexicans lived in urban areas (CONAPO, 2012: 21).

The following main features of the urbanization process stand out:

- The city system went from being a hierarchical model of capital and infrastructure concentration and specialization in a few metropolitan areas, mainly in Mexico City, Guadalajara, and Monterrey, to a set of city networks made up of territories benefiting from the change in the economic model – territories oriented towards export activities (*maquila*, manufacturing), services connected to global circuits, and/or tourism. This new structure hold place in a context of low economic growth at the national level and a weak integration of regional productive chains, as well as deepening socioeconomic inequality in the functioning of the city system (Sánchez Almanza, 2016: 31).
- The country has a consolidated metropolitan system. In 1995, the 31 identified metropolitan areas concentrated 43 percent of the national population (CONAPO, 1998: 59), whereas in 2010 there were already 59 metropolitan areas, accounting for just over half of the national population

(56.8 percent) (CONAPO, 2012: 35). In the border and port metropolitan areas, the population clustered in central urban areas; the industrial cities included suburbanization processes, whereas the bigger ones saw a depopulation of the central city (Guadalajara) or its repopulation (Mexico City and Monterrey) (Sobrino, 2014: 50–51).

- From the economic and functional points of view, in 2010 10 metropolises with a bifunctional structure were identified[2] – with economies based in manufacturing and tourism – and the larger metropolises transformed their structure becoming polycentric: these include Mexico City, Guadalajara, Monterrey, Puebla, and Toluca (Sobrino, 2014: 52).
- The population flow ceased to be rural-urban, and the exchanges made to and from the national urban system became more relevant. In 2010 alone, these migratory flows represented 73 percent of the total (CONAPO, 2012: 31).

These dynamics of the NUS responded to the very complex economic, social, and political scenarios of the country between 1996 and 2015, during which there were four governments.

The beginning of Ernesto Zedillo's administration (1994–2000) took place in a context of economic and political crisis. In December 1994, a few days after he came to power, the Mexican peso was devalued, unleashing one of the most important financial crises in the country. In 1995, gross domestic product (GDP) contracted by 6 percent, and between 1994 and 1996, income per capita decreased by 27 percent (INEGI, 2010a). In 1995, the 'open' unemployment rate reached 6.2 percent (CEFP, 2005) and poverty increased, particularly in urban areas. To reduce the effects of the crisis, a conditional cash transfer program – the Education, Health, and Food Program (PROGRESA) – was introduced in 1997.

In the context of this legitimation crisis of the government of the hegemonic party (Institutional Revolutionary Party, PRI) and the development of increasing political competition, there were changes of government in some states and municipalities that began to demand greater autonomy and resources for local governments (Ziccardi, 2003). In this way, the decentralization process moved forward, starting with the legislative reforms of 1999 that recognized the municipality as a unit of government within the federal system (Guillén and Ziccardi, 2004). Likewise, a fund was created to transfer resources directly to the state and municipal governments (Ziccardi, 2015b). Another important reform brought about during this period was the 1996 electoral reform, after which Mexico City was able to elect its head of government for the first time, electing Cuauhtémoc Cárdenas, an engineer and the candidate of the Partido de la Revolución Democrática (PRD) and a leftist coalition. This coalition has won the government on three other occasions and maintained a certain degree of autonomy in relation to the urban development and housing policy of the federal government.

The government of Vicente Fox (2000–2006) was the first change of government from the PRI, and it deepened the neoliberal economic policy implemented in Mexico since the mid-1980s. Although there were significant extraordinary resources – resulting from oil and non-oil industries – and the public debt increased considerably, the expected growth did not come about. On average, GDP grew 2.3 percent in these 6 years – less than in other countries of the region and during the previous 12 years. Unemployment increased between 2000 and 2006, and self-employment activities of low quality and low productivity were favored (Terrones et al., 2010: 84). Despite these problems, national and urban poverty decreased, inflation was controlled, and international reserves increased.

The restructuring of housing policy, which adopted financial profitability criteria, stands out in this period. To this end, the National Housing Development Commission (Comisión Nacional de Fomento a la Vivienda – CONAFOVI) was created as an entity with ample power, which led to the release of the resources from workers' funds (INFONAVIT and FOVISSSTE) to incorporate them into a protected housing market that allowed companies to obtain high rates of profit from the construction of massive housing projects in remote suburbs lacking basic urban goods and services (Ziccardi, 2015a).

During the second National Action Party (PAN) government, under Felipe Calderón (2006–2012), one of the most severe global financial crises took place, affecting the national economy and contributing to the fall in GDP. The unemployment rate and the informal sector increased,[3] adding to a sustained loss of the purchasing power of salaries (Center for Multidisciplinary Analysis, Faculty of Economics, CAM-FE, UNAM, 2012). According to the new multidimensional measure of poverty established in the Social Development Law of 2004, poverty in urban areas increased (CONEVAL, 2014b).

Shortly before the beginning of this six-year term, a new housing law (DOF, 2006) was enacted, repealing the prior 1984 law. The housing policy designed in the previous administration was consolidated and characterized as being disconnected from urban planning, resulting in the expansion of cities and an unresolved demand for urban goods and services for the lowest-income population. Housing agencies financed the massive housing construction and guaranteed high-profit rates to real estate developers, but without considering the quality of the resulting housing projects. At the same time, new financing lines were opened to renovate and improve housing and for the social production of habitat, but with very limited resources. During these last two governments, we could say, "lots of housing was built but very little city" (Ziccardi, 2015a).

From 2012 to 2018 under President Enrique Peña Nieto, poverty, unemployment, and low purchasing power persisted, particularly among the population living in urban areas. Although so-called structural reforms were approved in order to attract investment as a lever for economic growth, GDP growth was only 1.4 percent in 2013 and 2.5 percent in 2015 (INEGI, 2016a). Among the approved reforms, labor reform is one of the most important. It sought to increase employment by making labor regulations more flexible. However, low wages and longer working hours persisted, adding to the loss of purchasing power. This is reflected in urban poverty levels. In terms of urban development, there is evidence of some efforts to articulate a national urban policy; the institutional architecture was restructured, centralizing the functions of urban, agrarian, territorial, and housing development with the creation of the Office of Agrarian, Land, and Urban Development (Secretaría de Desarrollo Agrario, Territorial y Urbano – SEDATU). In addition, a new human settlements law was discussed and the housing law was modified. However, it is worth noting that the housing policy established in prior years is very difficult to transform (Ziccardi, 2015a).

National urban policies and urban governance

The national urban policies

Since the Habitat II Conference, the urban and territorial dimension of Mexico has been transformed by public policies. Several legal, normative, and policy instruments – housing, land use regulation, transportation, ecological planning, and water, among others – affecting the urban territory were designed. However, this normative framework works in a pragmatic and poorly articulated way. In each six-year period, strategies for urban areas were drawn in accordance with the priorities established by neoliberal economic policies that basically seek to attract domestic and foreign investment. Nevertheless, the subordination of urban development to housing finance policy and weak territorial and land-use planning processes in public policies, still prevail. There is also a tendency to transfer greater urban management responsibilities to local governments, without strengthening their institutional framework. Thus, it is fair to say that public action in relation to urban development and land-use planning has not adjusted to the profound transformations that have taken place in the economy, territory, society, and political life during the last 20 years. In particular, we perceive a lack of effectiveness to generate a better quality of life for all citizens.

Ernesto Zedillo's government (1994–2000)

The National Development Plan (Plan Nacional de Desarrollo – PND) is the instrument in which the federal government defines the objectives, strategies, and priorities for each six-year period and the specific programs for each sector. The PND of Zedillo's government had among its objectives to achieve "vigorous, sustained, and sustainable economic growth" and to extend to the entire country "opportunities for individual and community improvement, under the principles of equity and justice" (DOF, 1995). These proposals became – regarding the cities – the 1995–2000 National Urban Development Program, which established as its priority lines to "promote the spatial planning of economic activities and population according to the potential of cities and regions" and to "promote the orderly growth of cities under principles of environmental balance" (DOF, 1996).

To achieve such objectives, four strategic programs were developed:

- The "100 Cities Program" to promote the development of medium-sized cities and reduce the pressure on metropolitan areas;[4]
- The consolidation, regulation, and reordering program for the largest metropolitan areas;
- The spatial planning and promotion of urban development programs for the federative entities; and
- A program to promote social participation in urban development (DOF, 1996).

The federal government agency in charge at the time was the Under-Secretariat of Urban Development and Housing created within the Secretariat of Social Development.

This policy brought about a reduction of migration to the four large metropolitan areas – Mexico City, Guadalajara, Monterrey, and Puebla – and an increase in the population of the medium-sized cities. Large-scale urban infrastructure projects were built with federal, state, municipal, private initiative, and credit resources, which allowed local governments to increase their financial capacity. As part of the fiscal decentralization process, this program stopped operating in 1998, and the resources came directly under the control of the local governments through the creation of budget account XXXIII in the federal budget.

Another measure was the updating of the urban development programs for the medium-sized cities; most of them were legally approved and registered in the Public Registry. The government also approved the Territorial Planning Program for the Metropolitan Zone of the Valley of Mexico (POZMVM) and the installation of different metropolitan coordination commissions in this area. At the state level, laws and urban development plans were updated in almost half of the states (Government of México, 2000).

At the end of this period, the government began to implement a policy of territorial planning with an interdisciplinary approach. However, at the same time, the normative planning of the territory in governmental practice gradually began to lose legitimacy. Instead, the efforts focused decisively on social programs for poverty reduction – mainly PROGRESA – and environmental issues became more relevant in public policies (Ziccardi, 2008).

At the local level, the municipal governments of the National Action Party (PAN) promoted the creation of local planning bodies (IMPLANES). In Mexico City, ruled by the PRD, the General Program for Urban Development was approved, and an innovative participatory urban planning experience developed with the implementation of Partial Urban Development Programs in 31 zones of the city that had serious social conflicts and important urban problems (Ziccardi, 2003: 148).

Social participation gained ground in the framework of the democratization process of the political system with the creation of the "National Advisory Council for Urban Development, with representatives of the public, private, and social sectors in order to create a space for convergence and consensus-building aimed at strengthening the national urban development and territorial planning policy" (SEDESOL, 2000).

The Vicente Fox administration (2000–2006)

During this period, the territory was considered a strategic element for development and economic and social prosperity; new views on strategic planning were adopted with the aim of improving local conditions and competing in international markets. Likewise, the governmental discourse incorporated the notion of sustainability, and the strengthening of federalism gained relevance, leading to the creation of the National Institute for Federalism and Municipal Development (Instituto Nacional para el Federalismo y el Desarrollo Municipal – INAFED) in 2002. The 2001–2006 National Development Plan considered that cities fulfill a double role: "being the material and organizational support of the productive, social, and cultural activities of society" and a mechanism to "take development to large marginalized and poverty-stricken regions of the country" (DOF, 2001). Accordingly, the National Urban Development Program (PDU) (2001–2006) established three strategies: to develop a territorial planning policy, an urban and regional development policy, and a land and territorial reserve policy, as well as specific actions focused on the prevention and attention of impacts caused by natural disasters. In this context, changes were made in the institutional design and the Under-Secretariat of Urban Development and Housing became the Under-Secretariat of Urban Development and Territorial Planning, devoted to urban development, territorial planning, land and territorial reserves, regional development, and overcoming urban poverty; this last duty actually took up the greatest efforts of the under-secretariat.

The regional issue gained new impetus and gave origin to the Office for Strategic Planning in the Presidency of the Republic, which implemented mesoregional programs (Ziccardi, 2008; Fuentes, 2007). Other initiatives sought to specifically improve the conditions of the southern region and promote its "proactive insertion into the global economy" (the Puebla Panama Plan and the March to the South Program) (Hiernaux and Torres, 2008: 114). However, these initiatives had very limited resources and acted apart from other secretariats, so there were coordination and implementation problems (Garcés and Márques, 2007: 18).

One of the most important changes was the creation of a new decentralized body: the National Commission for the Promotion of Housing (Comisión Nacional de Fomento a la Vivienda – CONAFOVI). The commission reorganized the sector and laid the groundwork for freeing the workers' resources deposited in INFONAVIT and FOVISSSTE, designing financial actions that would allow large-scale projects.

The government of Felipe Calderón (2006–2012)

During the second PAN government, headed by Felipe Calderón, the subordination of urban development policy to housing policy – a process that had begun in the previous administration – became explicit. The National Development Plan (2007–2012) established as one of its goals "to expand access to financing for housing projects intended for the less privileged segments of the population, in a context of orderly, rational, and sustainable development of human settlements"(DOF, 2007). With this purpose in mind, it posed several strategies to generate a dynamic housing market and promote housing improvement, progressive housing, and social production of habitat. However, in reality, what was privileged was funding of new housing destined for employees with better incomes.

Even though sustainable human development was acknowledged as the guiding principle of public action, urban development policy was subordinated to housing policy, which, in turn, was closely linked to economic and financial policy. This was evident when the National Urban Development Program of the Calderon administration was not approved. This program weakened urban regulations, enabling the adoption of a dispersed city model fostered by the construction companies that developed large, low-quality residential complexes in distant peripheries, taking advantage of inexpensive land to obtain huge profits. This boost to housing was accompanied by heavy investments in infrastructure, mainly for roads in the center and north of the country.

A general assessment of this six-year period shows that territorial and urban planning, already delegitimized, was weakened further. In a context of relatively weak public institutions and a strong private sector, urban development was subordinated to the housing finance policy that aimed at solving the quantitative housing deficit of the country (OECD, 2015a: 162).

Enrique Peña Nieto's administration (2012–2018)

During the Pena Nieto administration, the normative instruments emphasized the importance of adequate planning of the territory to improve the quality of life of its people. Among the goals of the National Development Program (2013–2018) were "to achieve a society of full citizen and human rights" and "to promote greater productivity through policies facilitating a social and economically optimal use of the national territory" (DOF, 2013). The National Urban Development Program (PNDU, 2013–2018) established six goals:

- To control the expansion of urban areas and consolidate the cities;
- To have a model of urban development that guaranteed sustainability;
- To design and implement regulatory, fiscal, administrative and control instruments for land management;
- To promote a policy of sustainable mobility;

- To avoid human settlements in risk areas and reduce vulnerability in the face of natural disasters; and
- To consolidate the national regional development policy based on the local usage and economic potential.

Likewise, the government established a sectorial program for Agrarian, Territorial, and Urban Development (PSDATU), in which territorial and land-use planning were considered "focal points for the welfare of the people and the efficient use of the land."

The institutional design of this government changed so that all responsibilities pertaining to rural and urban land-use planning, housing, and sustainable development were brought together under a single secretariat. To this end, the Ministry of Agrarian, Territorial and Urban Development (SEDATU) was created in 2013, integrating the Secretariat of Agrarian Reform, the Under-Secretariat of Urban Development and Territorial Planning, the Commission for the Regularization of Land Tenure (CORETT), the National Fund for Popular Housing Trust (FONHAPO), and the National Housing Commission (CONAVI).

The investment in infrastructure, mainly roads, sought to revive previously abandoned transportation systems – such as passenger trains – in order to improve connectivity between the production, distribution, and domestic consumption centers (Government of México, 2015). However, some of these projects were affected by a lack of transparency that caused popular discontent (such was the case with the construction of the Interurban Train Mexico-Toluca) and led to the demand that the government put an end to the corruption permeating the construction of public works.

Regarding the link between housing and urban expansion, new systems were developed to direct subsidies towards well-located projects in terms of employment, with better urban facilities and adopting environmental technologies. This mechanism, however, has not been very effective because – among other things – it limited the planning competencies of municipalities. On the other hand, developers who own land outside the perimeters defined for the subsidies exert their influence to obtain approval for their more distant projects.

In short, in these 20 years, urban development policy was weakened and was subordinated to a housing policy promoting the territorial expansion of cities, with serious deficits in public facilities, infrastructure, and basic services, all of which leads to residential segregation processes and an increase in urban and social inequalities. An indicator of the poor quality of housing and its remote location is the fact that the 2010 census registered 4.9 million unoccupied homes (Ziccardi, 2015a).

The process of decentralization and urban governance

In recent decades, the country has carried out a decentralization process, with the central government delegating faculties and resources to local governments.

However, it has had limited scope and results (Martínez Assad and Ziccardi, 2000). In 1999, article 115 of the constitution was reformed and municipalities were recognized as government units within the federal system (Guillén and Ziccardi, coord., 2004). The 1997 reform of the Fiscal Coordination Law made it possible for the municipalities to be creditworthy and created the XXXIII budget account of the federal expenditure budget. Through this account, the federation transfers resources for basic education, health, and social infrastructure to the state and municipal governments. Since its creation, those resources have increased – but are still limited. Although there is a great difference in the efficiency with which local governments assume their responsibilities, in this process of fiscal decentralization, there is a greater exercise of public spending by subnational governments (Ziccardi, 2015b). In 2000, the federal government executed 71.2 percent of public expenditure, the states 23.7 percent, and the municipal governments 5.1 percent. Whereas in 2012, the federal administration executed 50 percent, the states 39 percent, and the municipalities 11 percent (Ziccardi, 2015b).

At the local level prevails a situation characterized by

> an obsolete institutional design that reproduces the sectorial and vertical structure of the central or state governments and their lack of institutional coordination; a strong dependence on federal or central government transfers in the case of Mexico City (former Federal District); government personnel are recruited for their political allegiance rather than professional qualifications; sectorial local public policies are disjointed and policies to promote local economic development are non-existent.
>
> (Ziccardi, 2008: 133)

At the same time, the situation of the municipalities deteriorated in recent years due to

> the massive production of housing, which affected the municipal governments by producing an increased demand for land as well as the private appropriation of large territorial reserves. The local governments had no legal, financial, and accountability instruments to regulate or control those speculative processes and corrupt practices.
>
> (Ziccardi, 2015a)

Constitutionally, the municipalities have the possibility of working together for the provision of public services, even if they do not belong to the same state, but they must request the approval of state legislatures (Ziccardi, 2003). There are also experiences of metropolitan coordination, mainly in Mexico City, where several sectorial coordination committees have operated among the entities of the city, but with little involvement from their municipalities (Ziccardi, 2003: 138–139).

Finally, among the financial instruments to promote urban development, it is worth mentioning the Metropolitan Funds made up of federal resources allocated to the metropolitan areas of the country. The Metropolitan Fund was included in the Expenditure Budget of the Federation in 2006 with a total amount of 1 billion pesos ($91.7 million dollars), purportedly intended for the metropolitan area of the Valley of Mexico (Zona Metropolitana del Valle de Mexico – ZMVM). In 2016, its resources increased to 10.4 billion pesos ($577 million dollars) distributed among 47 metropolitan areas in the country. In the case of the Metropolitan Fund of the Valley of Mexico, of the total resources obtained between 2006 and 2015, 27.6 percent went to road infrastructure projects, 25 percent to hydraulic infrastructure, and 20 percent to public transportation.

Citizen participation in land-use planning and management processes

The republic's constitution contains the legal foundations of citizen participation: it established democracy as the country's way of life and recognizes the existence of a planning system based on consultation and participation; it includes the right to information and rules that the local government administrations must guarantee citizen participation. Likewise, several federal and state laws refer to the participation of citizens and their organizations in different public matters. In the local sphere, 24 of 31 states have a citizen participation law and one more entity has a Popular Consultations Law.

Regarding the spaces for public participation, there are the Development Planning Committees (COPLADES) and the Municipal Development Planning Committees (COPLADEMUN). These are the first forms of institutionalized public participation and fulfill consultation functions in the resource allocation processes of the federation to local governments. They are formed by representatives of local interest groups (professionals, businessmen, neighbors, representatives of local organizations, etc.), but, in fact, they often tend to work as instruments for the legitimation of decisions taken within the local government apparatus (Ziccardi, 2008).

There are also the Municipal Planning Institutes (IMPLANES), decentralized public bodies of the city council that "act as local planning agencies and have introduced important participatory planning practices" (González and Ziccardi, 2015). The first institute was created in Guanajuato in 1994, and in 2015 there were already 52, most of them in cities in the north and central part of the country. Similarly, as of 2003, Local Urban Observatories (UOL) were created in the main cities as "organizations devoted to analyzing urban problems and formulating projects and public policies to address them" (SEDESOL and UN-HABITAT, 2011b). Other spaces for citizen participation appear in social programs, as was the case with the Habitat Program, which included citizen participation, consultation with the communities, and social audit and evaluation (Ziccardi, 2008).

As for the mechanisms used, the referendum is respected in 27 states, the plebiscite in 26, and the popular initiative in 19 states (Olvera, 2009). States such as Jalisco and Mexico City have other instruments, such as popular consultation – sporadically used when a government decision sparks conflicts – or participatory budgets. In terms of planning, innovative participatory methodologies have been developed for the design and updating of territory planning and management instruments in cities, metropolitan areas, regions, municipalities, population centers, neighborhoods, colonies and towns, and, more recently, historical centers. They are instruments of socially consensual government (Ziccardi, 2004; Cortés Rocha, 2015).

We must highlight the progress made nationally in terms of the recognition of economic, social, cultural, and environmental rights with the constitutional reform of June 10, 2011, which gives constitutional status to the treaties signed by Mexico on these matters. Locally, the Charter of the City of Mexico for the Right to the City stands out – signed in July 2010 by citizens, political organizations, and governmental authorities of Mexico City (Álvarez and Ziccardi, 2015). Furthermore, different laws regarding transparency and accountability have been passed at both the federal and local levels, and, in 2002, the Federal Institute for Access to Federal Public Information (IFAI) was created. In the local sphere, the recently approved law "to make Mexico City an open city" to improve the availability of public information and strengthen participation stands out.

Sustainability and environmental resource management

Policy and environmental resource management

The active and committed role of Mexico in the international arena has helped promote a national environmental agenda, creating modern institutions and legal and regulatory frameworks, which are constantly renewed.[5] Among their most important involvements are the Conferences of the Parties (COP 3, 13, 16, 17, 18, 20, 21), signing, among other agreements, the Kyoto Protocol and its amendment, the Bali Action Plan, the Cancun Agreements, the Lima Call for Climate Action, and the Paris Agreement. Moreover, since 1994 Mexico has been a signatory to the United Nations Framework Convention on Climate Change, has taken part in different working groups of the Intergovernmental Panel on Climate Change (IPCC), and has participated in the Commission for Sustainable Development of the United Nations (CSD).

Ernesto Zedillo's government (1996–2000)

Mexico's integration into the international economy – with the signing of the North American Free Trade Agreement (NAFTA) with the United States and Canada and its entry into the group of nations of the OECD – speeded up the regulatory, legal, and institutional modernization of environmental issues in the country (Domínguez, 2010; Lezama, 2010a). In this context, the government's first action was to create the Secretariat of the Environment, Natural Resources and Fisheries (Secretaría del Medio Ambiente, Recursos Naturales y Pesca

SEMARNAP), which represented a great advance for environmental resource management. It concentrated in a single government agency the responsibilities for the use and care of renewable natural resources and the environment, as well as the promotion of sustainable development (Domínguez, 2010: 281). This secretariat implemented strategic planning actions and transferred some responsibilities to the states while seeking to strengthen local capacities through the Institutional Environmental Development Program – although without achieving a great impact (Lezama, 2010a).

This new institutional design was based on the transition from a governmental vision to attaining an ecological balance based on sustainability and required legislative changes (Lezama, 2010a). In 1996, weighty changes to the General Law of Ecological Equilibrium and Environmental Protection (Ley General del Equilibrio Ecológico y la Protección al Ambiente – LGEEPA) – created in 1988 – were approved. With the reform of Article 1, achieving sustainable development – defined as "A process that can be assessed through criteria and indicators of environmental, economic, and social nature" – became an objective of the environmental policy (DOF, 1996b). It is worth noting that the assessment of the environmental impact and the ecological land-use planning became policy instruments (INECC, 2007).

Regarding ecological land-use planning, Antonio Azuela (2013) pointed out that these reforms increased the existing confusion between urban planning and environmental planning because they created two territorial areas whose limits and interactions are still a challenge in terms of planning for the territory.

The reform also broadened the margins of popular participation and represented a turnaround for the right to information, with the acknowledgment of the diffuse legal interests that opened the possibility for citizens to challenge acts of authority (INECC, 2007).

The most vital reform of this administration was made in 1999 to the fourth constitutional article, recognizing everyone's right to an adequate environment and establishing that it is the state's responsibility to promote comprehensive and sustainable national development (DOF, 1999).

All this resulted in new approaches to government programs. The aim of the Sectorial Environmental Program was "to slow down the tendencies of environmental deterioration and lay the foundations for an ecological restoration and recovery process based on sustainability criteria" (DOF, 1996c). Furthermore, it recognized the importance of the industrial system as a key element of regional and environmental transformations and established an agreement and negotiation policy with the polluting industrial companies to encourage greater participation, based on self-regulatory instruments (voluntary standards and product certification) and environmental audits (Micheli, 2000: 94). According to Vicente Ugalde (2010), thanks to this, progress was made towards translating environmental laws and regulations into concrete actions. In terms of budget, during this period there was a significant increase in resources. In 1994, the net expense in the environment and natural resources was 2,168,000 pesos (US$640 million)[6] – a 0.2 percent of the programmable spending of the federal government – but it increased considerably at the end of the six-year period. In 2000, it was just over 28,361,000 pesos (US$2,999,000) – representing 2.5 percent – (Centro de Estudios de Finanzas Públicas, de la Cámara de Diputados, CEF, 2012).

The government of Vicente Fox (2001–2006)

During the Fox administration, a lot of legislative productivity occurred and the institutional architecture was redesigned, expanding the institutions in charge of environmental matters. In 2000, the SEMARNAP was transformed into the Secretariat of Environment and Natural Resources (SEMARNAT). From this period on, sustainable development has permeated the discourse in public administration, and not just that of the offices in charge of environmental resource management. The federal government's program to promote sustainable development included specific commitments to the programs of 30 federal agencies coordinated by SEMARNAT and was based on tools called Cross-Cutting Agendas for Public Policies for Sustainable Development (Lezama, 2010a: 51).

The formalization and implementation of a national policy for the prevention, adaptation, and mitigation of climate change began by applying a cross-sectoral and cross-cutting perspective. In 2005 the Inter-Secretariat Commission on Climate Change was created and adopted a Climate Action Strategy for compliance with the commitments made in the UN Framework Convention on Climate Change.

In 2001, the net expense for environment and natural resources was just over 24,013,000 pesos (US$2,571,000), whereas at the end of Fox's term, it amounted to 38,529,000 pesos (US$3,533.72 million); that is, it went from representing 2.1 percent to 2.4 percent of the programmable spending of the federal government (CEF, 2012).

The government of Felipe Calderón (2006–2012)

As noted earlier, the vision of environmental sustainability had been strengthened as a cross-cutting issue of all public policies. The National Development Plan 2007–2012 placed sustainable human development as the premise and transformational driving force of the country, with environmental sustainability as one of its five guiding principles. However, this approach encountered tough obstacles in the sectorial structure of the federal public administration, as well as "the lack of a compulsory nature in the shared commitments and the inadequacy of the legal framework in the areas of integrality, cross-cutting and sustainable development" (SEMARNAT, 2006: 49, cited by Domínguez, 2010: 272).

In this six-year period, climate change was recognized as the main challenge in the global environmental agenda. For this reason, various measures were implemented to deal with its effects. In 2007, the National Climate Change Strategy was published, laying down the ranges, possibilities, and steps aimed at reducing greenhouse gas emissions and "outlined the needs of the country to build adaptation capacities" (CICC, 2007: 3). In 2009, the Special Climate Change Program (Programa Especial de Cambio Climático – PECC) was published with the purpose of developing a comprehensive policy to face climate change (CICC, 2012). Finally, in 2012, the General Law on Climate Change was published to guarantee the continuity of climate change policies and adjust the country's regulations to established international agreements (CICC, 2012). The law established an institutional framework for the convergence of mandates of different areas of government, based on the National System of Climate Change (CICC, 2012). It established an emission reduction target of 30 percent in 2020 and 50 percent in 2050 – compared to 2000 – and included regulatory mechanisms, such as the Inventory and the National Emissions Registry, and economic tools, such as the Climate Change Fund (CICC, 2012). Regarding the adaptation to climate change, it included diagnostic instruments such as the risk atlases, as well as prevention and urban planning mechanisms. Likewise, it established the foundations for an agreement with society in order to promote the transition towards a competitive, sustainable, and low-carbon economy (CICC, 2012).

The expenditures allocated to the environment and natural resources registered a slight decrease. In 2007, the allocated expenditure was 51,636,000 pesos (US$4,725,000), whereas in 2012 it amounted to 54,717,000 pesos (US$4,154.80 million) – representing 3.5 percent and 3.3 percent of the programmable spending of the federal government, respectively (CEF, 2012).

The government of Enrique Peña Nieto (2012–2018)

The National Development Plan 2013–2018 proposed "to promote and guide an inclusive green growth that preserves the natural heritage while generating wealth, competitiveness, and employment," advancing a cross-cutting approach that has fostered the adoption and inclusion of the concept of "green growth" by the agencies of the Federal Public Administration (APF). As a result, 14 sectorial programs in 14 federal agencies implemented actions with this objective in mind.

In terms of climate change, the institutional framework defined in the General Law on Climate Change was established in 2013 and 2014. A new National Climate Change Strategy was designed with objectives in terms of adaptation and mitigation and aims to accelerate the energy transition towards clean energy sources, reduce the intensity of energy consumption, and move to sustainable city models (Government of México, 2015b).

Also in 2014, the Special Climate Change Program for the six-year period was published, the Climate Change Fund began to operate, and a carbon tax was approved. It established conditioned mitigation commitments (made with its own resources) to reduce up to 36 percent of greenhouse gases and 70 percent of black carbon, and unconditional commitments (through assistance) to a reduction of 22 percent of greenhouse gas emissions and 51 percent of the emission of short-lived climate pollutants by 2030. In addition, it proposed to strengthen the adaptive capacity of at least half of the most vulnerable munici-palities in the national territory, adopt early warning systems and risk manage-ment in all levels of government, and reduce deforestation to zero (Government of México, 2015b).

In this context, various legal and practical actions have been taken to encour-age the energy transition and, at the same time, reduce energy consumption. The constitutional reform to energy stands out: implying the "transformation of the regulatory framework that currently sets the rules and manages the energy generation and distribution market" (Ruiz, 2015) and considers the possibility of private participation in the oil and gas sector – previously monopolized by a state company (Pemex) – which could increase the production of hydrocarbons and the greenhouse gas emissions of this sector.

The Nationally Appropriate Mitigation Actions (NAMA) of sustainable and urban transport were developed. The transport NAMA focuses on 29 met-ropolitan areas with more than 500,000 inhabitants and seeks to build a pedestrian infrastructure, optimize the existing transportation system with integrated systems, renew modal transfer centers to ease connections, and promote mixed-use urban development (SEDATU, 2015). Additionally, in 2015 the Guide for the Implementation of Transport-Oriented Develop-ment Policies and Projects was published with the goal of strengthening and expanding the technical capacities of local administrations to execute these projects, encouraging low-emission urban development. Likewise, Mexico was the first country to grant a sustainable housing NAMA, aimed at improv-ing the energy efficiency of housing and promoting the use of sustainable energy (SEDATU, 2015).

In 2013, the net expense allocated to the environment and natural resources was 56,471,000 pesos (US\$4,422,000) (CEF, 2013), whereas in 2016 the bud-geted expenditure for this branch decreased to 55,770,000 pesos (US\$3,092,000) (SHCP, 2016), which represented a variation in the total spending proportion, going from 3.2 percent in 2013 to 1.2 percent in 2016.

Subnational governments and their commitment to the environment

Although the federal progress in legislative, institutional, and programmatic terms is noteworthy, at the municipal level, it was much lower. Municipali-ties are responsible for the provision and sanitation of water, drainage and sewerage, collection and disposal of solid waste, local ecological planning, civil protection, and control and monitoring of land use and any changes. However, many municipalities lack the institutional capacity and resources to develop effective environmental governance (Arroyo and Rodríguez, 2014: 503–504). Until now, they have been unsuccessful in numerous issues – such as the definition of water and waste charges to cover the costs of providing these services – and have relied heavily on federal funding (OECD, 2013: 17). The coordination of the three levels of government in terms of environ-mental and energy policy is frequently unfeasible because they face confusing competencies.

Among the main environmental tools applied at the local level, the municipalities developed ecological land-use programs to regulate the use of land and its productive activities. Regarding climate change, the Municipal Climate Action Plan (Plan de Acción Climática Municipal – PACMUN) – aimed at creating local technical capacities in this subject and promoting local policies – is the main instrument at the municipal level. There are 70 PACMUNs in the country, representing only 2.84 percent of the country's municipalities, despite the fact that the Law on Climate Change states that all municipalities have the duty to design and implement programs to reduce their emissions and strengthen their adaptation capacities (Delgado et al., 2015).

According to Delgado et al. (2015: 118), the experience of Mexico City (formerly a federal district) stands out, given that the measures implemented there respond to the identified challenges of climate change, act transversally, and define indicators to assess its implementation. The Climate Action Program of Mexico City (PACCM 2008–2012) is significant as the first of its kind to perform an assessment of its performance; the results show that "Mexico City reduced its greenhouse gas [GHG] emissions by 4.5 percent with respect to its trend line, thus neutralizing the expected emission growth for 2012" (CMM, 2012).

However, this policy has been limited by the regulations of the spatial organization of urban growth, which "responds basically to a speculative logic and subsumes the socio-spatial equity and harmonious relations with the environment that serve as its support" (Puente, 2010: 379).

In the metropolitan sphere, there was a coordinated effort regarding the care and protection of the environment, and there is a Metropolitan Environmental Agenda, agreed between the State of Mexico and Mexico City governments, to deal with issues related to water, air, solid waste, land, and climate change.

Internationally, the Mexico City Pact (PCM) was signed in the World Mayors Council on Climate Change (WMCCC) on November 21, 2010, and represents one of the main agreements allowing cities and subnational governments to directly access multilateral, national, and regional international financing to undertake mitigation and adaptation projects (Sánchez, 2012, cit. in CMM, 2014: 33).

Environmental urban sustainability

The accelerated urbanization of the country has increased the pressure on the environment due to the consumption and settlement patterns of the territory. The demand for natural resources and energy, the emission of pollutants, and the waste produced have an impact on the environment that puts the sustainability of cities at risk (Ímaz et al., 2014). Among the main environmental problems faced by cities in Mexico are water scarcity and the unsustainable management of water resources, poor management of solid waste, growing consumption of energy from fossil fuels, mobility and environmental pollution problems, and the growing vulnerability of large sectors of the population – especially in the outskirts of the cities – in the face of increasing natural phenomena – mainly hydro-meteorological – related to climate change (SEDESOL and UN-HABITAT, 2011b).

Drinking water and wastewater

The average availability of water per capita in Mexico has decreased in recent years, from 5,011 m^3 in 1995 to 3,982 m^3 in 2015 – one of the lowest in the continent[7] – and 14 percent of it is intended for public urban use (Pineda et al., 2010: 124). Although the pressure exerted on this resource is considered moderate (17.32 percent), many of the administrative hydrological regions of the country present conditions of high or very high pressure due to asymmetries between availability and demand (Delgado, 2016). The greatest demographic and economic growth, where there is greater consumption, is in the north and center of the country, the areas with less water available. It should also be considered that the water operators perform poorly and have few resources to maintain and expand distribution systems. The losses in distribution networks are between 30 and 50 percent of the water resources (Ziccardi, 2015a: 121). As a consequence, water consumption and waste, as well as the population growth projections, indicate that the average annual availability per inhabitant could reach disturbing levels in the main metropolitan areas of the country, and in the hydrological region of Mexico City, it could reach 127 m^3 per inhabitant per year (Delgado, 2016).

According to some experts, this scenario could also be aggravated by the effects of climate change (Pineda et al., 2010: 125–126). Therefore, cities face the fundamental challenge of supplying a growing population, with low cost and consumption energy, in a context of growing scarcity (González and Ziccardi, 2013; Jiménez-Cisneros, 2014).

Given the scarcity and exploitation of the resource, wastewater treatment is an alternative; however, in the urban centers of Mexico, less than half of the wastewater is treated (48.64 percent) (SEMARNAT and CONAGUA, 2015).[8] To this scenario, we have to add pollution. In 2013, 22 basins with monitoring sites registered heavy contamination. There is a long way to go before the human right to water, recognized constitutionally in 2012, is a reality. Sustainable management of water involves reducing the extractions from overexploited underground aquifers,[9] with actions such as water reuse, rainwater harvesting, improving the efficiency of the distribution networks, implementing desalination technologies, and an adequate tariff structure according to the volume consumed and socioeconomic conditions.

Solid waste

Accelerated urbanization has changed the consumption habits in the country, and the production of urban solid waste (MSW) has increased (OECD, 2013). Between 2001 and 2012 there was an increase of 33.7 percent, but in per capita terms, an average Mexican produces less MSW per year (311 kg) than the average produced in the OECD countries (540 kg per inhabitant per year) (DOF, 2013b). However, the MSW collection improved marginally even though most municipalities do not have the adequate infrastructure for its disposal, which represents a serious environmental problem (DOF, 2013b).

A significant amount of MSW is organic (38 percent), and there is considerable potential to reduce GHG through proper management. MSW also contains recyclable materials that can be reused and, therefore, reintegrate in the economy. Although these actions are considered mitigation measures, very few municipalities in the country separate the different types of waste, which makes it difficult to reuse them (DOF, 2013b).

Climate change and energy consumption

In Mexico, improvements in mitigation and adaptation have not been enough to reduce polluting emissions. According to the National Gas Emission Inventory 1990–2010, in these two decades, the emission of GHG increased by 33 percent, with an average annual growth rate of 1.5 percent, a bit less than the world average (CICC, 2012: 195).

The country's growth has not been environmentally sustainable since the intensity of carbon in its economy increased between 2000 and 2012 (OECD, 2013: 26). Carbon dioxide (CO_2) is the main GHG derived from the use and burning of fossil fuels. In 2012, the country produced 436 $MtCO_2$ – representing 1.37 percent of the world total – being one of the 10 countries with the highest emissions of this gas. Nevertheless, if the per capita value (3.71 tCO_2) is taken into account, it is below the world average (4.52 tCO_2), which is related to Mexico's income level (International Energy Agency, IEA, 2015).

The latest update of the National Inventory of Greenhouse Gases (GEII) in 2013 estimated that 665 megatons of CO_2 equivalent ($MtCO_{2e}$) were emitted into the atmosphere (Government of México, 2015b). Energy production and use are the main sources of GHG (70.8 percent). Within this category, the sectors that contributed the most to GHG emissions were electricity generation (19 percent) and transportation (26.2 percent) (Government of México, 2015b; INECC, 2015). Trend analyses estimate that in the coming years these two sectors will be the ones with the highest GHG emission growth.

As of 2008, the country tried to diversify its energy matrix and set the goal of reducing its dependency on fossil fuels; however, fossil fuels continue to account for the largest percentage of energy supply (89 percent). Oil is the dominant fuel (63.4 percent), and natural gas – the second most important energy component – grew 30 percent between 1996 and 2014. During that same period, the use of renewable energies increased marginally – representing only 7.6 percent in 2014 – with biomass being the main primary renewable fuel (4.1 percent) (SIE-SENER, 2015).

Regarding energy consumption, during the last 10 years, per capita energy consumption grew an average 0.4 percent each year; hence, this sector faces a double challenge: to reduce the growth of energy demand in the country and satisfy the demand to produce fewer GHG emissions (CICC, 2009: 30).

In terms of energy consumption by sector, between 1990 and 2010, transportation had the highest increase in its relative share, whereas the residential and commercial sectors reduced it. This is partly due to the adoption of various initiatives aimed at increasing the efficiency of energy consumption in homes (CICC, 2012).

Urban spaces are highly vulnerable to the effects of climate change – such as higher frequency of heat waves, landslides, and floods – that increasingly affect the quality of life of their populations. It should be noted that in Mexico, 72.3 percent of the GHG emissions are produced in the NUS, and the 11 cities with more than 1 million inhabitants are responsible for just over a third of them (36.8 percent) (Delgado et al., 2015: 47). In 2012, Mexico City generated 30.72 $MtCO_{2e}$, representing 5 percent of the national emissions during that year. Energy consumption is responsible for 80 percent of the emissions:[10] transportation (37 percent), electricity (31 percent),[11] and waste (14 percent) (SEDEMA, 2014).

However, when considering the yearly GHG emission per capita in the three main metropolitan areas, Monterrey produces the highest emissions (6.9 tCO_2e), whereas the Valley of Mexico emits 2.4 tCO_2e and Guadalajara 1.09 tCO_2e (Delgado et al., 2015: 47).

According to Mexico's Fifth Communication to the United Nations Framework Convention on Climate Change (UNFCCC), "the technical potential for reducing GHG emissions identified in sustainable cities by 2020 is 26 $MtCO_2e$ per year." This implies better planning of the load capacity of the environment, the improvement of energy efficiency of buildings, investment projects in the urban transport infrastructure and optimization of transport systems, and measures to deal with urban solid waste management and water treatment (CICC, 2012).

Air quality and public transportation

The transportation sector is one of the main consumers of fossil energy and GHG emitters (23 percent of the total in 2013) in Mexico, and the contribution made by the automotive sector is very high. Between 2000 and 2013, the automobile rate in this country went from 169 vehicles per 1,000 inhabitants to 332 (INEGI, 2016b). The huge amount of low-cost used cars and fuel subsidies, the heavy investment in infrastructure for automobile circulation, the urban sprawl promoted mainly by recent housing policies, and the lack of efficient and high-quality public transportation have encouraged the use of private cars, which represent 66 percent of total motor vehicles (UN HABITAT, 2014a). This situation is clearer in the metropolitan areas: the Valley of Mexico, Monterrey, and Guadalajara have an average car rate of 300 cars per 1,000 inhabitants, and the whole of the 59 metropolitan areas concentrates 72 percent of the private cars (UN HABITAT, 2014a). It must be said, however, that only between 3 and 4 of 10 daily trips are made by this means, and most of the population uses public transportation. In the metropolitan area of the Valley of Mexico, 6 out of 10 trips are made by low-capacity collective public transportation (minibuses, station wagons, suburban bus, and taxi) and only 8 percent in higher-capacity means (metro, trolleybuses, and Bus Rapid Transit (BRT) buses). In some cities – such as León or

Guanajuato – BRT networks are responsible for 65 percent of trips (UN HABI-TAT, 2014a: 38).

In the cities, the transportation problem has increased traffic congestion and travel times, producing a negative impact on the environment. Among the measures taken to combat air pollution problems, air pollution monitoring systems were installed in 59 metropolitan areas – although most do not collect enough information to measure the air quality in at least 3 consecutive years (DOF, 2013b) – and updated standards to measure the efficiency of vehicles were developed.

Programs to improve air quality (Proaires) were implemented. They define specific measures to control pollutants and prevent future risks, based on better information on the emission of pollutants and their impact on air quality and human health (Delgado et al., 2015). Currently, nine Proaires are in force and another four are being developed or updated. According to some studies, the air quality has improved since their implementation and the number of days that exceed environmental standards in large cities has decreased. However, we must note that ozone pollution – mainly in Mexico City – and particulate matter emissions – especially in Monterrey and Ciudad Juarez – continue to represent major challenges (OECD, 2013: 33–34).

Mexico City was the first to have a Proaire program, inventories of air pollutant emissions, and a Metropolitan Air Quality Index (IMECA), measures taken in the 1990s when the city was considered one of the most polluted in the world (Delgado et al., 2015). Since then, concentrations of polluting substances have decreased and lead in the atmosphere has practically disappeared since it was eliminated from gasoline (Lezama, 2016). However, in 2016 the city faced a new environmental crisis that required a redefinition of the environmental policy of the region. After 14 years, an environmental emergency was declared, as well as several pre-emergency situations, all of which have demanded toughening of the "Hoy No Circula" Program (No-Drive Days).

In this context, it should be noted that, since 2013, the Environmental Commission of the Megalopolis (CAMe) was established as a coordinating body between the federal government, Mexico City, the State of Mexico, Hidalgo, Morelos, Puebla, and Tlaxcala to plan and take measures that contribute to the improvement of air quality.[12] The commission agreed to standardize the regulatory framework for all the entities that make up the megalopolis and the technical and methodological standardization of the vehicle verification programs and the control and surveillance system.

Despite these efforts, high levels of air pollution are still the rule. To this end, the Center for Atmospheric Sciences of the UNAM argues that the Program of Atmospheric Environmental Contingencies, recently approved, can only be considered a temporary emergency measure, because the real source of the problem is the disorderly urban expansion, which affects air quality, protected natural areas, crops, and water resources. Therefore, it is necessary to examine, standardize, and reinforce the land-use plan in all the entities, as well as to create a mega-metropolitan mobility program, privileging safe and top-quality public transportation.

In other cities, there has been progress through specific actions of sustainable mobility regarding these problems. The public bicycle programs in Mexico City (ECO Bici) and Guadalajara (Mi Bici – My Bike) have been important – especially ECO Bici – but their scope has been limited due to the lack of budget and infrastructure (bicycle lanes, bike parking, and wide coverage) (Delgado et al., 2015: 130–131). BRT systems have been introduced (Metrobús in Mexico City, Optibus in León, and Macrobús in Guadalajara), but their participation in terms of the number of trips is still low (UN HABITAT, 2014a). In addition, comprehensive mobility actions have been developed, such as the Non-Motorized and Intermodal Mobility Plan (León) or the passing of the Mobility Law of Mexico City; public parking control mechanisms (parking meters) in Mexico City, Victoria City, Tamaulipas, Guadalajara, and Jalisco; and programs to limit the circulation of automobiles (Hoy No Circula). Nevertheless, all those measures are still inadequate to face the magnitude of the problem.

Urban vulnerability, adaptation, and resilience

The urban growth model adopted favored urban expansion – both formally based on the housing policy of recent years and informally in self-produced settlements. This has produced changes in the land use of large territories, which in terms of environmental value, has deteriorated the ecosystems that provide important environmental services. Approximately half of the territory shows signs of soil degradation (DOF, 2013b). In the case of coastal systems, the real estate speculation and the tourism boom led to the construction of mega-projects that threaten these spaces: a constant of these projects includes a violation of the environmental law and acts of corruption by local authorities.

This situation has rapidly increased the vulnerability of the urban population and contributes to risk events turning into disasters (World Bank, 2013: 46). It is estimated that 87.7 million people live in risk areas, 70 percent of them in urban areas. Thirty-four percent are at risk of suffering the impact of hurricanes, and one in three Mexicans lives in areas subject to flooding. In addition, 59 percent of the population lives in zones of seismic activity (Aguilar, 2015).

In recent years, the country has begun to move from a reactive action model to a preventive approach, designed to face the impacts of natural phenomena. However, the development of adaptation capacities has been limited by the increase in poverty (Sosa, 2015).

Popular urbanization has produced precarious housing, located in risk areas such as mountain slopes, ravines, or areas susceptible to flooding. Their inhabitants do not have the resources to adopt prevention strategies or adapt to environmental risks (DOF, 2014b). Added to this is the fact that a housing policy disconnected from the local urban planning accentuated the vulnerability conditions of Mexican cities. Undoubtedly, the natural disasters of Acapulco in 2013, due to Hurricane Ingrid and Tropical Storm Manuel, revealed the excesses of the housing policy (González and Ziccardi, 2014: 49).

The urban and socioenvironmental resilience approach is presented in a context of adaptation to climate change. Among the measures adopted to build resilience are evaluation and vulnerability reduction studies, strengthening of strategic adaptation abilities, actions to reduce the risks of climate change, increasing the resilience of urban infrastructure, and risk prevention and mitigation.

However, "while the Federal Government of Mexico has a range of initiatives to strengthen disaster reduction and promote sustainable urban development, municipal governments still face important limitations in their ability to adopt these approaches" (World Bank, 2013). The PACMUNs include several measures to improve the adaptation capabilities of cities – including measures related to early warning systems and risk atlases – as well as establishing the need to review and rethink the land-use plans. Notwithstanding, the adaptation efforts are still incipient, as are the comprehensive vulnerability analysis and the definition of proper actions according to the reality of each urban settlement (Delgado et al., 2015: 129).

Discussion on sustainability

The increased concentration in urban areas requires the creation of sustainable cities, because the way in which these spaces are developed will affect national development (Molina, 2014). It is essential to promote the transition towards renewable energies and an efficient use of energy (Masera et al., 2010: 216–217). It is also vital to improve mobility in the cities, with efficient public transportation systems, using better fuels and that are connected to each other. This should include a reduction in the subsidies for fossil fuels and minimizing investments in the infrastructure for private transportation. In this sense, as noted by Nobel Prize winner Mario Molina,[13] the design for the expansion of cities plays an important role (Molina, 2014: 12). For that reason, an optimization of space should be promoted, as a basis "to implement adequately the other environmental and energy efficiency policies, making cities more sustainable and resilient to extreme weather events" (Molina, 2014: 13). One way to do this is to "recycle intra-urban areas" by promoting the creation of mixed-use spaces with housing for the low-income population and diversify the housing solutions offered (Molina, 2014).

According to Lezama (2010a: 55), there must be a link between the legal framework and a highly sophisticated institutional arrangement, with the development of better capabilities to take concrete steps or to enforce the existing legislation and regulations. Likewise, "solid and verifiable environmental commitments must be established in all areas of public policy, including specific economic measures that are compatible with environmental protection, as well as strengthening state and municipal environmental management capabilities" (Carabias et al., 2008: 40–41).

Finally, it is important to point out that the scientific community and the environmental groups consider the subject of climate change a priority and set it out in the public debate and the governmental agenda.

Housing and urban infrastructure[14]

Housing in Mexico today

The housing situation today has been influenced by demographic dynamics, the rapid urbanization process, poor employment conditions, and different financial crises.

Broadly speaking, in recent decades the housing stock has grown significantly, and the structural characteristics and access to the main public services have improved. Nonetheless, there are still large regional asymmetries in terms of guaranteeing adequate living conditions. The greatest shortcomings in access and quality, both in housing and in basic goods and services, are found in the southern region of the country.

At the same time, the current housing supply does not fully correspond to the social, economic, and cultural characteristics of new households in Mexico. Population dynamics have changed in the last two decades; life expectancy increased, the birth rate decreased, and the mortality rate was slightly higher (INEGI, 2010b). The age structure presents a tendency to aging and an increase in the economically productive population that is able to form a new family. Thus, there was a restructuring of Mexican households: nuclear family households decreased, while extended, nonfamily, and single-person households increased. At the same time, there have been important cultural transformations, such as the weakening of the patriarchal family and the social recognition of women heads of household. In addition, there is an intense migratory process, predominantly towards the United States. All of these factors produced a greater and more heterogeneous demand for housing, which requires the creation of a supply that meets these needs. However, the housing policy of recent years has not resolved this issue, because it privileged the mass production of finished housing without adequate urban and environmental habitability conditions (Ziccardi, 2015a).

The national housing policy in Mexico

The government of Ernesto Zedillo (1994–2000)

Since the end of the 1980s, a reduction in the state's regulatory role in the housing policy was promoted, and housing agencies abandoned their role as developers and focused instead on financing. During the administration of Ernesto Zedillo, housing policy was strongly influenced by the financial crisis of 1994–1995. With the devaluation of the currency and the increase in interest rates, the overdue portfolio increased significantly and gave rise to a social movement led by people who could not cope with their mortgage commitments.

With the banking crisis, government participation in housing finance declined and almost disappeared (Gonzales, 2002: 54). The resources came mainly from housing agencies, which financed mostly workers with better incomes (Maycotte and Sánchez, 2010). INFONAVIT (Instituto del Fondo Nacional de la Vivienda para los Trabajadores) was the organism granting the most credits in this six-year period – most of them to a population earning more than three times the minimum wages – and different agencies developed financing schemes based on prior savings (ASF, 2012: 27). The Fideicomiso Fondo Nacional de Habitaciones Populares (FONHAPO), the only federal organization focused on serving the population living in poverty, saw its funding sources and its role reduced, and was forced to transfer its functions to local housing agencies (OREVIS).

The government of Vicente Fox (2000–2006)

With the triumph of the right-wing opposition in the presidential elections, there was a profound transformation in housing policy. Housing was recognized as an element of development and revitalization of the economy, and the government set the goal of financing 750,000 homes per year, a figure that was exceeded. In this regard, the Sectorial Housing Program of this administration set out as objectives to consolidate the housing market, promote sectorial development and competitiveness, and reactivate development banking (Ziccardi, 2015a: 61). With this purpose, the National Housing Development Commission (Comisión Nacional del Fomento a la Vivienda – CONAFOVI) was created in 2001 as a decentralized body of the Social Development Secretariat, with technical autonomy and design functions, to promote and implement the housing policies and programs of the federal government. It involved a subsidy policy and institutional coordination.

The housing agencies were transformed, consolidating their financial role in response to demand. The Federal Mortgage Society (Sociedad Hipotecaria Federal – SHF) was created to promote the development of the primary and secondary credit markets for housing; FONHAPO began operating as a second-tier financial institution, and housing funds modified their allocation criteria to directly capture the demand, without the intervention of the unions. In addition, new mechanisms were created so that housing agencies could obtain resources from the capital market, housing co-financing programs were promoted, and housing supply was integrated into the Single Housing Registry (Ziccardi, 2015a).

The private sector began to play an extremely important role in the housing sector, both in financing from banks, limited-purpose financial corporations (SOFOLES), and multipurpose financial corporations (SOFOMES) to grant "bridge" credits to real estate developers.

With these reforms, housing policy acquired a new impetus, increasing the number of housing projects, which at the end of the six-year period were 4.6 million housing units. At the same time, an intense urban expansion process began on land that had previously been devoted to farming or environmental conservation, promoting a dispersed city (Ziccardi, 2015a).

The government of Felipe Calderón (2006–2012)

Shortly before the administration of Felipe Calderón, a new Housing Law was passed, repealing the law of 1984. This law placed housing as a priority issue on the national development agenda, defined the characteristics of decent housing, provided for the creation of housing quality and sustainability standards, and recognized the social production of housing (PUEC-UNAM et al., 2013). However, the housing policy of this administration was directly linked to economic and financial policy.

The Calderon government consolidated the Institutional Housing System (SIV), defined in the new law as a permanent coordination and negotiation mechanism between the public, social, and private sectors. This system was headed by CONAFOVI, which became the National Housing Commission (CONAVI), with the task of freeing up the resources from workers' housing funds and substantially increase the construction of housing. The housing funds (INFONAVIT and FOVISSSTE), SHF, FONHAPO, and local housing agencies, as well as banks, SOFOLES, and SOFOMES, were also made part of the Institutional Housing System in accordance with the law of 2006.

Based on this legal and institutional system, a housing policy that adopted the financial criteria was implemented. The policy increased the supply of housing only for those formally employed who have better salaries. The number of housing projects practically doubled those of the previous administration, with 8.7 million units (Ziccardi, 2015a). This model of massive housing construction was supported by the weakening of regulations on urban development, thus subordinating urban development policy to housing finance policy.

This enabled the adoption of, as noted earlier, "a dispersed city model fostered by the construction companies that developed large low-quality residential complexes in distant peripheries, taking advantage of inexpensive land to obtain huge profits" (Ziccardi, 2015a: 74). These developments were really thousands of homes built from low-quality prototypes reproduced throughout the national territory, without considering the specific features of each context. As a result, there was an unresolved demand for basic services and equipment, an alarming number of unoccupied homes, and a worrying past-due portfolio in some financial institutions (Ziccardi, 2015a).

Only towards the end of the six-year government was a methodology to assess the quality of the housing projects developed. Likewise, the procedures of the subsidy programs adopted a scoring system that granted differentiated sums according to location and sustainability criteria. These measures, however, were not enough to reverse the inertia of the housing policy applied since 2000.

Enrique Peña Nieto government (2013–2018)

In 2012, the PRI regained the presidency of the republic and promoted legal and institutional changes in housing, urban, and land-use development policies.

The Housing Law was reformed in 2013, 2014, and 2015, promoting the use of eco-technologies, the definition of a regional perspective to reduce gaps existing in the country, and the expansion of the concept of decent housing (Ziccardi, 2015a: 76).

The structure of the federal public administration was also modified, and the Secretariat of Agrarian Reform was transformed into the Secretariat of Agrarian, Territorial, and Urban Development (SEDATU), integrating the Under-Secretariat of Urban Development and Land-Use Planning. This new secretariat was in charge of planning, coordinating, and executing public policy for land use, housing, and sustainable development in the urban and rural areas of the country. CONAVI retained its specific powers in the housing policy, which – in this presidential term and by presidential mandate – were defined based on four strategic axes: a) greater and better inter-institutional coordination to guarantee the concurrence and joint responsibility of the three levels of government, b) moving towards a sustainable and intelligent urban development model, c) reducing the lag in housing and expand existing housing, and d) providing decent housing for all.

To advance these purposes, a National Registry of Territorial Reserves (RENARET) was created with updated urban containment areas to guide the granting of federal subsidies. To expand the financing options for the lower-income sectors, the operating rules of the Financing Scheme and Federal Housing Subsidies Program were redesigned, allocating additional support to the population with an income between 1.5 and 3.5 times the minimum wages and including into these subsidy schemes the beneficiaries of the lower-income workers' funds. In addition, specific support was announced for vulnerable sectors, and the social production of habitat and improvement continued to be financed. This included the "Un Cuarto Más" (One More Room) program, which assumed a gender perspective, prioritizing the improvement of the family environment and preventing situations of violence directed towards girls and young women as a result of the existing overcrowded living conditions.

A general assessment of that administration indicates that other housing solutions began to be institutionally recognized, but the resources were still mostly directed towards financing new housing, which between 2013 and 2016 accounted for 63 percent of total financing. The low-income population still received little attention, and, during the same period, only 14 percent of the resources went to households with incomes of less than 2.5 minimum wages. Likewise, despite the efforts made, almost a fifth of the current housing supply was located outside the established urban containment boundaries (i.e. cut off from the consolidated urban structure and therefore with great deficiencies in terms of equipment and services).

Quality of housing, infrastructure, and basic services

In recent years, the most common type of housing has been the single family house. In the SUN, these had a significant increase:[15] from 8 out of

10 homes in 2000 to 9 out of 10 in 2015. It should be noted that precarious housing – such as *vecindades*, roof rooms, and premises not built to be inhabited – decreased, a fact that reflects an improvement in habitability.

The existing material conditions in the housing stock improved. The proportion of dwellings with a dirt floor diminished, going from 6.5 percent to only 1.4 percent in 2010. In terms of structural features, in 2015, 9 out of every 10 homes in urban areas had partition walls made of brick, concrete masonry (CMU), stone, or cement – and 8 out of 10 had concrete slabs or brick roofs. The use of other materials such as wood and adobe has diminished. Overcrowding also decreased, and between 1990 and 2010 the average number of people per bedroom went from 2.6 to 2 (INEGI, 2000, 2010b).

Water and sanitation

The coverage of basic services has expanded in recent years. In 1990, urban dwellings with running water in their interior barely represented 68.3 percent, whereas in 2015 almost 9 out of 10 houses have this service (88.2 percent). However, this does not necessarily imply an improvement in the delivery and quality of this resource. In 2010, only 7 out of every 10 homes in the country had a daily water supply, whereas 8.2 percent had it only once a week and 3.5 percent only sporadically (INEGI, 2000, 2010b).

The municipality determines water service rates – so they vary considerably – and there is a tendency to increase water rates, representing a heavy expenditure for the poorest households. In addition, the population living in precarious areas usually has an irregular and low-quality supply, so they resort to other sources of supply that imply extra expenses. The water supplied by tanker trucks has an average cost of 40 pesos (2.5 dollars) per cubic meter (SEDESOL and UN HABITAT, 2011b). Likewise, the perception regarding the quality of tap water has encouraged the growth of the bottled water industry. Mexico is the main consumer of bottled water in Latin America, with an average annual per capita consumption of 234 liters (Delgado et al., 2015: 146). In urban areas, approximately 87.7 percent of households consume bottled water. The monthly expenditure on water jugs varies according to the city, from Villahermosa with an expenditure of 205 pesos per month (US$18.8) – representing almost 10 percent of minimum wage – to Mexico City, at 127 pesos per month (US$11.66) and Monterrey at 75 pesos per month (US$6.88) (Delgado and Ávila, 2014: 58).

Nine out of ten homes have sewage connected to the public network (89.9 percent), 7.28 percent to a cesspit, and just over 250,000 homes still have no service (INEGI, 2010b).

Electric power, street lighting, and pavement

The SUN has almost complete electricity coverage in terms of housing (99.2 percent), whereas public lighting has ample coverage in the municipalities and metropolitan areas. The paving and maintenance of secondary and tertiary roads is one of the most deficient services in the country, with an average coverage of 81 percent in the municipal headquarters (PUEC-UNAM et al., 2013: 120). There are differences in the coverage and quality of the infrastructure and services across different cities, due, among other things, to the rapid incorporation of new territories to the urban sprawl and the different technical and financial capabilities of local governments. Municipalities have very few sources of long-term financing and debt financing for infrastructure projects, leading to the development of private investment projects under concession agreements and contracting of services and public works.

Financing and housing market

The housing issue, historically considered a social policy, is now considered an essential link of the economic, financial, and low-skilled, low-paid employment policies. According to 2013 national accounts, the housing sector contributed 3.6 percent of GDP, and if one considers the value of the imputed income, this contribution would reach up to 14 percent (INEGI, 2016c).

Housing finance in Mexico is segmented, dividing the population according to income and type of housing solution to be purchased. Financing of mortgage loans is aimed at the high-income population, whereas the subsidies focus on the lower-income groups. There is also "a financial management platform for development banks to implement bridge loans for real estate developers" (PUEC-UNAM et al., 2013: 93).

It should be noted that recently, both public and private organizations have obtained resources from debt and equity markets "through the direct issuance of bonds (SHF and INFONAVIT) or from the granting of loan guarantees to commercial banking and other financial intermediaries" (PUEC-UNAM et al., 2013: 96).

Regarding the demand, the main limitations to accessing financing are "the structure of the labor market and the general level of wages" and "the regional differences in the structure of the real estate markets, which mean a significant variation in housing prices" (PUEC-UNAM et al., 2013: 104, 105).

Urban land

The large increase in credit supply for housing promoted a growing demand for urbanized land that the formal market has not been able to satisfy. In particular, lower-income sectors have had to resort to different types of "informal markets." According to some estimates, of the 300,000 households living in poverty that are annually included in urban areas, 41.7 percent occupy the land irregularly (PUEC-UNAM et al., 2013: 139–140). This results from the lack of supply of urbanized land for lower-income sectors, negligent authorities, and the lack of clear penalties for people who resort to these practices. Recently, authorities have implemented a policy of regularization and titling of properties located in irregular human settlements. Between 2006 and 2011, 214,625 were legalized, with an approximate total extension of 12,335 hectares (PUEC-UNAM et al., 2013: 138).

There is no land policy for the country as a whole that regulates land markets for urban development, but rather a complex regulatory framework in which the various governing bodies have their say. The *ejidos*, or communal lands, are federally controlled, whereas local governments manage the private ownership of the land. Municipal authorities are responsible for granting land-use permits, declaring the feasibility of provisioning and connection to infrastructure networks, granting construction licenses, and establishing their costs and deadlines, all of which means there are significant differences between the municipalities of the country (PUEC-UNAM et al., 2013: 136)

Although there are no statistics about the historical evolution of land prices, a study carried out by PUEC-UNAM et al. (2013: 135–136) found that the highest prices are in Mexico City, practically doubling the land prices of cities in the south such as Villahermosa (Tabasco). However, what really stands out is that the prices are inconsistent with the wages in the country.

Vacant housing

One of the consequences of the recent housing policy is the alarming number of unoccupied dwellings, which in 2010 reached 4.9 million, representing 14 percent of the housing stock and the highest within the OECD countries. Within the localities of the SUN, there are 3.6 million (14.3 percent), most of them located in the peripheries of the cities. Among the causes of this phenomenon are distance from employment sources, urban centers, and schools; the low quality and the size of the houses; the lack or deficiency of basic equipment and services; economic problems, such as the loss of employment and the cost overruns associated with the dwelling (mainly transportation);[16] as well as migration, violence, and insecurity, mainly in the north of the country. Regarding demand, the great financing opportunities opened to a segment of the population led to credits that were not associated with a need for housing (Ziccardi, 2015a: 88–89).

Most of the uninhabited houses were financed with resources from the workers' funds, which include employer contributions. Likewise, most of them are located in regions with higher levels of economic development and formal employment, so they do not match the needs of the purchasers. Additionally, they are an indicator of the degree of dissatisfaction with the property financed and – in many cases – the impossibility to continue paying for it. This phenomenon not only produces economic costs for families but also generates environmental, social, and legal effects assumed by governments and the local society (Ziccardi, 2015a: 137).

Poor neighborhoods

One of the main features of Latin American cities has been the development of a model of urban expansion that promotes poor neighborhoods on the outskirts of the central city. The processes tend to be of different types: organized or spontaneous, buying the land legally or invading risky and/or abandoned areas, self-built or through social programs that incorporate paid labor or access to government subsidies. Many of these peripheral popular neighborhoods have consolidated over time.

Between 2000 and 2010, the index of urban marginalization in Mexico reduced by 24.98 percent, going from 20.95 to 15.72 (CONAPO, 2010). This figure agrees with the information of United Nations Economic Commission for Latin America and the Caribbean (ECLAC), according to which the proportion of the urban population living in slums decreased significantly in the country, from 21.5 percent in 1995 to 11.1 percent in 2014 (ECLAC, 2016).

Among the local policies contributing to this improvement is the Housing Improvement Program (PMV) in Mexico City, an innovative initiative both in its design and in the involvement of different actors in the city. In essence, "it creates financial, technical and social conditions to improve the living conditions in popular neighborhoods, expanding, reinforcing, or consolidating houses; strengthening family solidarity networks; and overcoming overcrowding by building additional housing in family land, in addition to consolidating popular neighborhoods" (Ziccardi, 2015b). Another relevant program is the Neighborhood Improvement Program, whose main objective is to "promote collective organization practices to improve degraded public spaces or build new ones where they do not exist, to counteract the effects of urban segregation and social exclusion" and thereby guarantee the access of all inhabitants to the city (Ziccardi, 2015b).

Urban economy and productivity

Urban economy, productivity, and competitiveness of Mexican cities

Mexican cities are of vital importance to the performance of the national economy and constitute its main resource to generate international competitive conditions. In 1998, the metropolitan areas contributed 75.5 percent of gross national product (GNP) (SEGOB and CONAPO, 1998: 59).[17] In 2009, the 93 cities with more than 100,000 inhabitants contributed 88 percent of GNP, and the 56 metropolitan areas as a whole contributed 73.4 percent of the total. By that time, the 11 metropolitan areas of more than 1 million inhabitants generated half of GNP, and the medium-size metropolitan areas generated 11.8 percent (INEGI, 2012). The metropolitan border areas in the north and center of the country, as well as the tourist destinations and those with activities related to the oil industry, stand out (SEDESOL and UN-HABITAT, 2011b).

According to the data of the last economic census, carried out in 2014, 77.1 percent of GNP is generated in the 59 metropolitan areas and the metropolitan areas with more than 1 million inhabitants contribute the 49.8 percent of it. The largest number of economic units is in the trade sector (29.4 percent) and private nonfinancial services (24.3 percent) (INEGI, 2015a). According to

Góngora and Medina (2014), 69 percent of the trade with the United States comes from these sectors.

In recent years, several studies have addressed the economic performance of Mexican cities. In 2015, Banamex prepared the third edition of the *Competitive and Sustainable City Index*, which assessed the competitiveness of 78 cities with a population of more than 100,000 people. Within the group of cities with more than 1 million inhabitants, the Valley of Mexico, Monterrey, Guadalajara, Querétaro, and Aguascalientes were considered the most competitive cities. The study emphasized the need to strengthen the rule of law, address mobility problems, and improve water management. The main cities with 500,000 to a million inhabitants are Saltillo, Morelia, Cancun, Chihuahua, and Hermosillo, whose competitiveness is limited mainly by their performance in the use of energy and mobility (IMCO, 2015. The best performances are linked to cities in the center, west, and north of the country.

In 2012, the Center for Economic Research and Teaching (CIDE) prepared the third edition of the *Index for the Competitiveness of the Cities of Mexico, 2011.* According to this index, Mexico City stands out by having important infrastructure in terms of development. The following places are occupied by two cities in the northern part of the country: Hermosillo and Saltillo, with a weaker urban development component compensated for by their better economic position. In this way, 25 highly competitive cities were identified, 16 of them in the north of the country (4 border cities: Tijuana, Ciudad Juárez, Mexicali, and Nuevo Laredo). Only one highly competitive city is located in the south: Cancún. The results of this index show that there is a "group of 14 cities that have remained throughout these years among the twenty most competitive cities in the country" (Cabrero and Orihuela, 2012: 42).

An OECD study of Mexico states that the low productivity of urban agglomerations is related to a set of structural processes, such as the long distances between the place of residence and work, the plurality of administrative actors in the design and implementation of public policies, the lack of strategic regional planning frameworks, the lack of enough financial resources, and weak coordination and collaboration among governments (OECD, 2015a: 7).

Finally, in 2015, the National Population Council (CONAPO) calculated the Development Potential Index of the Cities and Metropolitan Areas of Mexico (Nava et al., 2014). It showed that the Valley of Mexico Metropolitan Zone (ZMVM) is the most competitive, but it lags far behind in issues related to equity and opportunities. The second most competitive city is the Metropolitan Zone of Guadalajara (ZMG), occupying first place in quality of life and urban sustainability but far below in productivity and equity opportunity. Third, the Metropolitan Zone of Monterrey (ZMM) had good performances in terms of urban sustainability, quality of life, productivity, and equity opportunity, but had a low evaluation in terms of government. The tourist cities had outstanding performances in terms of equity and opportunity, government, and productivity but have very low levels of quality of life and sustainability. Among the state capitals, better results were identified in equity and opportunity, productivity, and government but with low levels of quality of life and urban sustainability (Nava et al., 2014).

In short, although there are no unique limitations to generate conditions for urban competitiveness, we can identify a group of cities that are the "engine of national competitiveness" (Cabrero and Orihuela, 2012). A problem shared by many cities in the country is that urban expansion and dispersion have led to an increase in transport times due to an erroneous federal housing policy. The construction of low-cost and social housing in peripheral areas of several cities of the country has involved a series of new challenges for local governments in terms of urban management, such as land-use planning, public services provision, and respect for the environment. In addition, the transportation system does not increase its capacity and quality at the same pace as cities expand.

Employment, urban wages, and informal economy

In the last 20 years, there have been changes in the economic dynamics of the country. These changes have been accompanied by heavy capital investments in the creation of a road and communication infrastructure that connected cities. Although this promoted employment creation, in many cases, it was of poor quality, paid low wages, and was insufficient to respond to the demographic growth of Mexico (ILO, 2014). The slow response of the productive apparatus to the growth of the workforce produced a weak demand for paid employment. The increasing migratory flow of Mexicans to the United States did not prevent the gross unemployment rate from increasing between 2000 and 2010, a situation emphasized by the economic crisis of 2008 (Ruiz and Ordaz, 2011: 92).

Migration to the United States was a growing phenomenon, at least until 2016 with the advent of the Trump administration. Between 1990 and 2010, Mexicans migrating to the United States almost doubled, from 6.5 to 11.5 million people. Most migrants were from western, central, and southern states of the country (CONAPO and Fundación BBVA Bancomer, 2014: 35, 58). The counterpart of this demographic fact is that Mexico is currently the fifth country in the world receiving the most remittances and concentrates more than a third of the remittances in Latin America and the Caribbean. The economic dependence on remittances represented 1.8 percent of the national GDP in 2013, although there are states in which it represents between 5 and 7 percent of GDP (CONAPO and BBVA Bancomer Foundation, 2014: 160).

Regarding urban unemployment, there was an increase between 2004 and 2014, going from 3.8 to 5.8 percent. It also increased during the global financial crisis (ECLAC, 2015), particularly in cities with more than 100,000 inhabitants (SEDESOL and UN-HABITAT, 2011b). According to Bensusán (2013: 14),

the volatility of the jobs affected Mexican workers more than their peers in similarly developed countries – such as Argentina, Brazil or Chile – since the effects of the crisis were greater due to the exports to the United States, the serious deficiencies of the compensation system/severance packages before arbitrary dismissals, and the fact that only some cities have unemployment insurance.

Regarding the composition of unemployment, although generally increasing, there was a change in the composition of the unemployment rate as of 2009, being higher for men than for women (ECLAC, 2015).

The distribution of employment reflects an uneven development of productive capacities. In 2014, the 59 metropolitan areas absorbed 72.6 percent of the employed population, whereas almost half of the employed population (49.8 percent) lived in one of the 11 metropolitan areas with more than 1 million inhabitants (INEGI, 2015a). A reported 23.6 percent of the total employed population of the country worked only in the ZMVM (2013). Nonfinancial private services accounted for the highest participation in the employment of the metropolitan zones (27.1 percent), whereas 2 out of 10 people were engaged in trade and 17.5 percent in manufacturing (INEGI, 2015a). The country has heterogeneous labor markets in which wage differentials are noticeable. We also observe the persistence of nonsalaried workers who work informally on their own and/or establish microbusinesses and that this informality is found in all activities and levels. According to the National Survey of Occupation and Employment (ENOE), the national informal employment rate represented 58.79 percent of total employment in 2014.

Salary stagnation has also been a relevant issue in recent years. According to Bensusán (2013: 42), "the evolution of minimum wages since 1994 records a loss of more than 25 percent in almost 20 years, so today minimum wage is barely equivalent to a quarter of that of 1982." In 2011, the minimum wage was lower than the per capita poverty line (Moreno et al., 2014: 84).

This situation is even more alarming if one considers that Mexican workers work more hours and have a higher productivity compared to workers from other countries with better wages. "On average they work 10 hours per day, 500 hours per year more than the average of countries with a similar economy" (Alcalde, 2014). The Global Wage Report 2012–2013 of the International Labor Organization (ILO) indicates that "the minimum wage is below market levels, even for unskilled workers" (ILO, 2013: 42), and it has been pointed out that Mexico registers one of the worst performances regarding the growth of adequate salaries and its conditions of equality.

Among the countries of Latin America, Mexico's minimum wage is the one that has increased the least in the last decade (Moreno et al., 2014: 83). In comparison with 22 countries in the region, in 2011,

Mexico's minimum wage – equivalent at that time to US$112.2 – was the lowest, slightly surpassed by Nicaragua (US$117.50) and Bolivia (US$117.50) – countries whose productivity is four times lower – and equivalent to 40 percent of the minimum wage in Guatemala or Honduras, whose GDP per capita is well below that of Mexico, and less than a third of the minimum wage in dollars in Costa Rica and Argentina.

(Moreno et al., 2014: 81)

Thus, although unemployment rates are not as high compared to the regional average, employment in the country is precarious, without benefits and with low wages. There are also differences in the salaries received by workers in different parts of the national territory.

The 2014 Economic Census noted that the highest salary averages are earned in the boroughs of Mexico City: Miguel Hidalgo (US$15,200 per year) and Cuauhtémoc (US$13,070 per year), whereas the national average is only US$6,470 per year, per person (INEGI, 2015b).

In short, the labor market problems in Mexico are related to a development model based on intensive exports, unskilled labor, and flexible employment.

The metropolitan area of the valley of Mexico

The ZMVM has been evaluated as having low economic performance in relation to its size. Among the factors that affect its productivity are the fragmented governance structure in the Valley of Mexico and its territorial structure, which has led to an increase in the use of private vehicles and the resulting traffic congestion that produces annual losses equivalent to 3.1 percent of GDP (OECD, 2015b: 5, 9).

In the national context, the ZMVM concentrates a good part of the national economic activity and is the zone with the greatest commercial exchange with the United States (20.47 percent of the total) (Góngora and Medina, 2014). However, its participation in the GNP has declined in recent years, and in 2014, it represented a little more than a quarter of the national GNP (26.3 percent) (INEGI, 2015a). When analyzing its economic structure, we find a specialization towards the secondary and tertiary sectors of the economy. The central city has become a specialized center in high-added-value services, becoming a strategic point of connection between the national and the international economy. According to the Globalization and World Cities Research Network (GaWC), the ZMVM ranks 20 out of 55 global cities in the network of global cities, the first in Latin America (GaWC, 2010) (PUEC, 2012).

However, the ZMVM as a whole has not been able to intervene actively in the intense process of economic globalization and commercial openness to which it has been subjected. Rather, specific spaces have integrated globally, located on Paseo de la Reforma, Avenida Juárez, Santa Fe, Polanco, Insurgentes Sur, and Periférico Sur (Parnreiter, 2002).

In this sense, there is a relative deindustrialization but the metropolitan integration of the municipalities of Hidalgo and the State of Mexico has promoted a greater diversification of the economic activities, with an important emphasis on the manufacturing and building processes (PUEC, 2012). This last sector is driven by the expansive housing policy and the accelerated process of settlement in previously considered rural municipalities (PUEC, 2012).

Thus, according to the 2014 Economic Census, 50 percent of GNP is produced in the services sector; 30 percent in manufacturing industries; and almost 10 percent in extractive industries, electricity, and the commercial sector (wholesale and retail) (INEGI, 2015a). In the services sector, financial and insurance services stand out, contributing 17.62 percent of GNP, whereas information services in mass media contribute to 8.08 percent of total gross production (INEGI, 2015a).

The workforce of the ZMVM in 2015 was slightly higher (53.7 percent) than the national (50.26 percent). With regard to the employed population, almost a third receive up to two minimum wages per month (US$123.50), and almost a quarter corresponds to unwaged workers (26.4 percent).(INEGI, 2015c) In the economic sector, industrial activity occupies an increasingly smaller proportion of the population of the ZMVM: in 1980, 48 percent of the employed workforce was in this sector; in 2000, it was only 20.5 percent (PUEC, 2012). Currently, this sector employs 14.7 percent of the employed workforce in the ZMVM (INEGI, 2015a). Another characteristic is the transition to a service economy, with a strong tendency to informality in all activities and levels. Although in 2014 this sector concentrated 43.5 percent of the employed workforce (INEGI, 2015a), it is estimated that there are some 250,000 informal retailers in the ZMVM (PUEC, 2012).

Urban poverty, inequality, and social exclusion[18]

Poverty in Mexico

Poverty is the most serious social problem faced by Mexico, and despite the many efforts made to improve the quality of life of millions of Mexicans, it gives way very slowly and increases rapidly in times of crisis, such as in 2008. In Latin America, there is a trend towards poverty reduction, whereas in Mexico the tendency to increase poverty continues. Undoubtedly, this is because in Mexico the real minimum wage virtually has not changed in the last decade, whereas in Brazil it increased moderately and, in Argentina, it increased steadily after the economic crisis of 2001. In addition, well-paid jobs necessary for the huge number of young people joining the labor market each year have not been created. This leads to the idea that a generalized low income is an explanation for the increase in poverty (Ziccardi, 2015c).

Measuring poverty in Mexico

Between 1994 and 2014, "economic activity was marked by three critical years: 1995, 2001, and 2009, which together slowed down the economic growth rate of the period, although with different results and impacts on poverty" (Cordera and Provencio, 2016: 24). In 1995, there was a considerable increase in poverty, a decrease between 1998 and 2006, and between 2006 and 2008 a new growing trend began. In absolute terms, between 1994 and 2012, the urban population in patrimonial poverty[19] increased from 22.2 to 33.3 million Mexicans and went from representing 41.2 percent to 45.5 percent (CONEVAL, 2011).

The General Law of Social Development (2004) establishes, among other things, "the obligatory nature of multidimensional poverty measurement and notes that poverty involves a welfare dimension, a territorial dimension, and economic and social rights." According to this measurement, multidimensional poverty[20] increased between 2008 and 2014, from 38.9 to 41.7 percent in urban areas (CONEVAL, 2014b).

In these spaces, in the same period, there was a significant reduction in the national population with no health services (a 17.5 percent decline), social security (6.6 percentage point decline), and in the quality of housing and educational backwardness (2.8 percent decline). On the contrary, the population with no access to basic services in housing grew by almost 1 percentage point. The greatest increases were recorded in access to food and income gap indicators, which increased by almost 6 percentage points (CONEVAL, 2014b).

The most recent information, from 2014, shows that 7 out of 10 people living in poverty lived in urban areas. The most important deficiency was access to social security, affecting one out of every two people (52 percent). The second highest indicator of urban poverty was income below the welfare line, which also affects half of the population (50.5 percent). Both indicators are related to the trend in urban areas towards the insecurity of employment and an informal economy (CONEVAL, 2014b).

In absolute terms, poverty concentrates in the largest cities, probably in its peripheries. "In 2012, of the 36.6 million urban poor, half (18.8 million) lived in a locality of 100,000 inhabitants or more" (CONEVAL, 2014a: 21). However, in relative terms, the cities with the largest population have lower poverty percentages. According to Sobrino's (2016) poverty study in Mexican cities,

> the cities belonging to the SUN, with 500,000 inhabitants or more, are consolidating their generation and use of the economies of agglomeration for the performance of the urban labor market and of economies of scale for the provision of public services. Such performance translates into lower proportions of the population living in poverty and vulnerability conditions.
>
> (Sobrino, 2016: 156)

In 2010, in the 11 metropolises with more than 1 million inhabitants, 3 out of every 10 people lived in poverty.

Poverty and vulnerability

We must also include the notion of social exclusion (Castel, 1995) because it integrates the noneconomic dimensions of the phenomenon of poverty, touching on the weakening of the wage earners and social welfare regimes, the expansion of informal economy, and the insecurity of employment, as well as the discriminatory practices towards certain social groups – mainly of popular origin, due to their low educational level, gender, ethnicity, age, and region or area of the city in which they live. It is "a phenomenon that can be described as dynamic – insofar as it affects people and groups in a changing way, depending on their vulnerability to multidimensional marginalization dynamics" (Ziccardi, 2015c).

The poor indigenous population is among the main vulnerable groups. Between 2008 and 2014, it registered a slight decrease in percentage, going from representing 75.9 to 73.2 percent. However, in absolute terms, the poor indigenous population increased from 5.4 to 5.6 million (CONEVAL, 2014b).

In Mexico, 31.8 percent of the indigenous population lives in a condition of extreme poverty: 8 out of 10 natives do not have access to social security; 7 out of 10 have an income below the welfare line; half have deficiencies in both the quality of spaces and access to services in housing; and only 5 percent of this group is neither poor nor vulnerable (CONEVAL, 2014b). The vast majority of the indigenous population lives in rural areas, although 35.6 percent live in urban areas of more than 15,000 inhabitants. Of these, 23 percent live in cities of more than 100,000 inhabitants (CONEVAL, 2014d: 38). In Mexico City, for example, indigenous peoples have an important presence (Álvarez, 2008).

Another vulnerable sector is the population with disabilities. More than half of this group remained in poverty, registering a slight increase in percentages between 2010 and 2014, when they went from representing 50.2 to 54.1 percent (CONEVAL, 2014b).

In Mexico, according to CONEVAL's measuring, there are no significant gender differences among the population in poverty. It stresses that men are the most vulnerable because of social deprivation, but women are more vulnerable in terms of income. This vulnerability has increased from 6.1 percent of women in 2010 to 7.5 percent in 2014.

Similarly, regarding age, it is noted that these conditions distinctly affect the younger sectors of the population. The group under 18 years of age is the one with the highest poverty, with a little more than half the population (53.9 percent), that is, 20 million children and teenagers (Cordera and Provencio, 2016; CONEVAL, 2014b). In the case of urban areas, it is 52.8 percent in localities with a population between 15,000 and 100,000, and 40.6 percent in cities with more than 100,000 inhabitants (UNICEF and CONEVAL, 2013: 9). Some explanations for the high incidence of poverty in this age group attribute it to the fact that poor families have the highest fertility rates (Cordera and Provencio, 2016). According to UNICEF and CONEVAL (2013: 7), "poverty in childhood has particular characteristics that make attending it an urgent and priority matter: it has a greater probability of becoming permanent, its effects are – in many cases – irreversible, and its potential for reproducing in the future is greater."

The second age group with the highest concentration of poverty is the population of 65 and over, with an incidence of 45.9 percent in 2014, representing

4.2 million people. Among the characteristics that stand out is that, unlike what happens at the national level, the lack of access to social security is 41.3 percent lower in this age group (it represents 17.2 percent), whereas there is a greater educational lag (60.7 percent) (CONEVAL, 2014b)

Regarding young people between 18 and 30 years of age, the increase in poverty is strongly linked to their income – which is lower than the national average. This group has the greatest sensitivity to economic crises, and between 2008 and 2010, its income significantly reduced (Cordera and Provencio, 2016). In 2010, in urban areas, the population living in poverty accounted for less than half (41.2 percent) of the total of this age group. Due to their employment characteristics, the greatest deficiencies are recorded in the levels of income and the lack of access to social security, despite the fact that educational backwardness is much lower than in other age groups. It is a fact that "today, young people have more education, but fewer jobs; more rights, but they cannot exercise them; more information and less access to power" (Merielle et al., 2013: 15).

Urban inequality and social exclusion

In Mexico, income inequality has reduced, particularly in urban areas from the end of the 1980s until 2010. A UN-HABITAT study on inequality in Latin American cities indicates that "Mexico was the third country with the best results, narrowing the income inequality gap in urban areas by 14 percentage points between 1989 and 2010" (UN HABITAT, 2014b: 69). Nonetheless, there are still conditions of high inequality. "In Mexican cities, the average income of the richest 20 percent is equivalent to 13 times the income of the poorest 20 percent," which is more than twice the register in high-income countries and more than the average for Latin America. (SEDESOL and UN-HABITAT, 2011b: 45). In addition, there is an increase in poverty and low economic growth in the country.

It is stated that the bigger a city is, the better the conditions to reproduce and intensify inequality. This can be observed in the income distribution by size of the city, which presents great inequalities. In 2000, the average monetary income per household in the towns with fewer than 2,500 inhabitants was just 696 pesos (US$39.40), whereas in the cities of 500,000 or more inhabitants, it reaches 2,241 pesos, that is, 3.2 times more income on average (US$ 126.90) (CONAPO, 2005: 40).

Moreover, there is high inequality within many urban municipalities of more than 100,000 inhabitants, which presented Gini coefficients of extreme inequality. Municipalities located in the west of the country are illustrative of this situation (CONAPO, 2005). All these cities had a Gini coefficient above the national average. However, in some medium and large Mexican cities, the inequality index has decreased (UN HABITAT, 2014b: 60).

Apart from the conditions of poverty, social exclusion, and economic inequality in cities, there are the serious processes of territorial inequality that amplify the preexisting inequalities and create divided, fragmented, and segmented urban spaces, generated not only by structural causes of the labor market but also by a set of social practices that lead to the discrimination against lower classes.

Although inequalities are persistent, they change over time, and the old forms of inequality transform and intertwine with new disparities (Reygadas, 2008). In this sense, the new configuration of the economy – brought about by the neoliberal economic policies – has not only had repercussions in the labor markets and the income and wages structure but also in the forms of occupation and use of the land, all of which is clearly seen in urban spaces. These and the intention of renewing a socially degraded and urban deteriorated area create conflicts (Ziccardi, 2016).

In its territorial dimension, inequality expresses the differences that exist between enclaves of opulence – closed neighborhoods offering exclusivity and security to the minority upper classes – and the highly deficient conditions of the popular sectors in the poor peripheries of cities, but also in degraded central areas (Ziccardi, 2016). "This social and territorial division prevents social cohesion and constitutes a favorable climate for greater insecurity and violence." (Ziccardi, 2015a: 35)

In the case of Mexico City, although there is a moderate decrease in income inequality, it does not represent an improvement in the equity of access to urban goods and services. It should be noted as well that the city's urban expansion process has not been linked to a concept of spatial justice, and there are no actions supporting the redistribution of surplus value in order to improve the living conditions of the popular sectors.

The urban form of cities

Changes in the composition of the National Urban System

Since the 1990s, a restructuring of the distribution pattern of the population and more balance due to the economic model adopted by Mexico produced a relocation of the productive processes.

In less populated regions, urban poles arose, promoted by enclaves such as oil companies, tourism, industries, and metropolitan agglomerations (Aguilar, 2013: 187). There were also important investments in infrastructure through specific programs (100 Cities Program) and transportation and communications innovations that enabled connectivity between urban centers of different sizes.

Population flows to medium-sized cities increased, and those targeting large metropolises declined, losing the concentrating power of productive activities and population (Ziccardi, 2003; Eibenschutz and Goya, 2006; Aguilar, 2013; Sánchez Almanza, 2016). There are, however, differentiated dynamics within the group of metropolitan areas. The four main metropolitan areas that since 1990 exceed 1 million inhabitants – Mexico City, Guadalajara, Monterrey, and Puebla – showed a tendency to decrease their growth rate, whereas the metropolitan areas that joined this group during the last 20 years – Toluca, Tijuana, León, Querétaro, and San Luis Potosí, with the exception of Juárez and La Laguna – have had more dynamic growth rates (CONAPO, 2010). In spite of this, the four main metropolitan areas have retained their dominance in the national context and in 2010 represented 27.9 percent of the national population. Furthermore, in economic terms, in these areas there are spaces connected to global flows, articulating the national and international economies (Ziccardi, 2015a).

Likewise, in these years, there has been a consolidation and urban concentration process in the medium-sized cities, a trend that will continue for the next 25 years (SEDESOL, 2012: 9). In 2010, there were 84 medium-sized cities (between 100,000 and 1 million inhabitants) where 30 million Mexicans lived (29.5 percent of the total population). These centers, according to Aguilar (2013) "have received a large part of the repercussions of urban de-concentration in the phase of economic restructuring in the country, particularly in the form of productive relocation, foreign investment, and urban–urban migrations," showing a great power to attract population.

However, today a significant part of the population still lives in poorly connected areas, which in many cases exacerbate spatial inequalities (Corona et al., 2008: 181). The results of the de-concentration process of activities and labor in Mexico cannot be viewed in a positive light if we bear in mind that they have helped deepen regional inequalities (Ziccardi, 2003: 329).

The expansion of the Mexican metropolitan areas

The metropolitan areas in Mexico, like many others in the region, present a new spatial architecture. From the economic and functional point of view, the largest cities have transformed into a polycentric structure, organized around nodes. This polycentric structure has been identified in the largest metropolitan areas in the Valley of Mexico, Guadalajara, Monterrey, Puebla, and Toluca (Sobrino, 2014).

Similarly, the way in which metropolitan areas have expanded has generated a diffuse city model, with no clear limits, where activities are de-concentrated and services dispersed over an extense territory where urban, rural, and environmental uses are mixed. Among the factors that made this model feasible are the increasingly widespread use of cars (simplifying mobility, but with high environmental costs), the industrial relocation processes, the lack of urban regulation, and the housing policy developed in recent years (Ziccardi, 2016).

The appropriation of land and land-use processes has become apparent in these new urban forms. On the one hand, the self-production of neighborhoods under irregular conditions has facilitated this expansion (Ziccardi, 2016). A considerable part of the 17,500 hectares that the SUN occupies every year "[is] located in unsuitable areas and very far from the places of employment and services, which may even represent a risk to the population" (Fundación

CIDOC and SHF, 2015: 22). According to Priscilla Connolly (2012: 380), "informal settlements represent more than half of the urbanization." Although there are no precise figures on the number of informal settlements in the country, recent studies indicate that around 60 percent of the annual demand for urban land incorporation is for informal settlements. Moreover, it is considered that at least 3.5 million homes, of the almost 15 million located in the SUN cities, at some point occupied the land irregularly (Mansilla and Rubio, 2010: 10).

But these new forms identified in the cities are also the result of the commercialization of land and the collective assets of the city by a governmental apparatus in which the technical elite represents or is allied with the business interests – real estate developers and the construction industry – that promote the construction of residential mega-complexes in the far outskirts of cities. Thus, it is possible to affirm that in the last decade the main driver of territorial expansion has been the housing production resulting from the housing policy of the federal government, a policy disconnected from the urban development policy, whose main competencies are assigned to the municipal governments (Ziccardi, 2016). Between 2007 and 2011, 2,889,873 new homes were built, most of them located in the far outskirts of the cities (González and Ziccardi, 2015).

The distance between these large-scale residential complexes and the center of the city is considerable, being greater in the larger cities: 21.9 km in the megacities, 12.69 km in the large cities, 6.16 km in medium cities, and 4.81 km in small cities (Eibenschutz and Goya, 2009).

A study by the Secretariat of Social Development (2012) shows that between 1980 and 2010 the urban population doubled and the surface of urban fabric grew, on average, tenfold (SEDESOL, 2012). It also shows differences according to the size of the city. Within the cities with millions of inhabitants, Toluca and Queretaro are the most representative of this dynamic; in the former, its population multiplied by 3 in the last 30 years and its territory grew 26.9 times, whereas Queretaro's population grew 3.39 times and its territory 16 times (SEDESOL, 2012). In cities with 100,000 to 500,000 inhabitants, the tendency is stronger. For example, during the same period, the population in the metropolitan area of Tlaxcala-Apizaco grew 3.79 times and its area 57.14 times. It should be noted that the city with the largest surface growth was San Jose del Cabo, a city with fewer than 100,000 inhabitants, which increased 142.82 times its size and 20.67 times in population in the last 30 years. It is noteworthy that in this city there is a significant proportion of uninhabited housing.

Another feature of these complexes is that – being far from the city, along regional and secondary roads and with a closed urban design – they are isolated and disconnected from their surroundings and from urban centers, producing social and environmental effects and higher expenses for the municipalities. The latter have not been able to face the challenges imposed by this housing model because, in some cases, the size of these developments is totally out of proportion to the size of the municipality (Eibenschutz and Goya, 2009).[21]

This model is extremely inefficient, because it

> wastes the land (limited natural resource), produces high levels of pollution, and puts the population at risk by promoting the occupation of territories vulnerable to weather phenomena. Likewise, in economic terms, it is unproductive because it creates constant increases in time, distances, and transport costs, which in turn affect the air quality of the cities.
>
> (Molina, 2014: 12)

These changes are reflected in the density of the metropolitan areas. According to the *Atlas of Urban Expansion* (Angel et al., 2010), it is estimated that between 2000 and 2010, the decrease in the density of cities worldwide is 2 percent per year. In the case of Mexican cities, the National Population Council points out that the average urban density of the total metropolitan areas (MZ) declined from 124 inhabitants/ha to 111 inhabitants/ha between 2000 and 2010 (CONAPO, 2010).

However, the behavior of the metropolitan areas differs. The metropolitan area of Juarez, Chihuahua, in the north of the country, is the one with the highest loss of density, going from 91.1 inhabitants/ha to 67.9 inhabitants/ha between 2000 and 2010. Juarez also has the highest percentages of uninhabited housing and, in recent years, has suffered serious violence and insecurity. Other central metropolitan areas lost density; such is the case of Puebla-Tlaxcala and Pachuca. The four main metropolitan areas registered the highest urban densities in 2010, although it was lower than that registered in 2000.

Another process observed in the new configuration of cities is the recovery of central areas. In recent years, the Great Urban Projects Program (GPU) has changed the landscape of the great metropolises. This program includes a wide range of activities, including the recovery of historic centers, the creation of residential complexes, and the renovation of abandoned or underused areas. The aim is to promote the physical and functional transformation of the city and create new centralities under models of mixed land use. These processes are evident in the case of Mexico City and Monterrey. In recent years, Guadalajara – characterized by the depopulation of the central areas – has had a large investment in infrastructure, driven by the hosting of international events such as the Pan American Games.

These new dispersed urban forms that currently characterize the metropolitan areas of our country present residential segregation and urban fragmentation processes that amplify the pre-existing structural inequalities (Ziccardi, 2016).

The urban structure of medium-sized cities

According to Sobrino (2007), the most common typology of medium-sized metropolitan areas is monocentric. Cities with 100,000 to 249,999 inhabitants are formed by a smaller number of municipalities, and the central city is home to more than 70 percent of the population and more than 80 percent of employment, work-residence commutes between different jurisdictions exceed 90 percent (Sobrino, 2007: 608, 610). On the other hand, more recent studies conclude that medium-sized cities are no longer monocentric and that their structure is related to periods of urban growth (Álvarez de la Torre, 2011).

Border towns

In the case of the Mexican border, over the last 20 years, there has been a rapid urbanization trend with a tendency to concentrate the population in a few cities. Industry, usually located near the border crossing, is the most important activity of these cities and structures the way they function. With regards to trade and services, in Tijuana or Ciudad Juárez, there is a hierarchical structure of tertiary subcenters, with a large center that gathers the largest number of tertiary activities (Alegría, 2010: 302).

On the topic of the demographic characteristics,

> the higher income groups are concentrated near the old towns and a short distance from the border crossing. In contrast, people with lower incomes have two types of spatial patterns: in Tijuana and Mexicali it is dispersed, with few concentrations in the periphery; in Ciudad Juárez, people with lower incomes live in the periphery of the city.
>
> (Alegría, 2012: 106)

These metropolitan areas have created mechanisms to institutionalize cross-border or binational cooperation with American cities, and that has given them particular characteristics. These include possible solutions to urban development or infrastructure problems arising from the relationship between cities of different nationalities. Such is the case of the metropolitan areas of Nuevo Laredo, Mexicali, Ciudad Juárez, and Tijuana, among others (Alegría, 2012: 103).

The great metropolitan urban region of the valley of Mexico

The ZMVM is one of the mega-cities of the world. Its central nucleus is Mexico City, the capital of the republic. It is a polycentric and dispersed space, with a fragmented and low-density periphery. A large urban region in which large sectors of the population live in urban poverty amidst deep socioeconomic and territorial inequalities and other striking urban segregation processes (Ziccardi, 2016).

It has the highest population growth rates of the last decade in the periphery of the city, correlated with a noticeable growth of the urban surface. In 40 years, the population of the metropolitan area increased 1.42 times while its urban area increased 3.57 times (CONAPO, 2012, cit. In Ziccardi, 2016).

In the last decade, most of this territorial expansion was the product of new formal and informal settlements (16,500 hectares) (POZMVM-PUEC, 2012), with housing production – promoted by a federal housing policy disconnected from the urban development policy – as the main driver of this territorial expansion.

In the Valley of Mexico, housing production had a particularly accelerated dynamic between 2005 and 2010, when more than a quarter (26 percent) of the existing housing stock in 2010 was built (6.5 million homes). This housing production was focused in some municipalities of the State of Mexico that, due to their location, demand large investments in time and substantial resources for transport to and from these areas. These housing projects have actually promoted poverty conditions, increased structural inequalities, and produced residential segregation.

The most distinctive spatial feature of the economic reconfiguration of the territory is the appearance of new centralities that enable cities to continue fulfilling their main economic functions. In other words, the causes of urban expansion are not only the settlement processes and the income obtained from changing land use for rural to urban but also the restructuring of the local economy in a global context, towards increased deindustrialization process and a prevalence of the services sector. The spatial expression of this process is seen in the concentration of these activities in nodes of modernity and in the re-functionalization of the financial district, as the historic center was displaced by a new centrality defined by the Santa Fe area and the Masaryk–Reforma modernity corridor.

Thus, the metropolitan area has a grid pattern, with nodes of intense activity – both industrial and service sectors – connected by roads and highways as well as by informational technologies which have modified the distances between center and periphery – particularly in the Arco Norte and the Mexico City–Puebla exit (POZMVM, 2012).

The territorial expansion and population growth of the Valley of Mexico are characterized by intense processes of peri-urbanization resulting in a new polycentric urban form. In it, there are processes of residential segregation and fragmentation of the urban structure produced – to a large extent – by the housing policy of the Mexican state and the construction of luxury enclaves.

Conclusions

Between HABITAT II and HABITAT III, there were deep transformations in urban policies and urban governance in Mexico, in the framework of a neoliberal economic model that restructures the governmental and institutional apparatus.

Undoubtedly, the country experienced an intense urbanization process characterized by a growing number of metropolitan areas and the population living in them. However, there has been a progressive weakening of the institutional capabilities of the federal government to manage the urban development processes. The SEDATU was not able to position the urban agenda in the public policies context. In particular, it is very difficult to break the governmental inertia that leads to privileging a housing policy based on financial criteria and urban expansion.

At the same time, municipal governments have broad powers to govern land-use and urban planning processes, and are responsible for the supply of basic services. Although in this period their fiscal capacities were reinforced with the creation in 1997 of a budget account in the Federation Budget (XXXIII), the local capacities – in terms of human, technical, and administrative resources – were not strengthened. The inability of local governments to face a growing demand for basic goods and services, driven by a massive housing production, makes evident the absence of a local urban development policy that guarantees the proper city-making.

Although urban management processes and local land-use planning are generally subordinated to the federal government's housing policy, in some states and municipalities of the country, new instances were created to influence urban processes; such is the case of the Planning Institutes and the Urban Observatories. These organizations have had different performances according to local capacities and reality and – in some cases – have considered public opinion for their planning processes (IMPLANEG of the State of Guanajuato is an example). The new legislation regarding transparency and accountability and the use of new information and communication technologies is only starting to transform urban development management practices.

It is true that in the past 20 years there was an explicit and legal recognition of citizen participation in public decisions related to the life of cities, and there were different organizations and citizen or neighborhood committees in place. However, they were generally used to legitimize the implementation of urban policies already designed by the governmental apparatus. Although there are local experiences of innovative citizen participation, they face many difficulties surviving over time and being replicated on a large scale.

A general assessment shows that the Mexican state accepted the commitment to produce social housing without giving much importance to urban development. This is also evident in the legal field, where the legislative branch approved a new Housing Law without updating the Human Settlements Law that regulates land use.

A financial perspective dominated housing policy, while upgrading and social production of housing were incidental matters. In addition, the creation of SEDATU was not complemented with building the capacities of local governments to efficiently manage the territory.

Moreover, urban development planning and management are barely connected to environmental issues, and there is thus a territorial expansion that compromises natural resources. It should be noted that – unlike the lack of strength seen in Mexico's urban national policies – between HABITAT II and HABITAT III the issue of sustainability and environmental management received greater attention in public policies. This resulted in the creation and/or updating of regulations, the signing and fulfillment of important international agreements and innovation in issues on the environmental agenda – in particular, that of climate change. However, these efforts were not reflected at the local level; once again, decentralization processes are limited by the inadequate institutional capacities of local implementers. Among the commitments fulfilled by the Mexican state is the adoption of the sustainable development approach in the formulation of key environmental policies, and their legal framework. Climate change policy is included and prioritized in the governmental agenda, and the General Law of Climate Change has been approved. The notion of resilience, despite being a recently incorporated term, is already integrated into the national and local government agendas.

However, citizen participation in environmental issues remains at the heart of social mobilization, and a large number of social and nonprofit organizations created in the last 20 years have greatly contributed to the salience of these discussions in Mexico.

Notably, between HABITAT II and HABITAT III habitability criteria were included in the legislative framework defining dignified and decent housing. This legislative framework led to a redesign of social housing programs, however, the financing granted during these 20 years was aimed exclusively at those formally employed and having better salaries. Hence, housing supply barely corresponded to the needs of households – in terms of their composition and current social and cultural characteristics – houses were built following standard prototypes and usually in projects located in the peripheries of cities, which led to a dispersed city model. The construction companies developed large housing projects in the far outskirts of the cities, taking advantage of inexpensive nonurbanized land and obtaining huge profits. This is why we have stated that there was *a lot of housing but little city*. An indicator of the dissatisfaction produced by this policy is the high number of vacant homes. Although measures have recently been implemented to solve this problem, the bias of such a policy is difficult to change.

Over the last years, Mexican cities have become important contributors to the national economy, providing just over three-quarters of the country's GDP. In this dynamic, the largest metropolitan areas contribute the most. However, they face several obstacles to improving their competitiveness. Among them, the dispersed urban structure – a consequence of the federal housing policy of recent years – is seen as an element hindering the competitiveness of these areas: it produces an increase in commuting times and in the use of private cars, produces higher environmental pollution, and imposes challenges to local governments in terms of providing public services. In addition, the highly fragmented structure of its government does not generate incentives for economic development.

An important fact when analyzing the performance of the urban economy is the type of employment created – in this case, it is of poor quality, low productivity, low salaries, and insufficient to meet the labor demands of young people trying to join the labor market annually. Although unemployment rates are not as high as those of other countries in the region, it is important to bear in mind the significant proportion of the population in the informal sector: 6 out of 10 working people are without social protections and without a steady income.

In these 20 years, poverty in Mexico has not improved. Worse still, in times of economic crisis, as happened after 2008, it has increased. There is at stake a process of urbanization of poverty, that is, the share of urban population is increasing in the total of poverty headcount. While data indicate some improvement in access to social rights, there is undoubtedly a large majority receiving low incomes.

Although economic inequality has diminished in some cities, neoliberal policies have a territorial expression that manifests itself in divided, fragmented, and segmented urban spaces. Thus, serious territorial inequality amplify pre-existing structural inequalities.

The morphology of large metropolitan areas has produced a new low-density polycentric city model. In addition, the territorial expansion of cities outpaces population growth, and is paired with a decrease in their densities which has adverse social, environmental, and economic costs.

Altogether, these dynamics reveal that the recent federal housing policy has had a fundamental impact on land appropriation and land-use processes.

Notes

* The author thanks Cynthia Gómez Camargo for her help with this work; also, Teresa Ramírez, Karla Serrano, and Óscar Torres for their help in the process of gathering the information required for the preparation of this text.
1 The National Urban System is integrated by localities of more than 15,000 inhabitants.
2 Monclova, Saltillo, Torreón, Querétaro, Veracruz, Mérida, Puerto Vallarta, Cancún, Playa del Carmen, and Guaymas (Sobrino, 2014: 52).
3 Between 2006 and 2012, 3,411,000 Mexicans joined the informal sector and 2,137,000 were openly unemployed (CAM-FE, UNAM, 2012).
4 This program affected116 cities (DOF, 1995).
5 It has signed 92 international agreements and protocols related to climate change, waste, water, air, and environmental considerations (DOF, 2013b).
6 In all cases, the comparative value in dollars corresponds to the price on the referred date.
7 In Peru, it is 65,084 m³ per capita; in Argentina, 19,968; and in Brazil, 41,865 (DOF, 2013b).
8 With the exception of Monterrey, which has the capacity to treat 100 percent of the water it uses, whereas Mexico City only treats 20 percent (CEMDA, 2006: 51).
9 According to the OECD, 11.5 million m³ are extracted from nonsustainable sources (15 percent of the total), including 6.5 million m³ of overexploited aquifers (OECD, 2013: 29).
10 Energy consumption has increased by 25 percent, going from 443 petajoules (PJ) in 1992 to 554 PJ in 2012, with a per capita consumption of 27 gigajoules, which means that each year an inhabitant of Mexico City used the energy equivalent of burning 824 liters of gasoline (SEDEMA, 2013: 18).
11 The other branches within the energy sector are the residential and commercial sector, which contributed 8 percent, and manufacturing, with 4 percent.
12 In 1992, the Metropolitan Environmental Commission (CAM) was formed – consisting of Mexico City (formerly DF) and the State of Mexico – and as of 2005, some programs such as "Hoy no Circula" and Vehicle Verification were implemented (PUEC, 2012).

13 Mario Molina is a leading Mexican chemical engineer and a pioneer in atmospheric chemistry research. He co-authored, together with F.S. Rowland, the original essay that predicted the thinning of the ozone layer due to the emission of certain industrial gases and won the Nobel Prize in Chemistry in 1995 along with Paul J. Crutzen. Since 2005, he heads a center for research and promotion of environmental and energy public policies in Mexico, particularly in the fields of climate change and air quality. Source: Centro Mario Molina (CMM), http://bit.ly/1FTV73N

14 This section is based on Alicia Ziccardi's book. 2015. *¿Cómo viven los mexicanos? Un análisis regional de las condiciones de habitabilidad.* México: IIJ. It is also draws on previous work by PUEC-UNAM et al. (2013), "*Perfil del sector vivienda,*" Mexico.

15 The National Urban System includes localities with more than 15,000 inhabitants.

16 Transportation is the second item on which households spend their income – only below food, beverages, and tobacco – representing, on average, 18.5 percent of total net income (UN HABITAT, 2014b: 40).

17 In Mexican economic censuses, GDP is not calculated, but rather gross output is registered, which is why we use this measure. Total gross output is defined as the value of all goods and services emanating from economic activity as a result of the operations carried out by the economic units, including the margin of sale of the goods resold. It includes the production that was not released to the market because it was being produced or waiting for customers and the production of fixed assets for its own use (INEGI).

18 This section is based on the following essays: Ziccardi, A., (2016), *Poverty and Urban Inequality: The Case of Mexico City Metropolitan Región*, International Social Science Journal, UNESCO; Ziccardi, A., (2015c), *Pobreza urbana, marginalidad y exclusión social*, Academia Mexicana de Ciencias, número especial 75 años vol. III, Selección de artículos 2005–2015, México, pp. 206–215.

19 This refers to the population that can meet their minimum needs of food, education and health, but has a per capita income that is not enough to acquire essential minimum housing, clothing, footwear and transportation for each member of household.

20 People live in poverty when they have at least one social deficiency in the six indicators of educational lag, access to health services, access to social security, quality and housing spaces, basic services in housing, and access to food and their income is insufficient to acquire the goods and services required to meet their nutritional needs (minimum welfare line) and non-nutritional needs (welfare line).

21 In Mineral de la Reforma, Hidalgo, the target population of the developed housing projects exceeded the total resident population.

Bibliography

Aguilar, A. G., (2013), "Distribución Territorial de la Población en México. Elementos esenciales para una nueva Ley General de Población", In Valdés, L. (ed.), *Hacia una nueva Ley General de Población*, IIJ-UNAM, México. Available at: http://biblio.juridicas.unam.mx/libros/8/3538/11.pdf

Aguilar, A. G., (2015), *Trayectorias de Urbanización e Implicaciones Ambientales en México*, INEGI, México. Available at: http://bit.ly/2dPPAQ4

Alcalde, A., (2014), "La miseria de los salarios mínimos", *La Jornada*, August 9, México.

Alegría, T., (2010), "Estructura de las ciudades de la frontera norte", In Garza, G., and Schteingart, M. (eds.), *Los grandes problemas de México. II. Desarrollo urbano y regional*, El Colegio de México, México, pp. 259–304.

Alegría, T., (2012), "Estructura de las ciudades de la frontera norte", In Garza, G. and Schteingart, M. (eds.), *Los grandes problemas de México*, Edited version, El Colegio de México, México.

Álvarez, L. (ed.), (2008), *Pueblos urbanos. Identidad, ciudadanía y territorio en la ciudad de México*, Miguel Ángel Porrúa, CEIICH-UNAM, México.

Álvarez, L. and Ziccardi, A., (2015), "¿Cómo hacer efectivos los derechos ciudadanos? Las políticas de inclusión social de la ciudad de México", In *Revista de Ciencias Sociales*, # 27, Universidad Nacional de Quilmes, Buenos Aires, pp. 121–138.

Álvarez de la Torre, G., (2011), *Estructura y temporalidad urbana de las ciudades intermedias en México*, Frontera Norte, 23:46, July–December, México, pp. 91–124.

Angel, S., Parent, J., Civco, D. L., and Blei, A. M., (2010), *Atlas of Urban Expansion*, Lincoln Institute of Land Policy, Cambridge, MA. Available at: www.lincolninst.edu/subcenters/atlas-urban-expansion

Arroyo, J. and Rodríguez, D., (2014), "Gobernanza local urbana y medio ambiente en México", In Graizboard, B. (ed.), *Metrópolis: estructura urbana, medio ambiente y política pública*, El Colegio de México, México, pp. 497–555.

Auditoría Superior de la Federación (ASF), (2012), "Política Pública de Vivienda", In *Evaluación*, #1164, ASF, México.

Azuela, A., (2013), "El ordenamiento territorial en la legislación mexicana", In Sánchez, M., et al. (eds.), *La política de ordenamiento territorial en México: de la teoría a la práctica*, UNAM, Instituto de Geografía, Centro de Investigaciones en Geografía Ambiental, SEMARNAT, INECC, Mexico.

Bensusán, G., (2013), "Reforma laboral, desarrollo incluyente e igualdad en México", In *ECLAC, Estudios y Perspectivas*, # 43 ECLAC, Santiago.

Cabrero, E. and Orihuela, I., (2012), *Retos de la competitividad urbana en México*, CIDE, México.

Cabrero, E., Orihuela, I., and Ziccardi, A., (2009), "Competitividad urbana en México: una propuesta de medición", In *Revista Eure*, # 106, Instituto de Estudios Urbanos y Territoriales of the Pontificia Universidad de Chile, Santiago, pp. 79–99.

Carabias, J., de la Maza, J., and Provencio, E., (2008), "Evolución de enfoques y tendencias en torno a la conservación y el uso de la biodiversidad", In Sarukhán, J. (ed.), *Capital natural de México, vol. III: Políticas públicas y perspectivas de sustentabilidad*, CONABIO, México, pp. 29–42.

Castel, R., (1995), *La métamorphoses de la question sociale. Une chronique du salariat*, Fayard, París.

Centro de Análisis Multidisciplinario (CAM-FE, UNAM), (2012), "El desempleo y el empleo informal en el sexenio de Felipe Calderón, México, 2006–2012", Research Report #103 School of Economics, UNAM, México.

Centro de Análisis Multidisciplinario (CAM-FE, UNAM), (2015), "Desempleo y menos paga por más horas de trabajo: resultados a dos años de la reforma laboral", Research Report #118, School of Economics, UNAM, México.

Centro de Estudios de las Finanzas Públicas (CEFP), (2005), *Indicadores y estadísticas (macroeconomía)*, CEFP, México. Available at: http://bit.ly/2dBT9f4

Centro de Estudios de las Finanzas Públicas de la Cámara de Diputados (CEF), (2012), *Gasto Neto devengado del sector público presupuestario por clasificación administrativa, 1980–2012 (millones de pesos constantes 2012)*, México. Available at: http://bit.ly/2dp6VUo

Centro de Estudios de las Finanzas Públicas de la Cámara de Diputados (CEF), (2013), *Proyecto de Presupuesto de Egresos de la Federación 2014. Comparativo del Gasto Público por Unidad Responsable del Gobierno Federal 2013A – 2014P*, CEF, México.

Centro Mario Molina para Estudios Estratégicos sobre Energía y Medio Ambiente, (CMM), (2012), *Evaluación del Programa de Acción Climática de la Ciudad de México*, CMM, México.

Centro Mario Molina para Estudios Estratégicos sobre Energía y Medio Ambiente (CMM), (2014), *Estrategia local de acción climática. Ciudad de México 2014–2020*, CMM, México.

Centro Mexicano de Derecho Ambiental (CEMDA), (2006), *El agua en México: lo que todas y todos debemos saber*, CEMDA, México.

Comisión Intersecretarial de Cambio Climático (CICC), (2007), *Estrategia Nacional de Cambio Climático 2007 (Síntesis ejecutiva)*, CICC, México.

Comisión Intersecretarial de Cambio Climático (CICC), (2009), *Programa Especial de Cambio Climático 2009–2012*, Comisión Intersecretarial de Cambio Climático, México.

Comisión Intersecretarial de Cambio Climático (CICC), (2012), *Quinta Comunicación Nacional ante la Convención Marco de las Naciones Unidas sobre el Cambio Climático*, CICC, México.

Connolly, P., (2012), "La urbanización irregular y el orden urbano en la Zona Metropolitana del Valle de México de 1990 a 2005", In Salazar, C. (ed.), *Irregular: Suelo y mercado en América Latina*, El Colegio de México, México, pp. 379–425.

Connolly, Priscilla. and Cruz, Maria Soledad., (2004), "Nuevos y viejos procesos en la periferia de la Ciudad de México", In Aguilar (ed.), *Procesos metropolitanos y grandes ciudades. Dinámicas recientes en México y otros países*, UNAM, CONACYT, Mexico, pp. 444–473.

Consejo Nacional de Evaluación de la Política de Desarrollo Social (CONEVAL), (2005), *Mapas de pobreza 2005*, CONEVAL, México. Available at: http://bit.ly/2d0JKN3

Consejo Nacional de Evaluación de la Política de Desarrollo Social (CONEVAL), (2010), *Pobreza a nivel municipio 2010*, CONEVAL, México. Available at: http://bit.ly/1j3iGN8

Consejo Nacional de Evaluación de la Política de Desarrollo Social (CONEVAL), (2011), *Evolución de la pobreza por la dimensión de ingreso, 1992–2012*, Statistical Annex, CONEVAL, México. Available at: http://bit.ly/2dHknOu

Consejo Nacional de Evaluación de la Política de Desarrollo Social (CONEVAL), (2014a), *Pobreza urbana y de las zonas metropolitanas en México*, CONEVAL, México.

Consejo Nacional de Evaluación de la Política de Desarrollo Social (CONEVAL), (2014b), *Resultados de pobreza en México 2014 a nivel nacional y por entidades federativas*, Statistical Annex, CONEVAL, México. Available at: www.coneval.gob.mx/medicion/Paginas/PobrezaInicio.aspx

Consejo Nacional de Evaluación de la Política de Desarrollo Social (CONEVAL), (2014c), *Evolución y determinantes de la pobreza de las principales ciudades de México, 1990–2010*, CONEVAL, México.

Consejo Nacional de Evaluación de la Política de Desarrollo Social (CONEVAL), (2014d), *La pobreza en la población indígena de México 2012*, CONEVAL, México.

Consejo Nacional de Población (CONAPO), (2005), *La desigualdad en la distribución del ingreso monetario en México*, CONAPO, México.

Consejo Nacional de Población (CONAPO), (2010), *Índice de marginación urbana 2010*, CONAPO, México.

Consejo Nacional de Población (CONAPO), (2012), *Catálogo del Sistema Urbano Nacional*, CONAPO, México.

Consejo Nacional de Población (CONAPO), (2013), *Ciudades y Población 2004–2009. Dinámica de las ciudades de México en el siglo XXI*, CONAPO, México. Available at: http://bit.ly/2dp5BAR

Consejo Nacional de Población (CONAPO) and Fundación BBVA Bancomer, (2014), *Anuario de migración y remesas. México 2015*, CONAPO, Fundación BBVA Bancomer, México.

Cordera, R. and Provencio, E., (2016), *Informe del Desarrollo en México 2016*, Programa Universitario de Estudios del Desarrollo, México.

Corona, A., López, B., and Zamudio, S., (2008), "Un índice de ruralidad para México", In *Espiral, Estudios sobre Estado y Sociedad*, XIV:42, May–August 2008, Centro Universitario de Ciencias Sociales y Humanidades-Universidad de Guadalajara, México. Available at: www.scielo.org.mx/pdf/espiral/v14n42/v14n42a7.pdf

Cortés Rocha, X. (ed.), (2015), *Planeación participativa en centros históricos: tres casos de estudio: Campeche, Guanajuato y Zacatecas*, Facultad de Arquitectura, PUEC-UNAM, México, p. 300.

Dávila, H., (2014), "Evaluación de la política social durante la alternancia", In Rozo, C., Dávila, C., and Azamar, A. (eds.), *La economía mexicana en la alternancia panista*, UAM, México.

Delgado, G. C., (2016), "Vuelta al agua, disponibilidad, consumos, retos y perspectivas", In *Tierra Adentro*, #214, Fondo de Cultura Económica, México.

Delgado, G. C. and Ávila, S., (2014), "La industria embotelladora en México: negocio, regulación y apropiación de la agua", In Delgado, G. C. (ed.), *Apropiación de agua, medio ambiente y obesidad: los impactos del negocio de bebidas embotelladas en México*, UNAM, México.

Delgado, G. C., De Luca, A., and Vázquez, V., (2015), *Adaptación y mitigación urbana del cambio climático*, CEIICH-UNAM, México.

Delgado, J. and Suárez, M., (2014), "Ciudad de México ¿ciudad sustentable?", In *Ciencia*, Academia Mexicana de Ciencias, October–December, México.

Delgado, M., (2004), "El papel de las organizaciones de la sociedad civil ante el cambio climático global", In Martínez, J. and Fernández, A. (eds.), *Cambio Climático: una visión desde México*, SEMARNAT-INE, México, pp. 491–512.

Diario Oficial de la Federación (DOF), (1995), *Plan Nacional de Desarrollo 1995–2000*, May 31, Secretaría de Gobernación, México.

Diario Oficial de la Federación (DOF), (1996a), *Programa Nacional de Desarrollo Urbano 1995–2000*, March 27, Secretaría de Gobernación, México.

Diario Oficial de la Federación (DOF), (1996b), *Decreto que reforma, adiciona y deroga diversas disposiciones de la Ley General del Equilibrio Ecológico y la Protección al Ambiente*, December 13, Secretaría de Gobernación, México.

Diario Oficial de la Federación (DOF), (1996c), *Programa de Medio Ambiente 1995–2000*, April 3, Secretaría de Gobernación, México.

Diario Oficial de la Federación (DOF), (1999), *Decreto por el que se declara la adición de un párrafo quinto al artículo 4° constitucional y se reforma el párrafo primero del artículo 25 de la Constitución Política de los Estados Unidos de México*, June 28, Secretaría de Gobernación, México.

Diario Oficial de la Federación (DOF), (2001), *Plan Nacional de Desarrollo 2001–2006*, May 30, Secretaría de Gobernación, México.

Diario Oficial de la Federación (DOF), (2006), *Decreto por el que se expide la Ley de Vivienda*, June 27, Secretaría de Gobernación, México.

Diario Oficial de la Federación (DOF), (2007), *Plan Nacional de Desarrollo 2007–2012*, May 31, Secretaría de Gobernación, México.

Diario Oficial de la Federación (DOF), (2013a), *Plan Nacional de Desarrollo 2013–2018*, May 20, Secretaría de Gobernación, México.

Diario Oficial de la Federación (DOF), (2013b), *Programa sectorial de Medio Ambiente y Recursos Naturales 2013–2018* (Promarnat), 12 de diciembre de, Secretaría de Gobernación, México.

Diario Oficial de la Federación (DOF), (2014a), *Reglas de Operación del Programa Hábitat para el ejercicio fiscal 2015 y subsecuentes*, December 31, Secretaría de Gobernación, México.

Diario Oficial de la Federación (DOF), (2014b), *Programa Especial de Cambio Climático (PECC 2014–2018)*, Second edition, April 28, Secretaría de Gobernación, México.

Domínguez, J., (2010), "Integralidad y transversalidad de la política ambiental", In Lezama, J. L. and Graizboard, B. (eds.), *Los grandes problemas de México. Medio Ambiente*, El Colegio de México, México, pp. 257–293.

Eibenschutz, R. and Goya, C. (eds.), (2009), "Estudios de la integración urbana y social en la expansión reciente de las ciudades en México, 1996–2006", In *Cámara de Diputados LX Legislatura*, SEDESOL, UAM-Xochimilco, Miguel Ángel Porrúa Librero-editor, México.

Fuentes, N. A., (2007), "Las disparidades municipales en México. Un estudio desde la óptica de la desigualdad", *Revista Latinoamericana de Economía*, 38:150, July–September, pp. 213–234.

Fundación CIDOC and SHF, (2015), "Estado Actual de la Vivienda en México 2015", Centro de Investigación y Documentación de la Casa/Sociedad Hipotecaria Federal, Programa Editorial del Gobierno de la República, Mexico.

Garcés, C. and Márquez, B., (2007), "Políticas y Programas con Incidencia en la Migración Interna y la Distribución Territorial de la Población", In *National Workshop: "Migración interna y desarrollo en México: diagnóstico, perspectivas y políticas"*, April 16, ECLAC, CELADE, Ciudad de México.

Globalization and World Cities Research Network (GaWC), (2010), The World According to GaWC, *Research Bulletin*, 369. Available at: https://www.lboro.ac.uk/gawc/world 2010.html

Góngora, P. and Medina, S., (2014), "Las ciudades mexicanas y el TLCAN", *Revista Comercio Exterior*, 64:1. México.

Gonzales, G., (2002), "Evaluación de los instrumentos de crédito para vivienda en los mercados primarios de hipotecas: experiencias en América Latina", In *El crédito hipotecario y el acceso a la vivienda para los hogares de menores ingresos en América latina*, ECLAC, Santiago.

González, A. and Ziccardi, A., (2013), "Las inundaciones y el cambio climático en la Zona Metropolitana del Valle de México: conflicto y negociación entre sociedad y ámbitos gubernamentales", In Castañeda, F., Valverde, K., and Cruz, L. (eds.), *Dinámicas políticas, sociales, económicas y culturales frente al cambio climático*, UNAM/Colofón, México, pp. 287–323.

González, A. and Ziccardi, A., (2014), "Sustentabilidad y política de vivienda", *Revista Ciencia*, 65:4, Academia Mexicana de las Ciencias, México, pp. 46–51.

González, A. and Ziccardi, A., (2015), "Política de vivienda y municipios en México", In Ziccardi, A. and González, A. (eds.), *Habitabilidad y política de Vivienda en México*, PUEC-UNAM, México.

Government of México, (2000), *Sexto Informe de Gobierno*, Presidencia de la República, México.

Government of México, (2012), *Sexto Informe de Gobierno*, Presidencia de la República México.

Government of México, (2015a), *Tercer Informe de Gobierno*, Presidencia de la República México.

Government of México, (2015b), "Compromisos de mitigación y adaptación ante el cambio climático para el periodo 2020–2030", Report, Presidency of Mexico México. Available at: www.inecc.gob.mx/descargas/adaptacion/2015_indc_esp.pdf

Graizbord, B., et al., (2014), "Estrategia para la sustentabilidad urbana de la zona metropolitana del Valle de México: un enfoque programático", In Graizboard, B. (ed.), *Metrópolis: estructura urbana, medio ambiente y política pública*, El Colegio de México, México, pp. 557–608.

Guillén, T. and Ziccardi, A. (eds.), (2004), "Innovación y continuidad en el Municipio mexicano. Análisis de la reforma municipal en 13 estados de la república", In *Miguel Ángel Porrúa e Instituto de Investigaciones Sociales (IIS)*, UNAM, México, 541p.

Hiernaux, N. and Torres, R., (2008), "Desarrollo territorial en México. Un balance general", In Delgadillo, J. (ed.), *Política territorial en México. Hacia un modelo de desarrollo basado en el territorio*, IIE-UNAM, Plaza y Valdés, México.

Ímaz, M. (ed.), (2013), *Medio Ambiente. Recuperar y conservar el medio ambiente para mejorar nuestra calidad de vida*, Agenda Ciudadana de Ciencia, Tecnología e Innovación, CONACYT, Academia Mexicana de las Ciencias, UNAM, México.

Ímaz, M., Ayala, D., and Beristain, A., (2014), "Sustentabilidad, territorios urbanos y enfoques emergentes interdisciplinarios", *Interdisciplina*, # 2, pp. 33–49.

Instituto Mexicano de la Competitividad (IMCO), (2015), *Índice de Ciudades Competitivas y Sustentables*, Banamex, IMCO, CMM, BANOBRAS, INFONAVIT, México.

Instituto Nacional de Ecología y Cambio Climático (INECC), (2007[1996]), *Las Reformas a la LGEEPA*, México. Available at: www2.inecc.gob.mx/publicaciones/libros/384/cap2.html

Instituto Nacional de Ecología y Cambio Climático (INECC), (2015), *Inventario Nacional de Emisiones de Gases y Compuestos de Efecto Invernadero, 2013*, México. Available at: http://iecc.inecc.gob.mx/inventario-nacional-emisiones.php

Instituto Nacional de Estadística y Geografía (INEGI), (2000), *Censo de Población y Vivienda 2000*, INEGI, México.

Instituto Nacional de Estadística y Geografía (INEGI), (2010a), "Ingreso corriente total promedio trimestral per cápita en deciles de personas, 1992 a 2008", In *Encuesta Nacional de Ingreso y Gasto*, INEGI, México.

Instituto Nacional de Estadística y Geografía (INEGI), (2010b), *Censo de Población y Vivienda 2010*, INEGI, México.

Instituto Nacional de Estadística y Geografía (INEGI), (2012), "Zonas Metropolitanas de los Estados Unidos Mexicanos. Censos Económicos 2009", In *Monografía*, INEGI, México.

Instituto Nacional de Estadística y Geografía (INEGI), (2015a), "Las Zonas metropolitanas en México. Censos Económicos 2014", In *Mini monografía*, INEGI, México.

Instituto Nacional de Estadística y Geografía (INEGI), (2015b), "Las remuneraciones en México", In *Mini monografía*, INEGI, México.

Instituto Nacional de Estadística y Geografía (INEGI), (2015c), *Encuesta Intercensal 2015*, INEGI, México.

Instituto Nacional de Estadística y Geografía (INEGI), (2016a), *PIBT. Series originales. Variación anual de los valores constantes. SCNM. Producto Interno Bruto Trimestral 1993–2016*, México. Available at: http://bit.ly/2dqbWt9

Instituto Nacional de Estadística y Geografía (INEGI), (2016b), *Indicadores de medio ambiente*, México. Available at: www.inegi.gob.mx

Instituto Nacional de Estadística y Geografía (INEGI), (2016c), *Cuenta Satélite de Vivienda de México*, México. Available at: www.inegi.org.mx/est/contenidos/proyectos/cn/vivienda/default.aspx

International Energy Agency (IEA), (2015), *CO2 Emission from Fuel Combustion*, Database Anual Historical Series (1971–2013), IEA, Web. Available at: https://www.iea.org/statistics/?country=WORLD&year=2016&category=Emissions&indicator=CO2ByPop&mode=chart&dataTable=INDICATORS

International Labor Organization (ILO), (2013), *Informe mundial sobre salarios 2012/2013. Los salarios y el crecimiento equitativo*, OIT, Geneva.

International Labor Organization (ILO), (2014), *El empleo informal en México: situación actual, políticas y desafíos*, Programa de Promoción de la Formalización en América Latina y El Caribe, Geneva.

IPCC, (2014), *Cambio climático 2014. Mitigación del cambio climático Resumen para responsables de políticas*, Grupo intergubernamental de expertos sobre el cambio climático, Web.

Jiménez-Cisneros, B., (2014), "Agua, ciudades y futuro", In *Ciencia*, Academia Mexicana de Ciencias, October–December, México.

Lezama, J., (2010a), "Sociedad, medio ambiente y política ambiental, 1970–2010", In Graizbord, B. and Lezama, J. L. (eds.), *Los grandes problemas de México*, Tomo IV, Medio Ambiente, COLMEX, México, pp. 23–60.

Lezama, J., (2010b), "La contaminación del aire", In Lezama, J. L. and Graizboard, B. (eds.), *Los grandes problemas de México. Medio Ambiente*, El Colegio de México, México, pp. 105–139.

Lezama, J., (2016), "Contingencia ambiental y crisis de gobernabilidad", *José Luis Lezama Blog*. Available at: http://joseluislezama.blogspot.mx/

Lustig, N., (1995), "México y la crisis del peso: lo previsible y la sorpresa", *Revista Comercio Exterior*, 45:5, México.

Lustig, N., (2012), "El impacto de 25 años de reformas sobre la pobreza y la desigualdad", In Ordorica, M. and Prud'homme, J. F. (eds.), *Los grandes problemas de México. Economía*, COLMEX, México.

Madrigal, D., (2010), "Las movilizaciones ambientales", In Lezama, J. L. and Graizboard, B. (eds.), *Los grandes problemas de México. Medio Ambiente*, El Colegio de México, México, pp. 399–429.

Mansilla, E. and Rubio, I., (2010), *Diagnóstico nacional de los asentamientos humanos ante el riesgo de desastres*, SEDESOL, México.

Martínez Assad, C. and Ziccardi, A., (2000), "Límites y posibilidades de la descentralización", In Cordera, R. and Ziccardi, A. (eds.), *Las políticas sociales en México al fin del milenio, descentralización diseño y gestión*, IISUNAM, Miguel A. Porrúa, Coordinación de Humanidades, UNAM, México.

Masera, R., Salazar, A., and Martínez, R., (2010), "Mitigación del cambio climático y desarrollo sustentable en México: resolviendo necesidades locales con beneficios globales", In Delgado, G., et al. (eds.), *México frente al cambio climático. Retos y oportunidades*, Centro de Ciencias de la Atmósfera – Programa Universitario de Medio Ambiente, Centro de Investigaciones Interdisciplinarias en Ciencias y Humanidades, Programa de Investigación en Cambio Climático, UNAM, México, pp. 211–221.

Maycotte, E. and Sánchez, E., (2010), "Ciudades dispersas, viviendas abandonadas: La política de vivienda y su impacto territorial y social en las ciudades mexicanas", *Conference proceedings, Fifth International Conference Virtual City and Territory*, Barcelona, June 2–4, Centre de Política de Sòl i Valoracions, Barcelona.

Merielle, K., Peña, A., Gutiérrez, D., and Vargas, V., (2013), "Un panorama desalentador", In *Journal México Social, October special*, Juventud, México.

Micheli, J., (2000), "Política ambiental en el sexenio 1994–2000 (antecedentes y globalización del mercado ambiental mexicano", *El Cotidiano*, 17:103, UAM-Azcapotzalco, México, pp. 90–102.

Molina, M., (2014), "Expansión urbana y cambio climático", *En Revista Ciencia*, 65:4, pp. 46–51.

Moreno, J., Garry, S., and Monroy-Gómez, L., (2014), "El salario mínimo en México", *Economía UNAM*, 11:33, UNAM, México.

Nava, E., Ramírez, J., and Graizbord, B., (2014), *Potencial de desarrollo de las ciudades de México*, CONAPO, México.

Olvera, A., (2009), "Las leyes de participación ciudadana en México: proyectos políticos, estrategias legislativas y retos estratégicos en la democratización futura", *Document*. Available at: http://bit.ly/2dBTHBH

Organization for Economic Cooperation and Development (OECD), (2013), *Evaluaciones de la OECD sobre el desempeño ambiental*, OECD Publishing, México.

Organization for Economic Cooperation and Development (OECD), (2015a), *OECD Urban Policy Reviews: Mexico 2015: Transforming Urban Policy and Housing Finance*, OECD Publishing, Paris.

Organization for Economic Cooperation and Development (OECD), (2015b), *Estudios Territoriales de la OCDE: Valle de México, México*, OECD Publishing, Paris.

Parnreiter, C., (2002), "Ciudad de México: el camino hacia una ciudad global", *Revista EURE*, 28:85, Santiago, pp. 89–119.

Pineda, N., Salazar, A., and Buenfil, M., (2010), "Para dar de beber a las ciudades mexicanas: el reto de la gestión eficiente del agua ante el crecimiento urbano", In Jiménez, B., Torregrosa, M., and Aboites, L. (eds.), *El Agua en México: Causes y encauses*, Academia Mexicana de Ciencias, Comisión Nacional del Agua, México.

Programa Universitario de Estudios sobre la Ciudad (PUEC-UNAM), (2012), *Programa de Ordenación de la zona metropolitana del Valle de México (POZMVM)*, PUEC-UNAM, México.

Programa Universitario de Estudios sobre la Ciudad (PUEC-UNAM), (2015), *Foro Hacia Hábitat III. Síntesis de las sesiones de debate del documento preliminar de SEDATU*, UNAM, México.

Programa Universitario de Estudios sobre la Ciudad (PUEC-UNAM) and United Nations Human Settlements Program (UN Habitat), (2014), *Reporte nacional de movilidad urbana en México 2014–2015*, UN Habitat, México.

Provencio, E., (2004), "Política y gestión ambiental contemporánea en México", *Economía informa*, 328, July–August, UNAM, México.

Puente, S., (2010), "Una megalópolis en riesgo: la Ciudad de México", In Graizbord, B. and Lezama, J. L. (eds.), *Los grandes problemas de México*, Tomo IV, Medio Ambiente, COLMEX, México, pp. 373–397.

Reygadas, L., (2008), "La apropiación. Destejiendo las redes de la desigualdad", In *Anthropos*, UNAM, México.

Rockefeller Foundation, (2015), *Evaluación preliminar de resiliencia CDMEX. CDMEX resiliente: transformación adaptativa, incluyente y equitativa*, Rockefeller Foundation-100 Resilient Cities, México.

Romero, L., (2008), "Experiencias de acción colectiva frente a la problemática ambiental en México", *Revista Mexicana de Ciencias Políticas y Sociales*, 50:203, May–August 2008, UNAM, México, pp. 157–174.

Ruiz, V., (2015), "Los pros y los contras de la Reforma Energética de acuerdo con el paradigma del desarrollo sustentable", *Revista Digital Universitaria* [Web], 16:1, January 1. Available at: www.revista.unam.mx/vol.16/num1/art8/index.html

Ruiz Durán, C., (2005), "El reto del empleo en México", *Comercio Exterior*, 55:3, January 1, Mexico.

Ruiz Nápoles, P. and Ordaz Díaz, J. L., (2011), "Evolución reciente del empleo y el desempleo en México", *Economía UNAM*, 8:23, Meciso, pp. 91–105.

Sánchez, G., (2012), *Pacto de la Ciudad de México*, Fundación Pensar, México. Cited in: CMM, (2014), *Estrategia local de acción climática. Ciudad de México 2014–2020*, Centro Mario Molina para Estudios Estratégicos sobre Energía y Medio Ambiente, A.C., México.

Sánchez Almanza, A., (2016), "Sistema de ciudades y redes urbanas en los modelos económicos de México", *Revista Problemas del Desarrollo*, 184:47, IIE-UNAM, México.

Secretaría de Desarrollo Agrario, Territorial y Urbano (SEDATU), (2015), *Incidencia SEDATU en mitigación y adaptación al cambio climático (COP21-París, Francia)*", México. Available at: http://bit.ly/2dqczmK

Secretaría de Desarrollo Social (SEDESOL), (2000), *Resumen informativo 1994–2000*, México. Available at: http://zedillo.presidencia.gob.mx/pages/pub/informativo/sedesol.pdf

Secretaría de Desarrollo Social (SEDESOL), (2006), *Presentación ante la Comisión de Desarrollo Social de la H. Cámara de Diputados. Subsecretaría de Desarrollo Urbano y Ordenación del Territorio*, SEDESOL, México.

Secretaría de Desarrollo Social (SEDESOL), (2012), *La Expansión de las ciudades de México 1980–2010*, SEDESOL, México.

Secretaría de Desarrollo Social (SEDESOL) and United Nations Human Settlements Program (UN HABITAT), (2011a), *Guía metodológica para la constitución y operación de las Agencias de Desarrollo Urbano y los Observatorios Urbanos Locales*, SEDESOL, México.

Secretaría de Desarrollo Social (SEDESOL) and United Nations Human Settlements Program (UN-HABITAT), (2011b), *Estado de las ciudades de México 2011*, SEDESOL, UN-Habitat, México.

Secretaría de Gobernación (SEGOB) y Consejo Nacional de Población (CONAPO), (1998), *La situación demográfica de México, 1997*, Government of Mexico, Second edition, México.

Secretaría de Hacienda y Crédito Público (SHCP), (2016), "Informe sobre la situación económica, las finanzas públicas y la deuda pública. Gasto neto del sector público presupuestario", Report, México.

Secretaría del Medio Ambiente del Distrito Federal (SEDEMA), (2013), *Inventario de emisiones contaminantes y de efecto invernadero 2012. Zona Metropolitana del Valle de México*, SEDEMA, México.

Secretaría del Medio Ambiente y Recursos Naturales (SEMARNAT), (2006), *México Tercera Comunicación Nacional ante la Convención Marco de las Naciones Unidas sobre el Cambio Climático*, Semarnat-INE, México.

Secretaría del Medio Ambiente y Recursos Naturales (SEMARNAT) and Comisión Nacional del Agua (CONAGUA), (2015), *Situación del Subsector Agua Potable, Drenaje y Saneamiento, Edición 2015*, Government of Mexico, México.

Secretaría de Medio Ambiente del Distrito Federal (SEDEMA), (2014), *Estrategia Local de Acción Climática. Ciudad de México 2014–2020*, SEDEMA, Centro Mario Molina, México.

Secretaría de Medio Ambiente y Recursos Naturales (SEMARNAT) y Comisión Nacional de Agua (CONAGUA), (2014), *Numeragua, México 2014*, Government of Mexico, México.

Sistema de Información Energética – Secretaría de Energía (SIE-SENER), (2015), *Balance Nacional de Energía: Producción de energía primaria*, Government of Mexico, México.

Sistema Nacional de Información e Indicadores de Vivienda (SNIIV), (2016), *Financiamientos para la vivienda e Inventario de Vivienda*, CONAVI, México.

Sobrino, J., (2007), "Patrones de dispersión intrametropolitana en México", *Estudios Demográficos y Urbanos*, 22:3, Colegio De México, México, pp. 583–617. Available at: http://aleph.org.mx/jspui/bitstream/56789/21891/1/22-066-2007-0583.p

Sobrino, J., (2014), *Evolución y determinantes de la pobreza de las principales ciudades de México, 1990–2010*, CONEVAL, México.

Sobrino, J., (2016), "Medición y determinantes de la pobreza en las principales ciudades de México", In *La Situación Demográfica de México 2015*, SEGOB-CONAPO, México.

Sosa, R. F., (2015), "Política del cambio climático en México: avances, obstáculos y retos", *Realidad, datos y espacio. Revista Internacional de Estadística y Geografía*, 6:2, INEGI, México.

Terrones, A., Sánchez, Y., and Vargas, R., (2010), "Crecimiento económico y crisis en México, 1970–2009. Un análisis Sexenal", In *Expresión Económica*, 24, Universidad de Guadalajara, México.

Ugalde, V., (2010), "La aplicación del derecho ambiental", In Graizbord, B. and Lezama, J. L. (eds.), *Los grandes problemas de México*, Tomo IV, Medio Ambiente, COLMEX, México, pp. 227–256.

(UN HABITAT), Comisión Nacional de Vivienda (CONAVI), (2013), *México. Perfil del sector vivienda*, United Nations Program for Human Settlements, México.

United Nations Children's Fund (UNICEF) and CONEVAL, (2013), *Pobreza y derechos sociales de niñas, niños y adolescentes en México, 2010–2012*, CONEVAL, México.

United Nations Economic Commission for Latin America and the Caribbean (ECLAC), (2016), *Población urbana que vive en tugurios*, Databases and Statistical Publications, ECLAC-STAT, Santiago.

United Nations Economic Commission for Latin America and the Caribbean (ECLAC) and International Labor Organization (ILO), (2015), "Coyuntura laboral en América Latina y el Caribe. Protección social universal en mercados laborales con informalidad", *Bianual Publication #12*, May, ECLAC-ILO, Santiago.

United Nations Human Settlements Program (UN Habitat), (2014a), *Reporte nacional de movilidad urbana en México 2014–2015*, UN Habitat, México.

United Nations Human Settlements Program (UN Habitat), (2014b), *Construcción de ciudades más equitativas. Políticas públicas para la inclusión social de América Latina*, UN Habitat, Nairobi.

World Bank, (2013), "Las dimensiones sociales del cambio climático en México", Unidad Administrativa del Sector de Desarrollo Sustentable Región de América Latina y el Caribe, *World Bank*, Washington.

Ziccardi, A., (1985), "Problemas Urbanos: Proyectos y Alternativas ante Crisis", In González, P. C. and Aguilar Camín, H. (eds.), *México ante la crisis*, Siglo XXI, México, pp. 52–86.

Ziccardi, A., (2003), "Planeación urbana municipal ¿función normativa o sustento de la gobernabilidad local?", In Cabrero Enrique (ed.), *Políticas públicas municipales. Una agenda en construcción*, Miguel A. Porrúa, Centro de Investigación y Docencia Económicas (CIDE), México, pp. 129–154.

Ziccardi, A. (ed.), (2004), *Planeación participativa en el espacio local: cinco programas parciales de desarrollo urbano en el Distrito Federal*, PUEC, IIS, Posgrado en Urbanismo, UNAM, México.

Ziccardi, A., (2008), "La participación ciudadana en los procesos de planeación y gestión del territorio", In Delgadillo, J. (ed.), *Política territorial en México. Hacia un modelo de desarrollo basado en el territorio*, IIE-UNAM, Plaza y Valdés, México.

Ziccardi, A., (2015a), *Cómo viven los mexicanos. Análisis regional de las condiciones de habitabilidad de la vivienda*, IIJ-UNAM, México.

Ziccardi, A., (2015b), "Gobiernos Locales: federalismo, descentralización y autonomía", In *Repensando la agenda local*, Red MUNI, Argentina.

Ziccardi, A., (2015c), "Pobreza urbana, marginalidad y exclusión social", In *CIENCIA 75 años, vol. III: Selection of Articles 2005–2015*, Academia Mexicana de Ciencias, México, pp. 206–215.

Ziccardi, A., (2015d), "La dimensión urbana de la desigualdad", *Contrapuntos Blog*, El País. Available at: http://blogs.elpais.com/contrapuntos/2015/04/la-dimension-urba-na-de-la-desigualdad.html

Ziccardi, A., (2016), "Poverty and Urban Inequality: The Case of Mexico City Metropolitan Región", *International Social Science Journal*, 65, UNESCO, 217–218.

4 Chile

Housing without city

Alfredo Rodríguez and Paula Rodríguez

Introduction

Between Habitat II and Habitat III, Chile tripled its gross domestic product GDP per capita, reduced urban and rural poverty, built over 1.5 million affordable houses, and achieved near-total coverage in urban infrastructure (potable water, sanitation, electricity). Yet the seven commitments of Habitat II remain unfulfilled, including the right to adequate shelter for all, sustainable human settlements, and gender equality. The nature of the urban policy framework put in place at the country level partly explains this 'failure.' In practice, Chile's urban policy is less aligned with the protection of universal human rights and more with leveraging private–public cooperation, stronger markets, and financing for housing and infrastructure. As a result, urban policy in Chile – despite reference to Habitat II commitments – has not fostered socioeconomic and environmentally sustainable urbanization processes (United Nations, 2014).

The broader context of Chile's urban poverty reduction and higher average personal income is one where, in fact, income is more acutely concentrated. Today, the top 1 percent of the rich participates in 30.5 percent of the national income, and a woman is 23 percent less likely than a man to have a paid job (OECD, 2015). This is where we should focus the debate: on income inequality. New and better indicators are required to unmask the realities of the income gap and of women's poverty as the poorest households are still those headed by single mothers.

There is no improvement regarding the rights to adequate shelter for all and sustainable human settlements: in 1996, the housing deficit was 900,000 units; today it is 1.7 million units. In this period, Chile built more than 1.5 million houses that turned out not to be 'adequate,' therefore failing to reduce – and in fact, widened – the housing deficit. This process has generated entire neighborhoods that are socially violent, vulnerable, and unsustainable. In fact, Chile has had to demolish poorly constructed social housing projects built in the late 1990s.

Despite these challenges, since 2006 there has been progress in several areas. Minimum housing standards are now higher; a neighborhood upgrading program was set in motion, benefitting more than 500 neighborhoods across the country; and – as the National Report for Habitat III indicates – Chile has officially recognized the significant qualitative housing deficit. The latter is a crucial milestone for Chile's urban policy going forward.

Between 1990 and 2010, Chile relied on public–private cooperation to build all the social housing units and projects. Developers and the real estate sector grew stronger during this period to the point that public urban development initiatives practically disappeared. Because Urban plans in Chile are only indicative, economic return becomes the primary driver and fundamental criterion of urbanization and housing. As a result, construction benefits certain parts of the cities and neglects others that are bound to depend on focused housing subsidies. The *spatial* consequence of this process is that the bulk of construction happens in areas where high-income residents live and which provides greater incentives to developers (density, height, and attractive floor-to-area coefficients). The process is self-reinforcing, as more people with higher incomes want to live with similar standards, the demand for homes and services in those same areas is pushed further. This has been called spatial capital accumulation.

The *social* consequence has been a generalized trend of sociospatial segregation in the 2000s in all medium and large cities across the country. There can be social mobility, but it is not visible in the territory. The more affluent population segments are also creating new city centers, matching, if not surpassing, the economic importance (commercial activity and services) of the historic center. The real estate market has changed the demographics of Chile's cities. The egalitarian city project regressed, and the right to the city and to adequate shelter became commodified financial products: where a person lives strictly depends on their debt capacity and purchasing power. Indeed, the market is free and unregulated, but its action – entrenched in a state whose public policies protect the private interest – creates and segregates well-defined socioterritorial units.

Over the last five years, following the energy and education crises, the critique to Chile's public administration and development model has become more public. In 2011, groups of students and environmental activists turned the public attention to the extractivist and capitalist orientation of Chile's public policies, pointing toward the growing urban inequality, segregation, and fragmentation.

The period between Habitat II and Habitat III marked the rise and fall of the financing policies to build social housing in Chile and left lessons that other Latin American countries have not learned. Many countries with similar approaches are brewing similar problems at an even higher scale.

This chapter recounts in seven parts Chile's progress and setbacks since Habitat II. Part one examines the trajectory of urban and environmental policy and governance, including the set of policies Chile developed and implemented to address significant legislative gaps. Part two focuses on energy: the overrepresentation of private companies, the system's vulnerability and the need to transform the power grid to include more renewable and sustainable energies in the short term. Part three looks at the results of housing policies and the social problems that arose from the mercantilization of housing rights for low-income segments of the population. The fourth part describes the urban trends in Chile and the failure of urbanization to reverse inequality in cities, despite the net increase in urban infrastructure and coverage of basic services. The fifth part focuses on urban economy and productivity. This part concludes that having a job does not translate into overcoming urban poverty and looks at the precariousness of formal employment, functional income distribution, women and the labor market, and urban GDP. Part six reviews the issue of poverty reduction and growing social inequality and insecurity across Chilean cities. The last part describes the way urban forms have changed due to housing and social policies in Chile's cities. To end, we propose a set of patterns to explain the social and territorial variations caused by the market-oriented public policies in Chile.

Urban and environmental policy and governance: the new legislation

In 1996 Chile still had a National Policy of Urban Development (NPUD) enacted during the military dictatorship (1973–1989), which remained in place until the year 2000. A vague ruling allowed modifications to the legal text. Chile then created the "Urban Reform" Commission to develop a new NPUD, but nothing occurred until 2013 (MOP, 2013). The thirteen-year-long policy gap left sectoral state agencies operating in a somewhat disarticulated manner, following regulations yet lacking a common vision that could integrate their actions with civil society. Instead, sectoral state agencies favored their relationship with land agents (developers, real estate, etc.). Ultimately, the policy vacuum ended with the 2013 new NPUD (Rodríguez and Rodríguez, 2015), founded on the idea of 'sustainable development' to increase the opportunities of people without compromising the resources of future generations.

The 2013 National Policy of Urban Development

The 2013 NPUD set out to improve peoples' quality of life in five ways (MINVU, 2014):

- Social integration: facilitating equitable access to urban goods, addressing existing segregation and preventing segregation in the future, cutting down the housing deficit, promoting land use policies that favor social integration, and increasing connectivity, especially for remote communities.
- Economic development: fostering local productivity and employment generation, coordinating urban planning and investment programs, correcting flaws in the land market, and making cities more competitive and connected to the global economy.
- Environmental equilibrium: putting in place environmental planning and management tools to protect ecosystems, managing natural and human-made

risks, using natural resources sustainably, fostering sustainable urban land use and expansion, and promoting clean energy transportation, including more cycling and walking.
*   Identity and historic preservation: creating public awareness of the built and natural environment and its importance in forming cultural identity, as well as recognizing cultural diversity and managing cultural heritage.
*   Good governance and institutions: including decentralizing decision-making systems across administrative levels (neighborhood, metropolitan, regional, national), generating integrated planning systems (land use, financing, management), promoting citizen participation, establishing information systems to enable better decision making, acting upon urban challenges and rights, monitoring NPUD progress, and implementing public and private initiatives.

The 2013 NPUD is merely indicative – not mandatory – and, as such, it has neither a budget nor a set of indicators.[1] For this reason, it should be understood as a framework to guide principled and concerted state action (ministries and sectoral state agencies) on a more visible and better-understood social problem. The outcomes of the NPUD since its publication in 2013 are mostly attributable to the only policy instrument it formally created: the National Council for Urban Development (Consejo Nacional de Desarrollo Urbano, CNDU) (CNDU, 2014). The council has an executive secretary; a group of advisors who are experts on the five areas of the NPUD; and thematic working groups leading on three priority issues: land use and social integration policy, new institutional design for urban development, and integrated urban planning and development standards. The working groups include members of the council – or their delegates – and operate with support from the council's executive secretariat.

NCUD activities and initiatives

In September 2015, the council submitted to the presidency of Chile a set of land use measures to promote social integration across cities[2] and is currently working on another submission related to good governance and urban planning measures (new institutional framework). The impact of the NCUD measures will depend on the capacity of ministries involved to propose legislation to Congress for approval and financing. Meanwhile, the inclusion in the last five years of the NPUD in the government's political agenda is a promising sign that the work of the council might be successful. The council has set two goals toward a new institutional framework: First, to decentralize and democratize urban management, transferring planning and implementation capacity, and ensuring greater equity across administrative levels in the allocation of public resources. And second, to strengthen the linkage between urban planning, investments in infrastructure and transportation, and higher levels of citizen participation in the development and approval of urban plans and projects (Bresciani, 2014).

The 2016–2018 plan of the Housing and Urban Ministry (MINVU) aligns with the recommendations and measures of the council. MINVU will formally recognize metropolitan areas and create new norms and instruments so that regional governments take the lead in the provision of services that are currently centralized. For example, new specialized divisions within the regional governments will oversee land use, infrastructure, and transportation (CNUD, 2015a).

Similarly, the central government introduced two legislative initiatives. The first is a bill sent to the lower chamber of Congress proposing to create a levy on land price increases where urban expansion is permitted. The proposed bill, titled "Transparency in the land market and value increase of urban expansion," will capture and reinvest part of the income generated by higher land prices attributed to administrative decisions to expand the city limits. The second initiative is an amendment to the law on decentralization that creates a new planning instrument, the regional land use plan, to replace regional urban development plans. The amendment recognizes metropolitan areas and introduces new norms to transfer decision-making power and capacity to regional entities overseeing transportation, housing, environment, and public works.

It is too soon to tell whether these initiatives are influencing the quality of life in Chile's cities, but they do represent change in a new direction.

Environmental sustainability and management: a work in progress

Privatization is a cornerstone of Chile's environmental public policy. Between 1994 and 1996, following Chile's Water Code of 1981, state-owned water and sanitation companies serving urban and rural centers were privatized. Likewise, in the early 1980s, during the military dictatorship, Chile privatized its state-owned energy companies.

As stated in Energy 2050, Chile's Energy Policy:

> The country strategy to maintain sustained economic growth was based on the protection of the preponderant role of the private sector, leaving the State a subsidiary and regulatory role for those activities where competition was not naturally occurring. Energy policy, then, intended to promote economic efficiency in the sector. Economic efficiency was understood as generating favorable conditions for competition in the energy industries or, if this was not possible, to emulating these conditions in the respective markets by means of adequate regulation.
>
> (Ministry of Energy, 2015: 32)

Sustainability and environmental management of urban areas in the country are topics that have increasingly been placed in the public discussion at the national level thanks to natural events such as floods and droughts; the rise in air pollution, land pollution, and water pollution; and at the same time, the concern of a large number of people to have an energy matrix that does not harm the environment.

Looking back over the twenty years between Habitat II and Habitat III, one can see that there have been advances, from an incipient institution in 1996 to a very recent consolidation of the Ministry of the Environment and particularly of the Environmental Courts.

Regulatory framework

The General Bases Environmental Law (Law No. 19,300), approved in 1994, granted the National Environmental Commission (CONAMA) the responsibility to promote, care for, monitor, and compliance of environmental issues, as well as administer the environmental impact assessment system. These tasks were completed between 1994 and 2010.

During the 2000s, criticisms of CONAMA's institutional constraints were reinforced by the findings of a 1990–2004 Performance Assessment made by the Organisation for Economic Co-operation and Development (OECD) Environmental. These include the need to "develop and strengthen environmental institutions at the national and regional levels" (OECD and ECLAC, 2005). The OECD pointed out the necessity to strengthen the agency's "capacity for compliance and control, including through institutional reforms, such as the establishment of an environmental inspection body" (see Environmental Superintendence, http://www.sma.Gob.cl). This finally led to the government proposing a bill in 2008 creating the Ministry of the Environment, the Environmental Assessment Service, and the Superintendency of the Environment, which was finally approved in 2010 (Law No. 20,417).

The areas of competence of the Ministry of the Environment are, among others, the development and management of regulations, the protection of natural resources, and environmental education, as part of the right to live in a clean and protected environment.[3]

Among the set of instances that compose the ministry, it is interesting to highlight the Superintendency, the Environmental Assessment Service, and the Environmental Courts, given the functions they have performed in emblematic cases during the past few years:

- The Superintendency of the Environment (SMA) was created by Law No. 20,417. Its functions are to oversee environmental permits called Environmental Qualification Resolutions (RCA), environmental prevention, decontamination plans, and environmental quality standards, among others. In order to fulfill its tasks, the SMA operates in three modalities directly with its own employees, directly through sector institutions, and indirectly through third parties accredited by the SMA itself.
- The purpose of the Environmental Assessment Service (SEA) is to manage the National Environmental Impact Assessment System (SEIA), whose objective is to carry out the environmental assessment of the projects in

accordance with current regulations and facilitate the participation of the citizens in the evaluation of projects. The SEA operates on the basis of procedural guidelines, which allow it to standardize data (standard and technical requirements, background checks, certificates, and other procedures) according to what is established by ministries and other state agencies.

- The Environmental Courts are special tribunals of environmental justice under the Supreme Court of Justice (Law 20,600 of 2012).[4] The function of the Environmental Courts is to resolve conflicts related to, among others, demands for reparation of environmental damages, claims against the resolutions of the SMA or the resolution of the Committee of Ministers or the executive director of the SEA, and claims against acts that the ministries or public services dictate in environmental matters and that violate the law.

Air pollution in cities

Currently, air pollution in Chilean cities is a widespread environmental problem. According to the report by the government of Chile (2016) for Habitat III, "about 87 percent of the population in Chile is exposed to high levels of air pollution." According to the Second National Environmental Survey (2016) in the fifteen regional capital cities, air pollution is the main environmental problem in the country (33 percent), the second is garbage and dirt in the streets (19 percent), and third, pollution in general (8 percent) and cars that "generate noise, pollution or clogging" (8 percent) (Ministry of the Environment, 2016). What stands out from this survey is that air quality depends on the geographic conditions and the local energy matrix. Thus, Coyhaique a city of about 60,000 inhabitants, has the worst air pollution, (61 percent), Temuco (51 percent) on the order of 400,000, and Santiago (43 percent) about 6.5 million inhabitants.

As noted in Chile's report for Habitat III (Government of Chile, 2016), since the 1990s there have been partial plans for urban atmospheric decontamination. In this regard, "emission standards for primary and secondary air quality have been established, resulting in constant monitoring to determine the degree of contamination by type of pollutant in the main Chilean cities. As a result, different settlements have been declared latent or saturated zones, activating Atmospheric Prevention and Decontamination Plans whose general objective is to establish a guide for actions that protect the health of the population and reduce their exposure to harmful concentrations of pollutants that affect welfare and the physical quality of life of people" (Government of Chile, 2016). The current Chilean Atmospheric Decontamination Strategy: 2014–2018, which monitors the environmental quality of air in more than twenty-five cities in the country, aims to establish decontamination plans in areas declared to be saturated or dormant in the country (Ministry of the Environment, 2014). One of the prevention measures related to sustainable urban development is the implementation of a sustainable residential heating policy. Much of the air pollution from cities in the center and south of the country is associated with emissions from wood stoves and kitchens. Hence, different public entities have initiated programs to reduce or modify heating practices through the improvement of thermal insulation of homes and the introduction of solar energy for residential energy use (Ministry of the Environment, 2014).

Energy matrix

The primary energy matrix of the country is based mainly on oil (about 32 percent), followed by the use of coal (about 24 percent) and firewood and biomass (23 percent). It should be noted that Chile does not produce all the oil it needs and that, for that matter, 95 percent of that fuel is imported. As for the secondary energy matrix, oil also predominates, but electricity appears in second place, surpassing coal, wood, and natural gas (Ministry of Energy, 2015). With regard to electricity, Chile operates a system of concession areas for its generation, transmission, and distribution. The companies that produce, transmit, and distribute electricity are private. In total, there are about thirty energy generation companies, five companies that deal with transmission and thirty-six companies that distribute energy, all articulated in the national electricity system (Central Interconnected System, SIC).[5] This is system that gives freedom to companies that generate energy with respect to the obligation to invest. Companies that generate electricity but do not need to invest in guaranteeing energy supply; nor do they have a legal requirement to use efficient systems, renewable energy, or the best technologies. This favors the companies that are beneficiaries of the high marginal costs of generation, because they operate the system with maximum demand and with units that are very expensive to operate, because they use fossil fuels.

The state agencies that are involved in the regulation of this sector are the Ministry of Economy, the Superintendency of Electricity and Fuel, the National Commission of the Environment, the National Energy Commission, the Superintendency of Securities and Insurance, the municipalities, and eventually the National Consumer Service (SERNAC), as well as other organizations defending the rights of consumers. There is a large concentration of ownership in the electricity sector. Only three companies (Endesa, Colbún, and Gener) generate and market more than 84 percent of the energy in the SIC. This has been one of the results of policies implemented since 1990 to date. Governments have implemented modes of energy development that generate high profits for a small group of companies, but at the expense of public concerns and natural heritage. In addition, in Chile, industry and mining are the largest energy consumers (36 percent of the country's total consumption). Of this 36 percent, twenty-eight companies consume 60 percent (Sustainable Chile Program, 2013).

The cost of power generation, transmission, and distribution is high in Chile. By law, the tariffs charged to consumers must reveal the real cost of the entire process in order to "deliver the appropriate signals to both companies and consumers, in order to strive for an optimal development of electrical systems" (CNE, n.d.).[6]

The criterion for fixing prices is freedom in the segments where there is competition; but this does not happen in all cases. If a monopoly is identified (determined by connected power in excess of 2,000 kW), prices are regulated; otherwise, if there is competition, prices are released. In the case of regulated prices, the law distinguishes two prices: (a) 'node prices', which are defined for all the stations that generate and transport energy, and (b) distribution prices, which are determined on the basis of 'node prices' plus an aggregate value-added and a single charge for use of the backbone system (CNE, n.d.). From 1990 to 2013, governments had implemented an energy matrix that, as mentioned, generated enormous profits to a small group of companies, but at the expense of the consumption of the people and the natural heritage. This model has suffered a crisis of legitimacy and provoked mass protests, because it did not respond to the rights and aspirations of the majority of Chilean society. The critiques stressed:

- The lack of an energy development agenda.
- The overrepresentation of private companies in the definition of electricity generation technologies, whose objective was to increase the profitability of their investments.
- High energy prices and high energy dependence on primary energy imports.
- The vulnerability of the Chilean energy system, which exonerates generation companies from any obligation to invest. That is, they provide electricity to the country, but they are not required to do any investments to guarantee supply nor to use energy efficient systems and the best available technologies.
- The response to energy requirements focused on increasing supply. In recent years, the official discourse had insisted that the country should double the installed capacity of the SIC[7] by the year 2020, without taking into account that neither the historical rates reflected this growth rate, nor the projections of the National Energy Commission (CNE) meant that pace. This led to a false sense of urgency in the approval of new energy generation projects.

In search for a solution

Energy agenda

An energy agenda (Energy Policy 2050) is currently under review. The pillars of this policy are (a) security and quality of supply (security and flexibility at the centralized production level, decentralized production, and active demand management); (b) energy as an engine for social and economic development (inclusive energy development, equitable access to energy services and quality of life, and territorial inclusiveness, i.e. local, regional, and national coordination and competitiveness of the energy sector); (c) energy compatible with the environment (renewable energy matrix, local externalities, and climate change); and (d) energy efficiency and education.

The goals of the agenda have been set for the next twenty to thirty-five years. The main goals for 2035 are (a) about 50 percent of lower-income families would have access to energy services; (b) lower energy generation prices; (c) about 60 percent of the energy would come from renewable energies; (d) 30 percent of greenhouse gas emissions are reduced; and (e) increases the efficient use of energy in the mining and transportation sector. The main goals for 2050 are (a) 100 percent of the lower-income families would have access to energy services; (b) ensuring universal access to energy services for the entire population; (c) about 70 percent of the electricity generation, at the national level, would originate from renewable energies; (d) the growth of energy consumption would be decoupled from GDP growth; and (e) all construction and productive sectors would use or sell energy-efficient devices.

Environmental Tribunals

The Environmental Tribunals (ET), created in 2012, opened for environmental movements and organizations to present and prosecute their demands. In the opinion of the president of the ET, this court arose because "the country realized that, on the one hand, there was no agency capable of implementing environmental policy (. . .) and because monitoring the compliance with environmental legislation was very weak" (Asenjo, 2016). In practice, through the prosecution of cases, the ET supervises and, ultimately, implements environmental policies. Hence, the role that this court has played in the face of successful citizen demands that have actually stopped large extractive and infrastructure projects, is significant.

Public discussion of environmental sustainability

The criticisms that have been made of the process of institutionalization of environmental management in the country refer to the transversal character of sustainability and to the limited power of the existing organizations. The creation of the Ministry of the Environment is an improvement over CONAMA, but it shows that the issue of sustainable development continues to be considered a sectoral issue. In this line of criticism, the problem is that "sustainable development implies a paradigm change in how we think about development, that implies that all public policies that exist require drastic change."[8] Such an opinion is not different from that which is expressed in the document prepared by the Preparatory Committee for the United Nations Conference on Housing and Sustainable Urban Development (Habitat III), which notes "the persistence of a model of urbanization that is unsustainable on many fronts" (United Nations, 2014).

Mobilizations

Since 2010, environmental organizations and movements have followed two main paths. On the one hand, citizen protests have placed the issue in public opinion and, on the other, the prosecution of their demands through the Environmental Courts, which have managed to stop large extractive projects. The major urban protests of 2011 showed the strength of environmental movements over the last decade. The first major protest was the "Patagonia without dams" march against environmentally destructive power generation projects, which triggered a cycle from February to October 2011 of subsequent demonstrations by students and various other movements.

Reduction of the housing deficit: housing turned into ghettos, or the problem of "the ones with roof"

Social housing finance

It is common for international consultants and housing authorities in Latin America to believe that the social housing financing system implemented in Chile for almost forty years, has been very successful. From 1978 to date, around 2.5 million units have been built, financed under various types of housing subsidies, all of which are supported by the triad: family savings bank mortgage loan or SERVIU (Housing and Urbanization Service), and subsidies granted by MINVU. With this proposal, in its different variations and perfected over time, it was possible to give an important quantitative answer to the housing needs of the low-income sectors.

The balance shows us today that it was a financing policy for the construction of housing that had only positive results in quantitative terms, but in qualitative terms its results were not positive, because in the end, the total deficit has increased.

The period between Habitat II and Habitat III marks the rise and fall of this policy of financing social housing in Chile. The figures of building permits between 1996 and 2015 indicate that in that period, 3,249,933 dwellings (houses and apartments) were developed with 217,331,986 square meters of construction. The average area of housing in the country increased from 65 square meters in 1996 to 80.7 square meters in 2015. In the early 1990s, according to previous reports to Habitat II, there was a deficit of 970,467 units in the country, corresponding to 29.5 percent of the country's households. According to the Report of Chile to Habitat III (Government of Chile, 2016), there is a deficit of 1,707,237 units, corresponding to 34 percent of households. This means that, on the one hand, a lot has been built and the houses increased their average size, but, on the other hand, the deficit increased. This fact requires an explanation.

Deficit of adequate housing

The internal composition of the deficit provides a good explanation. In the 1990s, the total deficit comprised 29.5 percent of households and, among these, 18.5 percent were quantitative deficits and 11 percent were qualitative (ECLAC, 1996). Although the deficit of 34 percent of households in 2015 shows a substantial change in composition compared to that of the 1990s, the quantitative deficit is now in the order of 9 percent of households and the qualitative deficit is 25 percent.[9]

The origin of this situation dates back to 1990. When the first democratically elected government took over after the civil-military dictatorship, land occupations were likely, given the existing high housing deficit and the numerous 'homeless' organizations. At that time, it was thought that high, unmet housing demand could generate land occupations and create urban conflicts that would jeopardize the transition to democracy. The response of the first government was to dialogue with all organizations of renters and homeless, ensuring a housing solution in the medium term. To this end, the new government relied on existing subsidy programs, expanded them, and reduced the requirements for group enrollment on the application for housing subsidy programs. These proposals were well received by the homeless and the renters, within three years, the number of applicants enrolled in future programs doubled, and a growing number of social housing, transferred to the private sector, has been maintained to date with substantive modifications starting in 2006.

In this way the production of housing in the country was formalized (a little less than 1 percent of the country's population live in informal settlements), and no large land occupations have occurred, as had been the case before.[10] The current situation is the result of a policy that for many years was concerned only with the financial mechanisms and not with the products that were built according to its parameters: small, poor-quality homes, in peripheral places, without complementary services and with high densities. This reduced the quantitative housing deficit and increased the qualitative housing deficit. In recent years – from 2006 onwards – taking an important step in terms towards realism, the government has come to recognize the existence of this qualitative deficit.

In terms of the quality of the existing housing stock and considering the deterioration attributable to the use, passage of time, climatic conditions, and natural disasters, the government started to measure the qualitative housing deficit in 2009. Chile also uses this measurement to quantify the needs for housing repair expansion or relocation of homes those occupied by over-crowded households, and provision of basic health services (GoC, 2016: 9).

As shown in Figure 4.1, much of the construction activity takeoff was due to the increase of social housing programs launched in the early 1990s. The Habitat II Conference took place when Chile's housing subsidy policy was at its peak, via a combination of savings from applicants, subsidy from the Ministry of Housing, and bank credit (with state guarantee). From that time on, the social housing finance system began to decline. The 'Asian crisis' of the late 1990s sharply reduced the number of annual homes built, but not the annual number of square meters. This is due to a change in the real estate and construction sector, which found new niches of emerging middle buyers as a result of the country's strong economic growth in the 1990s. The country had grown at an annual average of 7.6 percent between 1985 and 1997, and between 1998 and 2005 it declined to 3.5 percent annually (Schmidt-Hebbel, 2006).

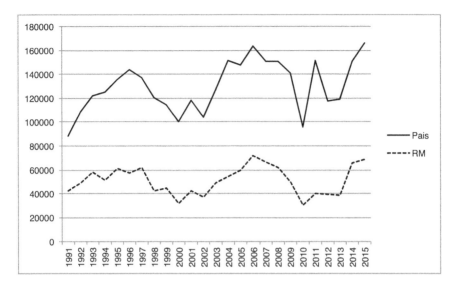

Figure 4.1 Number of housing according to approved building permits per year, 1996 to 2015

Source: National Statistics Institute (INE), Chile: Building: Authorized areas, Historical Series 1991 to February 1996. (www.ine.cl/).

With subsidies, but without rights

At the end of 2001 the first Social Housing Debtor Committees emerged[11] to prevent the foreclosure of the dwellings of defaulting debtors. From then on, the mortgage debtors were gaining notoriety, and in 2004, diverse groups of debtors were unified and the National Association of Debtors Housing (Andha Chile) was created. Through various actions – such as the takeover of the Ministry of Housing, street courts, and dramatic public demonstrations – they placed the issue of housing debtors into public opinion. Among their demands, they proposed debt relief to the poorest families, to the elderly with pensions below the minimum income, and to the families with members with catastrophic illnesses, as well as incorporation of all other types of debtors into the Dynamic Social Housing Without Debt Program (Carrasco, 2008).

In practice, between 2002 and 2006 the axis of what was the savings/ subsidy/credit trilogy was dismantled, and the Dynamic Social Housing Without Debt Program was launched, which reduced the initial down payment, reduced credit, and increased the amount of the subsidy. On the other hand, between 2005 and 2006, 70 percent of a total of 262,755 SERVIU debtors, had their debts forgiven. The Special Worker Program (PET) was suspended in 2006. In July 2008, in a report by the Chamber of Deputies, PET debtors were estimated at 204,011, of which between 33 percent and 40 percent would be delinquent.[12] Finally, in 2006 the MINVU, recognizing the existing problems in the social housing stock, began the

Quiero Mi Barrio program in 200 neighborhoods. Today this program is implemented in 500 neighborhoods.

The urban ghettos

The result of a successful social policy in quantitative terms has been the spatial concentration of poverty (Rodríguez and Sugranyes, 2005). The urban result was the consolidation of large homogeneous areas of poverty in the periphery of Santiago and other cities in the country. In these areas, we can observe the repetition of high-density residential units that are small and of poor quality, with difficult accessibility and without urban facilities.

A study published at the end of 2012 by Iván Poduje indicated that in twenty-five cities of the country lived 1.7 million people with populations classified as ghettos,[13] which is equivalent to 15 percent of the total population of these cities. Of the total, Santiago corresponds to 44 percent, and 56 percent to the rest of the cities studied. The largest ghettos are found in Santiago, such as Bajos de Mena (in the commune of Puente Alto, south of the city), where more than 122,000 people live in precarious urban conditions.

In Chile, the right to adequate housing is not met. On the contrary, its organic shortcomings are very visible in the sense that, when an attribute of the right to adequate housing is violated, this does not occur in isolation or alone, but also fails at the same time an important part of the seven attributes of this right. For example, when the right to adequate housing is violated, such a situation can also be related to a shortcoming in housing habitability.

What to do with a large stock of houses of poor quality?

What can be done with this huge stock of poor-quality housing? How can living conditions be improved in these neighborhoods? This was the question that was first raised in the 2000s by the organizations of settlers that sparked academic debate and then ignited a political discussion about public administration. The first demolitions began in 2000, even though some affected sites were not more than five years old. Among the reasons were construction issues – rain insulation, iron structures in a humid zone, seismic problems – or the need to reduce density.

The first major response was given by the MINVU in 2006, when the problem of the poor quality of construction of social housing was recognized and the *Quiero Mi Barrio* program begun, which intervened in 200 housing estates across different cities. This program implied a shift in MINVU's actions which had not engaged in popular neighborhoods for almost 30 years. At present, after ten years, the program works in the improvement of the public space and of the dwellings in 500 districts of the country, about 250,000 units.

A second response has been the Social Condos Recovery Program, which contemplates the demolition of 55,000 to 100,000 apartments and the regeneration of these neighborhoods. On May 16, 2013, the demolition of the first block of apartments started, with a total of 4,000 apartments. The program first started delivering a voucher so that families who wanted to leave the neighborhood sought the house they wanted in the market. The result of this program has not been positive: the housing blocks of families who decided to leave have been demolished, whereas the majority of the families stayed and live in even worse conditions than before. The families who left bought houses in the neighborhood, which increased the housing prices in the area, as prices quickly rose above the value of the voucher. Finally, 200 or 400 families may find a solution through the local housing market, but when it comes to the demolition of some 50,000 units, it is a matter of another scale and another problem altogether.

Reconstruction policies

According to the United Nations Office for Disaster Risk Reduction (UNISDR), Chile is one of the countries in the world that spends the most money as a result of earthquakes, floods, and volcanic eruptions, among other natural phenomena. According to Inter-American Development Bank (IDB) estimates, in the last twenty years, the Treasury has disbursed more than US$200 million annually in these disasters and had to help more than 350,000 people, making it the country that spends the most in emergencies in Latin America (De Solminihac, 2015).

Since the February 2010 mega-earthquake and tsunami, a great number of natural phenomena have occurred, which, due to the lack of urban policies, have had serious social consequences. Among the most notable events are: the earthquake in Iquique (2014), with a magnitude of 8.2; the earthquake in Coquimbo (2015), which affected the provinces of Elqui, Limarí, and Choapa, including the coastal towns of Peñuelas, Baquedano, Tongoy, and Los Vilos; the eruption of the Calbuco volcano (2015); and floods in the north (2015). To this set we added the fire in Valparaíso (2014), although it was not a natural phenomenon.

The replacement of housing has had a negative effect on the number of new social housing, as can be seen in Figure 4.2. Much of the funding for the new housing programs has been aimed at replenishing and repairing the affected stock, which, in quantitative terms, has been achieved.

As the only instrument of public policy in the field of housing remains the housing subsidy, the result is already known: in qualitative terms, greater segregation, expulsion of population to the periphery, increase in the real estate market, and success of the so-called public/private partnerships. Although housing standards – greater size, equipment, thermal insulation, solar panels – have improved since 2006, the model remains almost intact: the Ministry of Housing and Urban Development remains "basically a supplier of subsidies, citizens are consumers of housing who receive a voucher from the state to cover their ability to pay, and the private sector is in charge of designing, building and managing housing production" (Cociña, 2012).

Physical upgrading of cities

The provision of urban infrastructure, water, sewerage, electricity, health, and education services has improved in the last twenty years. However, its

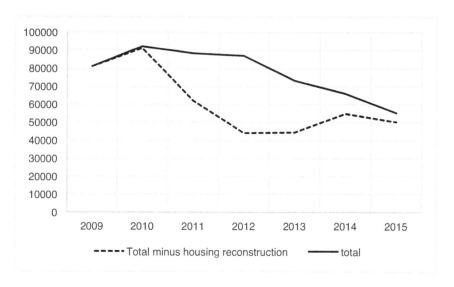

Figure 4.2 Total housing subsidies paid in Chile (2009–2015)

Source: Prepared based on data from the Ministry of Housing and Urban Development (Committee on Housing and Urban Studies (CEHU), "Subsidies paid regular program and reconstruction period 1990-December 2015, per year and program", Historical Statistics). Available at: http://bit.ly/2dqqvMk.

production and distribution have been totally privatized. It is part of a model that has been consolidated in Chile for some forty years and which, under the name of public/private partnerships has, on the one hand, reduced the investment and quality of public infrastructures and services and, on the other hand, transferred its production to the private sector. In the face of any crisis (Goyenechea and Sinclaire, 2013), the public sector appears incapable of responding and the private sector becomes the only one in a position to respond immediately by managing public subsidies aimed at solving temporary problems. What happens is that prices in one or the other system are very different, and the highest payment in the private system is presented as a failure of the public sector (El Mostrador, 2014).

Water, electricity, and urban sewerage

In the 1980s, the state initiated the privatization of electricity, water, and sewerage services. This process can be reviewed from changes in coverage and rates. As far as coverage is concerned, it is undoubtedly a positive figure. However, it must be considered that this increase was not due to the action of the private companies, but to public action. Through various subsidies, the state was able to increase coverage and increase the number of beneficiaries/users of services.

Currently, according to the National Statistics Institute (INE), 87 percent of the population lives in urban centers and the coverage of water, electricity, and urban sewage is close to 100 percent.[14] In 1980 (the year before the privatization of the drinking water service), the population in Chile was 8.89 million people, urban drinking water coverage was 91.4 percent, and urban sewerage coverage was 67.4 percent. In 1996, the population increased to 12.21 million, urban drinking water coverage reached 98.9 percent, and urban sewerage reached 90.4 percent. By 2014, the population was 16.5 million, urban drinking water coverage reached 99.9 percent, and urban sewerage, 96.7 percent (data from the Superintendency of Health Services [SISS]). Regarding electricity, in 1980, the coverage was 74.4 percent; in 1996, 92.2 percent; and in 2010, 98 percent (data from the Latin American Energy Organization [OLADE] and the IDB, 2012).

On the other hand, rates have increased, and lower-income households borrow to pay them. The costs of services are high, and payments can exceed the capacity of households, compromising a significant percentage of family budgets. In the case of households in the first quintile, the water and electricity bill can be equal to 20 percent of the average monthly income of the household. For the most part, households in debt correspond to single-parent households with female heads (or incomplete nuclear households), which are those with the lowest incomes.

People who cannot pay service bills can qualify for consumer subsidies. In the case of water, the subsidy is set according to the score in the Social Record or the Social Protection Record, which was gradually replaced in January 2016 by the Social Registry of Households, developed by the Ministry of Social Development to measure and record the degree of social vulnerability of families.[15] The Social Statement is the tool used by the state to target subsidies, bonds, and state funds. If a household succeeds in obtaining the subsidy for water consumption, the state directly pays the private company that provides the service. The amount of the subsidy is deducted from the amount that the person should pay. In 2014, the number of households with water consumption subsidies reached 731,213.[16]

Education and health

The cases of education and health are similar. In both, in the 1980s, at the same time as a privatization process, the budget lines and the contributions of the state decreased, and the capacity of coverage of education and public health also decreased.

In the case of education, the enrollment changed with regards to the type of school. If in the 1980s 80 percent of the enrollment was for tax schools,[17] in 2000, it had fallen to 56.5 percent, and according to the OECD, in 2015, it was 37.5 percent (OECD, 2016). The type of school that has increased during these years has been the subsidized (private but with a subsidy from the state). The percentage of private schools has not changed significantly.

With the return to democracy (1990) the privatization of Chilean education remained, with state subsidies. Since then, coverage has increased, reaching almost 100 percent, and the dropout rate has decreased. Since 1996, the full school day has been implemented, and since 2003, 66 percent of enrollment is with this schooling system. These are important figures and initiatives. But although years of schooling are not a problem (the law ensures twelve years of education for all children), the enormous gap in quality between public and subsidized education versus private education, is. The different types of schools, moreover, are spatially clustered: in the lower-income municipalities, there is a majority of municipal schools, whereas in high-income municipalities, private schools are more common.

Children living in lower-income municipalities are not only more likely to drop out of school but also receive lower-quality education in their municipal schools.[18] With this school base, very few of those coming from free public education or subsidized education tend to apply to traditional or state universities, rather than to private institutes or universities, although they know that in the latter they will not receive a good education.[19] High quality colleges are also part of the city that many eem not to deserve: without enough 'merits' some simply do not belong there. These students not only cannot afford the monthly fees of traditional or state universities, they also do not have enough knowledge to pass the entrance tests.

Despite this negative outlook, which was not changed in the 1990s, it should be noted that important discussions have taken place and that initiatives are being implemented. For example, since 2000 the coverage of parochial education has been increasing. The state is responsible for promoting a free system after the child's second or third year of age. The second level of transition (kindergarten) is compulsory and is a requirement to enter to the elementary school. As part of this process, in 2015 the Secretary for Pre-School Education, which is part of the Ministry of Education, was created.

Since 2014, a package of educational reforms has been discussed in Congress, including the Inclusion Act (now approved), to avoid the expulsion of students for reasons such as their physical appearance. The End to For-Profit, Selection and Copayment Act and the Law of Gratuity, which has already begun to be implemented in universities since the beginning of 2016, are also part of this set of laws.

As for health, in Chile the numbers are favorable. For example, the average life expectancy in 1996 was 75.3 years, and in 2016 it was 81.5 years, among other indicators (Expansion, 1996). The problem is that public health policy is focused (contrary to the universality of rights). It currently has a budget that exceeds 6 percent of GDP suggested by the World Health Organization (WHO), but this state contribution to the health system represents only 49 percent of the total of its financing, while the rest is delivered directly by people. The Chilean health system is composed of two public and private subsystems: the National Health Fund (Fonasa) and the Private Health Institutions (Isapres). These last ones account for the privatization process that was imposed during the military dictatorship and that was secured in the 1990s.

The public system has major shortcomings. Although there are good primary care centers, there are a low number of professionals and specialists

(1.7 professionals per 1,000 people, according to OECD figures). The deficiency of the system also results in an insufficient number of beds and long waiting lists for specialists or operations in public hospitals (lists that reach almost 2 million people).

As for the coverage of Fonasa and Isapres, with data since 1996, the split of users between both systems has changed. If, in 1996, about 60 percent of the population were Fonasa users, this figure increased to 80 percent in 2011 (Ministry of Health data). In the case of Isapres, in 1996, the users corresponded to 25 percent of the population, and in 2011, to 13 percent. However, there are large differences in the payment of benefits according to the type of hospital that users of the public system access. For example, if a person uses a bed in a private hospital, Fonasa pays about $1,000, but if the person uses a bed in a public hospital, he pays less than $100 (data from the National Federation of University Healthcare Professionals, Fenpruss). This state subsidy to private hospitals takes place within the framework of the Free Election Mode (MLE), which allows users of the public health system to attend the private system (with private prices). In this way, the state would seek to generate competition between both systems, which ultimately supports the private system and undermines the public health system.

If we revise the figures for 2011 by income level, we find that between the first and fourth quintile, about 90 percent of the population is a Fonasa user, whereas in the fifth quintile, the percentages of the population of Fonasa and Isapres are around 40 percent. Some of the reasons for these changes were the irregularities and over-charges of the private sector. It is also observed that, starting in 2000, measures were started to even out the quality between the two services. For example, in 2004, the Explicit Health Guarantees Regime (GES, ex AUGE: Universal Access Plan for Explicit Guarantees) was implemented, which imposes a Mandatory Health Plan for Fonasa, which includes the financing of treatment of a large number of illnesses, including catastrophic illnesses (BCN, 2013). However, people also fund the GES Plan: every time they pay their health insurance, a fee is added for that purpose.

Since 2015, some municipalities have begun to implement "popular or community pharmacies." These municipalities sell low-cost medicines directly, through nonprofit municipal corporations, to neighbors who live in the community. This measure, which was deemed by right-wing lawmakers as an attack on the free market, has spread rapidly to more than 100 (out of 348) municipalities in the country of different political colors. Even high-income municipalities adopted them, with pharmacies where anyone (regardless of the health system to which they belong) can register and obtain medicines at a low price.

New conflicts and urban mobilizations

Urban conflicts in Chile have traditionally been associated with the unsatisfied demands of the popular sectors, related to work, housing, health, and transportation. In this regard, there is an extensive bibliography on workers' struggles in cities, people's movements, and so on, covering the whole of the 20th century. With an initial protest of elementary and high-school students, urban mobilizations gained great force in 2011, expressing widespread discomfort in Chilean society regarding new realities: profit as a criterion of public policies (education, health), the destruction of the environment (energy matrix), and repression of native people, among others. The year 2011 was marked by protests of people in all the major cities of the country. Between February 26 and November 4, there were a total of 77 mass public demonstrations in Santiago, some of them with more than 200,000 people in the streets.

The initial milestone was an environmental march ("Patagonia Without Dams") against environmentally destructive power generation projects.[20] This was followed by marches of high-school students (then also university students) demanding the end of the for-profit education. There were eight months of mass demonstrations that made visible the structural and cultural violence that remains in this very unequal society.

Did these social mobilizations changed inequality in the country? No. But they did change the common opinions about it: the invisible begins to become visible. This implies that the role of the state in the provision of education and health, social security, and housing has begun to be part of the public conversation and the political agenda. Moreover, the issue of inequality in these areas was at the very heart of the speeches during the last presidential campaign and was the central theme of the current government agenda (Rodríguez et al., 2014).

Productivity and urban economy: working does not mean being out of urban poverty[21]

Currently, in the cities, the services and construction sectors predominate, whereas the industrial sector has reduced its participation in the GDP. This change in the productive structure has had important political and social repercussions. As the old industrial working class unions lost weight, the quality of jobs has also lessened to a large extent because the new jobs in services are deregulated, uncontrolled, and without contracts. This has led to a further reduction of the unionization rate and a fragmentation of the labor force, a situation sustained and reinforced by legislation that only allows negotiation by site not by company or by branch.[22] What currently exists is a large number of social organizations, articulated in a network in different areas. While they do not have a direct link with the traditional political parties, people with political capital or with experience working with grassroots communities participate.

Precariousness of wage labor

The reasons for the changes in the structure of employment in the city and in the country are related, according to the SOL Foundation (Durán, 2013), with some of the pillars that support the current neoliberal system in Chile: the

Labor Plan, subcontracting, and the pension fund system (the Pension Fund Administrators, AFP). These are parts of a process that, in the last decades, has increased precariousness of salaried work by increasing in working hours, decreasing wages or not paying for overtime work. Meanwhile, the prices of essential products (clothing, food, etc.) have increased.

Under these conditions, working for an employer, that is being a wage earner, is not equivalent to rising out from poverty. According to the SOL Foundation, data from the CASEN 2013 survey indicate that 580,000 salaried workers (considering all their income, subsidies, and state transfers) are in a situation of poverty.

From 1996 to date, unemployment rates range from 6 to 10 percent of the population. While new jobs have been created, mostly are precarious jobs (without social or health insurance), "flexible" jobs with low wages relative to GDP (Marinakis, 2006). The wages of lower-income people are supplemented by state subsidies, which are also low, because the structure of taxes is regressive and the funds redistributed by the state are scarce. Another way to 'supplement' low wages is by borrowing. For example, according to San Sebastián University, based on information from DICOM-Equifax, the number of indebted people in March 2015 in Chile was 10.6 million. If we compare that number with the 7.9 million employed by the INE's New National Employment Survey (in its January–March 2015 quarter), we find that there are 1.3 indebted people per job. In September 2011, according to the same source, the number of debtors was 9.5 million and the same indicator of 1.3 debtors per occupied person was given (Páez, 2015).

Functional distribution of income

In terms of functional income distribution, there is a reduction labor participation and a rise in profits. The conflict is that when the functional distribution of income by production sector is reviewed, the difference between both components increases considerably. For example, in the case of mining, the surplus mass reached 77.4 percent in the 1980s and 1990s. We are talking about the functional distribution of income as a way of measuring inequality, which is calculated by comparing two components of GDP – the global wage mass and the excess mass of exploitation of companies – which in the Chilean case is 80 percent of GDP (Schatan, 2005). For this measurement, data are used from the National Accounts of the Central Bank. As the ILO states (2013), there is a sustained trend in the world over time to lower labor participation and increase earnings in many countries. In this sense, Chile is no exception. According to Schatan (2005: 6), in Chile the relationship between the global wage mass and the mass of excesses of exploitation has varied remarkably in the last decades. In 1970, on average, the wage mass reached 52.5 percent and the surplus mass was the remaining 47.5 percent.[23] In the 1980s, the wage mass fell again, reaching 48.6 percent. And in the 1990s, it continued to decline, reaching 42 percent.[24]

Overall, functional distribution changed in the late 1990s to mid-2000s, when the relationship between the global wage mass and the surplus mass was reversed (Durán, 2009: 35). At the end of the 1990s, the global wage mass was 56.5 percent, on average, without disaggregating by productive sector. In 2005, the surplus mass returned to prevail over the global wage mass, due to the high capitalization of companies, commodity prices, redistribution in favor of capital, and "the null economic role of collective bargaining" (Durán, 2009). This trend has remained the same way until today.

Women and work: the world of care

The female participation rate in the labor force has increased in recent decades for reasons such as increased female education, outsourcing, and declining fertility rates. However, this rate remains low and is strongly affected by gender discrimination in the social division of labor, which is manifested in less income and precarious occupations in the case of women, among other factors.

One of the reasons that most strongly limits the economic autonomy of women is that housekeeping and the care of the children, the elderly, and the sick fall to them. In Chile it is still culturally accepted and promoted that women are responsible for the social reproduction of the workforce and those in charge of the care economy.

Among the almost 3.8 million inactive women at the national level (2015), in more than one-third of them, both in the country and in the Metropolitan Region, the reason for inactivity corresponds to the category "permanent family reasons." (See Table 4.1) And because women are included in this category (98.1 percent at the national level and 98.5 percent at the regional level), these data highlight the invisible tasks of women in terms of their contribution to the development of society (Segovia, 2016).

Cities and GDP

The sectors that generate more GDP are regionalized. In the cities of northern Chile, the sector that generates more GDP is linked to mining; in the Metropolitan Region, to the areas of commerce, construction, and services; and in the center and south, to agriculture and fishing. The report by Chile for Habitat III (p. 36) indicates that the proportion of domestic GDP generated in urban areas has increased from 81 percent in 1998 to 85 percent in 2013.[25]

Reduction of urban poverty, but inequality remains

Urban poverty in the country has declined in the last twenty-five years. It has been reduced from 38.8 percent in 1990 to 23.3 percent in 1996 and to 14.4 percent in 2011.[26] This is a multicausal process, from the increase in wages; subsidies focused on mining, services, and construction, among others; the greater coverage

Table 4.1 Population aged 15 and over outside the labor force, Chile and the Metropolitan Region, first quarter, 2015 (in thousands)

	Men		Women	
	Metropolitan Region	*National Total*	*Metropolitan Region*	*National Total*
Total population	3,498.73	8,897.78	3,671.40	9,066.56
Total inactive population	762.84	1,972.91	1,445.40	3,791.30
Initiator: still does not incorporate	15.2	30.98	16.54	38,21
Permanent family reasons	7.67	25.65	506.61	1,375.19
Study reasons	241.31	672.21	224.42	619.61
Retirement reasons	165.64	386.05	124.75	252.88
Pension reasons	30.34	155.98	151.99	449.23
Permanent health reasons	84.02	267.41	123.28	402.06
Temporary personal reasons	9.41	31.44	30.51	90.99
Without willingness to work	179.5	274.43	236.33	440.54
Seasonal reasons	9.38	26.37	9.12	23.51
Discouragement reasons	9.55	38.72	7.05	42.13
Other reasons	10.81	63.67	14.81	56.97

Source: INE, "Situation of employment and unemployment in the Metropolitan Region of Santiago. Mobile Quarter January-March 2015 (Results New National Employment Survey – INE)."

of technical education; and the entry of women into the labor market (formal or informal).

Overall, the country's economy grew, reflected in higher per capita income, and social spending more than tripled in real terms between 1990 and 2014 (Larrañaga and Rodríguez, 2014). However, income inequality was not reduced. Different studies indicate this, represented by the stabilization of the Gini index. In spite of economic growth, the reduction of poverty rates, the emergence of a middle-income sector in cities, and income inequality are issues that remain in the political debate "because of their negative effects on the concentration of power and influence of money in the public sphere" (ibid.).

Public social policies have increased social spending, without the results achieved. In the case of education systems (municipal and subsidized) and health (Fonasa, Plan Auge), these operate "through segmented allocations that result in the persistence of inequalities in the areas of capacities and opportunities." Also, as already mentioned, housing policy has been successful in quantitative terms "but it has deepened the residential segregation that separates social groups into differentiated territories" (Larrañaga and Rodríguez, 2014: 38). The problems described help explain the emergence of social issues in the public debate in recent years. This comes from the hand of a more empowered citizenship due to its own economic development, which rejects situations of abuse and discrimination that in previous decades could go unnoticed. This situation has become more evident from 2011 onwards.

Inequality

Traditional discussions on the issue of inequality focus on the extremes: the richest (or super-rich) and the poor. However, in recent years, several studies have focused on the participation of the richest (1, 0.1, and 0.01 percent richer) in the total income distribution in the country (López et al., 2013). Incorporating tax records, these studies present "a new dimension of the concentration of national income that goes beyond conventional estimates based on quintiles or deciles of income and the Gini coefficient that in Chile use the Casen data" (López et al., 2013) and estimate that, on average, between 2005 and 2012, the richest 1 percent had a 30.5 percent share of the country's total income, the 0.1 percent had a share of 17.6, and the 0.01 percent had a share of 10.1 percent of the total. These estimations modify the Gini inequality coefficient that, according to the National Socioeconomic Characterization Survey (Casen), was 0.55, on average, in the 2005–2010 period, leading to a higher coefficient of 0.63 (López et al., 2013).[27]

On the other hand, although poverty has reduced, the people and families who have left that condition still remain vulnerable, "without having reached a consolidated income situation that gives them economic security and [a] satisfactory quality of life" (Larrañaga and Rodríguez, 2014: 2). The characteristics of poverty refer to reduced wages and without social protections, such as contract security and social benefits (health, severance).

Gender and poverty

From a gender perspective, poor women in large cities outnumber poor men and among them, the most vulnerable are women heads of household in single-parent households (see Figure 4.3). In such cases, rising out of poverty entails several generations.

Social insecurity

In the country, manifestations of violence and insecurity are not crime-related or linked to situations of internal war, as in other cities in Latin America. They are, rather, the visible expression of structural violence, associated with the effects of economic or social policies that have restricted the solution of basic demands of the population. In that sense, they are linked to the widespread and growing economic and social inequality in a society guided by profit, and used to cultural violence: a neoliberal ideology that has legitimized the processes of concentration of wealth, segregation, and discrimination (Theodore et al., 2009). In this context, for example, Greater Santiago is a city with low crime rates compared to other cities in Latin America (UNDP, 2013). Despite this, the issue of insecurity prevails in the set of citizen perception surveys, it is clear that each year increases public and private investment in security. Some time ago, Lechner

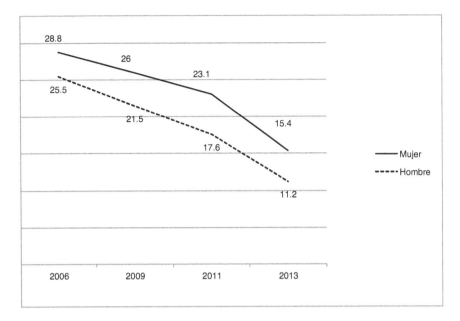

Figure 4.3 Percentage of households living in poverty by sex of head of household (2006–2013)

Source: Ministry of Social Development. Casen Survey.

(2002) compared the general rates of delinquency with the perception of violence of the people and was struck by the lack of causal relation between them. On the contrary, he believed that people's perception of violence was independent of criminal records. If this statement by Lechner is accepted, one can go further and affirm that, at the same time that the records of crimes are low, they are unrelated to the feeling of living in a 'dangerous' city. In Chile violence is related to the dismantling of a social state project and the implementation of a neoliberal state platform that has been considered one of the most radical applications of neoliberalism in the world (Harvey, 2007).

The autonomy of crime figures and the implementation of neoliberal policies have also gone hand in hand with the undermining of rights and freedoms that in Chile, up to the 1970s, were ensured by the state. In this context, Lechner (1986) posed two suggestive questions: Who is afraid? and What is he/her afraid of? According to this author, in Chile it seems that one fears delinquency, which is not a mere problem of civil insecurity. This is because criminals are often people who live in the low-income sectors of cities[28] and, according to Lechner (1986), they are the main victims of the (so-called) 'wars against crime'. This occurs, per Wacquant (2012), in the era of insecure employment, following the dismantling of social states (or their projects), as happened in Chile. That is, while the right to security is being canonized, the "'right to work' in its old form (that is, full-time, permanent and with social benefits and in exchange for a remuneration that allowed one to reproduce socially and project into the future), is abandoned"(Lechner, 1986: 36).

The urban forms have changed: concentration patterns in the built environment and dispossession of rights

As described throughout this chapter, the facilitation of markets has been fully achieved. In parallel, there have been changes in the spatial form and density of cities in Chile between 1996 and today. The concentrated urban pattern, has transformed into one that is both concentrated and diffuse. It is a scheme that expands the city but produces micro-zones of high concentration produced by market via capturing land-values via changes in land-use, densification of high- and middle-income sectors of urban areas, as well as urban expansion in the periphery (of low-density constructions for higher classes and of high densities for the lower classes).

A pattern operating through concentration and dispersion

In most of the cities of the country, this double trend is observed: cities are both more compact and more diffuse as a result of the real estate market that is capturing different niches over time.

In the case of Greater Santiago, the figures for building permits from 1990 to date point to dispersion and concentration tendencies that operate simultaneously, according to the opportunities for capturing land rents and social housing subsidies. In the 1990s there was a important urban expansion led by the construction of social housing in the southern periphery. In the 2000s this trend changed: with a consolidated real estate and construction sector, social housing was practically not built in the city itself – only in the periphery – and growth was concentrated in the higher-income areas.

The same pattern has occurred in the reconstruction of cities destroyed by the earthquake of 2010. For example, in Talca, the low-income sectors that traditionally lived in the center of the city in a low-density area were relocated to settlements in the periphery with high densities.

A pattern that develops the city but produces micro-areas of high concentration

If we consider the data of the built housing units, or if we look at the extension of the urban area, there remains the image of cities that are expanding, which are dispersed, which is true. However, his image is distorted if we stop talking only of housing units and consider instead the total number of square meters built. From this point of view, returning to the case of Santiago, we have a city in which construction activity is increasingly concentrated in six districts, accounting for almost half of the total area constructed in Greater Santiago over the last twenty years. And if we see this for various periods, we can see that the process is intensifying, reinforcing the fragmented structure of the city.

A pattern that promotes socioterritorial units of equals, which are segregated

In most of the medium and large cities in Chile, the aforementioned process of segregation occurs, which has become generalized by the year 2000. There may be some social mobility, as shown by numerous studies for Santiago on the reduction of poverty and extreme poverty, but it does not translate spatially in the territory. There is certain gentrification of some communities, but in a 'Chilean' version: there are no high-income sectors returning to the center of the city, but rather a population of slightly higher class among the displaced. High-income sectors are creating new centers that tend to outpace historic centers in terms of area built for nonresidential uses.

A pattern based on the commodification of housing and the city, that is, on the primacy of the exchange value over use value

Several studies show a process of commodification of the city. The spatial consequences of this process reveal a concentration of construction activity in the parts of the city where the higher-income population lives and in areas that display greater incentives for construction (higher heights, densities, building coefficients). Another consequence is the socioeconomic segregation of the population of the city. There where the higher-income sectors live this is where construction happens. This is a self-reinforcing trend: high-income sectors want to live among those similar standards and demand housing and services in those same areas.[29]

A pattern promoted by the state, which designs public policy with the interests of the private sector

As urban planning regulations are merely indicative and not compulsory, the production of urban land and housing is oriented solely by its profitability. This is evidenced by the fact that the construction activity is concentrated in specific sectors of the cities. In other areas, the activity has depends on housing finance through subsidies.

A pattern that does not remain static over time but is sensible to profit rates

Construction activity moves thoughout the city – depleating certain zones and redirecting itself in search of new businesses. As can be seen in the building permit registers. In the case of Santiago, in the 1900s, there was a great concentration of housing subsidy programs in the south and west peripheries; while in recent years, it is concentrated in the center of the city as a result of the addition of new subsidies, either for localization or urban renewal. The same trend can be observed in the reconstruction of cities that were destroyed by the 2010 earthquake.

The pattern described needs deregulation and creates clearly defined socioterritorial units, connected only by capitalist production chains

The spatial distribution of people by the market that has arranged them according to occupations and branches of activity shows the way in which the social division of labor manifests itself in the urban space. Thus, it can be observed how in cities in which the state has relapsed, the resolution of the right to housing is commodified: that is, housing is strictly a response to the purchasing power of individuals. The market may be deregulated, but it operates by ordering and segregating well-delimited socioterritorial units.

Notes

1 For example, the National Policy of Urban Development – and its implementation so far – is devoid of a clear gender perspective. Equality between men and women is more a declaration of intent than a policy objective translating into concrete action and programs (Segovia, 2016).
2 The policy proposal on land use and social integration in cities is part of the government's plan and includes twenty actions to improve land access for the lower-income sectors (Bresciani, 2014).
3 The functions of the ministry refer to the proposal of policies, programs, agreements and regulations that allow the realization of this right. The lines of action of the ministry are as follows: (a) review of the emission standards for industrial liquid wastes, (b) regulation of water quality, (c) opinion and review of air pollutants, and (d) the application of regulations, among others. See "Functions of the Ministry," http://bit.ly/2dNaQG9.
4 This and other laws mentioned are available on the website www.leychile.cl.
5 The SIC is Chile's main electricity supply system, which feeds 90 percent of the country. This system is used because the water is located in the south of the country and the consumption in the center and north.
6 See the introduction on the website of the National Energy Commission, http://antiguo.cne.cl
7 The SIC is composed of generating power stations; trunk, subtransmission, and additional transmission lines; electric substations; and consumer bars not subject to price regulation, operating interconnected from Taltal by the north (Region of Antofagasta) to the large island of Chiloé in the south (Los Lagos Region). The SIC is the largest of the four electric systems that supply energy to the country, a supply coverage of about 92.2 percent of the national population (www.cdecsic.cl).
8 "In 1998 there was an environmental policy for sustainable development in Chile, which was a policy to guide the activities of the different ministries, and it is one of the policies that never had weight. The Council of Sustainable Development, which was formed

in 1998, also with annual meetings, was not an executive institution, never managed to put issues such as Agenda 21 in the discussion, did not manage to pressure or guide the activities of ministries, services Public and private. If the State is not motivated, it is very difficult for the private sector to be added because the messages are unclear. There is the same situation with the civil society, which also try to do things, but fighting the state is very complicated" (Barton, 2011).

9 The National Habitat II Report explains that the quantitative deficit includes the "unrecoverable" houses, the "internal" and "external households," and "crowded secondary nuclei." The qualitative deficit includes "reparable" housing, the "expandable" that responds to the needs of enlargement from cramped households, and those with the potential to improve basic sanitation (GoC, 2016: 8–9).

10 In general terms, it can be said that the housing market is formalized, which does not mean that there is no informal market for subsidized housing or that there are no land occupations. Unlike two decades ago, the largest land occupations occur in provincial cities and not Santiago.

11 Among different modalities, mainly debtors of the public system (SERVIU) and debtors of the Special Workers' Program (PET), whose debts had been transferred to private banks.

12 The Special Committee on Historical Debt of the Chilean Chamber of Deputies agreed in 2009 that there was "state responsibility in the situation caused, since it is clearly the effects of a badly designed transition to new programs, in which the debtors were induced, both by prevailing conditions and by their natural interest in obtaining a home of their own, to underwrite credit incompatible with their income levels." However, as the MINVU has repeatedly expressed, in the case of a relationship between private actors, the government could not intervene.

13 In order to identify the ghettos, indicators were constructed considering four characteristics that distinguish a ghetto from a common neighborhood: social homogeneity (low income), concentration and size (important percentage of poor population in the city), service coverage (below city average), and accessibility (neighborhoods away from the main centers of the cities).

14 It should be noted that in the census cited, households are counted as having sanitation if they are served with a pit latrine, trench latrine, or chemical latrine.

15 The Social Register of Homes is a system built with information provided by the household and by different databases that the state owns, which places the household in a section of socioeconomic rating (www.registrosocial.gob.cl).

16 They subsidize 15 m^3 per month in variable percentages, which depend on the socioeconomic level and the current tariffs, and in some cases, they reach up to 100 percent of consumption. Source: Superintendency of Health Services, http://bit.ly/1fCc1Xx.

17 They are those schools that are funded by the Ministry of Education.

18 The mechanism used to evaluate the learning outcomes of education is the Quality Measurement System of Education (Simce), prepared by the Education Quality Agency, the Ministry of Education, the Superintendent of Education, and the Council of National Education (Quality Agency for Education, "What is Simce?," S/f, www.agenciaeducacion.cl/simce. Simce's goal is to account for the performance of students in different subsectors of the national curriculum, relating them to the school and social context in which they learn. Simce's educational results at the community level show that the distribution of the quality of education is unequal also at the socioeconomic and territorial level and that inequalities are widening as levels of education are advanced. The information generated by the Simce with the application of the measuring instruments is public and widely disseminated in the media.

19 The Chilean university system consists of three types of institutions: traditional universities, state universities, and private universities. The traditional universities – "the most traditional in the country" – are those belonging to the Council of Rectors of Chilean

Universities (CRUCH), among which there are state institutions, those belonging to the Catholic Church, and others to particular corporations. The state universities belong to the state of Chile, but it only finances them with a quarter of its budget. Finally, the enactment of the General Law on Universities in 1981 made it possible to create private universities without state dependence (see http://bit.ly/2dquicf).

20 HidroAysén, consisting of the construction and operation of five hydroelectric plants, two in the Baker River and three in the Pascua River, located in the XI Region of Chile (www.hidroaysen.cl/).

21 The analysis in this section is informed by previous work of Centro Latinoamericano para el Desarrollo Rural (RIMISP), as well as with national official statistics.

22 A bill that seeks to modernize the labor relations system by introducing amendments to the Labor Code is currently under discussion.

23 According to data from the Central Bank, this ratio was reversed in 1971 and 1972, when the wage mass increased over the surplus mass by more than 10 percentage points, which coincides with the drop in the Gini coefficient for the same period.

24 When the functional distribution of income by production sector is reviewed, the difference between both components increases considerably. For example, in the case of mining, the surplus mass reached 77.4 percent in the 1980s and 1990s (Schatan, 2005: 19) and in the chemical industry, 71.5 percent in the same period. Differences with the general (average) figures of the income distribution are due to the inclusion of the public administration in the global wage mass, which has zero excess mass of exploitation, and also as a result of the price that the commodities receive in some sectors, like in mining such as copper and gold.

25 In this report, the GDP generated in urban areas was estimated considering the percentage corresponding to the nonextractive activities, taking as its source the data of the Central Bank of Chile.

26 A new multidimensional poverty index has been introduced since 2013. For comparative purposes, we have maintained the old index. However, the variations between one index and the other one are not too noticeable, as well as being within the range of the vulnerability of poverty: one is not poor because of this or that score, but because of being within a margin of vulnerability.

27 Particularly illuminating is the comparison between the Gini coefficients from 2004 to 2010 in Chile against the participation of the 1 percent, 0.1 percent, and 0.01 percent wealthiest in the total income of the country, including retained earnings (and not including capital gains) (López et al., 2013: 23).

28 In the case of Greater Santiago, it is usual for the media to name places like the towns (*villas*) built in the 1980s as the result of eradications or housing policies. In other towns, the names reflect populations badly punished during the dictatorship.

29 Consider the development in recent years of the community of San Pedro de la Paz in the Metropolitan Area of Concepción, with a concentration of middle- and high-income sectors practically outside the city.

Bibliography

Asenjo, R., (2016), "Chile está bastante atrasado en algunos marcos normativos medioambientales", *Revista Técnicos Mineros*, interview, March 25. Available at: http://bit.ly/2a0BrQg. Revista eure, 32:96, pp. 27–45, Santiago de Chile, agosto de 2006.

Barton, J. R., (2011), "El desarrollo sustentable es un cambio paradigmático en cómo pensamos el desarrollo", Interview by Beatriz Mella, Plataforma Urbana, September 20, Web.

Biblioteca del Congreso Nacional de Chile (BCN), (2013), "Guía Legal Plan GES o AUGE", *Ley Fácil*, BCN, Web. Available at: www.bcn.cl/leyfacil/

Bresciani, L. E., (2014), *Planificación urbana integrada*, National Council of Urban Development (CNDU), Santiago de Chile. Available at: http://bit.ly/1YlY6rQ

Carrasco, I., (2008), "Los deudores habitacionales en Chile", In Aravena, S. and Sandoval, A. (eds.), *Política habitacional y actores urbanos*, Ediciones SUR, Santiago de Chile, pp. 93–98.

Cociña, C., (2012), "Por qué hemos construido guetos y lo seguimos haciendo", *Ciper Chile*, November 14. Available at: http://bit.ly/2acpB4s

Comisión Nacional de Energía, Chile, (n.d.), *Introducción a Electricidad*. Available at: http://bit.ly/2c7TV4s

Consejo Nacional de Desarrollo Urbano (CNDU), (2014), *¿Qué es el CNDU?*, Government of Chile, Web. Available at: http://cndu.gob.cl/

Consejo Nacional de Desarrollo Urbano (CNDU), (2015a), *Minutes of the Eight Plenary Session*, August 3, CNDU, Santiago de Chile. Available at: http://cndu.gob.cl/octava-sesion-plenaria-cndu/

Consejo Nacional de Desarrollo Urbano (CNDU), (2015b), "Propuestas para una política de suelo para la integración social urbana", Report, CNDU, Santiago de Chile. Available at: http://bit.ly/1GZu1oA

De Solminihac, H., (2015), "Desastres naturales: un gran problema para la población y sustentabilidad económica", *Diario Financiero*, April 7. Available at: http://bit.ly/1rd25KW

Durán, G., (2009), *Resultados económicos de la negociación colectiva en Chile*, Series *Ensayos sobre el Trabajo*, N° 2, Fundación SOL, Santiago de Chile. Available at: http://bit.ly/29M86dl

Durán, G., (2013), "Panorama Sindical y de la Negociaci´on Colectiva en el Chile de los US$ 22.655", *Revista de Derecho y Seguridad Social*, 3, 85–96.

El Mostrador, (2014), "Mañalich approved millionaire spent on day bed purchase in Las Condes Clinic", *Press*, May 6, Web. Available at: http://bit.ly/2auuWn5

Expansión, (1996), "Chile: Life Expectancy at Birth", *Datosmacro.com*, Web. Available at: http://bit.ly/2dNe8cw

Government of Chile (GoC), (2016), *Chile. Informe Nacional Hábitat III*, Government of Chile, Santiago de Chile. Available at: http://bit.ly/2abfQqf

Goyenechea, M. and Sinclaire, D., (2013), "Cómo se ha desmantelado la salud pública", *CIPER Chile, Opinión*, Centro de Investigación Periodística, Web, May 27.

Harvey, D., (2007), *A Brief History of Neoliberalism*, Oxford University Press, Oxford. Available at: http://bit.ly/OabaQO

Larrañaga, O. and Rodríguez, M. E., (2014), "Desigualdad de ingresos y pobreza en Chile 1990 a 2013", Working Paper, United Nations Development Program, PNUD Chile.

Lechner, N., (1986), *La conflictiva y nunca acabada construcción del orden deseado*, Siglo XXI, Madrid.

Lechner, N., (2002), *Las sombras del mañana. La dimensión subjetiva de la política*, LOM, Santiago de Chile.

López, R., Figueroa, E., and Gutiérrez, P., (2013), "La 'parte del león': Nuevas estimaciones de la participación de los súper ricos en el ingreso de Chile", Working Papers Series, SDT 379, Universidad de Chile, Economics Department, Santiago de Chile. Available at: http://bit.ly/1m5xZyS

Marinakis, A., (2006), "La rigidez de los salarios en Chile", *ECLAC Magazine*, N° 90, December, Santiago de Chile, pp. 135–150. Available at: http://bit.ly/29VESXS

Mella, B., (2011), "El desarrollo sustentable es un cambio paradigmático en cómo pensamos el desarrollo", Interview to Jonathan Barton, *Plataforma Urbana*, September 21. Available at: http://bit.ly/1YmDG27

Ministry of Energy, (2015), *Energía 2050. Política energética de Chile*, Chilean Ministry of Energy, Santiago de Chile. Available at: http://bit.ly/1TEnpBn

Ministry of Environment, (2014), *Planes de Descontaminación Atmosférica. Estrategia 2014–2018*, Chilean Ministry of Environment, Santiago de Chile. Available at: http://bit.ly/1imOPXW

Ministry of Environment, (2016), *Segunda Encuesta Nacional de Medio Ambiente*. Available at: http://bit.ly/1qc6rS3

Ministry of Housing and Urbanism (MINVU), (2014), *Decree # 78, Aprueba Política Nacional de Desarrollo Urbano y crea Consejo Nacional de Desarrollo Urbano*, March 4. Available at: www.leychile.cl/Navegar?idNorma=1059974

Ministry of Public Works (MOP), (2013), *Política Nacional de Desarrollo Urbano. Ciudades Sustentables y Calidad de Vida*, September 25. Available at: http://bit.ly/2a97IUz

Organization for Economic Cooperation and Development (OECD), (2015), *Todos juntos . . . en Chile. ¿Por qué reducir la desigualdad nos beneficia?*, May 21. Available at: http://bit.ly/29UU9F4

Organization for Economic Cooperation and Development (OECD), (2016), *Education at a Glance: Chile*. Available at: http://bit.ly/1jlnOMj

Organization for Economic Cooperation and Development (OECD) and United Nations Economic Commission for Latin America and the Caribbean (ECLAC), (2005), *Evaluaciones del desempeño ambiental Chile*, OECD/ECLAC, Santiago de Chile. Available at: http://bit.ly/29U3Z0i

Páez, A., (2015), *Trabajar en una economía de la deuda*, Fundación SOL, Available at: http://bit.ly/29U3Fyt. Also published by Centro de Investigación e Información Periodística (CIPER), Chile. Available at: http://bit.ly/29U3HGB

Poduje, I., (2010), *Estudio Guetos en Chile*, ATISBA, Santiago de Chile. Available at: http://bit.ly/1iULAgS

Poduje, I., (2012), "Guetos Urbanos en Chile", *Mensaje*, June, pp. 198–200.

Rodríguez, A. and Rodríguez, P., (2015), "Case Study. National Urban Development Policy of Chile 2013", Paper presented at Forum on Best Practices United Nations Human Settlements Program Regional Office for Latin America and the Caribbean, Rio de Janeiro, October. Available at: http://bit.ly/28L4T9U

Rodríguez, A., Rodríguez, P., Saborido, M., Segovia, O., and Mires, L., (2014), "Visible and Invisible Violence and Inequality in Neoliberal Santiago", *Environment and Urbanization*, 26:2, October, pp. 359–372.

Rodríguez, A. and Sugranyes, A. (eds.), (2005), *Los con techo. Un desafío para la política de vivienda social*, Ediciones SUR, Santiago de Chile, Anational. Available at: www.sitiosur.cl/r.php?id=81

Schatan, J., (2005), "Distribución del ingreso y pobreza en Chile", *Polis Revista Latinoamericana*, 11, p. 6. Available at: https://polis.revues.org/5865

Schmidt-Hebbel, K., (2006), "El crecimiento económico de Chile", Working Paper N° 365, Chile Central Bank. Available at: https://dialnet.unirioja.es/descarga/articulo/2112278.pdf

Segovia, O., (2016), *¿Quién cuida en la ciudad? Oportunidades y propuestas en la comuna de Santiago (Chile)*, Gender Issues Series, N° 132, ECLAC. Available at: http://bit.ly/29VQzeY

Sustainable Chile Program, (2013), *Energía en Chile. ¿Para qué y para quién?*, Heinrich-Böll-Stiftung – Cono Sur. Available at: http://bit.ly/29Z6z3j

Theodore, N., Peck, J., and Brenner, N., (2009), *Urbanismo neoliberal: la ciudad y el imperio de los mercados*, Temas Sociales, N° 66, Ediciones SU, Santiago de Chile. Available at: www.sitiosur.cl/r.php?id=898

United Nations Economic Commission for Latin America and the Caribbean (ECLAC), (1996), "Alojar el desarrollo: Una tarea para los asentamientos humanos", Latin America and the Caribbean Habitat II Preparatory Meeting, ECLAC Santiago de Chile, November 13–17 1995. Available at: http://bit.ly/29M8por

United Nations General Assembly (UNGA), (2014), "Progresos logrados hasta la fecha en la aplicación del documento final de la segunda Conferencia de las Naciones Unidas sobre los Asentamientos Humanos (Hábitat II) y determinación de los problemas nuevos y emergentes del desarrollo urbano sostenible", Secretary General Conference Report, New York. Available at: A/CONF.226/PC.1/5. http://bit.ly/2acqNVd

United Nations General Assembly (UNGA), (2014), "Progresos logrados hasta la fecha en la aplicación del documento final de la segunda Conferencia de las Naciones Unidas sobre los Asentamientos Humanos (Hábitat II) y determinación de los problemas nuevos y emergentes del desarrollo urbano sostenible", Preparatory Committee to Habitat III Conference, First Round of Sessions, New York, September 17–18. Available at: http://bit.ly/29VFrAR

United Nations Human Settlements Program (UNHABITAT), (1996), *Habitat II Conference Report II*, June 3–14, Istambul. Available at: http://bit.ly/2acqLNr

United National Development Program (UNDP), (2013), *Seguridad ciudadana con rostro humano: diagnóstico y propuestas para América Latina*, United Nations Development Program, New York.

Wacquant, L., (2012), "Three Steps to a Historical Anthropology of Actually Existing Neo-liberalism", *Social Anthropology*, 20:1, pp. 66–79, Doi: 10.1111/j.1469-8676.2011.00189.x

5 Brazil: confronting the urban question in Brazil: 1996–2016

A politico-institutional assessment[1]

Edesio Fernandes

This chapter provides a general assessment of the main developments in Brazil during the 1996–2016 period regarding the core urban policy areas highlighted in the commitments of the Habitat II agenda. It starts with a general introduction in which the chapter argues that, rather than the lack of laws, actions, or resources, it was the lack of an articulated urban policy framework what determined the contradictory dynamics of urban development, policymaking and management in the country. Next, the chapter discusses the broader historical context in which significant legal and institutional changes were promoted in Brazil prior to the 1996 event. This is followed by a critical analysis of the main policies, programs, and actions undertaken by both the federal government and municipal administrations in Brazil over the last two decades, with emphasis on the sociopolitical and politico-institutional conflicts and disputes that have led to the current situation of utter and widespread political instability. As a conclusion, it will be argued that, if the post–Habitat II period was marked by many ups and downs in Brazil, advances and backlashes, euphoria and depression, the current mood is one of uncertainty. Ultimately, the future of cities – social justice or big business, collective creations of commodities – will depend on the Brazilian people's capacity to redefine and expand sociopolitical mobilization so as to influence the decision-making processes at all governmental levels.

General remarks and the need for an analytical framework

The purpose of this chapter is to provide a general assessment on the core urban policy areas highlighted in the commitments of the Habitat II agenda and which are now under discussion for a New Urban Agenda. As indicated by the editors of this book, these key areas include:

- Adoption of **national urban policies**, including prioritizing urban issues in national development and macro-economic policies, and strengthening **urban governance**, including identifying inter-governmental roles, urban planning, urban finance, citizen participation, and access to information;

- Strengthening the **sustainability** of urban areas, particularly, mitigation of the urban effects of climate change and resilience of communities and urban areas;
- Improving access to **affordable urban shelter and urban infrastructure services**, including water, sanitation, electricity, solid waste, and management;
- Improving the **productivity of urban economic activities** and thereby generating employment and incomes;
- Reducing **urban poverty, intra-urban inequality, and social exclusion**, including discrimination based on gender, race, and ethnic or regional origin; and
- Assuring more **equitable, dense, and efficient urban forms** to generate employment, reduce energy consumption, promote infrastructure-intensive spatial development, as well as counter negative impacts of climate change and the environment.

Besides providing general information on such issues, the chapter will provide a critical, and rather personal, analysis of what has been happening in Brazil in the field of urban policy since Habitat II, especially from the viewpoint of the main ongoing, and intertwined, politico-institutional and sociopolitical processes in the country. I would argue that, although the production of further information on matters related to urban development is always useful, the formulation of a broad and articulated politico-institutional analytical framework is even more necessary as it allows for a critical and constructive assessment of the country's urban realities.

In fact, generally speaking information on the phenomenon of urban development is not a major problem in most Latin American countries and in Brazil, although it can certainly be better organized and articulated in many of them. Unlike other parts of the developing world, the urbanization process in Latin America, and in Brazil, was long consolidated by the time Habitat II took place in 1996. There is a strong tradition of urban research in the region, and relatively reliable data on all sorts of urbanization-related aspects have been systematically produced and revisited by several governmental, academic, and nongovernmental agencies and institutions in most countries. In particular, a wide range of urban indicators has been provided and updated by regular national censuses. The lack of proper governmental action, though, and especially the lack of urban policy, planning, and financial resources for investment in urban areas, has long been considered to be one of the main reasons for the enormous stock of urban, social, and environmental problems existing in Latin American cities.

However, perhaps more so than in other Latin American countries with the possible exception of Colombia, in Brazil the last two decades following Habitat II were marked by a number of significant attempts – especially at the federal level – to address in many ways the urban, social, and environmental problems that had accumulated in cities nationally following decades of rapid urbanization and inadequate governmental action. Important urban policy efforts were also made at the municipal level in a number of cities across the country.

Directly or indirectly, totally or partly, deliberately or coincidentally, such attempts were aligned with most of the afore-mentioned Habitat II directives. Urban sustainability, urban governance, urban shelter, urban infrastructure, urban poverty, urban economic inclusion: to different extents and to different degrees, in more or in less organized ways, all such notions were incorporated in the country's public agenda, and as such they were dealt with by the federal and sub-federal governments. In fact, they were not new in Brazil: they were already part of the broader philosophical notion/political banner/institutional platform/social movement that had been constructed in Brazil since the early 1980s, namely, the urban reform agenda. Perhaps the directive of "promoting a more equitable, dense and efficient urban form" has been less evident, but at least nominally it can be said that urban policy in Brazil reflects Habitat II's agenda.

On the whole, though, the nature of the news coming from Brazil since the 1980s has been mixed. Very significant progress has been made towards the creation of a legal framework to govern urban development processes nationally, especially with the enactment of the 2001 City Statute and several subsequent federal laws; however, the promising progress at the municipal level, especially in the 1990s, and the reach and implications of the more recent federal laws and relevant federal programs have been undermined by the tensions inherent in the country's politico-institutional system and renewed sociopolitical disputes within civil society, as well as jeopardized further by the ongoing political crisis motivated by the orchestrated impeachment of President Dilma Rousseff.

Since the mid-1980s and especially throughout the 1990s, an important process of urban reform was being slowly, but consistently, promoted in the country, especially at the municipal level. Following the enactment of the 1988 federal constitution, significant legal and institutional changes were introduced at the federal level, creating a whole new legal-urban order that was consolidated with the enactment of the 2001 City Statute and the installation, in 2003, of both the Ministry of Cities and the National Council of Cities. Throughout the post–Habitat II period (1996–2016), several efforts were made at the federal level to achieve a balance, albeit an elusive one, among institutional reform, legal change, and governmental action. Enormous financial investments were made by the federal government in urban areas through a number of groundbreaking national programs. It is important to stress that all such governmental efforts were always fueled by several very dynamic sociopolitical mobilization processes taking place all over the country. However, from the perspective of the urban reform agenda, on the whole, the last 15 years or so have been particularly difficult, and there has been a gradual, notable backlash at all governmental levels insofar as the articulated processes of urban development, policy, planning, and management are concerned.

I would argue that the enormous public investment in cities made by the Brazilian government especially since 2003 – said to be the largest in the history of Latin America – has been significantly jeopardized, if not partly wasted, by the lack of a clearly defined and integrated conceptual framework, and its corresponding institutional context, governing the overall management of the "urban question" in the country. Far from redressing the long-standing urban, social, and environmental problems, it is fair to say that the nature of governmental action at all levels throughout most of this post–Habitat II period worsened the pattern of urbanization in the country even further through a perverse pattern of combined sociospatial segregation, environmental degradation, economic inefficiency, fiscal crisis, administrative irrationality, and social insecurity, as well as rampant land and housing informality. If that was ever the case, the current process of "urban spoliation" in Brazil can no longer be blamed on the lack of laws, planning, or financial resources.

Politico-institutional tensions and disputes

The 1996–2016 period was strongly characterized by several intertwined politico-institutional tensions and sociopolitical conflicts in Brazil, as well as increasingly marked by a manifest conceptual sociopolitical dispute with regard to the very definition of *what cities are, for whom are they managed, who makes decisions and how*, and *who pays and how* for the financing of urban development. Federal policies on and in cities were, and remain, sectoral, isolated, and fragmented, thus reflecting the same institutional fragmentation existing among several federal ministries and even within the Ministry of Cities itself, as revealed by its conflicting internal organization. Created in 2003, this ministry comprises four parallel secretariats dealing with housing, sanitation, transportation, and mobility, as well as so-called "urban programs", which mostly aim to provide support to municipal urban plans and to municipal programs for the regularization of consolidated informal settlements. There has been little communication among such secretariats, as well as among the Ministry of Cities and all other national ministries that have a significant presence in cities, especially the Environment Ministry and the Planning Ministry.

On the whole, it can be argued that, in conceptual terms, that the federal government in Brazil has failed to understand what cities really are in the contemporary world, especially in the current stage of postindustrial capitalism in the country. Nor has the federal government understood the nature and implications for the country of the ongoing process of urban development, especially within the context of rapidly globalizing land, property, and rental markets.

While most political parties, politicians, and managers do not have or follow a clearly defined and articulated urban policy, especially at the federal level, investment in cities has been viewed by the government merely as a means of "creating infrastructure for economic development" and/or "formulating social policy". The enormous investment of public resources by the federal government, especially through the massive "Plano de Aceleracao do

Crescimento – PAC" (Plan to Accelerate Growth) and "Programa Habitacional Minha Casa, Minha Vida – MCMV" (My House, My Life Housing Program), has taken place without a previous definition of an integrated land, territorial, and urban national policy. The equally massive "Bolsa Familia – BF", a poverty eradication/income redistribution program, has also been largely conceived without a solid understanding of its impact on urban areas and on the overall pattern of urban development and management. Moreover, several economic policies – such as incentives to the national automobile manufacturing industry – were implemented with little understanding of their impact on cities, whereas other economic development policies – such as the construction of a system of huge dams – had little concern for their environmental impact.

The 1996–2016 period was also marked by a national context of intense, excessive, and rather artificial politico-institutional decentralization, as well as by tense, volatile, and largely manipulated intergovernmental articulation. Many analysts have said that Brazil has one of the most decentralized federal systems internationally: there are currently 27 states and over 5,550 municipalities, the latter with an unrivalled level of legal, administrative, political, and, to a lesser degree, fiscal autonomy. However, the original problem with Brazilian "municipalism" is that the same formal constitutional treatment has been given to completely different socioeconomic, sociopolitical, and socioterritorial realities, thus rendering the politico-institutional system deeply flawed and fundamentally ineffective.

An extreme polarization between federal and municipal governments grew over the last two decades, and as a result the roles of the federated states are no longer clear, especially in the northeast, southeast, and south of Brazil, where the vast majority of the population lives. Moreover, the "map of territorial development" effectively resulting from decades of urban development was not properly reflected in the traditional political-institutional order defined by the 1988 federal constitution, thus creating further distortions. Of particular relevance is the fact that the growing number of metropolitan regions and urban agglomerations in the country – totaling over 30 – are still unsupported by any adequate legal-institutional apparatus, and as such they exist in ambiguous political realm and gray legal zones.

The pressure for politico-institutional decentralization during the 1986–1988 constitution-making process was largely justified as a fundamental means to promote sociopolitical democratization in the wake of a long-standing military regime. But only more recently has there been an understanding that decentralization, especially in the unqualified way that it has taken place in Brazil, and democratization are not necessarily synonymous, so the search for new politico-institutional formulas is imperative.

Although their legal obligations have increased over the years, Brazilian municipalities on the whole are still fundamentally lacking the capacity to act, and thus to formulate, implement, and monitor urban policies. The inexistence of sufficient resources explains only part of the problem. However, there has also been widespread poor utilization mismanagement of existing fiscal and financial resources by municipal administrations. Municipalities have often opted for maintaining their dependence on federal and federated-state financial transfers for political reasons, especially regarding their hesitation to make full use of their legal power to implement adequate land and property taxation and thus antagonize powerful local groups. By doing so, they have reinforced historical patterns of political patronage, as well as renovated long existing dynamics of political clientelism. The electoral system prevailing in Brazil has long worsened this state of affairs, as it allows for a stronger representation of rural areas and less populated federated states in the National Congress.

Another consequence of the unqualified way decentralization has been promoted, and of the formal municipalism system that has prevailed, is the widespread lack of attention to such rural areas. A myth has emerged that municipalities only have legal powers – including of territorial organization – over their urban areas, and as a result many municipalities have simply abolished their rural areas from their perimeter laws, despite the existing conditions of agricultural production and/or vocation. Even those municipalities that have been trying to formulate and implement municipal master plans have largely failed to develop specific regulations and policies for their rural areas – as well as articulated rural-urban strategies. Moreover, although municipalities have the nominal power to promote territorial organization and urban policy, most of the economic policy is dictated at the federal level, often ignoring or even at odds with whatever the existing municipal plans propose.

In this confused political-institutional context, only in recent years has there been a more consistent and critical discussion on the inadequacies of the prevailing "federative pact" and the shortcomings of the formal municipalism in place, thus questioning the notion that the role of federal government is merely to provide financial support to municipalities. According to this still-dominant view, even the voluminous federal resources from both PAC and MCMV have necessarily to be spent by municipalities alone. As a result, in many cases significant amounts of financial resources have been left unused or have even been returned to the federal government, given the lack of municipal capacity to formulate projects, open tendering processes, and monitor the implementation of public contracts. In the cases in which nongovernmental organizations (NGOs) and the private sectors have been included in the process of urban management through public–private partnerships (PPPs) and other such schemes, mismanagement and corruption have also been common. As a result, there has been a growing call for the formulation and implementation of truly national policies to govern the phenomenon of urban development and all its implications and consequences.

The damaging impeachment process

To complicate a chronically difficult situation even further, for all its long-existing shortcomings, contradictions, and constraints the action of the federal government in Brazilian cities was severely affected by the worsening political, institutional, economic, and fiscal crisis that virtually paralyzed the country since January 2015, when President Dilma Rousseff took office to undertake her second mandate.

This has been a lamentable situation that has already had serious implications for the existing set of sectoral federal policies. The prospects for the future of the country's patchy national urban policy are now even worse, as ultimately what was at stake in the core of the impeachment process were two different national sociopolitical projects – with the one opposing the Rousseff government being more unambiguously in favor of neoliberal policies, privatization schemes, flexibilization of labor relations, and unqualified property rights, as well as of the deregulation of economic activities and urban development processes.

The warnings were clearly there long before the impeachment process started, especially since countless street demonstrations, many of them involving forms of police violence, happened all over Brazil for several months in 2013 mobilizing hundreds of thousands of people – ultimately being about the worsening conditions of cities and urban living in the country. The result of the October 2014 election was fiercely contested by many parties and socioeconomic groups since its announcement, and the legitimacy of the President Rousseff's very small majority was questioned after the election. Given the serious accusations of corruption involving her party and several political allies, she was subjected to a long, draining impeachment process, as well as to systematic sabotage by rivals and allies alike – such is the confusing nature of Brazil's unviable "coalition presidentialism". Motivated in part by the fiscal deficit generated by the government's previously mentioned social policies, the strict fiscal adjustment policies the president was forced to introduce in 2015 led to a profound economic recession, which was aggravated further by the international context as much as by the spiraling domestic political crisis.

In 2006, the Ministry of Cities had already been sacrificed in the name of "governability", handed over to a conservative party, and gradually turned into little more than a "clientelistic business desk". However, as the 2014–2015 sociopolitical polarization gripped the country and brought the federal government to a standstill, the main federal programs such as BF, PAC, and MCMV were significantly affected.

The situation was confusing. In May 2016 the elected president was suspended by both Houses of the National Congress, and the federal Senate decided to impeach her by mid-August. In the meantime, the vice-president acted as a so-called "interim president". However, given his close links to the political group supporting the aforementioned neoliberal project, he did not waste any time replacing all the ministers and main federal authorities. While he promptly signaled his support for further orthodox austerity in terms of fiscal and economic measures, several decisions taken by the elected government over the last 12 years were without any discussion or consultation, especially those of a social nature. This shocking backlash meant that significant cuts were announced to the main federal programs, including BF. The Minister of Cities seemed to be more strongly committed than the previous one to a widespread program of privatization, PPPs, and support to land developers and property promoters; his very first measure was to abolish the dimension of the My House My Life (MHML) program that encouraged collective self-construction by housing cooperatives and residents' associations. Major cuts to this program were also announced.

At the time it was impossible to predict with any certainty what the outcome of this impasse would be, impeachment or no impeachment. But, following the impeachment of the president, it was to be expected that Brazilian cities would have an even harder time in the near future. Such changes have been met with increasing hostility on the part of a growing number of people and organizations, and all sorts of daily sociopolitical protests have taken place. As a result, some decisions have been fully or partly reversed or suspended, worsening further a general situation of political uncertainty. It is impossible to say with any degree of clarity what the future is holding in reserve. Although new sociopolitical pacts were forming, and the level of social mobilization has gradually decreased. While daily revelations of the extent of all sorts of corruption practices have gripped the nation's attention, the political crisis has made the economic and fiscal crises even worse, especially at the federated-states level – many of which are in a desperate fiscal situation.

Not unlike most low- and middle-income and transitional countries, Brazil is in the very uncomfortable position of having to "change the wheels with the car moving". This task has been complicated further by the changes in the nature and dynamics of the urbanization process in the global economy. More than ever, the importance of getting the conceptual framework and corresponding politico-institutional systems right cannot be underestimated. Once the current political crisis is over, the promotion of urban reform will take time and will require continuity and systematic responses at all governmental levels in order to address the scale of the existing problems, as well as other fundamental factors such as capacity building, approval of articulated policies according to a clearly defined urban agenda, and the allocation of the necessary resources.

There is still a long way to go in Brazil, and many serious obstacles to be overcome. This is an open-ended process, the political quality of which resides ultimately in the Brazilian society's capacity to effectively assert its legal right to be present and actively participate in the decision-making process. The rules of the game have already been significantly altered; what remains to be seen is whether or not the newly created legal and political spaces will be used to advance the urban reform agenda in the country.

Main antecedents

Brazil has experienced one of the most drastic processes of socioeconomic and territorial reorganization in the developing world as a result of rapid urbanization since the 1930s: 84 percent of the total population currently lives in urban areas, and there is an enormous concentration of population and economic activities in a very small part of the national territory. All the relevant figures and available data clearly indicate the staggering scale and complex nature of this process, which has been widely discussed in an extensive literature.

Urban development rates have decreased since the 1980s, although they are still high in parts of the country such as the Amazon and the southern border. According to the latest census, what is different in today's urbanization process is the fact that fewer people have been migrating towards the capital cities and more people have been migrating towards middle-sized and smaller cities. Moreover, there is a growing phenomenon of metropolitanization taking place nationally, but no longer only around the traditional capital cities. In old and new metropolitan regions alike, there has been a consistent process of peripherization of the urban poor. The pattern of urban development, though, remains the same, namely, one of sociospatial segregation. Even given due respect to some municipal attempts at expanding their – precarious, insufficient, and expensive – public transportation networks, urban expansion has reinforced a long-standing car-centered culture. Commuting to work regularly involves long hours, and millions of people have to walk long distances to work. In other areas, the level of service provision has improved in some respects – electricity and water notably – but sanitation remains an enormous challenge: much of the solid waste is not collected, especially in the poorer regions of the country and urban neighborhoods, and most of what is collected is not treated.

Another relatively recent development concerns the growing land, property, and rental prices in many cities, often breaking historical levels, now within a globalizing market. Moreover, even where poverty has decreased, land informality has increased – thus showing that there is more to land informality, particularly resulting from the exclusionary nature of the urban territorial organizations, such as that determined by municipal administrations.

Of particular importance is the nature of the land structure prevailing in the country. The escalating housing deficit has been estimated to be around 6,000,000 units, while 12 million other families live in inadequate conditions. At the same time, there are about 5.5 million underutilized built properties in the country, of private and/or public ownership, as well as an enormous stock of serviced, but vacant, plots of privately owned land, which is as high as 20 percent in some cities – a number sometimes sufficient to accommodate twice the existing population of these cities, while they have around 20 to 25 percent of people living in favelas and other informal settlements. Further information is required on the significance of public-owned land in urban areas that could be used to promote inclusive development and social housing.

Despite a long-standing tradition of political, legal, and financial centralization during most of the urbanization process, until the beginning of this century the federal government has failed to formulate and implement comprehensively any national land and urban policies, or even to put together a basic institutional infrastructure to deal with the many concerns affecting cities and their growing urban population. At the most, there have been some isolated, usually half-baked and ill-fated, federal programs.

Prior to the creation of the Ministry of Cities in 2003, the lack of a proper governmental response at the federal level – given the elitist and exclusionary nature of the actual governmental intervention through the few existing programs such as the "Banco Nacional de Habitacao – BNH" (National Housing Bank) was one of the main factors determining the exclusionary nature of land and urban development in Brazil.

This was aggravated further by the conditions of political exclusion resulting from the legal system in force prior to the promulgation of the 1988 federal constitution, especially during the 1964–1986 military rule. This legal system not only undermined the legal-political powers of municipal government but also the intrinsic quality of the representative democracy system at all governmental levels.

Another fundamental factor in the creation and reproduction of this process was the prohibitive and obsolete legal order entrenched the anachronistic paradigm of the 1916 Civil Code, that reinforced the historical tradition of unqualified private property rights. As a result, until recently, the scope for public intervention through land and urban planning was very much reduced, especially at the municipal level. Whereas most Brazilian municipalities still have only a set of basic laws – determining the urban perimeters and traditional constructions codes – only from the mid-1960s did a new generation of more ambitious planning laws start to be enacted in some of the main cities, although initially they were often legally contested.

From the mid-1970s, and especially from the early 1980s on, important cracks appeared in the long-standing military regime as a result of a powerful combination of factors: the growing social mobilization through trade unions, civic organizations, social movements, residents' associations, groups linked to the progressive branch of the Catholic Church, and other collective channels; the reorganization of traditional political parties and creation of new ones expressing renewed political claims for politico-institutional change, particularly through democratic elections and the strengthening of local government; and, to a lesser extent, to the rearrangements within land and property capital, as some urban promoters and property developers were also affected by land and property speculators and the overall constraints of the planning system in force. Although Brazilian cities had been growing systematically since the 1930s, the first significant attempts at the democratization of urban management at the municipal level could only be identified in the mid-1970s.

As a result of the growing process of social mobilization and political change, an important federal law was approved in 1979 aiming to regulate urban land subdivision nationally, as well as providing basic elements for the regularization of consolidated informal settlements in cities. Soon afterwards, some progressive environmental laws were also enacted, including a groundbreaking legal recognition in 1985 of a civil public action to defend diffuse interests in environmental matters, *locus standi* being extended to the emerging NGOs. At the municipal level, the first land regularization programs were formulated in 1983 in Belo Horizonte and Recife.

A national urban reform movement then emerged and started to gain momentum within the broader political opening process, aiming to promote the re-democratization of the country. With the increasing strengthening of a new sociopolitical pact, there was a wide recognition of the need for deeper legal and political changes in the country, thus leading to the remarkable, though, in many respects flawed, constitution-making process from 1986–1988.

The 1988 federal constitution

The urbanization process in Brazil started in the 1930s and had its peak in the 1970s, during which period several federal constitutions were promulgated – 1934, 1937, 1946, 1967, and the 1969 general amendment. However, until the 1988 federal constitution came into force, there were no specific constitutional provisions to guide the processes of land development and urban management. It was the original chapter on urban policy introduced by the 1988 constitution that set the legal-political basis for the promotion of urban reform in Brazil.

Since the constitution-making process was itself the subject of an unprecedented level of popular participation, much of this constitutional chapter resulted from what was developed based on the "Popular Amendment on Urban Policy" that had been formulated, discussed, disseminated, and signed by more than 100,000 social organizations and individuals involved in the Urban Reform Movement.

This "Popular Amendment" recognized the following general principles:

• Autonomy of municipal governments;
• Democratic management of cities;
• The social right to housing;
• The right to the regularization of consolidated informal settlements;
• The social function of urban property; and
• The need to combat land and property speculation in urban areas.

Another important "Popular Amendment" proposed the approval of a series of constitutional provisions recognizing the collective right to a balanced environment. Following a process of intense dispute in the Constituent Congress, a progressive chapter on environmental preservation was eventually approved, together with a groundbreaking, though limited, chapter on urban policy. Most of these popular claims were recognized to some extent in the final text of the 1988 federal constitution. The right to the regularization of consolidated informal settlements was promoted through the approval of new legal instruments aiming to render such programs viable, both concerning settlements formed on private land (*usucapiao* rights, that is, adverse possession rights in five years) and on public land ("concession of the real right to use", a form of leasehold). The need to combat land and property speculation in cities was explicitly addressed, and new legal instruments were created for this purpose, namely, subdivision, utilization, and construction compulsory orders; progressive property taxation; and a punitive form of expropriation.

The principle of the democratic management of cities was fully endorsed, as the 1988 constitution provided a series of legal-political instruments aiming to widen the conditions of direct participation in the overall decision-making process. The autonomy of municipal government was also recognized in legal, political, and financial terms to such an extent that Brazilian municipalities have been compared to Swiss cantons in terms of political autonomy. However, the 1988 constitution did not take a proper stand on the matter of metropolitan administration, transferring to the federated states the power to do so.

At that juncture, there was no political consensus on the recognition of the social right to housing. Regarding the recognition of the principle of the social function of urban property, which had been repeated in all constitutions since 1934 but was largely a rhetorical notion, there were heated debates between antagonistic groups, and as a result the following formula was approved: private property is recognized as a fundamental private right, provided that it accomplishes social functions, which are those determined by municipal master plans and other urban and environmental laws. By making the principle of the social function of urban property conditional on the approval of municipal planning laws, the intention of conservative groups seemed to be to keep the rhetorical nature of this principle.

The limited Brazilian experience with city planning so far had been largely ineffective in terms of its power to reverse the exclusionary conditions of urban development. On the contrary, informal land development had largely resulted from the elitist and technocratic nature of city planning. Faced with the impossibility of approving another, more progressive constitutional formula, the Urban Reform Movement then decided to make the most of the situation and subvert the approved provision, by consciously investing in the formulation of municipal master plans throughout the country that were both inclusive and participatory.

A new legal–urban order in the 1990s

A whole new legal-urban order was inaugurated with the promulgation of the 1988 constitution, and its possibilities began to be realized throughout the 1990s by means of a series of progressive local experiences.

Many municipalities embraced the banner of the urban reform movement and approved new urban and environmental laws, including some master plans; in fact, Brazil became an interesting urban planning and management laboratory, with new strategies and processes establishing new relations between the public, the community, the private, and the voluntary sectors where urban land development was concerned. New land regularization programs were formulated and began to be implemented by several municipalities.

Special emphasis was placed on the political quality of all such processes, with popular participation being encouraged in various areas, from the definition of urban policies in "City Conferences" to the introduction of innovative participatory budgeting process. Since then, municipalities such as Porto Alegre, Santo Andre, Diadema, Recife, and Belo Horizonte, many of which were associated with the "Partido dos Trabalhadores – PT" (Workers' Party), have gained international recognition. The Participatory Budget initiated in the 1980s was taken to a new dimension, and the constitutional notion of the "social function of property" was particularly materialized through the demarcation of several "Special Zones of Social Interest" (ZEIS) corresponding to the long-ignored consolidated informal settlements. Limited attempts at a new urban-fiscal policy were introduced in some municipalities.

However, the lack of regulation of the urban policy chapter in the 1988 federal constitution through specific federal legislation, as is the tradition in Brazil, led to a series of legal-political difficulties, which were fomented by groups opposed to the advance of the new legal-urban order. This undermined the extent and the scope of the promising municipal experiences. As a result, the organizations involved in the Urban Reform Movement decided to consolidate and expand the urban reform movement itself initially by creating the National Forum of Urban Reform (NFUR) in the early1990s.

Comprising a wide range of national and local organizations and movements, the NFUR was instrumental in promoting the urban reform banner and agenda nationally. Three of its main targets in the 1990s were, first, the incorporation of the social right to housing into the 1988 federal constitution. Second, the approval of a specific federal law regulating the constitutional chapter; and third, the approval of a bill of law, originating from a popular initiative using the new possibilities created by the 1988 federal constitution, which proposed the creation of a National Fund for Social Housing. At the same time, the NFUR also called for the creation by the federal government of an institutional apparatus at the national level to promote urban planning and policy in Brazil.

A long process of social mobilization and a fierce political struggle lasted throughout the 1990s and into the new century, within and outside the National Congress. In 1999, a new federal law regulated the action of "civil society organizations of public interest" so as to allow them to receive public money when involved in urban management processes. The social right to housing was eventually approved by a constitutional amendment in 2000, and the federal law creating the National Fund for Social Housing was finally enacted in 2005. Of special importance was the enactment, in 2001, of the internationally acclaimed "City Statute", the federal law on urban policy

The 2001 City Statute

Brazil's national urban policy law – the 2001 City Statute – has been widely regarded as a groundbreaking effort to conceive a regulatory framework more conducive to providing adequate legal support to governmental and social attempts to promote urban reform. The City Statute was approved after 12 years of intense discussion and fierce disputes within and outside the National Congress. Since then, it has been acclaimed internationally, with Brazil having won UN-Habitat's Scroll of Honor in 2006 for having approved it. Envied by policymakers and public administrators in several countries, the ambitious City Statute has been proposed by the Cities Alliance as a paradigm to be considered internationally.

The City Statute regulated and expanded on the previously mentioned constitutional provisions, and it explicitly recognized the "right to the city" in Brazil. It widened the fundamental legal-political role of municipalities in the formulation of directives for urban planning, as well as in conducting the process of urban development and management. The City Statute broke with the long-standing tradition of civil law and set the basis for a new legal-political paradigm for urban land use and development control. It did this especially by reinforcing the constitutional provision, recognizing the power and the obligation of municipal governments to control of the process of urban development through the formulation of territorial and land use policies, in which the individual interests of landowners necessarily coexist with other social, cultural, and environmental interests of other groups and the city as a whole. Moreover, the City Statute elaborated on the principle of the "social function of property and of the city", thus replacing the individualistic paradigm of the 1916 Civil Code. In addition, the statute provided a range of legal, urban planning, and fiscal instruments to be used by the municipal administrations, especially within the context of their master plans, to regulate, induce, and/or revert urban land and property markets according to criteria of social inclusion and environmental sustainability. All such instruments can, and should, be used in a combined manner aiming not only to regulate the process of land use development but especially to induce it, according to a "concept of city", to be expressed through the municipal master plans.

Municipalities were given more scope for interfering with, and possibly reversing to some extent, the pattern and dynamics of formal and informal urban land markets, especially those of a speculative nature, which have long brought about social exclusion and spatial segregation in Brazil. In fact, the combination of traditional planning mechanisms – zoning, subdivision, building rules, etc. – with the new instruments – compulsory subdivision, construction, and utilization orders; extra-fiscal use of local property tax progressively over time; expropriation-sanction with payment in titles of public debt; surface rights; preference rights for the municipality; onerous transfer of building rights; etc. – opened a new range of possibilities for the construction by the municipalities of a new urban order that can be economically more efficient, politically fairer, and more sensitive to the gamut of existing social and environmental questions.

Moreover, the City Statute offered new spaces for municipalities to integrate urban planning, legislation, and management to democratize the local decision-making process and thus legitimize a new, socially orientated urban-legal order. Several mechanisms were recognized to ensure the effective participation of citizens and associations in urban planning and management: audiences, consultations, creation of councils, reports of environmental and neighborhood impact, popular initiative for the proposal of urban laws, public litigation, and, above all, the practices of the participatory budgeting process. The new law also emphasized the importance of establishing new relations between the state and the private and the community sectors, especially through partnerships and linkages of "urban operations" to be promoted within a clearly defined legal-political and fiscal framework.

The 2001 legislation also improved on the legal order regarding the regularization of consolidated informal settlements in private and public urban areas, enabling municipalities to promote land tenure regularization programs and thus democratize the conditions of access to land and housing. As well as regulating the earlier mentioned constitutional instruments of *usucapiao* and concession of the real right to use, the new law went one step further and admitted the collective utilization of such instruments. Subsequently, still in 2001, given the active mobilization of the NFUR, the Provisional Measure no. 2.220 was signed by the president, recognizing the subjective right (and not only the prerogative of the public authorities) of those occupying public land until that date to be granted, under certain circumstances, the "concession of special use for housing purposes", another form of leasehold rights.

All municipalities with more than 20,000 inhabitants, among other categories, were given a deadline of five years to create and approve their master plans.

Ever since, the federal legal order has been complemented by several other important laws: Provisional Measure 2.220/2001 (Special Concession of Use for Housing Purposes); Federal Law 11.079/2004 (Public-Private Partnerships); Federal Law No. 10.931/2004 (Land and property credit and registration); Federal Law 11.107/2005 (Public consortia); Federal Law (of popular initiative) 11.124/2005 (National Fund for Social Interest Housing – FNHIS); Federal Law 11.445/2007 – (Sanitation); Federal Law 11.481/2007 (Federal land and property); Federal Law 11.888/2008 – (Technical assistance to communities); Federal Law 11.977/2009 ("My House, My Life" National Housing Program and regularization of informal settlements); Federal Law 11.952/2009 ("Legal Amazon"); Federal Law 12.305/2010 (Solid waste); and, more recently, Federal Law 12.608/2012 (National Policy for Civil Protection) and Federal Law no. 13.089/2015 ("Metropolitan Statute").

All those federal laws are currently in force, together with several international conventions and treaties signed/ratified by the country (especially on housing rights); federal laws on environment, historic heritage, expropriation, and registration; bills of laws being discussed (land subdivision); "white papers" being discussed (especially on the resolution of land conflicts); and countless decrees and resolutions of the National Council of Cities and of the National Environmental Council, as well as endless directives of the public bank, Caixa Economica Federal.

A new legal-urban order has thus been consolidated – sophisticated, articulated, and comprehensive – including the constitutional recognition of urban law as a field of Brazilian public law with its own paradigmatic principles, namely, the socioenvironmental functions of property and of the city and the democratic management of the city. The collective right to sustainable cities was explicitly recognized, and there is a clear commitment in the legal system to the urban reform agenda. These significant and structural legal changes have been expanded at all governmental levels – federated states and especially municipalities – particularly as mentioned through the approval of more than 1,450 municipal master plans (MMPs).

This gradual fundamental process of legal reform was also supported by a significant process of institutional change. The creation of the Ministry of Cities in 2003 deserves special mention. National Conferences of Cities have been promoted every two years since then; the National Council of Cities meets regularly; Caixa Economica Federal – said to be the world's largest public bank – has promoted several federal plans and projects, especially PAC and MCMV.

The Ministry of Cities and the National Council of Cities

Perhaps given President Fernando Henrique Cardoso's celebrated academic and political background, the lack of a national urban policy and a corresponding institutional apparatus during his government (1995–2002) was particularly frustrating. There were some isolated, sectoral programs scattered through several ministries dealing with aspects of the broader urban question, but there was no national urban policy to articulate them, especially because the then-existing urban policy secretariat had insignificant powers and few resources. Fernando Henrique Cardoso's administration will be better remembered for its greater emphasis on economic and monetarist policies, as well as its liberalization and privatization programs.

Only with the election of President Lula in 2003 was a decision made to create the Ministry of Cities. It is important to stress that the new ministry was not created by executive decision by the newly elected president, but as his response to the social claim long defended by the NFUR and other stakeholders, is what confers a special form of legitimacy on the Ministry of Cities.

As mentioned, the ministry consisted of an executive secretariat presiding over four national secretariats, namely, housing, environmental sanitation, public transportation and mobility, and land and urban programs. Among other tasks, the executive secretariat focused on building the capacity of municipalities to act, initially through a national campaign, for the elaboration of multipurpose municipal cadasters. As well as formulating national programs on their respective subjects, the four secretariats were involved in negotiations with the National Congress to promote further changes in the regulatory framework in force, with a relative degree of success.

Perhaps the most remarkable aspect of the new political-institutional apparatus that was created in Brazil was the installation of the National Council of Cities. In April 2003, President Lula called for a national mobilization to discuss a list of land, urban, and housing policy goals, through a series of

municipal "City Conferences" in which delegates would be elected to participate in State Conferences, and eventually in the National Conference planned
to take place in October 2003. It was expected that some 300 or so municipalities, out of the 5,571 existing, would have the time and the conditions to
organize local conferences. As it happened, over 3,000 municipalities did so,
as did all 27 federated states. Over 2,500 delegates discussed the initial national
policy directives on urban development, as well as the range of specific proposals on sectoral housing, planning, sanitation, and transportation national policies. They all voted on the definition of the final list of principles that should
guide the formulation of national policies by the Ministry of Cities.

Moreover, one of the most important deliberations of the First National
Conference of Cities was the creation of the National Council of Cities, with
representatives from all sectors of stakeholders being elected. The National
Council consisted of 86 members, 49 representing segments of civil society
(popular movements, workers' unions, NGOs, academic institutions, and the
business sector) and 37 representing federal, federated-state, and municipal
administrations. All the members were elected for a two-year term. Citizen
participation in the council's deliberations was thus widely ensured, and the
Ministry of Cities was legally required to follow and respect such deliberations.

The Second National Conference of Cities took place in December 2005,
again as the culmination of a nationwide mobilization process. Some 2,500
delegates and 410 observers from all federated states and different social segments discussed a more articulated National Urban Development Policy, aiming to generate "fairer, democratic and sustainable" cities. The Third National
Conference of Cities took place in November 2007, again involving the participation of over 2,500 delegates; it aimed to take stock of previously approved
plans and programs, as well as to discuss the National Housing Plan. Perhaps
involving a lesser degree of popular participation, the Fourth National Conference took place in June 2010, discussing "Advances, difficulties and challenges
in the implementation of the urban development policy". The Fifth National
Conference of Cities took place in November 2013, discussing "We are the
ones who change the city: urban reform immediately", involving around 3,000
participants, 1,689 of them elected in regional conferences.

Despite its promising start and the approval of important new federal laws
and sectorial national programs, the PT-controlled Ministry of Cities was soon
handed over in 2006 to the very conservative Partido Popular – PP (Popular
Party), as a means of obtaining this party's support for the increasingly more
beleaguered federal government that did not have a majority in the National
Congress. Unfortunately, ex-President Lula and his advisors never fully understood the political nature of cities and of urban policies. More familiar with
the traditional capital-labor disputes within the confines of factories, they did
not understand that cites are no longer only the place where industrial economic development takes place, with urbanization providing support to capitalist accumulation, but they have also become the very object of postindustrial,
financial, and services capitalism.

Led by backward, often dodgy politicians more clearly committed to the interests of urban developers, builders, and other dominant socioeconomic groups, the Ministry of Cities quickly became involved in old-style practices of political patronage. The fact that the ministry's institutional structure had been basically consolidated by 2006 has made it possible for some of the initial programs to be maintained, albeit in a fragmented way. Some of the original urban reform agenda was kept alive by remaining members of the original staff.

But, on the whole, the ministry has never been able to achieve a proper degree of recognition vis-à-vis other federal ministries, has failed to promote interministerial articulation, and has repeatedly lost vital budgetary resources. No national urban policy has been formulated, let alone implemented, no comprehensive national policy for the use of federal land and property has been approved, and no national territorial organization proposal has been systematically discussed.

The National Council of Cities has struggled to revive the decaying level of sociopolitical mobilization, and despite the interesting resolutions it has passed, its consultative nature has meant that it has not been able to influence decision making at the federal level, including inside the Ministry of Cities itself. On the contrary, both the Ministry of Cities and the National Council of Cities have been repeatedly bypassed by the president, including when deciding on the two main national programs that have eventually prevailed, namely PAC and MCMV, which are not part of any broader urban policy formulated by the ministry and approved by the council.

Actions at the federal level

As mentioned earlier, the bulk of the action of Brazil's federal government in the country's urban areas has resulted from the unplanned combination of three massive programs, namely, BF, PAC, and MCMV

Bolsa Familia and poverty eradication

In 2003, President Lula formed BF by combining pre-existing social programs "Bolsa Escola" with "Bolsa Alimentação" and "Cartão Alimentação" – all part of his "Fome Zero" anti-hunger program – and Auxílio Gas (a transfer to compensate for the end of federal gas subsidies). This also meant the creation of a new Ministry – the Ministério do Desenvolvimento Social e Combate à Fome (Ministry for Social Development and War Against Hunger). This merger reduced administrative costs and eased bureaucratic complexity for both the families involved and the administration of the program.

The resulting BF was a social welfare program that provided financial aid to poor Brazilian families; if they have children, families must ensure that the children attend school and are vaccinated. The program attempted to both reduce short-term poverty by direct cash transfers and fight long-term poverty by increasing human capital among the poor through conditional cash transfers. It also gave free education to children who could not afford to go to school, stressing the importance of education.

The program was a centerpiece of President Lula's social policy and is believed to have played a role in his own re-election, as well as the election and re-election of his successor, President Dilma Rousseff. It became the largest conditional cash transfer program in the world, and it has been mentioned as one factor contributing to the reduction of poverty in Brazil, which fell 27.7 percent during the first term of the Lula administration. Improvements in the job market and real gains in the minimum wage also contributed towards a sharp reduction in the number of poor people in Brazil up to the end of 2016. About 12 million families received funds from BF. Altogether, some 30 million people were lifted out of poverty, and a "new middle class" or "precarious working class" was created.

The Plan to Accelerate Growth

The PAC is a major infrastructure program launched on January 28, 2007, by President Lula, consisting of a set of economic policies and investment projects with the objective of accelerating economic growth in the country. The program forecasted investments by the federal government, state enterprises, and the private sector in construction, sanitation, energy, transport, and logistics, mostly in urban areas and including the upgrading of informal settlements. The program had a budget of $503.9 billion Reais for the 2007–2010 *quadriennium*. The Rousseff administration continued the program under the name PAC-2 in March 2010, with estimated investments of US$526 billion (R$958.9 billion) for the period from 2011 to 2014.

Similar to the first phase of the program, PAC 2 focused on investments in the areas of logistics, energy, and social development, organized under six major initiatives: Better Cities (urban infrastructure); Bringing Citizenship to the Community (safety and social inclusion); My House, My Life (housing); Water and Light for All (sanitation and access to electricity); Energy (renewable energy, oil and gas); and Transportation (highways, railways, airports). Because of the economic and political crisis affecting President Dilma's second term, PAC 3, announced for July 2015, did not materialize as expected.

The My House, My Life program

Launched by President Lula in 2009, the ambitious My House, My Life Program was continued by President Dilma in her first term (2011), and the third stage was launched in 2016. Promoted through Caixa Economica, the program was aimed at families earning up to R$5,000. In six years, 2.3 million houses were completed, with a remaining 1.4 million still to be completed. The total investment so far has exceeded R$270 billion.

Assessments and criticisms of the federal programs

Regarding BF, the first thing to be said is that, whatever its intrinsic shortcomings, constraints, and failures are, the program has been widely recognized and praised by World Bank, Food and Agriculture Organization (FAO), and many other international institutions. The fact that the living conditions of 50 million people have been improved is no small feat and should not be underestimated. Nevertheless, several orders of legitimate criticism have been increasingly made of the program, especially about its remedial, not structural, nature. It was not supported by sufficient job creation and economic growth and led to artificial consumption levels. Also criticized is the lack of proper integration of the social distribution program with a solid educational reform. While the level of schooling has increased, high school education remains a bottleneck. Formal illiteracy has decreased, but functional illiteracy remains high. The racial and poverty quotas system has had promising results in public universities, but the system remains strongly questioned by the elites.

The growing economic crisis since 2015 has confirmed how precarious the "new middle class" was, as more and more people have lost their newly obtained formal jobs – an emblematic case in point being domestic servants turned into workers in other areas who are now back to working as domestic servants – and many have been left with enormous debts as a result of excessive spending. Of special relevance is that this wide-reaching social welfare program, which has had a major impact on urban areas, albeit indirectly, has never been remotely articulated with the other national programs being implemented in cities.

PAC has also been widely criticized on several grounds: the ad hoc nature of many projects in the absence of clearly defined policies; interventions by the federal government that contradict municipal land use and zoning laws; an enormous amount of resources being transferred to municipalities that lack a basic capacity to act; irregular or illegal tender processes with corrupt urban management practices; wasted resources, given the lack of suitable technical projects and of social control; lack of popular participation in the decision-making processes; old-fashioned, inadequate technical solutions adopted; lack of adequate environmental-impact assessments, and so on.

Also MCMV housing programs have also been widely criticized, despite the recognition that an impressive number of houses were delivered within a relatively short period – scale was rarely in the essence of public policies in Brazil.

Poor location in peripheral areas; lack of sociospatial integration of the newly built housing estates; precarious public services, collective facilities, urban equipment, and public spaces; poor architectural and building quality – these are some of the most recurrent criticisms. MCMV is also heavily criticized for having favoring construction companies, thus producing houses, but not cities, and for having reinforced long-existing patterns of sociospatial segregation. Moreover, the program has been criticized for not supporting a denser and more efficient urban form. In particular, the program has been condemned for its failure to intervene in the concentrated land structure and for placing emphasis on individual freeholds. Although it has done more than previous housing programs to cater to the very poor, who comprise the bulk of the housing deficit, it has not reduced informality, and in fact, many estates risk soon becoming informal settlements.

Other than those three federal programs, there are currently no other significant wide-ranging and significant policies and programs of the same scale in urban areas, especially as sectoral policies and programs have been undermined by the all-encompassing PAC. Some environmental programs – for example, on coastal protection and preservation of the Atlantic forest – have had erratic results. A misguided, half-baked, ambiguous, and ultimately ineffective program was approved to govern the development of the Amazon, which is one of the regions currently showing the highest rates of urban development in the country.

In any case, as mentioned, the political, institutional, economic, and fiscal crisis since January 2015 has had a major impact on all national programs. While BF has so far been kept without significant changes – although the interim president has mentioned the intention of excluding some 10 million beneficiaries – drastic cuts have led to many PAC projects being interrupted, whereas MCMV has changed focus and has had its scope significantly reduced.

Actions at the municipal level

The new legal-urban order consolidated in Brazil with the enactment of the 2001 City Statute has placed in the hands of the municipalities much of the power to promote urban policy, planning, and management. However, now that more than 15 years have passed since the approval of the 2001 City Statute, there are significant debates about its efficacy.

As mentioned, the main dimensions of the new urban land governance framework proposed by the City Statute are the following:

- It firmly replaced the traditional legal definition of unqualified individual property rights with the notion of the social function of property so as to support the democratization of the access to urban land and housing.
- It defined the main articulated principles of land, urban, and housing policy to be observed in the country.
- It created several processes, mechanisms, instruments, and resources aiming to render urban management viable, with emphasis placed on the capture for the community of some of the surplus value generated by state action that has been traditionally fully appropriated by land and property owners.
- It proposed a largely decentralized and democratized urban governance system, in which intergovernmental articulation as well as state partnerships with the private, community, and voluntary sectors are articulated with several forms of popular participation in the decision- and law-making process.

- It recognized the collective rights of residents in consolidated informal settlements to legal security of land tenure, as well as to the sustainable regularization of their settlements.

Together, these intertwined dimensions of the City Statute certainly constituted a new urban land governance framework in Brazil.

Given the previously mentioned highly decentralized nature of the Brazilian federative system, the materialization of this legal framework was largely placed in the hands of the municipal administrations through the formulation of MMPs. Prior to the enactment of the new law, the vast majority of municipalities did not have a adequate regulatory framework in place to govern the processes of land use, development, preservation, construction, regularization, etc. Most of them did not have basic information, maps, photos, and other relevant materials, either. Out of some 1,700 municipalities that had a legal obligation to approve such MMPs so as to apply the City Statute, some 1,450 have already done so – which fact in itself is undoubtedly remarkable.

However, since the enactment of the City Statute, Brazilian cities have undergone significant changes. As mentioned, the rates of urban growth have decreased but are still relatively high, especially in middle-sized and small cities, thus leading to the formation of new metropolitan regions – with 30 such regions having been officially recognized. Economic development and the emergence of a so-called "new middle class"/"precarious working class" have aggravated further long-standing urban problems of transportation, mobility, environmental impact, and urban violence. Infrastructure and energy provision problems have increased, and the fiscal crisis of the public administrations is widespread, especially at the municipal level.

Above all, the long-existing land and housing crisis has escalated. The housing deficit is still enormous, and despite the impressive number of units already built/contracted, the MCMV national housing program has not fully reached the poorest families and has been criticized for having reinforced long-standing processes of sociospatial segregation. The levels of land, property, and rental appreciation – and speculation – have broken historical records, now within a clearly globalized market, there remains an enormous stock of vacant serviced land and abandoned/underutilized properties, as well as of public land and property without a social function.

Informal development rates are still high, with the densification/verticalization of old settlements and the formation of new settlements, usually in peripheral areas, and it has also been taking new shapes – backyarders, informal rental transactions, etc. The proliferation of gated communities in peripheral areas and other metropolitan municipalities means that for the first time rich and poor are competing for the same space. Urban development in the new economic frontiers – especially in the Amazon – has largely taken place through informal processes, and there is a growing number of land disputes and socioenvironmental conflicts throughout the country.

Over the last two decades or so, an enormous amount of public resources – land, fiscal incentives, all sorts of credits, tax exemptions, building and development rights – has been given to land developers and urban promoters/builders, usually within the context of urban renewal and revitalization programs; rehabilitation of downtown areas and historic centers; large-scale projects; modernization of harbors, ports, and infrastructure; and global events such as the World Cup and the Olympic Games.

The number of forced evictions – estimated by some at 250,000 people only insofar as the World Cup is concerned – is staggering, not only in Rio de Janeiro and Sao Paulo but even in municipalities such as Belo Horizonte and Porto Alegre that were long committed to the urban reform process. The urban reform process, which was so vivid in the 1980s and 1990s, and which was instrumental for the enactment of the 2001 City Statute, seems to have lost momentum, and from several sectors many stakeholders have been asking "what cities, and for whom" – and have demanded to know who has actually benefitted from the enormous transfer of public resources.

What has happened to the City Statute, then? Has it failed, as a growing group of skeptical groups seems to believe? Rather than contributing to the promotion of sociospatial inclusion, has it perversely contributed to the current escalating process of commodification of Brazilian cities – and to the further peripheralization of the urban poor – as some have argued? ((Cymbalista and Santoro, 2009), (Santos and Montandon, 2011), and (Schult et al., 2010)). There are also several published case studies, and a "bank of experiences" was created by the Ministry of Cities. Both the legal and the institutional orders are fundamentally social conquests, having largely resulted from a historical process of sociopolitical mobilization involving thousands of stakeholders – associations, NGOs, churches, unions, political parties, and sectors of land and property capital – which since the late 1970s have claimed for the (rather late) constitutional recognition of land, urban, and housing questions, as well as for the decentralization and democratization of, and popular participation in, law- and decision-making processes.

However, at the same time, over the last decade or so several stakeholders have increasingly denounced the growing process of property speculation in Brazil; the elitist utilization of the enormous amount of financial resources newly generated, especially through the sale of building and development rights in public auctions; the way the so-called "unlocking of land values" by large projects and events has reinforced sociospatial segregation; the recurrent abuse of the legal arguments of "public interest" and "urgency"; and the enormous socioenvironmental impact of federal programs and others.

Growing land conflicts, growing rental prices, growing urban informality, growing number of eviction and removals, worsening of transportation, mobility and sanitation problems, and especially a growing process of commodification of Brazilian cities, which are currently at once both venue and object of postindustrial capitalist production, are now at a global level, given the aggressive penetration of international land and property capital. This new stage of urban development and financialization of cities in Brazil has led to the strengthening of the individualist and patrimonial legal culture that had long prevailed prior to the enactment of the City Statute: property viewed merely as a commodity; consideration of exchange values but not of use values; and the right to use, enjoy, and dispose of the property, often meaning the right not to use, enjoy, and dispose – in other words, to freely speculate.

What has happened to the urban reform process? How does one explain the growing gaps between the progressive new legal order and the exclusionary urban and institutional realities? How does one explain the enormous legal and institutional gaps? Indeed, there is an enormous gap between the legal-urban order and the urban and social realities. The legal-urban order is still largely unknown by jurists and society, when not an object of legal as well as sociopolitical disputes. There is a gigantic challenge of implementation so as to give it legal and social efficacy.

There is also a huge gap between the institutional order and the urban and social realities. As mentioned, the Ministry of Cities has often been emptied or bypassed by the federal budget or by other ministries; the National Council of Cities has often been emptied or bypassed by the Ministry of Cities or other ministries, compromising the renewal of social mobilization. Whenever there is not a lack of projects, duplicity, inefficiency, waste, lack of continuity, and bottomless corruption have marked the fragmented urban management at all governmental levels.

It is in this context that there is a growing skepticism among planners, managers, academics – and society – regarding the City Statute. The federal law has been demonized by some, who have blamed the 2001 federal law for the recent processes of sociospatial segregation and the fact that the new urban management tools have been appropriated by conservative sectors, as well as for the fact that new forms of old processes of "socialization of costs and privatization of benefits" have emerged also with the re-concentration of public services and facilities.

What has actually happened, then, with the new generation of MMPs? The existing studies have clearly shown that there has been progress on many fronts: the general discourse of urban reform has been adopted by most MMPs; specific sectors – environment, cultural heritage – have been dealt with; there has been a widespread creation of ZEISs corresponding to the areas occupied by existing informal settlements; and, whatever the variations – which naturally express the different political realities in the Brazilian municipalities – the participatory nature of the discussion of the MMPs was remarkable. Perhaps the main achievement has been the record production of data and all sorts of information about Brazilian cities.

However, there are several problems of legal efficacy undermining the new MMPs: the excessive formalism and bureaucracy of municipal laws; requirement of further regulation by several subsequent laws for full enforcement; punctual changes have been promoted without participation; and both the obscure legal language and the imprecise technical legal writing (urban laws are rarely written by legal professionals) have widened the scope for legal and sociopolitical disputes.

There are also several problems of social efficacy undermining the new MMPs: most plans remain traditional plans, merely technical and regulatory, often failing to territorialize the proposals and intentions, as well as to intervene in the land structure and in the land and property markets. The emphasis on the new tools created by the City Statute has been placed without a clearly defined project for the city. The vast majority of MMPs have failed to recapture any surplus value resulting from state and collective action, and when this has happened, there has been no or limited social redistribution of the newly generated financial resources.

Moreover, most MMPs have placed no or limited emphasis on social housing in central areas, having failed to earmark central, serviced, and vacant land for social housing. Generally speaking, there are no specific criteria for the expansion of urban areas, public land and property have not been given a social function, and there has been no clearly articulated socioenvironmental approach. Large projects have often bypassed the MMPs – and presumed collective eviction. Above all, land, urban, housing, environmental, fiscal, and budgetary policies have not been integrated, and the regularization of informal settlements is still largely viewed as an isolated policy, with most MMPs imposing enormous technical difficulties to the legalization of informal settlements. Bureaucratic management and technical complexity have also meant that there has been a widespread lack of administrative capacity to act at municipal level. Many MMPs are mere copies of models promoted by an "industry" of consultants. Obscure planning language has been as problematic as obscure legal language.

As mentioned, at the other governmental levels, the precarious institutional systems have experienced several problems. At the federal level, sectoral policies have not been integrated within and outside the Ministry of Cities; urban policy has not articulated with environmental policy; there is no national urban/metropolitan policy or system of cities, as well as no national territorial policy generally, most especially regarding the Amazon. The institutional and legal action of the federated states has been very limited.

Above all, at all governmental levels, there is a profound lack of understanding that cities are not only about "social policy" and "infrastructure for economic development", but they are about also the economy itself, as well as having a deeply political nature.

Plus ça change . . . plus c'est la même chose? The confirmation post–City Statute of old sociospatial segregation processes by the Brazilian state at all governmental levels, despite the possibility of significantly changing the course of things through the formulation of profoundly different and inclusive MMPs, seems to demonstrate that – with the support of conservative lawyers – urban planners and public managers remain, and have seemingly become increasingly more, hostages to exclusionary land and property markets that they have created and fomented in the first place, as well as of segregating public policies that they have implemented.

The fact that decreasing poverty rates coexist with growing informal development rates has clearly shown that, although it remains a significant factor, poverty can no longer be viewed as the sole reason for informal development, or even the main one. Other factors need to be considered to explain the phenomenon, and they have largely to do with the nature of the territorial organizational order and its relation to the land structure: there lies the reason for the Brazilian state's structural inability to provide accessible, adequate, sufficient, well-located, and affordable access to serviced urban land and housing.

Perhaps more so than ever in the past, the current public services crisis has demonstrated that the building of walls, imaginary or concrete, is insufficient to protect the more privileged socioeconomic groups. If in the past the lack of basic sanitation only affected the urban poor, today's public health crisis has no borders, especially given the combined impact of the ongoing Zika, Dengue, and Chikungunya pandemics. If the urban poor remain more directly affected, the impact has been widely felt.

The same applies to the growing failure of other public services and infrastructure systems, such as the widespread energy crisis, especially given the saturation of the electricity and water provision models. The serious problems now regularly experienced by the gigantic urban population concentrated in Sao Paulo, Minas Gerais, and Rio de Janeiro, among others, tend to be aggravated further by severe droughts and other consequences of extreme weather patterns and related variations that were not common in the country in the past. And yet, urban policies, plans, projects, and laws at all governmental levels have failed to seriously consider the new environmental scenarios that are clearly forming. On the contrary, economic development is still promoted in an unqualified manner, public works such as the gigantic Belo Monte dam and many PAC-sponsored projects do not have a clear environmental impact dimension, and the deforestation of the Atlantic rainforest, as well as of the Amazon, keeps happening at alarming rates.

All in all, the inadequacy of the politico-institutional system and resulting governance processes is manifest from the lack of a metropolitan sphere, intergovernmental articulation, and a national territorial policy/system of cities to conflicting "green" and "brown" agendas and inefficient environmental policies regarding coastal protection, river basins, vegetation, global warming, gas emissions, and the Amazon. The largest socioenvironmental disaster in Brazil's history developed in 2015–2016 – initially in Mariana, Minas Gerais as a result of the wastewater released by the bursting of a dam and subsequently affecting 40 cities of two federated states, a large stretch of the Atlantic Ocean, the whole valley of the Rio Doce, several communities, and economic activities – received minimal and delayed governmental attention.

At the root of all such problems is the lack of a comprehensive and articulated land policy. The "urban question" in Brazil has been up for grabs, when it has not been auctioned off by the government. Had the federal government understood that, perhaps the current political crisis would not have taken place.

The growing sociopolitical unrest: June 2013 and beyond

Recent social movements in Brazil, characterized by diffuse claims and a diversity of actors, have ultimately been about the elitist nature, as well as inefficiency, of recent urban policy in the country.

The social demonstrations that took place in Brazil on and off from May 2013 through 2014 puzzled many analysts, who were at a loss to understand what exactly was going on in the country and what the real meaning of these demonstrations was. Conflicting assessments about the events were made, and in fact some commentators from different sides of the political spectrum only saw what they wanted to see, often passing premature judgment without solid information and proper research. It is tempting to reduce this confusing collective phenomenon to a single cause: on the international scale, many people have interpreted the phenomenon almost exclusively as a reaction against the absurd costs and implications of the 2014 World Cup and the 2016 Olympic Games in Brazil. Yet the diffuse nature of the claims and the diversity of the stakeholders involved require a broader analytical framework – especially because the street demonstrations have been taking place even after the World Cup, although it lost momentum or was diluted into the equally frequent and powerful social mobilization around the political strategies for President Dilma's impeachment.

If there is a common base to these apparently disparate social claims, it is the fact that, consciously or not, directly or indirectly, they all denounced the exclusionary nature and the sociospatial segregation pattern that have long characterized urban development in Brazil. Over time, it has become increasingly clearer to many involved in the social mobilization process that, because they are ultimately denouncing the same basic problems, they would greatly benefit from regrouping their fragmented claims under the umbrella of the analytical framework that has long inspired the urban reform movement in Brazil. Indeed, only such a renewed social mobilization in Brazil was seen as leading toward the effective and full implementation of the "right to the city" promised by the country's groundbreaking 2001 City Statute.

In 2014–2015, street protests occurred more sporadically and in fewer cities, such as Sao Paulo, Porto Alegre, Recife, and Belo Horizonte, although many analysts believed that they might gain strength by the time of the Olympic Games in Rio de Janeiro. Initially, there was a widespread perplexity regarding the causes and timing of the social demonstrations: no one knew the exact identity of the actors involved, nor what their goals were. Several lessons have gradually emerged for Brazil and countries everywhere, especially regarding the relationship between urban planning, policy, management, and urban law. It is not easy to explain what has happened since 2013, given the general lack of focus of the demonstrations, as well as the absence of clear leaders.

The first demonstration in Sao Paulo back in May 2013 was a specific protest against increased bus fares. Fomented by violent police reaction, the demonstrations then grew and spread to many other cities, as well as incorporing several other claims, such as the quality of public services (especially health and education) and the cost of the 2014 World Cup, the 2016 Olympic Games, and several large projects funded by the public authorities such as the "urban revitalization programs" in Recife and Porto Alegre. They also denounced specific laws and politicians, as well as widespread corruption.

The diffuse composition of this social mobilization has also been intriguing. Demonstrators were largely young people, initially from the so-called "new middle-class", which has – ironically – emerged out of the social policies adopted by the federal government over the last 15 years. They were later joined by the members of the traditional middle classes and eventually by residents in favelas. Regardless of their different backgrounds, they all shared a profound distrust of the official institutional actors – political parties, powers of the state, governmental levels, unions, students' organizations, NGOs, media, etc. Fomented by the repeated use of police violence, this broad popular agenda often risks being taken over by largely obscure radical right- and left-wing groups. They indeed included both groups, seemingly supported by conservative and even reactionary segments – some of which have publicly declared a longing for the military regime – and the supporters of the still-little-studied "Black Bloc tactic". The action of this latter group seems to be based on unclear notions of forms of acceptable "anarchy" and "vandalism" – depending on one's perspective – as well as the place of "symbolic violence" in the confrontation of exclusionary political systems.

Many largely peaceful demonstrations ended in some form of violence by minority groups. The recurrence of both police violence and violent actions of such minority groups in the street demonstrations seems to have led to the declining popular participation in some cases, although hundreds of thousands of people again took to the streets to either protest against or support the presidential impeachment process. However, even when they were violent, this social mobilization process dialogued with the state and demanded an overall "political reform", even though in vague terms.

Amidst all these uncertainties, two things are certain: the street demonstrations have an urban nature and – consciously or not, directly or indirectly – they are ultimately about the so-called "urban question", that is, the nature of the social process of production of urban space in Brazil. No wonder, then, that the ideas of Henri Lefebvre (1968) and Manuel Castells (1977) are back in vogue among the demonstrators.

Even when they are conveyed in specific or narrow terms, their claims ultimately address, and condemn, the general urban development pattern in the country: sociospatial segregation deeply affecting 84 percent of the people living in cities; the increasing peripheralization of the urban poor, who can no longer afford to live even in more centrally located favelas and other informal settlements; the concentration of public services, equipment, facilities, and opportunities; and growing taxation and limited access to public services. For the last eight decades, Brazil has experienced an unparalleled increase in urban risk and spoliation, with an enormous socioenvironmental impact.

Cities in Brazil are the sociospatial expression of an exclusionary and perverse sociopolitical pact: as stressed earlier, a gigantic housing deficit coexists with an equally gigantic stock of vacant built properties and serviced urban land, as well as tens of thousands of informal settlements. Going to work for most people requires long, precarious, and expensive commutes. Interestingly, "better housing" as such has not been a significant claim of the demonstrators: in some specific cases, people have opposed the eviction of favela dwellers. Residents in favelas have made it clear that they want sanitation, not cable cars; but few people seem to have directly questioned the official housing policy and the process of informal development.

It has also become increasingly clear to all that the underlying question determining the growing social unrest concerned the increasing financialization of land, property, and rental markets, and corresponding commodification of Brazilian cities. As mentioned, if they were originally the *place of* and provided *support to* the urban-industrial economic development model, they are currently both the *place* and the *object* of the postindustrial model (i.e. a globalizing and highly speculative development model). Indeed, new, still largely ignored, powerful stakeholders working at the global level – developers and promoters, banks, pension funds, hedge funds – have increased their presence, thus leading to land and real estate speculation.

Has this exclusionary urban development pattern resulted from the lack of urban planning, as many have argued? The answer is no. Brazil's urbanization has largely been a state-led process. What is at stake is the kind and nature of traditional urban planning (theory, education, and, above all, practice), which has long been viewed merely as a "technique of territorial organization", as well as being "neutral" and "objective" socially and politically. The fragmented approach has dissociated urban policy from land policy and housing policy, as well as from transportation, environmental, fiscal, and budgetary policies. What's more, urban planners and managers have no understanding of the exclusionary and speculative dynamics of the property markets they create, seeing themselves as poor hostages of such aggressive markets.

As a result, this elitist planning tradition has led to informality. Moreover, there is no attempt to share with the community some of the gigantic surplus value resulting from state action (through public works, services, and urban laws), and when there is, as is the case of Sao Paulo, it reinforces sociospatial segregation, as most of the newly gained resources are invested in the same areas in which there is already a higher concentration of services and equipment. Mistaking effects for causes, well-intended governmental actions have generated ill effects: as described, the massive social program implemented by the federal government has already built over 2 million houses in precarious peripheries; costly, but isolated, regularization programs have led to higher land, property, and rental prices and thus to displacement.

Urban planning has also long been dissociated from urban management. Lengthy, bureaucratic procedures and the lack of intergovernmental articulation, as well as of transparency and accountability, have significantly contributed to the urban crisis. This was the case especially at the local level, given the widespread lack of municipal capacity to implement more complex proposals. Although nominally recognized and even required by the legal-urban order in force, popular participation has not taken place in all stages of decision making, and it has often been manipulated, reinforcing the long-standing tradition of political patronage.

The street demonstrations also told an important cautionary tale: legal reform is not sufficient. For all the country's undeniable progress towards confronting poverty and inequality, there still is an enormous amount of work to be done to redress several forms of historical injustices, to provide better public services, and to promote effective inclusive socioeconomic and urban policies. This requires an articulated set of public policies, ranging from the creation of a truly redistributive tax system – in a country dominated by regressive and indirect taxation – to more incisive land policies.

Brazil's legal-urban order has undeniably significantly changed, but urban managers have not assimilated the new principles, and civil society has not awakened to the new legal realities. Playing the game according to the new rules is fundamental for the collective construction of sustainable and fairer cities for the present and future generations.

It is in this context that the street protests have increasingly led to the revival of the urban reform movement, which was very influential in the 1980s and 1990s but then lost momentum. There was a concerted attempt to articulate all the specific claims defended by the demonstrators under the umbrella of the "Right to the City". Achieving this goal would require new political strategies way beyond representative democracy, involving direct participation, but also recognizing the scope for confrontation, occupation, and radical action. Independent media and community planning strategies, with support from committed academics, have had a growing influence in this search for original collective emancipation processes.

The future of the City Statute urgently requires a thorough renewal of the sociopolitical mobilization around land, urban, housing, and environmental matters so as to advance urban reform nationally. It is everyone's task to defend the City Statute from the proposed (essentially negative) changes being discussed at the National Congress and to fight for its full implementation. If decades of sociopolitical disputes were necessary for the enactment of the City Statute, a new historical stage has been opened, namely, that of the sociopolitical disputes for its full implementation. Let us hope that the resolution of the ongoing politico-institutional crisis and, beyond, a renewed social mobilization process, fully embraces the urban reform agenda in Brazil so as to affirm, and enforce, the collective right to sustainable and inclusive cities.

Conclusions

The post–Habitat II period has been marked by many ups and downs in Brazil, advances and backlashes, euphoria and depression, but the current mood is one of uncertainty. Although there has certainly been greater public intervention in urban areas at both the federal and the municipal levels, especially through a number of laws, programs, and plans, the fact is that the lack of a consistent, articulated urban policy framework has undermined much of the efforts, often reinforcing patterns of waste, inefficiency, exclusion, and segregation rather than promoting productivity, sustainability, and inclusion. Long-existing structural problems, obstacles, and bottlenecks have not been removed, thus determining the limited, elitist nature of urban governance, and long-standing tensions and disputes have gradually come to the fore.

Given the evolving and spiraling political and economic crises, much of what had been achieved – especially through poverty reduction policies – has turned out to be fragile. Shortly before President Dilma Rousseff was suspended by the National Congress, the Brazilian delegation expressed the country's commitment to promoting urban reform and defended the inclusion by the UN of the "right to the city" in the zero draft of the New Urban Agenda. However, given the nature of the policies already proposed by the interim president – favoring privatization, deregulation, PPP, and a drastic reduction of social programs – it was difficult to see this commitment ever becoming a reality.

If during the 1996–2016 period Brazil struggled to support the directives of the Habitat II agenda, the risk is that, far from embracing a "New Urban Agenda" approved in 2016, the new political direction in the country might lead towards the rejection of the 1996 agenda. Ultimately, the future of cities – social justice or big business, collective creations of commodities – will depend on the Brazilian people's capacity to redefine and expand sociopolitical mobilization so as to influence the decision-making processes at all governmental levels.

The right to the city is still to be conquered.

Note

1 This chapter was written prior to the 2018 presidential elections in Brazil. (Note from the editors.)

Bibliography

Castells, M., (1977), *The Urban Question: A Marxist Approach*, A. Sheridan (trans.), Edward Arnold, London.

Cymbalista, R. and Santoro, P. F. (eds.), (2009), *Planos Diretores – Processos e Aprendizados*, Instituto Polis, Sao Paulo.

Lefebvre, H., (1968), *Le Droit à la Ville*, du Seuil (ed.), Collection Points, Paris.

Montandon, J. S. A. O., and Montandon, D. T. (eds.), (2011), *Os Planos Diretores Municipais Pos-Estatuto da Cidade: balanco critico e perspectivas*, Observatório das Metrópoles – Letra Capital, Rio de Janeiro.

Schult, S. I., Silbert, C., and Souza, L. A. (eds.), (2010), "Experiências em planejamento e gestão urbana: Planos Diretores Participativos e Regularização Fundiária", *Conference Proceedings, Seminário de Avaliação das experiências em planos diretores participativos e de regularização fundiária*, Edifurb, Blumenau, Santa Catarina.

6 Colombia

The singularity of housing policy in urban development

Jorge Enrique Torres Ramírez

Introduction

Colombia's urban policy is characterized by the salience of housing policy, which in turn is characterized by its emphasis on the construction of new social housing. This focus leaves many other important topics relatively out of range, making it more difficult for the national government to guide urban development in the way specified in the Habitat II agenda.

Colombia's current population is 48.7 million inhabitants, most of whom live in the central Andean region. Seventy-six percent of the population dwells in "municipal seats" (*cabeceras municipales*), which are urban areas including those adjacent and beyond the administrative boundaries of the municipalities. Colombia has five main cities with a population of more than 1 million inhabitants and 62 cities with more than 100,000 inhabitants. The capital, Bogotá, concentrates 16 percent of the total population. The process of urbanization in Colombia has been influenced by forced displacement of the population from rural areas to the cities due to an internal armed conflict that persisted for more than 50 years.

Colombia's gross domestic product (GDP) per capita was US$7,903.9 at current prices in 2014. Also in 2014, monetary poverty (defined as those receiving less than US$105.05 per month) was 24.1 percent and the Gini coefficient was 0.514, one of the highest in the region. Bogotá generates 25 percent of the national GDP and, together with the other three main cities, accounts for 80 percent of Colombia's GDP. However, the Colombian system of cities is fragmented due to the poor development of the intermodal transport infrastructure, causing economic isolation among the main urban centers and agglomerations.

The pledge made by the government of Colombia in 1996 at the Habitat II World Conference in Istanbul covers a diverse and complex set of issues. Indeed, the Habitat agenda that was approved has more to do with the rights of citizens than with human needs. In this sense, the fulfillment of the commitments assumed by the government in 1996 must be understood as the steps taken in pursuit of the effective enjoyment of the collective and individual rights inherent to the attributes of Habitat. This understanding is also in line with the exercise of the rights enshrined in the Political Constitution of Colombia of 1991, in particular, those that have to do with decent housing, freedom of mobility, public space, and the right to a healthy environment, among others. Moreover, in Colombia the principle of adequate housing is part of constitutional law by virtue of the Colombian government's subscription to General Observation No. 4, a concept that the Constitutional Court has taken as a reference for rulings related to the enforcement of the right to decent housing.

Assessing the progress towards the Habitat II agenda goes beyond the mere examination of the quantitative outputs of the sectoral policy by the different governments since 1996. Instead, it is a matter of verifying the degree of development of the rights of the citizens in relation to Habitat. Throughout this chapter, the analysis will focus on the actual results rather than on the institutional and legislative arrangements implemented in the country to meet the commitments established. In doing this, it is particularly interesting to observe how public expenditures were actually oriented in the sector, as they are a testimony of the effective realization of urban and housing policy *mandates*.

Hence, this chapter presents a qualitative assessment of the fulfillment of the commitments undertaken by the government of Colombia in the Habitat II conference. To this end, the text has been divided into four parts. The first corresponds to this introduction. The second provides a synthetic vision of population distribution, urban primacy, and the system of cities in Colombia. The third section has six subsections, which were agreed between the authors of this volume. The first subsection addresses the evolution of urban policy in Colombia since 1996: its objectives, components, outputs, and impact on other national policies. This part also considers aspects of urban governance, like institutional changes, decentralization processes, and other procedures. The second subsection deals with issues of urban management and sustainability; it delves into the actions taken by national and local governments to improve urban resilience. This part touches upon the urban use of natural resources and the existence of public debates on urban sustainability. The third subsection refers to housing and urban infrastructure. It begins with an overview of the evolution of housing conditions since 1996: the barriers to affordable housing, mortgage credit, precarious settlements, accessibility to urban land, changes in housing policies, access to urban infrastructure, and the marginal cost of water.

Urban economy and productivity are the topics of the fourth subsection, with includes aspects of urban employment behavior, urban wages, informal employment and production, labor productivity and commuting times, and urban share in national terms. This fourth part also examines urban poverty, intraurban inequality, and social exclusion. This part studies social exclusion, urban poverty trends, and characteristics and trajectories of intraurban inequality since 1996. The final subsection of the third part of this chapter refers to urban form. It deals with spatial urban configurations, density of cities, and metropolitanization. It also examines the decentralization of economic activities and changes in the spatial distribution of the urban population in large, medium, and small cities.

The fourth and final section of this chapter is devoted to identifying Habitat II's outstanding tasks. Hence, it details a set of recommendations that the author has considered appropriate.

Population and urbanization

The process of urbanization in Colombia has been fast paced. In addition to the natural growth of the population, urbanization has been influenced by significant migration flows of a diverse nature: labor, forced displacement, demand for goods and services, and others. As in most countries of the region, the population is concentrated in urban centers, a visible trend ever since the 1960s and consolidated in the 1980s. According to figures from official population censuses and housing surveys in 2005 (the last available measurement), about three-quarters of the population reside in areas known as the "municipal seat",[1] which for the purposes of this publication will be referred to as "urban". Table 6.1 presents an evolution of the total national population, as well as by urban and rural areas for the period 1938–2005. Covering a total of seven censuses, this information shows a reversal in the urban-rural proportion of the population over a period of 67 years.

In terms of the spatial distribution of the population in the context of the urbanization phenomenon, factors such as the location of economic activities, as well as the housing supply and the provision of basic services (health, education, etc.), led to a process of densification of the main urban centers. This densification has occurred both in the formal city (where the compact city model has been adopted) and in residential areas of informal origins. In recent years the informal production modality has shifted from being predominantly produced via new urban expansions to re-densification.

Furthermore, in light of the Urban Primacy Index, the case of Colombia is special among the countries of Latin America due to the existence of a set of predominant cities (see Table 6.2). The biggest city, Bogota (the capital city), has the size of the three following cities: Medellín, Cali, and Barranquilla. All

Table 6.1 Evolution of the total national population by urban and rural areas, 1938–2005

Census	Census Population			% Urban	% Rural
	Total	Urban	Rural		
1938	8,701,816	2,533,680	6,168,136	2.91E+01	7.09E+01
1951	11,228,509	4,441,386	6,787,123	3.96E+01	6.04E+01
1964	17,484,508	9,093,088	8,391,420	5.20E+01	4.80E+01
1973	20,666,920	12,637,750	8,029,170	6.11E+01	3.89E+01
1985	27,867,326	18,710,087	9,157,239	6.71E+01	3.29E+01
1993	33,109,840	23,514,070	9,595,770	7.10E+01	2.90E+01
2005	41,489,253	30,846,231	10,643,022	7.43E+01	2.57E+01

Source: National Administrative Department of Statistics, DANE. Revista IB Virtual Vol. 2 No. 2 (http://bit.ly/2dchCVH).

Table 6.2 Population statistics, 1973–2015 (thousands of inhabitants)

Feature	Year			
	1973	*1993*	*2005*	*2015**
Total population	22,862	37,662	42,888	48,203
Population in municipal head	13,548	25,856	31,886	36,847
% total	60%	69%	74%	76%
4 main cities	5,600	10,099	12,099	13,931
Cities with more than 100,000 inhabitants	8,920	17,421	21,512	29,143
No. of cities with more than 1 million hab.	2.00	4.00	4.00	5.00
No. of cities with more than 100,000 hab.	18.00	33.00	38.00	62.00

* DANE 2015 projections

Source: National Administrative Department of Statistics, DANE.

of these four cities have their own economic and demographic dynamics, a characteristic that has been referred to as urban four-headedness (Universidad Externado, 2007).

It is important to note that the current distribution of the Colombian population has not been the result of processes of economic or land-use planning nor population policy. The population dynamics of the urban areas respond to the existence of a large landownership structure, precarious socioeconomic conditions, and, in a prominent way, two periods of armed conflict generating violence against the civilian population. The first period between the years 1948 and 1964 initially had a political-partisan character but it later degenerated into banditry. The second period, from 1962 to the present,[2] was the result of disputes between several guerrilla groups, paramilitaries, drug traffickers, and state actors. One of the most prominent consequences of the armed conflict in Colombia has been the forced displacement to cities (see Figure 6.1). These figures are so pronounced that the current official records of the Unit for Attention and Integral Reparation to Victims (UARIV) state that it is 7,121,912 people as of February 2016, that is, a total of 1,960,034 households. It is worth mentioning that official statistics reveal an exacerbation of this problem from the 1990s, with a peak in the period 1998–2002.

These two antecedents confirm that contemporary Colombian cities are the result of the post-conflict during the years 1950–1960 and also of the current confrontation, which has taken the form of social production of habitat.[3] This form of urban production, together with the migration triggered by factors associated with poverty and low income, has been a key determinant in the formation of the housing stock in Colombia. It is estimated that the social production of habitat contributes to two-thirds of the national housing stock (CENAC, 1993), producing and reproducing precarious settlements. Despite the important number of units currently being affected through programs

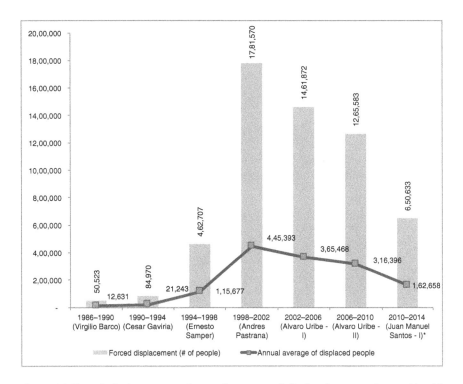

Figure 6.1 Forced displacement and annual average of displaced persons by presidential period (1986–2014)

Source: CODHES. Forced displacement and the imperative need for peace. Displacement Report 2013 (http://bit.ly/2cOLwhb).

seeking to improve the conditions of houses already built, less than 16 percent of the total resources allocated to housing subsidies are allocated to upgrading programs, as will be discussed later. This means that public expenditures on family housing subsidies are mainly concentrated in the acquisition of new housing.

Notwithstanding the relatively low geographical dispersion of the urban system in Colombia, the economic isolation between the main cities and the urban centralities in the periphery is persistent due to the low development of an intermodal transport infrastructure. Relatedly, the legislation that allows supra-municipal association schemes has not been implemented. Ultimately, failure to invest public resources in improving the housing conditions of built areas is playing against reaping the benefits of agglomerations. Although other important factors are at stake, this underinvestment inhibits the advantages of urban agglomerations, and hence, urban areas cannot serve as a tool for closing regional gaps in equity and poverty.

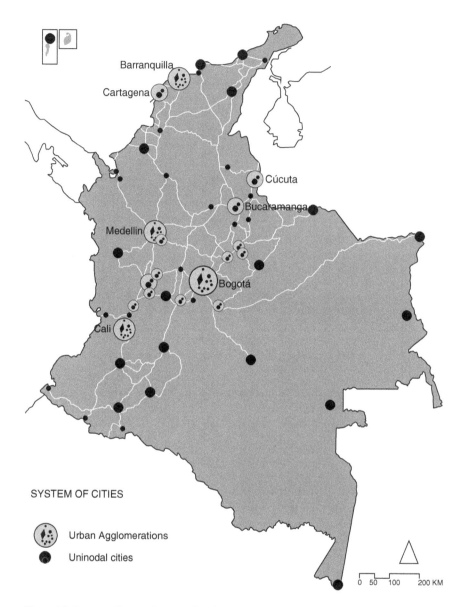

Figure 6.2 System of cities: functional and mononodal cities

Source: CONPES (2014). Available at: http://bit.ly/2dHpuyk.

In facing this situation, Colombia defined its system of cities[4] favoring the notion of commuting times as a way to establish relationships between different urban centers. The Colombian system of cities is composed of a set of 56 cities, 18 of which fall under the category "functional areas" (group of settlements usually concentrated around a main city or nucleus that have functional relations in terms of economic activities and of supply and demand for goods or services) and 38 called mononodal (urban centers whose functional area remains within the political boundary of an administrative municipality). In this way, the system of cities in Colombia gathers 65 percent of the total population of the country and about 80 percent of the urban population. Figure 6.2 shows the set of cities defined as a system for the case of Colombia.

These conceptual developments and the government programs associated with the system of cities have helped make visible again the relevance of urban and regional issues in Colombia. They render evident that sectoral policy has an excessively narrow vision focused exclusively in the production of social housing.

National urban policy and urban governance

The commitments of Habitat II

The Habitat agenda arising from the Habitat II conference held in Istanbul in 1996 states that the sustainable development of human settlements, particularly those undergoing processes of accelerated urbanization, will increasingly depend on the capabilities of all levels of administration (UN-Habitat, 1996).

In fact, one of the strategies established in the global plan of action is precisely "capacity building and institutional development". This implies, inter alia, the adoption of policies and legal frameworks that support decentralization and strengthen the capacities of local authorities, their associations, and networks; promote planning, development, and management strategies for entire metropolitan areas or their regions; create legislative frameworks and adopt organizational structures to ensure adequate provision of services; expand financial mechanisms to support economic development; mobilize public, private, bilateral, and multilateral resources to monitor expenditures and efficiently manage budgets; and put in place institutional and legal frameworks to facilitate broad participation of all citizens in decision making and in the implementation and monitoring of policies and programs, which should be governed by the principles of accountability and transparency.

Colombia's urban policy since 1996

Colombia has not had a national or long-term urban policy. In each presidential period, the National Congress approves the national economic and social development plan that is prepared by the incoming government and must include some degree of participation. This plan includes sectoral policy, which encompasses housing policy. Despite the fact that the value chain of this public policy is much more encompassing, urban policy ends up being reduced to the allocation and execution of public expenses related to housing, potable water, and sanitation. This is the way historically that the national policy on the urban sector in Colombia has been managed, and it has determined the limited incidence of urban planning on the growth of cities. In turn, the gaps in urban planning have been filled by other forms of urbanization that are neither legal nor optimal, giving rise to the formation of dual cities, where high standards in the built environment coexist with marginality, poverty, and inequality.

The attention of the public sector in the urban area has been wavering, but the balance of the last 20 years indicates a predominance of a vision that considers the urban as part of the building construction sector, especially housing, whose potential to influence employment and economic growth is well recognized.

Six urban policies have been implemented since 1994. In that year, and prior to Habitat II, the urban policy "Cities and Citizenship" was issued (administrative period 1994–1998), which asserted an integrated urban vision and positioned housing as one of the attributes of the city. It was intended that this urban policy would

> be the navigation chart for Colombian cities to serve the great social goals, and in turn, that national policies, when deployed in the urban space, help construct cities that are more competitive, governable, fair, environmentally sustainable, and with higher levels of collective identity.
>
> (Ministry of Economic Development, 1995)

A notable fact of this period was the issuance of Law 388 of 1997, the Land-Use Planning Law, which endowed urban managers with urban management tools; in particular, it mandated public management of urban land through mandatory land-use plans (POT). Curiously, Law 388 makes it possible for the state to intervene in Colombian cities, six years after the housing policy shifted from a model of direct provision to a market-based one and focused on direct subsidies in response to demand.

During the following period, 1998–2002, there were no major changes in the direction of urban policy. The sector's attention was mainly focused on the economic crisis of 1999, recognizing the problem of forced displacement, and paying attention to the housing needs of this population.[5] From 2002 to 2010, the two administrative periods of President Álvaro Uribe, CONPES[6] 3305 of 2004, titled "Guidelines for Optimizing Urban Development Policy", was issued. This document submitted to the council "a set of actions aimed at optimizing the urban development policy of the National Government", including a "proposal and strategies to improve the management of urban development in Colombia". The predominant policy in this period was the strategy of "Friendly Cities", which although focused on poverty, employment, and equity, in the end it almost exclusively focused on housing programs, implementing the strategy "Colombia, a Home-Owners' Country". In addition, there were attempts to formulate urban policies able to transcend presidential terms, like CONPES 3604 of 2009 for Comprehensive Neighborhood Upgrading (MIB) and CONPES 3658 of 2010 for Renewal of Historic

Centers. Notably, CONPES 3583 of 2009 for Macro-projects of National Social Interest (MISN) was also issued in this period, but because it enabled the nation to surpass municipal autonomy, it was declared unconstitutional.

In 2011 the program "Housing and Friendly Cities" was implemented. Then, in 2011, Law 1444 was issued, giving rise, in its fourth article, to the Ministry of Housing, City, and Territory (MVCT). With the creation of this ministry, the construction of social housing was scaled up as part of a national strategy to mobilize strategic sectors called "growth locomotives". Housing was among the small set of sectors that were identified as being able to speed up rest of the economy and have a direct and indirect impact in economic growth and job creation. In 2011 a much-awaited law was issued, Law 1454 Organic Law on Territorial Planning (LOOT). A pending task from the 1991 political constitution, this law has had minor developments and applications, especially with regard to the expectations of it being able to facilitate processes of intermunicipal association. In 2012, CONPES 3718 was approved, establishing the national policy for public space. In this regard, Colombian cities have a significant backlog compared to the optimal international indicator established by the World Health Organization of 10 to 15 m^2 per inhabitant. It was estimated that in 2010, Colombia had an average of 3.3 m^2 of public space per capita. Hence, overcoming the quantitative deficit of public space is one of the most important challenges of Colombia's urban future (Document CONPES 3718, 2012).

Currently, the MVCT is working on the development of a national policy to consolidate the system of cities, framed in CONPES 3819 of 2014, and in the strategic document "Smart Territories 2035", which envisions the "implementation of a new agenda of planned territorial and urban development, with a special focus on the regional axes of the Colombian system of cities" (MVCT, 2015). Also, in close relation with urban policy, a CONPES document on climate change was approved in 2011.

In conclusion, it is important to state that urban policy in Colombia has not evolved as a result of an intense process of citizen participation, although this is legally stipulated as part of the discussion and approval process of the national development plans. What is really at stake here is a procedure of concertation among elites, of which the most outstanding are the economic guilds, professional associations, and institutional specialists. The academics are seldom consulted, and if they are, they do not participate much, and in general, their input has a low level of impact.

However, it is also important to mention that after Habitat II, urban policy has gained space in the formulation of the national development plan. Unfortunately, its implementation has been limited due to the lack of greater fiscal support, which focuses almost exclusively on housing. This mismatch between policy aims and implementation is reflected in the current conditions of the Colombian cities, which are discussed later. Table 6.3 shows the most important aspects and policy instruments during each presidential period.

Table 6.3 National urban policies under different presidential governments

Period	President	Urban policy designation	Outstanding elements and policy instruments
1994 1998	Ernesto Samper Pizano	Urban Policy, Cities and Citizenship	Law 388 of 1997 (Land-Use Planning Law)
1998 2002	Andrés Pastrana Arango	Change for the Peace Building	Declaration of the state of economic emergency to deal with the earthquake in the coffee axis and the crisis of the UPAC system. Law 546 of 1999, a housing law that establishes the new financing system for housing, giving rise to the real value unit (UVR).
2002 2006	Álvaro Uribe Vélez	Towards a Country of Home-Owners	CONPES 3305 of 2004: Guidelines for optimizing an urban development policy
2006 2010	Álvaro Uribe Vélez	Friendly cities	CONPES 3604 of 2009: Comprehensive Neighborhoods Upgrading; CONPES 3583 of 2009: Macro-projects of National Social Interest (declared unconstitutional); CONPES 3658 de 2010: Historic Centers
2010 2014	Juan Manuel Santos	Friendly Housing and Cities	Law 1444 of 2011-Article 4, with which the Ministry of Housing, City, and Territory is created; Law 1454 of 2011: Organic Law of Territorial Planning, LOOT; CONPES 3700 of 2011: Institutional strategy for the articulation of policies and actions on climate change in Colombia; CONPES 3718 of 2012: National policy of public space
2014 2018	Juan Manuel Santos	Smart Territories 2035	CONPES 3819 of 2014: System of cities

Source: Author.

A prominent historic outlier in the evolution of urban policy in Colombia is the sectoral policy "Cities Within the City" formulated by Professor Lauchlin Currie,[7] which was in place in the period 1974–1978. This was a special period in which urban policy in Colombia was integrally articulated with the strategy for long-term economic growth.

Impact of urban policy on national development policies and resource allocation

In Colombia, the relationship between urban policy and development policies is inverse. That is, the main objective of the national economic and social development plan is economic growth, and the different sectors must contribute to the increase of the GDP. In this context and in terms of urban policy, the emphasis has been placed on the construction of social housing, which has become the sole focus of housing policy. Cities and housing are understood as important contributors to the GDP of the construction sector and hence to total GDP via its multisectoral effects. Consequently, public expenditures in housing production are seen as an instrument for employment generation, having countercyclical effects during times of economic recession.

That is to say, the inclusion of urban and housing policy in the national development plan does not come from the recognition of the urban as a relevant sector in and of itself, but rather, it is assigned a set of national economic and social objectives and targets it must carry out. The allocation of public spending resources to the sector is consistent with this vision. In sum, the development plan does not contain sectoral proposals, but rather it is only concerned with aligning and defining its direction.

But urban policy ought to be broader, as was documented in the previous section. Despite this, during the period 2010–2014, the proportion of public expenditures allocated to social housing construction has increased significantly. What is happening is that the conception, formulation, and program development of urban policy increasingly has an integrated overall vision, but its implementation is singularly focused on housing. This is clearly illustrated by the fact that 84 percent of the ministry's funds for housing subsidies are allocated for new housing (IDB, 2011).

It should be noted that in relation to the production of housing, both social housing and for higher-price segments, significant expenditures have been made in expanding the networks of basic public services for drinking water, sanitation, and electricity, as well as equipment, mainly in health and education.

Evidence and indicators of impact and outcome of these policies

Although urban planning in Colombia has a longer trajectory, land-use planning has a 19-year history, based on Law 388 of 1997. An important feature of this process is the adoption of such plans in 99 percent of Colombian municipalities (Herrera, 2014), starting in the year 2000. Despite the fact that they exist, their level of effective application, their quality, and relevance are debatable. According to the National Planning Department (DNP), to date, there are three groups of problems identified in the land-use plans (Gaviria, 2016):

Technical, methodological, and data flaws in the formulation

- Sixty percent of the municipalities inadequately define their urban perimeter in land-use planning schemes (EOT) (municipalities with fewer than 30,000 inhabitants).
- Fifty percent of the municipalities determined to expand land without clear criteria or adequate information.
- Sixty-one percent of the municipalities established protection areas incorrectly.
- Twenty-one percent of the plans lack geo-referencing.
- Sixty percent of the plans do not consider agricultural, livestock, and forestry uses.

Outdated plans:

- By the end of 2015, 83 percent of all municipalities (916) had expired and were not updated.
- No municipality includes regional determinants in its plan.
- In all cases, the land-use planning did not go beyond its political- administrative boundaries.

Little prominence of the land-use development plans as a development tools:

- Low application of land-use development instruments (recovering capital gains, valorization, project announcement). The resources derived from capital gains were only 0.02 percent of what could be charged and 0.13 percent in the case of valorization.
- Only 12 percent of municipalities capture land value through capital gains charges or valorization.
- Only 3 percent include strategies and programs to develop the rural component.
- In 2014, valorization ranked 16th and capital gains charges 28th in terms of income contributions to municipal budgets.

With regard to the implementation of urban policy in Colombia, there are currently no impact indicators to assess the programs implemented by the MVCT, because the ministry is not directly responsible for the policy's implementation, but rather it concentrates exclusively on institutional support to local administrations in issues such as public management of urban land, risk management, land-use planning, housing macro-projects, neighborhood upgrading, public space, property titling, and urban renewal. The ministry is responsible for the development of regulations on land management, but its application is the responsibility of municipalities.

An evaluation of the results of the MVCT (CENAC 2012, 2013) program for the integral neighborhood upgrading (MIB) reported that the objectives set for the physical component of the projects were met. The program indeed provided greater coverage of public services, access to formal transport due to the partial paving of roads, treatment of geological risk, new public space, basic social services, and so on. In addition, the evaluation documented other results derived from community involvement in project management, such as improvements in community life, community participation, and a higher recognition of their local organizations. At an economic level, it is noteworthy that after the program, households invested in their own homes, which rose real estate values an average of 41.2 percent, rendering as well greater real estate liquidity, expressed in an increase in the demand for rent in these areas. The coverage of this program comprised eight settlements with a total population of 2,824 households.

The MIB program, however, has not had a stable allocation of national resources to scale up its coverage and ensure its sustainability and institutional quality in the long term. The reason for this has already been discussed and is related to the almost exclusive focus of housing policy on the new social housing construction program.

There are other results of urban policy corresponding to programs that have a low public cost but about which available information is scarce. The urban attribute in which important investments have focused in the last years is urban mobility, given the backlog of road infrastructure in the main cities of Colombia.

Urban governance in Colombia since 1996

Key normative developments have taken place since 1996. Urban governance in Colombia advanced considerably with the enactment of Law 388 of 1997, the Land-Use Development Law, which mandates the participation of civil society organizations and citizens in the processes of territorial development and urban planning. The most prominent and effective participation instrument is the POT, which must go through a process of consultation and participation at the level of municipalities and districts, based on a proposal presented by the local authority. This process also involves the environmental authority, the Land-Use Planning Council,[8] and culminates with approval by the Municipal Council.

It is important to mention that this law has as its antecedent Law 9 of 1989, the Law of Urban Reform. After the introduction of the new Political Constitution of Colombia was issued in 1991, it became urgent to update this urban law. However, as was mentioned before, those who participate more actively in the discussion of the POTs are the private guilds of urban construction, professional associations, public officials, and to a lesser extent, academia. Notably, these laws recognize community housing organizations as providers of social housing programs, social housing (VIS), and housing of priority interest (VIP).

Another front related to urban governance is Law 1454 of 2011, Organic Law on Territorial Planning (LOOT), which also establishes responsibilities for departments (similar to states in the United States) for territorial planning. It also regulates supra-municipal and regional association processes, the direct participation of citizens and nongovernmental actors to ensure the legitimacy of these association schemes, association around strategic projects, and so on. This law has been only barely applied. It should also be considered that since 1996, administrative decentralization advanced in urban development and land-use planning. Whereas Law 388 completely delegated the municipalities all powers in the field of territorial planning, the LOOT enabled the nation and the departments to so articulate multilevel competencies, helping mediate some conflicts that were being generated between the municipalities and higher-level territorial units.

Institutional changes that have affected urban planning and policy

Since 1996 in Colombia there have been institutional, decentralization, and procedural changes that have affected policy and urban planning. The issuance of a set of detailed urban regulations strengthened the sector, as there was a previous situation of normative dispersion. In terms of urban licensing, Colombia implemented the urban "curatorship" system, which is recognized as a good practice internationally. According to the Law 388 of 1997, the urban curator is an individual in charge of studying, processing, and issuing licenses for parceling, urbanizing, construction, or demolition, and for the subdivision of buildings, at the request of the interested party to advance subdivision, urbanization, building, demolition, or subdivision projects, in the areas or areas of the municipality or district that the municipal or district administration has determined as its jurisdiction. Urban curators exercise a public function of verifying compliance of a proposed building or urbanization with the urban and building regulations in force in the district or municipality, and it grants urbanization and construction licenses.

The urban curators were created by Law 388 of 1997 in response to the fact that municipal planning offices were not able to study and approve on time the requests for construction licenses. This led to corrupt practices, as charges were imposed to expedite certain procedures, and in turn, this opened possibilities of negotiating the urban norms. Private professional associations often pointed to this inefficiency as the cause of hidden costs and delays in initiating projects. The objective of creating urban curators was geared towards curbing corruption in urban planning, reducing transaction costs, and, importantly, freeing municipal or district planning offices from the burden involved with the urban licensing process, letting them focus instead on land-use planning.

Optimization of construction procedures has been a major concern in the larger cities of Latin America, and it has prompted the establishment of a "single window" instance to expedite the urban permits. In the case of Colombia, the curators have contributed to streamlining these procedures, but controlling compliance to the norms during and after construction is still an unresolved issue without a watchdog. This situation spurred a heated debate recently due to the collapse of a residential building in Medellín. After this incident, a series of community complaints led to the identification of several housing projects with high structural vulnerability in Bogotá and especially in Medellín.

The urban curators in Colombia have responded to a need of the formal construction sector. However, even though it is within its functions to issue "recognition acts" for the construction of socially produced housing, their track record in this arena is not optimal. In addition, the costs of these permits, and even the physical location of the curator's offices within the city, deter those producing housing outside of the formal circuits from getting the formal paperwork. These reasons and other considerations have given rise to discussions about the need for "social curators" who would deal with the procedures derived from the social production of housing.

New forms of citizen participation

The new forms of citizen participation are operating both prior to and after Habitat II with notable influence in the processes of territorial development and urban planning. Most importantly, there has been an emergent dynamism of new political actors at the local urban level: ethnic, cultural, and LGBT organizations, as well as more women empowerment. The "prior consultation"[9] predicament has helped give voice to Afro descendants, indigenous, and gypsy communities in the development of projects that affect their territorial and cultural environment. Notwithstanding, there is no evidence of a significant effect of urban governance on people's lives, considering that there have been no changes in the main problems affecting citizens, such as insecurity, inequality, and spatial segregation. Although there have been changes in poverty reduction, these are mainly due to macroeconomic performance and health and education programs targeting the population, and there are significant concerns about their quality (Escallón, 2014).

Future trends in urban governance

Given the exacerbation of problems in terms of mobility, the poor quality of urban life, the effects of climate change, and the persistence of inequality and social exclusion, it is relevant to foresee deepening of nongovernmental actors participating in all processes related to the development of urban public policies. On the other hand, because the association between municipalities (and other territorial entities) has been legally enabled, we can expect to see more strategic supra-municipal projects in the future. There is also a definite trend towards the promotion of alternative development models at the local, regional, and national levels.

However, the expansion of participation to incorporate new types of actors and organizations that represent the diversity of civil society tends to maintain a relatively low impact on urban governance, considering that there is no equality of power (or capacity to apply pressure, or capabilities to archive results) between them. That is to say, the lobbying capacity of private professional associations will continue to prevail in urban policy decisions, as long as are no effective conditions for participation and a more democratic composition of legislative bodies and entities of the executive level.

In closing this first topic of the assessment on national urban policy and urban governance in relation to the fulfillment of Habitat III commitments, it is crucial to state that in Colombia this sectoral policy has been subordinated to the economic guidelines of the national development plan. At the territorial level, there continues to be two factors that fuel each other: the lack of coordination between local authorities and the impossibility of constructing regional agreements for the formation of associations between municipalities and departments, which has limited the viability of metropolitan projects where they are needed. In addition to this, there is the fiscal fragility of municipalities due to the low generation of their own resources, which has deepened regional gaps. On the other hand, the supposed integrality of urban policy has been reduced in practice by the effective allocation of public expenditure resources. In fact, housing policy has co-opted urban policy, and housing construction, in turn, has captured housing policy. All of this occurs within a framework of restricted participation that engages only a few urban agents, while citizens end up with low incidence on the formulation and implementation of urban policy.

Sustainability and environmental management

In the Istanbul Declaration, governments committed themselves to "adopting sustainable modes of production, consumption, transport and settlement development; to prevent pollution, to respect the carrying capacity of ecosystems and to ensure that the opportunities of future generations are preserved". They recognize the need to adopt these measures "in a manner consistent with the precautionary approach, which will be applied widely according to the capacities of the countries". They also establish a commitment to promote and

> recognize that we must take these actions in a manner consistent with the precautionary principle approach, which shall be widely applied according to the capabilities of countries. We shall also promote healthy living environments, especially through the provision of adequate quantities of safe water and effective management of waste.
>
> (UN-Habitat, 1996)

Sustainability and environmental management in Colombian urban areas

Urban areas in Colombia have presented an ambiguous balance in terms of sustainability and environmental management during the last 20 years. Although progress has been made in consolidating an institutional framework and the corresponding legislative development, it cannot be said that this effort has been translated into effective improvement in this field. The reason for this assertion has to do with the lack of development regulations at the local level and the low investment in upgrading programs for precarious settlements. Social production of housing is particularly vulnerable to climate change and is an important contributor to emissions. Currently, these types of interventions are currently directed and financed by the national government, but they require further local intervention and the development of regional norms.

Settlements resulting from the processes of social urbanization and housing production are generally of low density, which is due to the fact that, from the urban point of view, the plot dimensions are small[10] and constructed as single-family dwellings. However, despite the low housing densities per hectare, there are high proportions of population overcrowding, due to the presence of several households in each dwelling, in turn due to poverty constraints or renting.

With regard to the construction process, Centro de Estudios de la Construcción y el Desarrollo Urbano y Regional (CENAC) found evidence to support that a socially produced dwelling uses twice as many building materials per square meter compared to another of formal origin in the price segment corresponding to social housing (ASOCRETO, 2012).

The greatest vulnerability to climate change of these settlements originates in their location in areas that are not suitable for construction, on high slopes and often in sectors of high geological risk. Vulnerability is exacerbated by the lack of water and sanitation networks and the consequent direct discharge of wastewater on the slopes, canyons, and aquifers. Likewise, these same places are dump sites for solid waste, which affects the absorption capacity and hydraulic circulation of the soil. These conditions contribute to the destabilization of the land, causing numerous landslides, which in Colombia have generated a large number of disasters in urban areas with loss of human lives.

The regularization and the integration into the consolidated city of those settlements that were socially produced, when feasible, imply extending public services and transportation networks. The economic precariousness of these households induces the use of secondhand or recycled kitchen and bathroom appliances, which have a higher level of emissions than the urban average. This situation led the Nationally Appropriate Mitigation Actions (NAMA) Habitat of Colombia to identify as a priority the MIB, aimed at addressing the precarious habitat conditions of these settlements.

Environmental management in Colombia has acquired significant weight since 1991 with the new Political Constitution. The new constitution mentions the right of citizens to enjoy a healthy environment, defines environmental responsibilities to the state and civil society, and promotes citizen participation. In 1993, there was an institutional breakthrough with the creation of the Ministry of Environment, which was a way to state that the institutional status of a sector ought to be consistent with the importance of the challenges with which it deals.

The most outstanding norms in environmental management also spring from Law 388 of 1997, the Law of Land-Use Development, which includes the concept of sustainability in land-use planning. This normative process continues with a set of CONPES: MIB, Public Space, the System of Cities, and Climate Change. Derived from this last one is the Colombian Low Carbon Development Strategy (ECDBC) which links five ministries: Energy, Transport, Agriculture, Housing, and Environment. Within this institutional framework, the DNP generates the National Plan for Adaptation to Climate Change, upon which each sector prepares its own Sectorial Adaptation Plan.

In the field of urban environment, at the national level, the MVCT is in charge of establishing the criteria for incorporating climate change into land-use planning. At the regional level, the public entities that lead this topic are the Regional Autonomous Corporations (CAR) and, at local level, the municipal administration. In all levels, and despite legislative developments, there are management deficiencies that are starker in medium and small cities, in part because of a lack of resources, but especially in the case of CARs, due to inefficiency, politicization, and corruption of these organizations. In fact, after several recent critical environmental situations generated by *La Niña* and then *El Niño* phenomena in 2016, a debate arose about eliminating or reforming these organizations.

Evidence of improved sustainability and environmental management

Evidence of improvements can be found mainly in the normative developments. However, as it is a recent institutional initiative, there are currently few ongoing projects. Environmental action plans have been devised, and in Bogotá and the metropolitan area of the Aburrá Valley (Medellín and nine neighboring municipalities), progress has been made with the formulation of sustainability and environmental management policies. What is really at stake is not the capacity of developing plans and regulations, but rather bringing them into effect. The challenge is to implement these regulations and go beyond the diagnostic phase (emissions, risk, urban footprint, etc.), which has taken a long time already. It cannot be said that funding is currently a constraint; instead, it seems that progress seems slow because this is a new policy.

Ultimately, the current situation of sustainability and environmental management in Colombian cities is contradictory, considering that important progress has been made in the creation of legislative structures and public institutions, but this has not evolved, with few exceptions, in the formulation of local policies, in the implementation of action plans, or in the development of strategic projects.

Urban resilience measures taken since 1996

The measures taken since 1996 that have contributed to strengthen urban resilience have taken the form in Colombia of what is known as risk management. In Colombia there are both adaptation and risk management programs, issues led by the MVCT and dealt with in an integrated manner. Nevertheless, although public management in this field is partially centralized, urban resilience initiatives happen mainly in larger cities and some intermediate ones, due to the availability of fiscal resources. In this sense, a major concern is the fiscal weakness of 86 percent of Colombian municipalities,[11] as it poses critical limitations on urban resilience actions.

The fact that such a high proportion of the municipalities in Colombia are fiscally unsound portrays acute regional disparities and large development gaps between the big cities and the countryside, with its small municipalities and rural economic activities. This situation has taken shape for decades, fueled by the centralism of planning, policies, and public spending. Outdated cadasters also contribute to this situation, as property tax rates have restrained the generation of municipal resources. Consequently, such a precarious fiscal scenario is a barrier to the development of urban resilience in much of the national territory, as it requires resources to implement its management.

Furthermore, this situation evidently affects the implementation of the New Urban Agenda set in Habitat III. That is to say the efforts of countries in achieving the urban development objectives over the next 20 years, bringing their citizens a better life and improved cities, is contingent on the fiscal reality of the municipalities.

Changes in urban use of natural resources

One of the most salient changes in the urban use of natural resources has been a significant reduction of water consumption, which has been the result of rationing in the early 1990s, educational campaigns, and high tariffs. Also notable is the extent of the switch in electric power of residential and industrial arenas into natural gas. Wind and solar energy projects have also been initiated. Starting in 2015, land-use planning norms set limits on the consumption of water and electricity in new buildings.

In terms of energy efficiency, Colombia's energy matrix is defined as clean because 70 percent of its power generation is hydraulic. However, this overdependence on hydro is problematic in light of the effects of the recent *El Niño* phenomenon, which makes the water supplies vulnerable. Already Colombia has seen its energy generation and coverage threatened to the point that it was necessary to ask for voluntary savings by consumers.

In terms of sustainable construction practices, the first national regulation for saving water and energy in buildings was announced in 2015 by Resolution 549 of the MVCT. In relation to this, it is estimated that about 5 million square meters have been licensed and constructed in more than 200 buildings that are qualified as Leadership in Energy and Environmental Design (LEED) projects.

An important conquest in the area of environmental justice is that a May 2016 ruling from the Constitutional Court repealed an article of the Mining Code that prevented territorial administrations (mayors and councils) from closing mining sites. From now on, municipalities can take actions through community consultations and reforms of the land-use plans.

A diagnosis of environmental sustainability in the system of cities in Colombia, carried out by the DNP in 2012 as part of the mission of the System of Cities (Costa, 2012), highlighted important issues related to the supply of natural resources and ecosystem services available for the sustainable growth of cities:

Hydrological resources:

- Water supply per capita in Colombia is five times higher than the world average. However, the resource is not evenly available across the national territory.
- Interregional differences in water supply availability in Colombia depend not only on environmental conditions but also on technical, institutional, and financial factors that have drastic effects on the living conditions of the population.

- Although Colombia has water surpluses in a large part of its territory, the areas with the highest demographic concentration and economic activity are in those with resource deficits.
- There is a direct relationship between the category in which municipalities are classified and the water quality of its aqueduct systems, with lower standards in smaller municipalities.
- Only major capital cities are able to guarantee a continuous water supply.
- Although important advances have been made in the country in the water infrastructure, the capacity of treatment plants is uneven.

Air quality:

- The pollutant of greatest concern in the country is the particulate matter (PM10). Bogotá, Medellín, and Bucaramanga have average concentrations of PM10 above the normative values.

Climate change adaptation:

- Progress in this area has been limited in Colombia.
- Although Instituto de Investigaciones Marinas y Costeras "José Benito Vives de Andréis" (INVEMAR) has carried out studies on the impact of sea-level rise in coastal cities, suggesting recommendations, no adaptation plans have been developed, and recommendations have not yet been included in the development plans.

Adapting cities to climate change:

- Progress in this area has been limited in Colombia.
- Although for coastal cities INVEMAR has carried out studies on the impact of sea level, making recommendations for adaptation, no adaptation plans have been built and recommendations have not been included in the development plans.
- In 2008, INVEMAR identified three types of adaptation measures: protective infrastructure works (dykes, flooding protection barriers, silt fences), civil works in ports (dredging and infills), and the protection and restoration of coastal ecosystems.

Disaster risk management:

- A significant proportion of the Colombian population of households (close to one in two households) lives in conditions of high vulnerability to natural hazards due to inadequate land management and inappropriate building standards. About 6 million homes were built before 1984, when Colombia's first building code including seismic design standards came into effect.

- In terms of municipal investment, only 13 percent of the local budgets goes to disaster management, with a concerning disconnect between public investments and the effectiveness of these actions.
- Seismic risk management has more legal and institutional tools than flooding, which is more prevalent. This started to change after the 2010–2011 winter season, when DNP estimated that losses exceeded US$15 billion (the famous earthquake of the Coffee Axis cost the nation between $2 and $3 trillion).

Wastewater and solid waste:

- The highest levels of water pollution occur in water basins where the greatest economic development is concentrated.
- Only 35 percent of municipalities have wastewater treatment plants. Water systems in large cities allow only for 32 percent of the wastewater to be treated before it is discharged to the water bodies.
- The increased generation of solid waste has been matched with the improvement of final disposal sites across the country.

Primary ecological structure:

- Although all municipalities must identify and protect the primary ecological structure in their land-use development plans, in most cases, they only identify existing protected areas.
- Plans for watershed management should be identified and protect the main ecological structure. However, very few basins are well equipped, and the priority basins to be managed have yet to be identified.

Public discussion on urban sustainability in Colombia

Public discussion about urban sustainability in Colombia circles around the consultation process of the land-use development plans (POT), controversial large mining projects, illegal mining and its incidence on urban water sources, corporate responsibility for sustainable development, and the constitutional protection of the high mountains ("páramos"). However, this discussion takes place mostly in social networks, and local governments have had little to do with its promotion.

The fulfillment of Habitat II commitments in terms of sustainability and environmental management provides an ambiguous balance, given that the public sector, in part through consultation with the private economic associations, has responded by developing and updating a set of norms and an institutional framework. However, these efforts are not followed up by rulings and the consequent formulation and execution of policies, plans of action, and projects at the local level. Evidence of this is the low investment in housing maintenance programs, especially in programs for upgrading informal neighborhoods, which are highly vulnerable to climate change. Urban resilience has improved in large cities, but is not workable in most municipalities in Colombia due to the weakness of their fiscal resources. The balance of public policies in this field warns about shortcomings in water resource management, lack of implementation of recommendations to prevent the future effects of sea-level rise, and a risk management focus that is inconsistent with the magnitude of the threat of floods and landslides throughout the national territory. It is also crucial to point out that the primary ecological structure and the key watersheds in the municipalities are not well incorporated into municipal land-use plans and hence are not adequately managed.

Housing and urban infrastructure

The various documents emanating from the Habitat II conference ensure the commitment of governments to adapt their legal, fiscal, and regulatory frameworks, as well as to adopt policies aimed at "progressively guaranteeing everyone the full exercise of the right to an adequate, safe and secure housing, that is accessible and affordable, has basic services, facilities and amenities, and has legal security of tenure so people are protected against evictions". The narrative also addressed "the need for housing policies to adopt a multi-sectoral approach in their design, seeking to articulate macroeconomic, social, demographic, land, environmental and cultural heritage policies, which promote sustainable patterns of spatial development and improve the population's access to goods and services". Governments also committed themselves to "decentralize housing policies and their administration to the subnational and local levels", to improve coordination mechanisms, and to build appropriate institutional structures to facilitate this. Documents pointed to the need to promote the rehabilitation, renovation, and upgrading of housing and to promote other forms of tenure such as "rental housing, community-ownership, cooperative, and nonprofit property". In addition, the Habitat II agenda highlighted the importance of "facilitating individual or collective production of housing by the inhabitants and the communities themselves ". Another point of emphasis was the need to support the housing market by guaranteeing and expanding access to credit; mobilizing new sources of financing; integrating housing finance into the general financial system; and fostering new financing systems through credit unions, cooperation banks, insurance cooperatives, and other nonbank financial institutions.

Evolution of the housing situation in Colombia since 1996

Before 1991, Colombia had a universal model of public management for the housing sector that was later replaced by a market model of direct demand subsidies. This shift implied a deep rethinking of the role of the state from a direct provider to a mere facilitator of the housing services markets. In this regard, the evolution of Colombia's housing policy was not fully aligned with the commitments made in Habitat II. An important change in the national sectoral policy was the introduction of a new so-called ABC subsidy model incorporating savings (*Ahorro*), bonds (*Bono*), and mortgage (*Crédito*). These three elements ought to be harmonized to help households achieve financial closure. It is important to note that the ABC model predated Habitat II and even influenced the recommendations of this summit. Curiously, despite the emphasis of housing policy on the production of new units and access to property, ever since 1993 there has been a steady decline in the proportion of owners and a rise in the percentage of tenants. The proportion of owners versus tenants has inverted over a span of 23 years, as can be seen in Table 6.4.

Setting aside changes in the economic capacity of the households, gaps in the sectorial policy, and other market failures, this changeover between the two main forms of housing tenure can be attributed to the fact that both housing production and housing stock are lagging behind the size of the population. Also contributing to this change in tenancy is the difference between the formation of new households (280,000 per annum) and formal housing production (which recently reached an average of 220,000). Such an imbalance has been compensated for by households resorting either to the social production of housing or via rental options. In the first case, as mentioned, this form of production represents 66 percent of the housing stock. In the second case, Colombia is the Latin American country with the highest proportion of renters.

In terms of housing, the two fronts with most notable changes in Colombia are the increase in urban coverage of public services (utilities) and the reduction of the quantitative housing deficit (see Table 6.5).

In contrast to the behavior of the quantitative housing deficit, the qualitative housing deficit is inelastic (see Table 6.6), because of the steady increase in the proportion of tenants and the consolidation of informal housing production, which represents more than 50 percent of the housing stock in Colombia (Habitat District Secretariat – CENAC, 2011).

Table 6.4 Evolution of the distribution of the form of housing in Colombia, 1993–2015

Year	Source	Type of tenure			
		Owner, fully paid	Owner, payment in process	Lease or sub-lease	Other type
1.99E+03	Census	49.70	10.90	33.90	5.50
2.00E+03	ECV	46.20	6.10	36.80	10.90
2.01E+03	Census	45.10	7.10	36.90	10.90
2.01E+03	ECV	43.30	7.30	37.70	11.70
2.01E+03	ECV	41.10	5.60	40.70	12.60
2.02E+03	ECV	38.90	5.00	44.10	12.00

Source: National Administrative Department of Statistics (DANE). National Census of Population and Housing; Quality of Life Survey, (ECV).

Table 6.5 Access to public utilities in urban areas[1]

Year	Data source – Unit of measurement	Water	Sanitation	Electricity
1993	Census – Percentage of occupied houses with connection	94.6	81.8	88
2005	Census – Percentage of occupied houses with connection	94.3	89.7	98.4
2015	ECV – Households	97.6	93.1	99.9

Source: Water and electricity 1993 and 2005: National Administrative Department of Statistics (DANE). Statistical Atlas of Colombia; Sanitation 1993: CONPES 3383 of 2005 (Development Plan of the Water and Sanitation Sector) – National Population and Housing Census 1993; Sewerage 2005: DANE – Census tables 2005; water, sanitation, and electricity 2015: Quality of Life Survey, ECV.

[1] In this case, the DANE asks if the house has infrastructure of domiciliary services. The service can be provided through a legal or illegal connection, and the service can be managed by a public, private, or community-owned company, although at the time of the interview, the service might or might not be functioning (DANE, 2010).

Table 6.6 Total national housing deficit, urban and totals, 1993, 2005, and 2014

Year	Feature	Urban		Total	
		#	%	#	%
	Total households	5,374,990	100	7,159,825	100
1993[1]	Households without deficit	2,940,183	54.7	3,318,525	46.3
	Households with deficit	2,434,807	45.3	3,841,300	53.7
	Quantitative deficit	1,093,077	20.3	1,217,056	17
	Qualitative deficit	1,341,730	25	2,624,244	36.7
	Total households	8,210,347	100	10,570,899	100
2005[1]	Households without deficit	5,993,484	73	6,742,844	63.8
	Households with deficit	2,216,863	27	3,828,055	36.2
	Quantitative deficit	1,031,256	12.6	1,307,757	12.4
	Qualitative deficit	1,185,607	14.4	2,520,298	23.8
	Total households	10,631,027	100	13,598,823	100
2014[2]	Households without deficit	8,686,809	81.7	10,245,275	75.3
	Households with deficit	1,944,219	18.3	33,53,548	24.7
	Quantitative deficit	746,030	7	1,273,334	9.4
	Qualitative deficit	1,198,189	11.3	2,080,214	15.3

(1) Census of Population and Housing, 1993, 2005
(2) Great Integrated Household Survey, GEIH, 2014, estimation

Source: National Administrative Department of Statistics (DANE). Population and housing census 1993 and 2005; Great Integrated Household Survey, GEIH, 2014. Own elaboration.

The housing policy in Colombia has concentrated in the production of new units and public expenditure for the improvement of the housing stock has not been consistent with its magnitude, nor with the volume of the population that lives in substandard housing. Most households satisfied their housing needs with the housing stock historically produced in cities. However, although some programs have been formulated, public spending on housing upgrades, structural reinforcement, titling, neighborhood upgrades, urban renewal, and regeneration is low.

Housing accessibility and affordability

A large proportion of the population that are subject to the housing policy in Colombia is of low income and an informal nature, with very limited capacity to save and remain marginalized outside of mortgage credit markets. This is a key access barrier to the programs and instruments of the housing policy. In the case of housing finance, the barrier is more restrictive – since 1991 there has not been any massive direct public credit nor rediscount programs with the private sector. There is a rediscount line in the Territorial Development Finance Fund (FINDETER), but it has a very low coverage. These conditions make it impossible for households to achieve the financial closure required to apply for state subsidies and to receive a subsidized unit in the market, either of social housing or in the higher segments.

Several indicators illustrate the severe access limitations: the dynamism of informal housing production, the high rate of renters, and the reduction of households whose status is "homeownership with payment in process", which has reduced from 10.9 percent in 1993 (National Population and Housing Census) to 3.8 percent in 2014 (Great Integrated Household Survey, GEIH).

Another limitation to housing in Colombia is that mortgage payments represent a large portion of household expenditures for those who can access credits and subsidies. Data on the distribution of household expenditures by type of housing tenure show that those who are in the process of paying the mortgage spend 40 percent less on food than the national average. This is very concerning because it signals that for many, owning a house can lead families into poverty. A situation like this not only has important economic implications; more alarmingly, it calls into question the concept of "adequate housing" and the effectiveness of the housing policy. This ultimately means that in Colombia purchasing social housing represents a high opportunity. It also means that social housing is not really affordable, because so many households must reduce spending on essential goods and services in order to keep up with their mortgages' monthly installment.

Another barrier to housing affordability is the recent real estate boom in Colombia. Construction of this type of housing (and construction in general) had an unprecedented peak that coincided with the behavior of total GDP, which boosted the prices of new houses. In fact, these prices grew by 1.4 percent in 2002, then increased by 13.5 percent in 2004, and in 2007 they rose up to 19.7 percent (IVPN-DANE). In all these years there was an imbalance between the behavior of this indicator, inflation, and housing construction costs, which triggered a heated debate about the existence of a housing bubble in Colombia. Because social housing occurs with the market, when price increases exceed by a large amount increases in the purchasing power of low and middle wages, then more people end up being marginalized from affordable housing.

Recognition of these access barriers led to a partial modification of the rules of the pure market-based housing model, and the first measures were taken in 2012. For instance, a free housing program was introduced for people in poverty, those internally displaced, and those affected by natural disasters. Another program was introduced for the non-poor population whose head of household has formal employment (the program was called *My House Now* with three alternatives: *Savers, Initial Fee,* and *Subsidy to the Interest Rate.* In these cases, the Family Housing Subsidy (SFV) was increased, meaning less savings are required from households. At a complementary level, the National Savings Fund (FNA)[12] recently initiated a rental program for social housing claimants.

Because these actions have been taken, the situation changed from a severe affordability crisis of social housing to another one in which this failure of public policy has become more or less accepted. Still, there are doubts about the continuity of the free housing program and the interest rate subsidy, because the effect the tax revenues from oil and other commodities exported by Colombia has shrank substantially.

Absence of the *"houses without people"* phenomena in Colombia

In Colombia, the problem of *houses without people* is not occurring, because the annual production of social housing has been a number of new units lower than the aggregate annual formation of new homes. Moreover, the qualitative deficit is very high, and the population in need of resettlement by risk and those displaced by internal conflict is also on the rise. On the other hand, such a phenomenon has been prevented by the sales model that the business sector adopted in Colombia after the 1999 real estate crisis. After the crisis, developers implemented a scheme of anticipated sales. That is, housing projects only begin construction once they reach a financial equilibrium point, which is generally higher than 75 percent of the total residential units offered. This scheme applies to social housing, to other types of housing, and even to commercial buildings.

Housing mortgage

Housing finance, especially for poor households, is one of the structural flaws of sectoral policy. Furthermore, it is one of the consequences of delegating the operation of the mortgage credit market to private banks, implementing the ABC model, and renouncing to a regulation more in favor of social housing. That is, public entities were completely excluded from the management of any form of housing finance, with the exception of the FNA. It is also important to note that after 1991, when the model of public-sector management changed, housing finance in Colombia was restricted to mortgage loans for home purchase (including microcredit since 2003),[13] leaving aside other important elements of housing's production chain such as land acquisition, construction, housing improvement, structural reinforcement, progressive development, renovations, change of use, etc.

As can be seen in Table 6.7, housing credit has grown over the last 10 years in terms of the number of mortgages and in the amount of resources disbursed for purchasing new housing.

The used housing market shows a sharp growth, even matching the resources for new housing, a situation unprecedented in Colombia. However, the participation of mortgage portfolio recovery is not reflected in the GDP. In the years before the 1999 crisis, it reached 8.6 percent (1998), whereas in 2012, it was 5.26 percent.

The loan-to-value (LTV) ratio (that is, the proportion of a loan to the value of the housing purchased is very low) is especially low in Colombia. For instance, during the third quarter of 2015 it was only 49.1 percent for nonsubsidized housing and 61.4 percent for subsidized housing (*Vivienda de Interés Social*, VIS[14]) (see Figure 6.3). Also, it is notable that the proportion of the population in the process of paying off their house has been consistently shrinking, being currently only 3.8 percent. Furthermore, despite the efforts made, Colombia does not have a functioning micro-finance system for the housing market, as it currently has a very narrow coverage, failing to reach houses and neighborhoods of 'progressive development' that are in need of upgrading.

To guarantee the long-term financial stability of the social housing market, the Constitutional Court instructed that the interest rate for social housing ought to be the lowest in the market. So, in order to increase the availability of mortgage credits, the government created an interest rate subsidy for mortgages aimed at new housing in both the VIS and middle-income segments. This subsidy operates as a countercyclical measure of employment protection.

Table 6.7 Mortgage portfolio in Colombia, 2005–2015 (Q3 July–Sept. each year)

Year	Capital balance (millions of US$)*	Cumulative number of mortgage loans
2005	4,693.9	749,285
2006	4,700.5	727,784
2007	5,308.8	732,282
2008	6,184.4	750,771
2009	6,677.5	741,807
2010	7,585.4	766,182
2011	8,749	801,297
2012	10,359.1	864,779
2013	11,801.6	906,485
2014	13,477.6	958,734
2015	15,055.4	997,621

*Original data in millions of current pesos. (Exchange rates using representative exchange rates US$ 2,983.82 by May 15, 2016.)

Source: DANE. Housing mortgage portfolio, for years 2005 and 2006: Colombia and 13 areas, and for 2007 to 2015: Colombia and 14 departments.

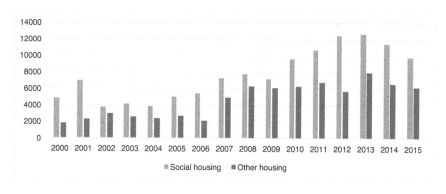

Figure 6.3 Number of housing units financed in Colombia between 2000 and 2015 (Q3 July–September each year)

Source: DANE. Housing Mortgage Portfolio.

The precarious settlements

A significant proportion Colombian households, estimated at 13.2 percent in 2014, live in precarious settlements, generally located in areas of high risk. Although this percentage has not increased since 2000, Colombia has not met the target for this Millennium Development Goal (MDG). In fact, a baseline of 19.9 percent was established and a target for 2014 of 12.36 percent was set. As mentioned, the proportion Colombian households dwelling in informal settlements was estimated at 13.2 percent in 2014, 1 percentage point off the target. But the extent of noncompliance is better appreciated once one considers that the target is to reach 4 percent of households in 2020. This means it took Colombia 14 years to reach just 42.1 percent of this MDG (DNP, 2014b).

Access to urban land

The failures in the urban land market are one of the structural problems of the housing policy in Colombia. In big and mid-sized cities, such failures have led to severe limitations in the supply of urbanized land and have created a distorted price system that constitutes a critical barrier to the production of social housing. It is important to note that the urban regulations and licensing fees are the source of these failures, given that municipalities have full autonomy to define the urban perimeters and land-use processes. The source of the problem lies in the structure of land ownership and in the speculative nature of the land prices, as they are a key input to the construction's supply chain.

Under these conditions, the application of the instruments of public management for urban land proposed in Law 388 of 1997 is practically nonexistent. Even though the law allows Colombian municipalities and districts to directly intervene in the land market in order to expand the supply of urbanized land (by identifying priority development zones, sanctioning idle property, creating land banks, and so on), local governments have not been able to overcome the uneven and speculative nature of the land market.

Currently, urban land prices have also made it unfeasible to produce single-family social housing in the main cities of Colombia. The cost of land accounts for approximately 20 percent of the sale price of the home, both in the social housing price segment and above (CAMACOL, 2014). This has a profound impact on social housing in Colombia, whose price is regulated.[15] For instance, the Bogota Land Price Index of the Banco de la República de Colombia (Central Bank), whose base (100) corresponds to 1960, reached 749.90 in 1996 and 1,533.86 in 2013, according to the last published data.[16]

Changes in housing policy over the last two decades

Housing policies change every presidential period alongside national development plans, which, in principle, implement the proposal made during the electoral campaign. However, what remains unchanged is the underlying market-based model of direct subsidies to the demand, which was previously referred to as the ABC model (*Ahorro + Bono + Crédito*, that is, *Savings + Subsidy + Credit*). In this model the savings of the income of households is supplemented with both soft credits to the households and a state subsidy in order to help the developers arrive at a financial closure of the housing projects. In principle, there are subsidies for new and used housing, housing improvement, structural reinforcement, and urban renewal. There is also a prioritization system for special types of populations (internally displaced people, those affected by natural disasters, and the poorest households).

Between 1996 and 2016 some adjustments to the ABC model were introduced, most notably the reform of the housing finance system (Law 546 of 1999) that created a measure for mortgage credit, the real value unit (UVR). The UVR replaced the 1972 units of constant purchasing power (UPAC), which was later declared unconstitutional by the court, even though it had already financed approximately 1.5 million homes.

Also noteworthy is the creation of the MIB and the macro-projects.[17] The first generation of macro-projects was declared unconstitutional by the Constitutional Court on the grounds that the national-level government was overrunning municipal government in matters of land-use planning and unlawfully making direct decisions on local urban regulations. In the period between August 2010 and October 2015, 14 macro-projects were launched in 13 cities and 46,096 new homes were built. The expectations were far larger than these. In fact, the actual level of implementation of these macro-projects, as of October 31, 2015, was 17 percent of what was originally expected, according to the MVCT.

As was described in the last section, the basic housing policy model (the ABC model) has suffered profound changes, most especially after 2012. In this year, modifications were introduced to the housing policy that were literally intending to rethink the role of the state in this public policy. In fact, the current model entails a greater intervention of the state in the operation of housing market variables, such as housing supply and finance. Hence, it can be argued that today, Colombia housing policy operates under different assumptions than those stipulated by the ABC model in 1991.

Access to urban infrastructure

In Colombia, larger fiscal resources have been invested and contribute to a clear increase in the rates of coverage of water, sanitation, and electricity public services, as well as education, health, and housing infrastructure. In terms of public space, achievements are less significant, as well as in sports and cultural infrastructure and other types of urban services. By far, the most lagging sector is transportation infrastructure.

Notwithstanding the improvements in the coverage of basic urban public services, there are important regional gaps in the coverage and quality of infrastructure, as well as gaps within cities. An illustrative case is that of Bogotá, where studies have identified the existence of an additional mode of socioeconomic segregation produced by inequality in the distribution of urban facilities across different localities (UNDP, 2008).

The supply of potable water in Colombia is carried out by private or mixed capital companies that are subject to regulations proper of such natural monopolies. In principle, the long-run marginal of this service tends to be decreasing, especially in cities that can ensure a high volume of users.

However, the cost of water to the final customers is not determined by the curve cost alone. Instead, a representative cost is calculated by considering the costs of operation of the service, as well as the expansion of networks. This reference cost is what middle-income families pay, without receiving any subsidies or giving any contributions. Low-income households receive subsidies, which are paid for by a surcharge in the tariffs of higher-income families. Hence, public services like water, electricity, and gas operate via a cross-subsidization system.

Summing up this section on housing and urban infrastructure, it can be said that with the adoption of the model of subsidies to demand, housing policy in Colombia has solely been focused on new social housing through two instruments: savings and state subsidies. Hence, housing policy has allocated minimum public resources to other types of programs (even though they are formulated) geared to the improvement and upgrading of the existing housing stock. This overemphasis in the construction of new social housing comes with an overemphasis on full formal property ownership, leaving little room for other forms of tenure and other forms of production like the cooperatives or organized processes of social production. This is what I refer to as the singularity of housing policy in Colombia, a rather narrow understanding of what housing policy can encompass. Anything that is not constructing new units of social housing to be sold in the market is not considered seriously as housing policy. This singularity of the housing policy is problematic, because it is of little help in solving the barriers of access to housing and the market in urban land, which by now have acquired a structural character. All of this occurs in a market mechanism characterized by a real estate boom that expands housing production without lowering the prices of new housing. Hence, sectoral policy in Colombia has not been entirely consistent with the principles of adequate housing agreed on at Habitat II.

Productivity and urban economy

The Habitat II Action Plan established the need for governments to, among others: strengthen urban economies so that they may be competitive in a globalizing economy; establish an effective financial base for urban development; support -as appropriate- public and private enterprises in their efforts to adapt to the changing requirements of technological and human resources development; offer opportunities for urban economic activities by facilitating the access of new and emerging businesses, and small and medium-sized enterprises, including the informal sector, to credit and finance, and by streamlining legal and administrative procedures.

(HABITAT II, 1996)

Over the last 10 years the Colombian economy has experienced sustained rates of growth at an average rate of close to 4.8 percent, and of 3.6 percent in terms of GDP per capita. These facts constitute a reference for the issues raised next.

Urban employment

Employment and urban unemployment figures in Colombia since 1996 show a cyclical behavior, with two clearly defined periods marked by the 1999 economic crisis. In fact, in 1999, Colombia's GDP registered the only historical decrease statistically documented in the two decades between 1996 and 2016.

From 1990 onwards, the occupied population in Colombia began a process of growth, until 1994, when the effects of the crisis became evident. At the end of the 1990s, there was a period in which unemployment reached double digits and remained so until 2014, when the economically active urban population fell to 9.9 percent. Urban unemployment reached 9.8 percent in 2015, as shown in Figure 6.4.[18] The first months of 2016, however, show a slower pace of economic growth that brought the unemployment rate to 10.2 percent as of in March 2016.

Evolution of urban wages

In Colombia there is a legal monthly minimum wage (SMML), which for 2016 was set unilaterally by the national government at US$231.10 (COP 689.454, at a RER from COP 2,983.82 to May 15, 2016). As a rule, the annual increases of the minimum wage are made in a percentage equivalent to the inflation of the previous year, plus an adjustment for productivity. These adjustments are agreed on with organizations of employers and trade unions, but in 2016, these organizations could not reach an agreement. The urban legal monthly minimum wage

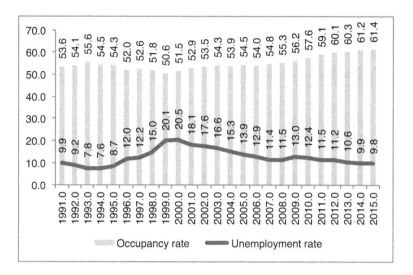

Figure 6.4 Occupancy rate and unemployment rate between 1991 and 2015*

*1991 to 2000: Seven cities and metropolitan areas; data dated September for each year, 2001 to 2015: 13 cities and metropolitan areas; average data from January to December of each year. Source: DANE. Continuing Household Survey, ECH; Great Integrated Household Survey, GEIH.

1991 a 2000: DANE. Serie histórica 1984–2000. 7 ciudades y áreas metropolitanas. Dato a septiembre de cada año

2001 a 2015: DANE. 13 ciudades y áreas metropolitanas. Promedio enero a diciembre

registered real increases in years prior to 1996. In the public sector, the annual adjustments of salaries above the minimum wage are generally done in lower percentages, which ultimately means that at higher levels there is a notable – yet unconcerning – deterioration in purchasing power. On the other hand, in the private sector, salaries for middle management and directive positions in an independent regime is applied, which includes extras and bonuses.

For 170 years until 2006, urban real wages in manufacturing increased less than the GDP per capita increases; this has produced a clear asymmetry in income distribution across households in Colombia. Among seven economic sectors analyzed in the period 1982–2006, only the *Provision of public services* and *Financial firms'* sectors had increases in their real salary. Instead, *Manufacturing industries, Retail, Construction, Services,* and *Transportation,* had minor real wage dynamics (Urrutia and Ruíz, 2010). The economic crisis of 1999 explains the decline in wages of the final years of the period 1892–2006.

Urban informal employment and urban informal production

The proportion of the population occupied in activities within the informal economy has declined five points in the period between 2000 and 2013. When considering the total number of employed people in Colombia, it is evident that up to 2012, more than 50 percent of the employed population were engaged in activities of the informal economy, as seen in Figure 6.5. In 2012 informal employment reached 51.2 percent. In subsequent years there was a decline in urban informal employment, which reached 47.7 percent in 2015. The capital Bogotá reports the second lowest proportion of informality in the country: 43.3 percent (GEIH, 2014).

Now, in terms of the participation of informal production in the total economy, there are two types of estimations. One considers compliance with firm requirements (accounting, commercial registration, payment of social benefits to workers); this type estimates that 39 percent of Colombian companies are informal. For the second calculation, based on contribution to GDP, informal production in Colombia oscillated between 45 percent and 65 percent in the period 2000–2007 (Hamann and Mejía, 2011). An alternative measurement estimates a participation of Colombia's informal economy in total GDP by 38.2 percent for 2006 (Bustamante, 2011).

Statistics on productivity in urban areas

The main factor explaining the per capita GDP gaps between urban agglomerations in Colombia is productivity. The average productivity in Colombia's 13 metropolitan areas in the period 2005–2010 was US$4.6 (at a RER of COP 2,983.82).

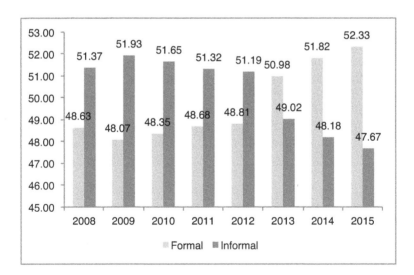

Figure 6.5 Percentage of informal and formally employed populations in 13 main cities (2008–2015, September–November)

Source: National Administrative Department of Statistics, DANE. Continuing Household Survey, ECH (2001–2006); Great Integrated Household Survey, GEIH (2007–2014).

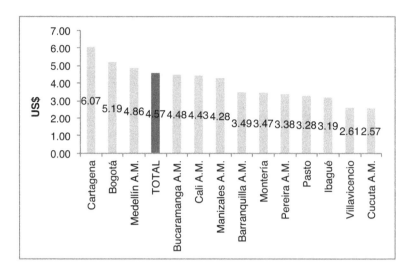

Figure 6.6 Average productivity per hour in 13 main cities between 2005 and 2010

* Original data in thousands of constant pesos ($) of 2005.

Source: Bustamante, Juana Paola. The challenges of the formal growth of the economy. In: Fiscal Notes No. 9 (August 2011). Bogotá, D.C. Ministry of Finance and Public Credit.

The highest productivity was recorded in Cartagena, a city that is the site of Colombia's main petrochemical center. But Cartagena is also one of the cities with the highest levels of poverty in the country. As shown in Figure 6.6, which shows productivity per hour worked in Colombia's 13 metropolitan areas, the second most productive city is Bogotá (Fedesarrollo, 2014).

According to 2007 data from the Urban Mobility Observatory of the Latin American Development Bank (CAF), in Bogotá the mean commuting time is 40.5 minutes for people in cars, 58 minutes for those using traditional buses, and 49 minutes for those using *Transmilenio* buses (BRT system). In Pereira the average commuting times in 2009 were 21.5 minutes for car and 25 minutes for the BRT system. These are the only two cities are included in CAF's observatory so far.

Participation of cities in Colombia's GDP

Eighty percent of Colombia's GDP is currently generated in cities. Bogotá, Medellín, Cali, and Barranquilla generate a product that reaches the largest shares in the national GDP. While currently only Bogotá calculates and monitors its own GDP performance, Table 6.8 shows the breakout of the GDP for Colombia's 16 departments, plus Bogota Capital District.

Table 6.8 Contribution of the departmental GDP to the national GDP by economic activity, 2013

Department	Economic Activity									
	−1.00	−2.00	−3.00	−4.00	−5.00	−6.00	−7.00	−8.00	−9.00	−10.00
Antioquia	13.40	3.50	15.90	22.40	15.20	15.20	12.50	15.10	11.50	13.70
Atlántico	1.30	0.20	5.00	8.40	4.20	4.40	4.80	4.10	3.90	4.80
Bogotá DC	43.70	27.20	32.40	27.90	21.60	28.10	17.40	23.80	0.70	25.90
Bolívar	3.40	1.30	7.40	4.20	5.40	3.00	4.10	2.30	3.40	7.40
Boyacá	6.30	3.90	3.00	4.10	2.40	2.50	3.30	1.20	2.50	2.00
Caldas	2.70	0.10	1.60	2.70	1.80	1.20	1.50	1.20	1.70	1.30
Cesar	2.90	10.00	0.60	2.00	1.00	1.30	1.50	0.70	1.70	0.80
Córdoba	4.30	2.90	0.50	2.30	2.00	1.70	1.60	1.30	2.50	0.80
La Guajira	0.80	7.80	0.10	1.70	0.60	0.50	0.80	0.20	1.10	0.50
Magdalena	3.10	0.10	0.60	1.60	1.70	1.60	1.70	0.70	2.10	0.90
Nariño	3.60	0.30	0.70	0.80	1.80	2.30	1.60	0.80	2.50	0.80
N. Santander	2.60	0.50	1.00	2.30	1.70	1.70	2.20	1.30	2.40	1.00
Quindío	1.70	0.10	0.40	0.80	1.30	1.00	0.80	0.50	1.00	0.40
Risaralda	2.10	0.10	1.70	1.50	1.70	1.40	1.70	1.40	1.70	1.40
Santander	6.30	4.40	11.00	5.00	13.30	5.00	6.10	4.30	3.90	11.90
Sucre	1.70	0.10	0.50	1.10	0.80	1.00	0.80	0.30	1.60	0.40
Valle del Cauca	8.00	0.30	13.50	12.00	7.30	9.50	10.10	13.10	8.70	10.70

Source: National Administrative Department of Statistics, DANE. Departmental Accounts Colombia.

Structure of Colombia's GDP

During the last 20 years the Colombian economy has undergone an important structural transformation. The most notable change was the decrease in
manufacturing industries and the increased share of mining and extractive
industries in the national economy. The numbers do not reflect this change
clearly because the prices for oil (Colombia's main export), coal, and other
minerals fell.

The *Agriculture, livestock, hunting, forestry and fishing* sector also contracted, while
the sectors *Financial, Services,* and *Construction* rose. Figure 6.7 shows Colombian
GDP's recent performance broken down by sector or economic activity.

Colombian GDP has similar characteristics to other Latin American
countries – the structure of the economies reveals limited job creation and
job quality. Indeed, in Colombia there is a process of deindustrialization of
the economy and a very low growth rate of the agricultural sector. This has
increased the dependence on food imports, which together with the revaluation of the dollar, has a strong impact on the cost of living. The increase in
the share of the *Construction* sector has been driven by a real estate boom, that,
although it drives employment up, a high proportion of these jobs are informal.

Perhaps the most adverse aspect of Colombia's economic structure is the
dependence on large-scale mining for GDP growth, as it generates multiple
environmental risks as well as conflicts with the communities. This economic
structure reveals a low share of labor and negatively affects the programs to
combat inequality and exclusion.

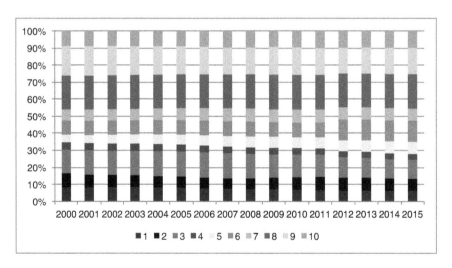

Figure 6.7 Participation of economic activities in total GD in Colombia, 2000–2015

(1) Agriculture, hunting, forestry, and fishing; (2) Exploitation of mines and quarries; (3) Manufacturing;
(4) Electricity, gas, and water supply; (5) Construction; (6) Restaurants and hotels; (7) Transportation,
storage, and communications; (8) Financial establishments, insurance, real estate, and business services;
(9) Social, communal, and personal services activities; (10) Taxes. Source: DANE – National Accounts.

Main constraints to urban productivity

The main limitations to urban productivity are derived from the lack of investment in physical capital and a shortage of employment that reflects the low educational levels of the labor force and the limited incidence of human capital formation processes. It is estimated that 4.5 Colombian workers generate, on average, the output of one US worker. Overall, labor productivity in Latin America as compared to that of the United States is low: Chile's is 47 percent, Mexico's 36.3 percent, Argentina's 33.7 percent, Brazil's 24.8 percent, and Colombia's is only 23 percent – one of the lowest labor productivities in the region (Conference Board Total Economy, 2014).

Low urban productivity also has to do with the use of dated technologies, which in turn reflects a lack of science, technology, and innovation programs both in companies and in the public sector. Also noteworthy is the lack of clusters of economic activities with high-added value on one end and, on the other, high economic and labor informality.

In addition to these factors companies lack specialization, which prevents the creation of productive chains based on complementarities. A poorly connected system of cities is partly to be blamed, preventing the formation of economies of agglomeration and scale. Indeed, the intermodal network of the transportation and communications infrastructure is so underdeveloped that it hinders the integration and proper access of the companies located in the cities to the national and foreign markets.[19]

Regarding the productivity of the urban economy itself, it can be said that for more than a decade there has been a process of economic growth that has reduced unemployment, although it coexists with a high rate of informality (slightly below 50 percent of the labor force). Economic growth has not been distributed symmetrically within the population, and GDP per capita has increased below the rates for total GDP. As in other countries in the region, 80 percent of the country's economic output is generated in the four main cities of Colombia. Notwithstanding the earlier indicators, the structure of the Colombian GDP shows a deterioration of the economy associated with deindustrialization, stagnation of the agricultural sector, and rise of the mining sector, especially of the services sector. This has led to an economic growth that does not generate quality employment and that inhibits the reduction of income and regional inequality gaps.

Urban poverty, intra-urban inequality, and social exclusion

Promoting equitable, socially viable and stable human settlements is inextricably linked to eradicating poverty . . . The eradication of poverty requires sound macroeconomic policies aimed at creating employment opportunities, equal and universal access to economic opportunities . . . education and training that will promote sustainable livelihoods through freely chosen productive employment and work . . . People living in poverty must be empowered through freely chosen participation in all aspects of political, economic and social life. Other key elements of a poverty eradication strategy include policies geared to reducing inequalities . . . recognizing the needs and skills of women; developing human resources; improving infrastructure, making it more accessible; and promoting domestic policies for meeting the basic needs of all.

(HABITAT II, 1996)

In addition to these global urban trends, forced displacement by Colombia's internal armed conflict is seen as a cross-cutting aggravation of poverty, intra-urban inequality, and social exclusion.

Urban poverty

Since 1996, urban poverty has declined in Colombia in terms of monetary poverty, extreme poverty, and multidimensional poverty. Recent statistics at the national level show monetary poverty for urban areas of 24.1 percent in 2015, compared to 26.6 percent in 2014 and 37.4 percent in 2008. For the same years and months, extreme poverty has plummeted from 11.2 percent in 2008, to 5.1 percent in 2014, and 4.9 percent in 2015. In line with these statistics, over the last five years (2011 to 2015), the urban population living in poverty has declined by 1.6 million people and the number of people living in extreme poverty by a little more than 620,000 people (DANE, 2015) (see Figure 6.8). As for multidimensional poverty, the affected population represented 23.5 percent in 2010, a percentage that fell to 15.4 percent in 2015 (ibid.).

However, the behavior is not homogenous across different areas. Colombia is characterized by the existence of acute gaps between the rural areas and the city, between regions, and between cities (see Figure 6.10).

Notable features of urban poverty in Colombia

In 2015, monetary poverty was higher than the national average in the urban areas, and in turn, monetary poverty was higher in the urban areas than in the main 13 cities of Colombia. These are important statistics, demonstrating that urban dwellers do have better economic conditions than those in the rural areas and that big cities have, on average, better economic conditions than smaller cities.

Table 6.9 shows that monetary poverty is higher when the household head is female (28.3 percent) than when it is male (21.7 percent). Likewise, monetary poverty has a higher incidence, 35.3 percent, in young adults with a very low educational level (none or primary). The highest poverty rates are those of households whose head is unemployed (46.5 percent), and the lowest are those whose head has a college or postgraduate education (5.1 percent), followed by heads of household who have access to social security (8 percent).

Regarding other household members, monetary poverty has more incidence in households with more children over 12 years old, and it has less incidence when there are more household members, as shown in Table 6.10.

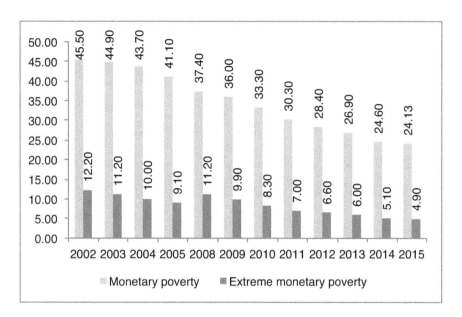

Figure 6.8 Incidence of monetary poverty and extreme monetary poverty

* Urban (%). 2002–2015
* Expanded data with population projections, based on 2005 census results. Data for 2006 and 2007 are not calculated due to comparability issues in the employment and poverty series, as a result of the methodological change involved in the transition from Continuous Household Survey to the Great Integrated Household Survey.

Source: National Administrative Department of Statistics, DANE – Continuous Household Survey, ECH (2002–2005); Great Integrated Household Survey, GEIH (2008–2015)

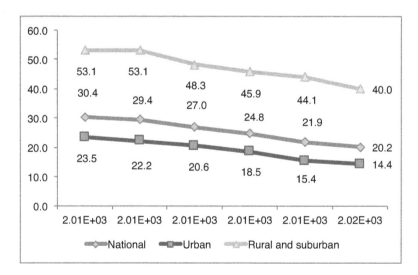

Figure 6.9 Incidence of poverty in urban and rural areas and national total (%), 2010–2015

Source: National Administrative Department of Statistics, DANE. Calculations based on the Quality of Life Survey, ECV 2010–2015 (Technical Bulletin, March 2016: http://bit.ly/2aNP32v).

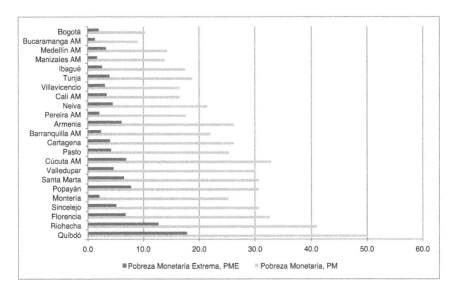

Figure 6.10 Incidence of monetary poverty and extreme monetary poverty for 23 cities in 2015*

*Expanded data with population projections, based on the results of the 2005 census. Source: National Administrative Department of Statistics, DANE – Great Integrated Household Survey, GEIH.

Table 6.10 shows that extreme monetary poverty follows the same trends as monetary poverty in relation to head of household (but here its incidence is twice as much if the head of the household is female), educational level, occupational position, and affiliation to social security, among others (see Table 6.11). Likewise, the same relationship can be found between extreme poverty and the characteristics of the household in terms of the number of children and the number of household members who work.

Overall, urban poverty in Colombia reveals two key features affecting specific population groups. First, as observed in many other countries, the feminization of poverty has a high inelasticity, that is, it remains difficult to curb with the current public policy programs. Second, there are major limitations in both training programs promoting human capital and in those intending to reach the most vulnerable populations with basic social services.

Although there are not causation links between household characteristics and poverty, the general conclusion is that poverty reduction programs and socioeconomic improvements resulting from GDP growth are not reaching the most vulnerable population groups. This reflects an outstanding targeting problem, as poverty is maintained and reproduced across generations, with significant social costs and impacts on quality of life indicators in cities.

Table 6.9 Poverty rates according to the characteristics of the head of household, 2015 (%)

Characteristics of the head of household		National average	Urban areas	Main 13 cities*
Gender	Man	26.30	21.70	13.70
	Woman	31.00	28.30	18.10
Age	25 years or less	32.10	29.50	20.00
	Between 26 and 35 years	32.90	29.40	20.80
	Between 36 and 45 years	32.30	27.70	18.40
	Between 45 and 55 years	24.80	21.60	13.50
	Between 56 and 65 years	22.40	18.60	10.80
	More than 65 years	22.60	19.40	10.10
Education Level	None or elementary	38.60	35.30	22.80
	Secondary	25.10	23.80	16.30
	Technical or Technological	10.70	10.40	6.60
	College or graduate school	5.30	5.10	3.40
Occupational Status	Unemployed	48.00	46.50	35.90
	Employed	26.60	22.50	14.30
	Inactive	28.90	25.20	14.50
Occupational Position	Salaried worker	15.60	14.70	9.80
	Patron or self-employed	35.70	29.90	19.50
Social Security	Affiliated	7.80	8.00	6.40
	Not affiliated	38.00	34.50	23.30

*The 13 cities are Barranquilla (Metropolitan Area), Bogotá, Bucaramanga (Metropolitan Area), Cali (Metropolitan Area), Cartagena, Cúcuta (Metropolitan Area), Ibagué, Manizales (Metropolitan Area), Medellín (Metropolitan Area), Montería, Pasto, Pereira (Metropolitan Area), and Villavicencio.

Source: National Administrative Department of Statistics, DANE. Calculations based on the Great Integrated Household Survey, GEIH 2015 (Technical Bulletin March 2016: http://bit.ly/2aNP32v).

Table 6.10 Poverty rates according to household characteristics, 2015 (%)

Household's characteristics		National total	Urban areas	13 main cities*
Number of children under 12 years old	None	14.40	12.30	7.40
	One child	24.80	22.10	14.10
	Two children	41.00	38.30	26.70
	Three or more	64.90	61.60	49.40
Number of occupied persons in the household	None	45.10	41.20	30.30
	One Occupied	36.40	33.10	23.30
	Two or more Occupied	21.00	17.40	10.10

*The 13 cities are Barranquilla (Metropolitan Area), Bogotá, Bucaramanga (Metropolitan Area), Cali (Metropolitan Area), Cartagena, Cúcuta (Metropolitan Area), Ibagué, Manizales (Metropolitan Area), Medellín (Metropolitan Area), Montería, Pasto, Pereira (Metropolitan Area), and Villavicencio.

Source: National Administrative Department of Statistics, DANE. Calculations based on the Great Integrated Household Survey, GEIH 2015 (Technical Bulletin March 2016: http://bit.ly/2aNP32v).

Table 6.11 Rate of incidence of poverty according to the characteristics of the head of household, 2015 (%)

Characteristics of the Head of Household		National Total	Urban Areas	13 Main Cities*
Gender	Man	7.10	3.70	2.00
	Woman	9.60	7.00	3.90
Age	25 years or less	9.90	6.70	3.80
	Between 26 and 35 years	9.90	6.80	4.30
	Between 36 and 45 years	9.60	5.40	3.10
	Between 45 y 55 years	6.60	4.00	2.00
	Between 56 and 65 years	6.00	3.80	1.90
	More than 65 years	5.90	3.70	1.80
Education	None or elementary	12.20	7.70	4.20
Level	Secondary	5.90	4.40	2.70
	Technical or Technological	2.00	1.70	1.20
	University or graduate school	1.40	1.40	0.90
	Unemployed	21.20	19.10	13.80
	Employed	6.80	3.60	16.20
	Inactive	10.00	6.70	3.40
Occupational	Salaried Worker	1.80	1.20	0.50
Status	Patron or Self-Employed	10.90	5.90	3.40
Social	Affiliate	0.30	0.20	0.20
Security	No Affiliate	10.60	6.40	3.70

*The 13 cities are Barranquilla (Metropolitan Area), Bogotá, Bucaramanga (Metropolitan Area), Cali (Metropolitan Area), Cartagena, Cúcuta (Metropolitan Area), Ibagué, Manizales (Metropolitan Area), Medellín (Metropolitan Area), Montería, Pasto, Pereira (Metropolitan Area), and Villavicencio.

Source: National Administrative Department of Statistics, DANE. Calculations based on the Great Integrated Household Survey, GEIH 2015 (Technical Bulletin March 2016: http://bit.ly/2aNP32v).

Table 6.12 Rate of incidence of extreme poverty according to the features of the household, 2015 (%)

Household Characteristics		National Total	Urban Areas	13 Main Cities*
Number of children	None	3.70	2.60	1.60
under 12 years old	One child	6.10	3.90	2.20
	Two children	10.90	7.30	3.70
	Three or more	24.50	15.80	10.70
Number of	None	23.90	19.60	14.00
occupied in the	One occupied	10.70	7.00	4.10
household	Two or more occupied	4.60	2.10	0.90

*The 13 cities are Barranquilla (Metropolitan Area), Bogotá, Bucaramanga (Metropolitan Area), Cali (Metropolitan Area), Cartagena, Cúcuta (Metropolitan Area), Ibagué, Manizales (Metropolitan Area), Medellín (Metropolitan Area), Montería, Pasto, Pereira (Metropolitan Area), and Villavicencio.

Source: National Administrative Department of Statistics, DANE. Calculations based on the Great Integrated Household Survey, GEIH 2015 (Technical Bulletin March 2016: http://bit.ly/2aNP32v).

Intra-urban inequality

Recently, inequality in Colombian cities shows a decreasing trend. At the national level, the Gini coefficient for the urban areas decreased from 0.517 in 2013 to 0.514 in 2014, and in the 13 metropolitan areas, the Gini coefficient was 0.505 in 2013 and 0.504 in 2014.

In Bogotá, the average Gini coefficient for the city as a whole is 0.542, but when measuring within localities, the Gini coefficient is lower (around 0.400). The lowest inequality measures are recorded in four of the poorest localities: Bosa, Ciudad Bolívar, Usme, and San Cristóbal, as shown in Table 6.13. Candelaria and Santa Fé are those with the highest Gini coefficient: 0.587: these are also some of the poorest localities in Bogotá. Chapinero, the locality with the highest per capita income in 2011, had a Gini coefficient of 0.513 in that year, whereas the second highest-income town, Teusaquillo, had one of 0.415. These differences illustrate that there is significant inequality between localities, but poorer localities tend to be more even (SDP, 2013).

Table 6.13 Per capita income, Quality of Life Index, and Gini coefficient for Bogota localities, 2011

Locality	Income per capita (US$)*	Income in Chapinero/Income for each locality	Quality of Life Urban Index	Gini Coefficient	Quartile
Ciudad Bolívar	118.40	9.23	0.57	0.38	1.00
Usme	118.40	9.22	0.55	0.39	1.00
San Cristóbal	128.40	8.51	0.57	0.40	1.00
Bosa	134.30	8.13	0.58	0.37	1.00
Rafael Uribe	155.10	7.04	0.59	0.43	1.00
Tunjuelito	182.00	6.00	0.61	0.42	2.00
Kennedy	213.20	5.12	0.60	0.41	2.00
Antonio Nariño	238.30	4.58	0.62	0.45	2.00
Los Mártires	241.50	4.52	0.59	0.48	2.00
Puente Aranda	262.40	4.16	0.63	0.42	2.00
Engativá	268.50	4.07	0.62	0.41	3.00
Santa Fe	273.60	3.99	0.59	0.59	3.00
Bogotá average	194.50	5.62	0.64	0.54	3.00
La Candelaria	332.60	3.28	0.61	0.59	3.00
Suba	355.20	3.07	0.62	0.52	3.00
Fontibón	380.50	2.87	0.65	0.51	4.00
Barrios Unidos	410.00	2.66	0.63	0.50	4.00
Usaquén	647.40	1.69	0.64	0.54	4.00
Teusaquillo	695.80	1.57	0.67	0.42	4.00
Chapinero	1.092.1	1.00	0.66	0.51	4.00

* Original data in pesos of 2011. Conversion to a representative exchange rate of US$ 2,983.82 as of May 15, 2016.

Source: National Administrative Department of Statistics, DANE.
– Bogota Secretariat of Planning, SDP. Bogota Multi-Purpose Survey, EMB
– 2011 and CID, 2012 (Bogotá, D.C. City of Statistics, Bulletin No. 56)

Table 6.13 shows that intra-urban inequality, per capita income, and urban quality are closely related in Bogotá.

The Gini coefficient for Medellín's localities – called communes – is not available. For this reason, we have used two proxies: the Quality of Life Index (QLI) and the Multidimensional Indicator of Living Conditions (MILC), whose methodology can be consulted in the document of the Administrative Department of Planning of Medellín, 2012.

Table 6.14 shows the significant differences in quality of life among households in Medellín's localities. In terms of the QLI, conditions deteriorated in 2011 for some of the poorest families. This increase was mainly associated with shortages in water provision, sanitation services, and garbage collection. It is also observed that between 2010 and 2011, the gap between the best and poorest performers in the QLI has widened.

The MILC for 2010 and 2011 presents a scenario of general improvement across Medellín between 2010 and 2011, as shown in Table 6.15. Medellin passed from 47.26 in 2010 to 47.62 in 2011; that is a rise of 0.76 points. The lowest scores of the MILC composite indicator are recorded in two poor localities: Candelaria and, unexpectedly, in the Poblado, one of the localities with most high- and high-middle-income settlers in Medellín.

Notable features of intra-urban inequality

In principle, intra-urban inequality and inequality between the different Colombian cities have the same main qualitative characteristics, explained by gaps in productivity and in GDP per capita (FEDESARROLLO, 2014). This

Table 6.14 Quality of Life Index by communes, Medellín, 2010 and 2011

Commune	2010	2011	% Variation
1 Popular	76.27	75.98	−0.38
2 Santa Cruz	77.73	79.21	1.9
3 Manrique	79.67	78.31	−1.71
4 Aranjuez	81.9	82.72	1
5 Castilla	84.41	84.58	0.2
6 Doce Octubre	81.16	81.6	0.54
7 Robledo	83.35	83.61	0.31
8 Villa Hermosa	79.71	79.46	−0.31
9 Buenos Aires	83.74	84.97	1.47
10 Candelaria	87.55	87	−0.63
11 Laureles	91.01	91.18	0.19
12 América	88.66	89.31	0.73
13 San Javier	80.52	80.77	0.31
14 Poblado	92.76	93.41	0.7
15 Guayabal	86.49	85.44	−1.21
16 Belén	87.6	88.17	0.65

Source: Quality of Life Survey. Medellín 2010–2011 (Mayor of Medellín – Administrative Department of Planning, Poverty and living conditions of the inhabitants of Medellín, 2011).

Table 6.15 Multidimensional Indicator of Living Conditions in Medellín by communes, 2010 and 2011

Commune	2010.00	2011.00	% Variation
50 Palmitas	65.71	61.94	−5.74
60 San Cristóbal	75.16	71.62	−4.71
70 Altavista	70.65	68.33	−3.28
80 San Antonio de Prado	79.48	80.19	0.89
90 Santa Elena	77.21	75.45	−2.28

Source: Quality of Life Survey. Medellín 2010–2011 (Mayor of Medellín – Administrative Department of Planning, Poverty and living conditions of the inhabitants of Medellín, 2011).

is results in a certain duality among Colombian cities. Some sites of modern economic sectors coexist with others of precarious economic growth. Furthermore, there is social and spatial segregation, differentiated access to natural resources, to financial and productive assets, and to local opportunities. Still, in Bogotá, inequality between localities is high, but in the poorer localities it tends to be low, much lower than in the wealthier ones.

Patterns of social exclusion

Social exclusion in Colombia operates from several fronts. The most relevant are the violation of civil and political rights (displacement, political violence), poverty, labor informality, limited access to education, limited access to credit and banking, capital and stock concentration, limited access to productive assets (financial, human capital, productive capital), skewed access to public services, and income inequality, as well as female head of household and its impact on the intergenerational reproduction of social exclusion (Garay, sf).

Reasons behind recent changes in poverty and inequality

In Colombia, changes in poverty levels are more visible than those reported by the dynamics of inequality. In the case of poverty, the main causes that have contributed to the reduction of monetary poverty, extreme and multidimensional, are related to the performance of the Colombian economy in the last 10 years (average growth of 4.8 percent of GDP), the progress in human capital (education, social security, formalization of labor), social programs focused on vulnerable population, and a significant increase in the public expenditure for poor population and for those displaced by the internal conflicts.

In terms of inequality, the results are less effective, and the little progress made has had a slow pace. This is also the case in Latin America overall, where it seems that the Gini coefficient and other indicators have stagnated to the extent that indicators regularly point to this region as one of the most unequal in the world. The causal explanations continue to be under study. However, it is agreed that the model of economic growth in the region has reduced the share of labor in GDP. Also, the share of the services sector has increased, which produces a greater asymmetry in the distribution of household income, among other consequences.

Urban form

> *Governments at the appropriate levels should . . . develop and support the implementation of improved land-management practices that deal comprehensively with competing urban land requirements for housing, industry, commerce, infrastructure, transport, green spaces and forested areas, taking into account the need for spaces for everyday activities – for playgrounds, parks, sports and recreation areas and areas suitable for gardening and urban agriculture . . . promote land-use patterns that minimize transport demands, save energy and protect open and green spaces. Appropriate urban density and mixed land-use guidelines are of prime importance for urban development.*
>
> (HABITAT II, 1996)

Recent changes in density and the spatial form of Colombian cities

Colombian national urban policy has made mandatory land-use development plans for all Colombian cities since 2000. Moreover, the legislation explicitly privileges the compact city model. What is more, the high prices of urban land have induced high densities, and indeed, building single-family housing in Colombia's major and intermediate cities has become unfeasible (DNP, 2014a). In fact, densification has occurred mainly in the larger cities and pertains to urban modern and formal sectors, which exist in a close yet segregated way with sectors of informal origin (i.e. social production of housing) where the low densities prevail. Unfortunately, when examining current urbanization processes, it is evident that land-use plans have not yet become effective drivers of city growth. Instead, city growth has been largely market driven. Alas, it can also be said that land-use planning has been divorced from transportation planning, to the point that the road network is not guiding urban growth, but on the contrary, mobility infrastructure is marching behind the growth of cities.

Furthermore, urban planning in Colombia applies mostly to the formal production of nonresidential buildings, whereas the majority of the housing stock is produced informally. This produces, among other results, urbanization processes that are incomplete and are of low densities.

At a broader territorial level, many urban centers, regional corridors, and urban agglomerations are being formed and consolidated in the country. These processes have significant shortcomings because they lack informed development orientation and do not make use of any of the financing instruments available (CONPES, 2014).

Urban form of metropolitan areas and smaller territorial units

Unregulated urban growth, conurbation, and suburbanization processes in urban corridors are the main characteristics of the urban form of metropolitan areas and of smaller territorial units. Also, economic agglomerations have developed outside any institutional platform or norms for supra-municipal association (ibid.).

The Metropolitan Area of the Aburrá Valley (Medellín and its surrounding municipalities) is perhaps the only exception, because it is a metropolitan area clearly derived from metropolitan planning. In this case, the layout of urban infrastructure and the allocation of urban land for future expansion have determined – and balanced – the distribution of the population across the territory.

One remarkable fact of Colombia's urban and territorial development is the lack of a metropolitan area in Bogotá and its neighboring municipalities, especially Soacha, a city of more than 500,000 inhabitants that is contiguous with the capital of the country. This absence is more inexplicable if one considers that 19 municipalities in the Bogotá savanna create a single functional area, together with Bogotá, especially in terms of commutes. The nonexistence of a metropolitan area in Bogota is more alarming considering that the metropolitan area of Medellín was legally established almost four decades ago.

Although several joint initiatives to formalize some type of associativity in the region have been undertaken by Bogotá and the Cundinamarca department (state), this has not been achieved, mainly because municipalities do not want to lose their legal and financial autonomy. On the other hand, the new metropolitan area that would be formed would assume the functions of environmental authority in its jurisdiction, which would deprive significant resources from the CAR, the organization that currently has that competence. Hence, this situation prevents the district of Bogotá and its neighboring municipalities from adequately managing metropolitan issues related to mobility, public utilities, waste management, and so on. In addition, Soacha, as well as the rest of the municipalities that would potentially be part of the metropolitan area of Bogota, are depriving themselves of the benefits and investment opportunities that such an administrative change could bring about.

At a more general level, the lack of a metropolitan institutional framework has inhibited the formation of a shared regional vision, hindering the coordination of planning and development initiatives with an integral territorial conception, to the point that municipalities, rather than neighbors with common purposes, are actually competitors. This situation has contributed to the geographical dispersion of industrial zones, which is economically detrimental to the establishment of well-linked productive chains.

Other relevant spatial forms

In the case of Colombia, four factors stand out as having incidence in spatial forms: uncontrolled suburbanization; accelerated growth of rural housing in rural, nonsuburban areas; and the re-densification of the informal city. Deregulated urban sprawl is the most salient of these phenomena, which includes industrial zones, hotels, universities, and colleges, whose building permits are usually negotiated with high levels of corruption.

Decentralization of economic activity

There has been no decentralization of economic activity in Colombia during the post-1996 period. The location of central institutions and productive infrastructure has reaffirmed the economic primacy of the capital, Bogotá, which concentrates 16.3 percent of the country's population and accounts for 25.9 percent of total GDP. Besides being the seat of the national government, the capital has a considerably well-sized market: Bogota's GDP represents the eighth largest economy of Latin America (Goueset, 1998).

Distribution of urban populations between large, medium, and small urban areas

Small urban areas in Colombia are recording population loss, except for the neighboring municipalities of the big cities, as has happened with those of the Bogotá savanna region. In general, the population is increasing in medium and bigger urban centers and agglomerations, as well as in regional corridors. Some of the factors influencing these demographic changes are labor force attraction, resettlement due to high geological risk, and, most importantly, the process of forced displacement by the internal conflict. However, it can be said that these demographic features are not unique to the period 1996–2016. Colombia is indeed a decentralized country with a system of cities.

In sum, modern and high-density sectors are present in large and medium-sized cities of Colombia, whereas small cities are characterized by low densities and informal urban sprawl formed by low-income households. In large and medium-sized cities, urban growth is guided by market mechanisms, which have prevailed over the forecasts of the land-use plans. Another outstanding feature is the low number of associations of municipalities and departments, which has deprived cities and regions of the advantages derived from the supra-municipal associativity. Overall, uncontrolled suburbanization processes are occurring, together with the growth of populated centers and the re-densification of the informal city. Bogotá has confirmed its urban primacy and its role as the center of national economic activity, contributing 25 percent of the national GDP.

Pending tasks and recommendations

Pending tasks with respect to Colombia's Habitat II commitments

Regarding the commitments made by Colombia in Habitat II, it is worth noting that it has not been possible yet to coordinate efficiently different levels of government. There are still serious limitations in the coordination between urban and territorial planning, as well as a lack of cooperation between nation, departments, districts, and municipalities, which affects the sustainable development of urban settlements across the country.

As far as decentralization is concerned, there has been progress on the political-administrative level, power devolution for land-use planning, and management of public services, including health and education facilities. However, the housing policy maintains a high degree of centralization. It is important to reiterate that urban policy is very weak in the region, as 86 percent of Colombian municipalities are classified as financially unviable.

Colombia has made little progress in supra-municipal associative processes, despite the fact that it has a system of cities with an important number of relatively large agglomerations, as well as regional corridors and urban centers that operate as a de facto metropolis. Lack of metropolitan formalization prevents the country from capitalizing on the advantages of this institutional framework.

The financial base of Colombian municipalities and departments is very limited. Several factors have to do with this: outdated cadasters, low property tax rates, and the low participation of other sources of income, which makes the municipalities more dependent on the transfers from the central government. Besides, very few municipalities make use of land-value capture instruments that allow them to finance urban interventions without affecting other parts of the municipal budgets.

Another aspect that needs much improvement is the quality of urban participation processes, which need to ensure greater input from citizens, transcending the almost exclusive involvement of economic and professional associations.

The commitments of sustainability and environmental management have been fulfilled in terms of institutional and regulatory development, although this is mainly relevant at the national level. This is to say that sustainability and environmental management at the municipal level is still very weak, as its regulations are much more recent, especially those related to sustainable modes of production and transportation (rather than consumption). With relation to urban development, the outcome is negative because settlements, both formal and informal, are characterized by low densities and high generation of emissions.

Housing policy in Colombia has not implemented in full the concept of *adequate housing*, which is one of the main commitments acquired in Habitat II. Despite the fact that this concept is part of the constitutionality block issued by the Colombian Constitutional Court (General Comment No. 4), which rules "the right to decent housing".

With regard to housing policy, Colombia is in the process of making further progress in measures aimed at generating urban land and coordinating it with a demographic policy. In the same vein, the sectoral policy is overfocused on the housing subsidies. Furthermore, it can be said that the construction of new housing is the single most important item on the housing policy. Other issues, like the upgrading of the housing stock in cities, receives very low levels of public expenditure.

Despite being enshrined in Article 51 of the 1991 constitution, since 1991 the central government has not promoted "adequate financing systems" or "associative forms of implementation" of social housing programs in the spirit of Habitat II commitments. Moreover, there is no funding for other components of the housing production chain, nor for cooperative production and financing systems. Poor and low-income households and those in informal occupations are excluded from access to bank mortgages.

Over the last 10 years the country's larger cities have taken the most advantage of Colombia's GDP. Cities overall have improved their economy, although there is still a high proportion of informal employment that affects the distribution of the benefits of this growth. In terms of employment quality, local governments have little leeway, as this is considered to be a function of the central government. Likewise, local governments' influence in promoting entrepreneurship is low, although the main cities are currently more proactive in this type of work. Efforts have been made to simplify procurement processes and to support financially small and medium enterprises. Although the situation is changing favorably, citizen insecurity and internal armed conflict provide an adverse environment for companies in some areas of the country.

On the other hand, leveraging city resources linking private capital in public projects, such as public–private partnerships and concessions, among others, is relatively new in Colombia, being first implemented by the national government for infrastructure works for multimodal transport.

The correlation between poor housing conditions and poverty has been well documented in Colombia. Interestingly, households affected by housing precariousness (qualitative deficit) have twice the probability of being poor than those who require housing (quantitative deficit). In the face of economic shocks, housing policy has emphasized public spending on programs aimed at the construction of new housing. This orientation of the sectoral policy prevents it from contributing to the fight against poverty. Additionally, this inclination towards new housing rather than upgrading lessens the potential for urban and housing policy to have an effect in inequality. Given the limited nature of public land management, urban land availability is driven by the market. The urban land price system has also influenced the location of settlements originating in informal housing production, inducing it to the peripheries, increasing its dependence on motorized transportation, and making nonpolluting alternatives less viable.

Recommendations

The New Urban Agenda should have considered recommending governments apply the concept of "adequate housing" as one of the guiding principles of housing policy. Although this notion is frequently found in the text of sectoral policies, its actual implementation in terms of public expenditures is insignificant. Paradoxically, the "adequate housing" concept has remained largely unknown in the initial phases of the value chain of the housing policy, that is, diagnosis and dimensioning of the housing needs of households, which ought to be the basis for all formulation of programs and policy instruments. This helps explain the difference between the aims of public policy and the orientation of public spending. These considerations allow us to argue that the concept of "adequate housing" is barely applied in practice, both in the production of housing (low income and beyond) and in the social production of habitat processes (self-management and self-construction).

In Colombia, the attributes of adequate housing that are notoriously absent from formal production and social production of housing are those referred to as "cultural appropriation" and "sustainable expenditure."

It is important for governments to consider housing policy programs and instruments aimed at requalification of the built environment and the existing housing stock, considering that this represents a greater proportion of the housing supply. Also, the built housing stock is a determinant of both housing prices and prices for urban services. So consequently, it should be a priority of the government to make itself responsible for satisfying the housing needs of most of the population.

The coexistence of urban land management instruments present in the legislation and a speculative system of prices for land remains a contradiction that affects in a profound way the availability of urbanized land required for the production of social housing and of housing of other prices. In this sense, more state intervention in this market is needed in order to expand the supply via the alternatives offered by Law 388 of 1997 and, by this means, to modulate surges in prices.

Housing finance must transcend mortgage credit and move towards the implementation of a housing financing system that includes different types of credit, whose conditions are defined according to the socioeconomic characteristics of the population that is the object of the national housing policy: mortgage credit and not mortgages from commercial banks and nonbanking establishments, both short and long term, with subsidized interest rates and with rediscount operations of public entities for social housing, as well as direct credit to households originating in public social housing institutions.

In the field of other financial instruments, housing subsidies must be conceived and implemented as a broader system: direct and indirect subsidies to demand and supply, in money and in kind, as well as subsidies to the origination of credits. In all cases, these should operate as a complement to the payment capacity of households with insufficient income to autonomously meet their housing needs.

The relevance of proposing a system-based conception for the financial instruments of the housing policy lies in the fact that borrowers are households with different characteristics with regard to the nature of their occupations (formal and informal), level and periodicity of income, and availability of collateral (personal, collective, real, etc.). That is, it is not viable to sustain housing financing with commercial mortgage credit alone, which excludes –as is currently happening – a very high proportion of the applicants to social housing.

Colombia, like Latin America overall, accumulated until 1990 a remarkable trajectory of organized processes of the social production of housing, first in the form of mutual funds (1930–1950), then as part of the cooperative movement

(1960–1970), and then in the form of housing associations (1980–1990). At the same time, the public sector consolidated an institutional framework to support this form of social production of housing, with the Territorial Credit Institute (ICT), the National Learning Service (SENA), the General Directorate of Community Development (DIGIDEC), and the Ministry of Government, among others. The range of these public services integrated the resources required for communities to originate and manage their housing projects.

Later on, all these forms of community organization were gathered in the Organizations for Popular Housing (OPV), recognized by the 1989 Urban Reform Law and the 1997 Territorial Development Law as formal providers of publicly funded social housing projects (both VIS and VIP). However, the change in the model of public management in 1991, from universal provision to that of subsidies to demand, implied the disbanding of institutional services directed to support self-construction and self-management processes. As an alternative, several types of collective subsidies for the production of new housing were tried, but they did not render much success. The organized housing movement in Colombia was almost completely dissolved, depriving the housing policy of important actors with a high potential to contribute to satisfy the country's housing needs. My claim therefore is that it is important to include programs and instruments in the housing policy that promote and support the whole chain of production of social housing, starting with the initial process of organizing the communities. In addition to being included in the Habitat II commitments, this recommendation follows up on the final content of Article 51 of the constitution of Colombia (the right to decent housing), which states that "(. . .) The State (. . .) shall promote forms of associations of the implementation [. . .] of these housing programs".

Urban development is carried out through actions that require specific financing. In Colombia, notwithstanding the provisions of the current legislation, most municipalities and districts have in fact ignored land capture resources. Municipalities could capture increased land values from capital gains derived from the urban action carried out in the city by public administrations in the form of investments in public goods and urban services. These uncaptured resources have an important dimension, considering the recent real estate boom of the Colombian cities. To have a sense of the extent of the inactivity of the municipalities in this field, I mention again that only 0.02 percent of the current income of local governments has been generated by participation in capital gains (Gaviria, 2016). However, this potential source of resources should be understood as a payment for the added value for urban development, rather than a discouragement to private investment in social housing.

This concluding section cannot avoid mentioning the severe effects of Colombia's internal conflict, specifically the humanitarian crisis created by forced displacement of rural populations towards the cities. This violent process has been one of the important determinants of the de facto occupation of the territory and the processes of social production of housing (i.e. informality) that have characterized the growth of Colombian cities since the 1950s. The resulting settlements concentrate political and socioeconomic problems transcending the general state of denial of the rights of citizens, as was confirmed by the ruling T25[20] of Colombia's Constitutional Court.

In this sense, it is important to note that if a final agreement is reached in the negotiation process between the Colombian government and the FARC, one of the main characteristics of the post-conflict era will be a significant reduction of migratory pressure towards the main urban agglomerations. The post-conflict reality can be better appreciated in its demographic dimension: currently, more than 7.1 million displaced people are housed in settlements located generally on the periphery of cities. Public urban and housing policy will then face a double burden. It must deepen and produce results in the programs directed towards displaced households in a context that will also involve a process of restitution of rights. In addition, public policy ought to pay more attention to public spending, broadening its target to include other population groups with housing needs, as is the case of households in conditions of poverty and vulnerability. However, the greatest challenge will transcend the scope of sectoral policy and will relate to the capacity of Colombian society to recognize the reality and diversity of cities, which have accumulated the effects of the conflict. The challenge includes overcoming current levels of segregation, exclusion, and social inequality and, in a higher sense, consolidating just cities.

Finally, it must be said that it would have been very productive if the preparatory process for Habitat III in Colombia had developed during a longer period of time and if they had had a more intense participation of civil society organizations, academia, and citizens. This would have generated a reflective process on the urban reality of the country, which would have contributed to the discussion and identification of long-term purposes for cities and regions. This approach is even more valid if it is considered that overcoming the armed conflict will create conditions on which urban knowledge has no antecedents on the types of challenges ahead, the emerging problems, and the possibility of capitalizing on a situation of greater welfare opportunities.

Notes

1 The National Administrative Department of Statistics (DANE), responsible for ensuring the production, availability, and quality of strategic statistical information and to direct, plan, execute, coordinate, regulate, and evaluate the production and dissemination of basic official information in Colombia (Decree 262 of 2004), defines administrative divisions following these basic concepts. *Urban area*: Consists of groups of buildings and contiguous structures grouped in blocks, which are mainly delimited by streets, alleys, or avenues. It is usually provided with essential urban services such as aqueduct, sewerage, electric power, hospitals, and schools, among others. This category includes the capital cities and other municipal seats. *Rural area or municipal remainder*: It is characterized by dispersed houses and agricultural plots. It does not have a layout plan or nomenclature of streets, roads, avenues, and others. Neither does it generally have public services and other facilities of the urban areas. *Municipal seat*: It is the geographical area defined by an urban perimeter, whose limits are established by the Municipal Council. It corresponds to the place where the administrative headquarters of a municipality is located.

2 This chapter was produced before the peace accord between the government of Juan Manuel Santos and the FARC was signed and ratified by Congress. (Note from the editors.)

3 The concept "social production of habitat" (SPH) is used in the chapter instead of "informally produced housing". "Although its definition is still in a deliberative process in the making, the Social Production of Habitat should be understood as a mode of production of housing and/or urban environment, in which a family or a community participatory in an organized manner. The Social Production of Habitat is considered an alternative to the mercantile production of housing, in which housing has lost its character as an inalienable human right, and has become a commodity, excluding a large part of the population. According to his exponents, the Social Production of Habitat presents a great number of advantages, in the sense that such production is flexible and is created from the genuine cultural, social, and housing needs of the residents" (Enet et al., 2008).

4 The Mission for Cities of the National Planning Department (DNP) "proposed a characterization of the Colombian System of Cities, based on the concept of agglomeration economies developed by Duranton (2008 & 2013) that uses urban equilibrium models based on variables of urban productivity and quality of life. It also used concepts associated with functional relationships between urban centers measured in commuting times, following the methodology proposed by the United States census office to define the extent of metropolitan areas (United States Office of Management and Budget, 2010). Moreover, conceptual elements employed by the Organization for Economic Cooperation and Development in shaping urban functional areas (OECD, 2013) were also considered. For the initial characterization of the system of cities, the Mission used four criteria. The first one considers the functional relations between the municipalities, the second considers population size, the third the political-administrative function of the municipalities, and the last one, the strategic importance of the municipalities in the regions" (National Council of Political and Social Economy, 2014).

5 "The issuance of sentence T-025 of 2004 of the Constitutional Court on the treatment that the State must give to internally displaced population, in particular on their right to a decent housing, declared an unconstitutional state of affairs and established that both National and territorial authorities, within the scope of their powers, must adopt corrective measures to overcome this state of affairs. This court sentence put more pressure on the output of the housing policy and exposed the dramatic limitations of the policy based on a subsidy to the demand" (CONPES, 2014).

6 The National Council for Economic and Social Policy (CONPES) was created by Law No. 19 of 1958. This is the highest national planning authority and serves as an advisory body to the government in all aspects related to the economic and social development of the country. To achieve this, it coordinates and guides all the agencies responsible for economic and social management in the government, through the study and approval of documents on the development of general policies that are presented in session. The National Planning Department serves as the executive secretariat of CONPES and therefore is the entity in charge of coordinating and presenting all documents for discussion (http://bit.ly/13gbViS).

7 Lauchlin Currie was a Canadian-born American economist who served as an aide to the Roosevelt administration during World War II. He later joined the World Bank, where he led the first comprehensive country survey in Colombia in 1949. After the report, the Colombian government invited him to implement his own recommendations (in stark opposition to those of Hirschman, who was also part of the survey (Sandilands, 2015)). (Note from the editors.)

8 The Territorial Planning Councils (CTP) are territorial planning bodies created by a constitutional provision to guarantee citizen participation in the development and monitoring of public policies at the territorial level, under the principle of participatory planning.

9 "The prior consultation is a fundamental right of the indigenous and tribal peoples of the world, recognized by the UN, which seeks to safeguard the people, institutions, property, work, cultures, and environment of these peoples, as well as recognize and protect their social, cultural, religious, spiritual, and institutional values and practices. However, for companies, the first step is to comply with when they want to carry out extractive activities (or those linked with transport, mining, and energy infrastructure) in any region of the country. In Colombia, this function is assigned to the Ministry of Interior and Justice and operates through permanent dialogues within working groups where these minorities are represented (. . .) this is a responsibility shared between representatives of the projects and the state, through the ministry." (Dinero, 2013).

10 For decades, in the larger cities in Colombia, the preference of the households is to have individual plots of 72 m², an area that is affordable and that enables undertaking progressive development of a house which, in addition to providing a roof, can generate income to the household through rents and holding productive activities within the dwelling.

11 The DNP found out that 956 of the 1,107 municipalities of Colombia are classified in fiscal category 6, that is, they have a population of fewer than 10,000 inhabitants and have available an annual disposable income of less than 15,000 monthly minimum legal wages (US$3,465,963, at an exchange rate of COP 2,983.82).

12 The FNA was created by Extraordinary Decree 3118 of 1968 to administer the severance packages of public employees and official workers. Through Act 432 of 1998, it was transformed into a state industrial and commercial company (a national financial company), which allowed it to expand its market to the private sector. Its purpose is to fulfill the rights of all Colombians to have decent housing and access to education (www. fna.gov.co).

13 Real estate microcredit (Law 795 of 2003) has not had a significant impact on the financing of housing because its regulations included conditions that limited their acceptance by households and banks. In the first case, the mortgage guarantee was established, which was a discouraging factor for the households, which in Colombia do not have a positive perception on the collection practices of banks. In the case of banks, the interest rate for these microcredits was integrated into the existing regulation for the purchase of housing of social interest, that is, it was defined as the "lowest market", certified by the Bank of Republic. This measure generated the disinterest of the banks, which generally provide for housing improvement and other types of actions included in the progressive development process at the rates corresponding to consumption and free investment, which imply interest rates close to usury. On the other hand, in order to compensate for the cost of the process of analysis of these microcredits mainly related to the verification of income of an informal nature, the banks were authorized to charge a commission. On this point, a debate was generated because the possibility was raised that this commission, if added to the interest rate of credit ("the lowest"), could imply for the bank a violation of the existing regulation for social housing loans. This situation was classified as legal insecurity for the banks and was presented as a reason for not promoting and placing real estate microcredit resources.

14 ASOBANCARIA, based on statistical reports by several leading banks (i.e. AV Villas, Banco Caja Social, Bancolombia, BBVA, Colpatria, and Davivienda).

15 The price of the VIS is the equivalent to 135 current minimum monthly wages (or US$31,193.70) and the VIP price is US$16,174.50 (at a RER of COP 2,983.82).

16 Bank of the Republic of Colombia. Land price index in Bogotá, relative to the Consumer Price Index (CPI), total CPI Bogotá.

17 Macro-projects of national social interest are interventions promoted by the national government that link instruments of planning, financing, and land management to carry out a large-scale operation that contributes to the territorial development of certain municipalities, districts, or regions of the country. The objective of these macro-projects is to increase the supply of urbanized soils for the development of priority and social housing programs (VIS-VIP), especially in the municipalities and districts of the country

that have a large housing deficit and where difficulties have been found in obtaining land for the development of VIS–VIP programs (www.minvivienda.gov.co).
18 In both cases, the data correspond to the January–December monthly average of 13 cities and metropolitan areas (DANE, 2015).
19 Sustainable Cities and Competitive Platform (CSC), FINDETER program in partnership with the Inter-American Development Bank (IDB), inspired by the Emerging and Sustainable Cities Initiative (ICES) that the IDB carries out in more than 30 cities in Latin America and Caribbean.
20 See endnote 5.

Bibliography

Alcaldía de Medellín – Departamento Administrativo de Planeación, (2011), *Pobreza y condiciones de vida de los habitantes de Medellín*, Medellín City Government, Medellín.

Asociación Colombiana de Productores de Concreto, ASOCRETO – Centro de Estudios de la Construcción y el Desarrollo Urbano y Regional, CENAC, (2012), *Estimación del consumo de materiales de construcción en la vivienda informal en Bogotá*, ASOCRETO-CENAC, Bogotá, DC.

Bustamante, J., (2011), *Los retos del crecimiento formal de la economía, Notas fiscales No. 9*, Ministerio de Hacienda y Crédito Público, Bogotá.

Cámara Colombiana de la Construcción, CAMACOL, International Finance Corporation, IFC, and Economía Urbana, (2014), *Escasez de suelo e incidencia en la actividad edificadora*, Julio Miguel Silva (consultant), Bogotá.

Ceballos, O., Saldarriaga, A., and Tarchopoulus, D., (2008), *Vivienda social en Colombia: una mirada desde su legislación 1918–2005*, Editorial Pontificia Universidad Javeriana, Bogotá.

Centro de Estudios de la Construcción y el Desarrollo Urbano y Regional, CENAC, (1993), *Estudio de las necesidades habitacionales de la población residente en algunos municipios de Colombia*, CENAC, Bogotá.

Conference Board Total Economy, (2014), *International Labor Comparisons Program 2014*. Available at: www.conference-board.org/ilcprogram/

Consejo Nacional de Economía Política y Social, CONPES – Departamento Nacional de Planeación, DNP, (2012), *Document CONPES 3718: Política nacional de espacio público, PNEP*. Available at: http://bit.ly/2dHpuyk

Consejo Nacional de Economía Política y Social, CONPES – Departamento Nacional de Planeación, DNP, (2014), *Document CONPES 3819: Política nacional para consolidar el Sistema de Ciudades en Colombia*. Available at: http://bit.ly/2dHpuyk

Consultoría para los Derechos Humanos y el Desplazamiento, CODHES, (2013), *El desplazamiento forzado y la imperiosa necesidad de la paz*, Report 2013. Available at: http://bit.ly/2cOLwhb

Costa, C., (2012), *Sostenibilidad ambiental, cambio climático y gestión del riesgo de desastres*, Misión del Sistema de Ciudades – Departamento Nacional de Planeación, DNP. Available at: http://bit.ly/2dcf49a

Departamento Administrativo de Planeación, DANE, (2010), Dirección de Metodología y Producción Estadística, DIPME, *Manual de recolección y conceptos básicos*, ECV, Report, Bogotá.

Departamento Administrativo de Planeación, DANE, (2015), "Monetary Poverty Results for July 2014–July 2015 Database, Calculations According to *Gran Encuesta Integrada de Hogares GEIH*", Government of Colombia, Web.

Departamento Administrativo de Planeación – Subdirección de Metroinformación – Observatorio de Políticas Públicas, (2012), *Pobreza y condiciones de vida de los habitantes de Medellín, 2011*, Database, Government of Colombia. Available at: http://bit.ly/1Qg8akD

Departamento Administrativo Nacional de Estadística, DANE, (2007), *Revista ib virtual*, 2:2, Government of Colombia. Available at: www.dane.gov.co/revista_ib/html_r4/articulo2_r4.htm

Departamento Administrativo Nacional de Estadística, DANE, (2014), *Gran Encuesta Integrada de Hogares*, GEIH, Government of Colombia, Web.

Departamento Administrativo Nacional de Estadística, DANE, (2016), *Technical Bulletin*, March 2016, Government of Colombia, Available at: http://bit.ly/2aNP32v

Departamento Administrativo Nacional de Estadística, DANE – Secretaría Distrital de Planeación, SDP. Encuesta Multipropósito de Bogotá, (2012), *Ciudad de Estadísticas*, Bulletin No. 56, Government of Colombia, Bogotá.

Departamento Nacional de Planeación, DNP, (2005), *Visión Colombia II Centenario: 2019*, Government of Colombia, Available at: http://bit.ly/1VNd46R

Departamento Nacional de Planeación, DNP, (2014a), *Evaluación de operaciones y línea de base de los programas de subsidio familiar de vivienda y subsidio familiar de vivienda en especie. Volumen 1: Política nacional de vivienda en Colombia*, Government of Colombia, Bogotá, DC.

Departamento Nacional de Planeación, DNP, (2014b), *Plan Nacional de Desarrollo 2014–2018: Todos por un nuevo país*, Law 1753 June 9 2015, Government of Colombia. Available at: http://bit.ly/1K5wzST

Development Planning Unit, DPU, (2006), *Suelo urbano y vivienda para la población de ingresos bajos. Estudios de caso: Bogotá, Soacha, Mosquera; Medellín y Área Metropolitana*. Available at: http://bit.ly/2dPVIb5

Dinero.com, (2013), "10 pasos para realizar consulta previa en Colombia", *Dinero Magazine*, February 12, Web, Available at: http://bit.ly/2cQOqld

Echavarría, J., Arbeláez, M., and Rosales, M., (2006), *La productividad y sus determinantes. El caso de la industria colombiana*. Available at: www.banrep.gov.co/docum/ftp/borra374.pdf

Enet, M., Olivera, R., and Romero, G., (2008), "Herramientas para pensar y crear en colectivo: en programas intersectoriales de hábitat", Ciencia y Tecnología para el Desarrollo, CYTED, Hábitat International Coalition, HIC, Buenos Aires 2008, In Secretaría Distrital de Hábitat – CENAC, *El Proceso de la Ciudad Informal*, Noviembre 2011, Association Agreement No. 082, 2011.

Escallón, G. C., (2014), "Gobernanza en proceso de regeneración urbana. Aproximaciones al caso de Bogotá", *Monography CIDER: Universidad de Los Andes*, 28, pp. 11–134.

FEDESARROLLO, (2014), *Productividad y competitividad del sistema de ciudades*, Available at: http://bit.ly/2dPVH6N

Garay, L., *En torno a la economía política de la exclusión social en Colombia*. Available at: https://dialnet.unirioja.es/servlet/articulo?codigo=2329127

Garay, L. J., (2003), "En torno a la economía política de la exclusión social en Colombia", *Revista de economía institucional*, 5:8, pp. 15–31.

Gaviria, M. S., (2016), *Sistema de ciudades en Colombia. De cara a la nueva agenda urbana*, Keynote presentation at: Primer Foro Camino HÁBITAT III, mayo 10, Bogotá.

Goueset, V., (1998), *Bogotá: Nacimiento de una metrópoli. La originalidad del proceso de concentración urbana en Colombia en el siglo XX*, Tercer Mundo Editores, Observatorio de Cultura Urbana, CENAC, IFEA, FEDEVIVIENDA, Bogotá.

Government of Colombia, (1991), *Political Constitution of 1991*, Article Government of Colombia, Bogota.

Government of Colombia, (2014), *Informe de seguimiento de los Objetivos de Desarrollo del Milenio*, Available at: http://bit.ly/2dqja0o

Hamann, F., and Mejía, L., (2011), "Formalizando la informalidad empresarial en Colombia", *Borradores de economía: Banco de la República*, 676, pp. 1–30, Bogotá.

Herrera, C. G., (2014), Hacia la construcción de territorios equitativos, Conference presentation at World Urban Forum 7, abril 9, Medellín.

Interamerican Development Bank, IDB, (2011), *Estudio sobre el mercado de arrendamiento de vivienda en Colombia*, Jorge Enrique Torres Ramírez (consultant). Available at: www.iadb.org/es/

Ministry of Economic Development – Government of Colombia, (1995), *Ciudades y Ciudadanía. La política urbana del salto social*, Tercer Mundo Editores, Bogotá.

Ministry of Housing, City and Territory, MVCT – Centro de Estudios de la Construcción y el Desarrollo Urbano y Regional, CENAC, (2012, 2013), *Evaluación del Programa de Mejoramiento Integral de Barrios, PMIB*, MVCT-CENAC, Bogotá.

Ministry of Housing, City and Territory, MVCT – Centro de Estudios de la Construcción y el Desarrollo Urbano y Regional, CENAC, (2015), *Territorios inteligentes al 2035. Una estrategia para el desarrollo territorial y urbano planificado*, MVCT-CENAC, Bogotá, DC.

Organisation for Economic Co-operation and Development (OECD), (2013), "Definition of Functional Urban Areas (FUA) for the OECD metropolitan database", *OECD*, September, Web, Paris.

Programa de las Naciones Unidas para los Asentamientos Humanos, ONU Hábitat; CAF – Banco de Desarrollo de América Latina, (2014), *Construcción de ciudades más equitativas: Políticas públicas para la inclusión en América Latina*. Available at: http://bit.ly/RJjz00

Report of the United Nations Conference on Human Settlements (HABITAT II), (1996), *Istambul Declaration on Human Settlements*, United Nations General Assembly, Istanbul, 3–14 June.

Roger J. S., (2015), "The 1949 World Bank Mission to Colombia and the Competing Visions of Lauchlin Currie (1902–93) and Albert Hirschman (1915-2012)," *History of Economic Thought and Policy*, Franco Angeli Editore, 1, pp 21–38, Milan.

Secretaría Distrital de Hábitat – Centro de Estudios de la Construcción y el Desarrollo Urbano y Regional, CENAC, (2011), *El Proceso de la Ciudad Informal*, Government of Bogotá, Bogotá.

Secretaría Distrital de Planeación, SDP, (2013), *Bogotá, DC, Ciudad de estadísticas. Índice de desigualdad de Bogotá*, Bulletin No. 56. Available at: www.sdp.gov.co

United States Office of Management and Budget, (2010), "Standards for Delineating Metropolitan and Micropolitan Statistical Areas", *Federal Register*, 75(123), June 28, Notices, Washington.

United Nations Development Program UNDP Colombia, (2008), *Bogotá, una apuesta por Colombia. Índice de desarrollo humano*. Available at: http://hdr.undp.org/sites/default/files/idh_2008_bogota.pdf

Universidad Externado de Colombia. Centro de Investigación sobre Dinámica Social, (2007), *Ciudad, espacio y población: el proceso de urbanización en Colombia*. Available at: http://bit.ly/1Fwj5f6

Urrutia, M., and Ruíz, M., (2010), "Ciento setenta años de salarios reales en Colombia", *Ensayos sobre política económica: Banco de la República*, 28:63, pp. 156–189, Bogota.

7 Argentina

20 years of Habitat II: the pending subjects

Andrea Catenazzi and Eduardo Reese, with Agustín Manuel Mango

Introduction

This chapter seeks to assess the way the commitments assumed by the government of Argentina at the Second United Nations Conference on Human Settlements (HABITAT II, 1996) had an impact on public policies. After 20 years of Habitat II, the housing panorama in Argentina shows significant achievements but also several pending issues in terms of "adequate housing for all and sustainable human settlements", as indicated in the main agreements of the Istanbul Declaration.

Before starting our assessment, we think it necessary to give an explanation of the low visibility of the commitments and recommendations emanating from Habitat II in Argentina's public policies. The materials surveyed and the analysis carried out for this work show that they were referred to in very few documents, both governmental and from social organizations. This does not mean that the problems set out in Habitat II have not been addressed, but it suggests a series of questions about the reasons for the very limited relevance of that summit in the public debate.

To understand the tortuous trajectories of the policies aimed at improving habitat, we have reconstructed and differentiated the network of problems, actors, and public policies into three cycles. The first cycle extends from 1996 to the internal crisis (2001–2002), which marked an economic, political, social, and state legitimacy turning point in our country. Those years were characterized by the strengthening of a neoliberal regime based on policies of economic deregulation, privatization of public enterprises (including those for the provision of urban services), deterioration of the living conditions of the middle and poor sectors, and targeting of social policies. The cycle was conditioned by the convertibility regime (1991–2002), which established a fixed exchange rate between the national currency and the US dollar. The second cycle, from 2003 to 2015, shows various signs of rupture with the previous regime. This period was characterized by an active role of the state in the economy through a series of neo-developmentalist[1] policies, among which stood out the incentives to the domestic market; the expansion of policies aimed at expanding rights; territorial planning; and an increase of public investments in infrastructure, social services, and housing. Finally, the third cycle begins with the government that won the general elections held at the end of 2015. In the last six months, Argentina's socioeconomic model – promoted by the national government – has experienced a drastic change that, in general terms, can be described as a return to the principles of economic liberalism: less state intervention in the general functioning of the economy, a strong reduction of public spending, the hegemony of financial capital, and the instability of work relations.

Even though it is possible to differentiate three cycles, it is no less evident that there are pending subjects that go through them. In particular, there are two key issues essential to progress towards the commitments expressed in Habitat II: urban and land market regulations and the territorial integration of sectoral policies. Both issues are vital to breaking the chain of factors that impede full access to a decent habitat and sustainable territorial development.

The land market regulation is an incipient policy and loosely connected to the problems of access to housing. However, conflicts over access to urban land are a fact in all cities of the country, regardless of their size and geographical location. During the last two decades, the increase in prices derived from real estate speculation has further exacerbated these historical problems.

The weak integration of sectoral policies shows that the subject of unequal access to a decent habitat has not been set out in the agenda of the different governments. On the contrary, the formulation of public policies has kept a sectoral and centralized vision of territorial and environmental problems, reflected in the institutional and organizational division of the state administration. On the one hand, it is assumed that the problems of the formal city are solved by the agencies responsible for urban planning and, on the other hand, the problems of the informal city are subject to social policies in general, and low-income housing policies in particular.

Urban and land market regulation and the territorial integration of public policies are especially important because Argentina is a country with an early and high urbanization rate. By the 1930s, together with Cuba and Uruguay, it was considered an urban country, and in the 1950s, more than 62 percent of its population lived in cities. In 2010, it had a total population of slightly more than 40 million inhabitants and less than 10 percent lived in rural areas.

The territorial distribution on the national scale was notoriously unequal. The highest concentration of human settlements is in the Pampas region, especially in the Buenos Aires–Córdoba area, with about 22 million inhabitants – 61 percent of the country's population, living in approximately 25 percent of its area (Plan Estratégico Territorial, 2008). In keeping with this situation, the Pampas region is the most densely populated in the country and has the highest levels of connectivity and infrastructure coverage. In this context, the three main urban agglomerations (Buenos Aires, Córdoba, Rosario) consolidated as industrialized metropolitan areas with a broad and dynamic tertiary sector, benefiting from a development model that focused in them the most substantial part of the human, economic, and innovation resources of the productive process in Argentina. In general, the growth of the cities took place at the expense of the smaller settlements and the dispersed rural population (especially peasants or smallholders) as a consequence of the migration from neighboring countries.

Cities have played a fundamental role as promoters of development and are where social tensions and territorial inequalities are most clearly seen. Thus, and coinciding with some lines of the current debate on the urban issue in Latin America, we note that the current urbanization model in Argentina has not been able to associate urbanization with the democratization of social relations, maintaining a simultaneous and contradictory process of expansion of citizenship with a sociospatial exclusion that will be difficult to reverse.

Starting from these first notes on the urban and housing problems in Argentina, we now present a series of analyses and reflections on the fulfillment of the commitments accepted in Habitat II. The work is organized in the six dimensions proposed by the framework project: urban policy and governance, sustainability and environmental management, access to housing and urban infrastructures, productivity of economic activities, urban poverty and social exclusion, and urban morphology. Each of these dimensions is addressed from three aspects. First, reference is made to the commitments made in Habitat II (in particular, the agreements presented in the global plan of action and the strategies for its implementation). Second, we examine the way those challenges were included in the national agenda. Third, we identify the key issues in our country associated with these commitments. These central concepts make it possible to reconstruct the main problems, policies, and actors, highlighting in some dimensions the role of social organizations and the main collective actions in defense of a decent habitat. The assessment is presented in terms of continuities and ruptures regarding the first two cycles aforementioned. The still incipient changes of the third cycle are revisited in the conclusion.

The work concludes with a series of reflections on the scope and limitations of the analyzed period, together with a set of challenges and new issues on the urban agenda in Argentina as a proposal for Habitat III.

Policies and urban governance

The Habitat program, which is part of the Istanbul Declaration, raises at least three issues closely related to forms of urban governance. On the one hand, it addresses the promotion of institutional and legal frameworks – at a national, subnational, and local level – that favor the deployment of resources destined to an urban planning process, based on a vision that guarantees and protects human rights; on the other hand, the promotion of decentralization and the strengthening of local authorities and their associations or networks is considered. Finally, it acknowledges the recognition and respect of the rights of all through their participation in the urban planning process – in particular of women, children, people with disabilities, people living in poverty, and vulnerable and disadvantaged groups.

These issues have registered changes and continuities in the two cycles mentioned. In effect, the aforementioned institutional crisis of 2001–2002 marked the emergence of a new scenario in which devaluation was the starting point for changes in the economic policy that affected the national agenda, the experiences of local governments, and collective action.

An initial institutionalization of urban problems

Argentina is a federal republic with three government levels: national, provincial, and municipal. Due to different reasons, and in spite of the early urbanization process, the metropolitan phenomenon was never included in the national or provincial legislation. The "metropolitan issue" does not seem to be considered a relevant issue for society or the state in Argentina, which – until now – is nothing more than a summation of municipal realities (Pírez, 2001). These characteristics of the state organization define the institutional framework in which urban problems are registered. Moreover, they condition the way in which those conflicts were included in the national agenda for the last 20 years.

During the first cycle, national governments deepened and concluded the fiscal adjustment initiated during the civil–military dictatorship (1976–1983). The economic and political program combined the privatization of public service companies with a great impact on the concentration and foreignization[2] of the economy (Azpiazu and Basualdo, 2004), together with a profound reform of the state based on the principles of subsidiarity and neutrality, in which the policies of deregulation, privatization, targeting, and decentralization were the central points of an "exclusive modernization" (Barbeito and Lo Vuolo, 1992).

The licensing of urban services, which until then had been managed by state enterprises, was a response to the difficulties that the state as a whole was facing and in the context of the growing legitimacy of a privatizing discourse, promoted by the national government and multilateral credit organizations (especially the World Bank). The effectiveness of the official discourse of Carlos Menem's first government (1989–1995) was to present as "the only solution" one inspired by technical considerations or administrative reform, unrelated to any political controversy. The privatization program was part of a policy to modernize the state and – in that context – privatization was defined as a discussion among experts that had nothing to do with the material benefits or the distribution of power.

The outstanding features of the Argentine privatization experience were the haste, the extent of the process, and the diversity of the privatization methodologies prioritized in each case (Azpiazu et al., 2004). Unlike other processes in Latin America, Argentina's peculiarity was the absence of parliamentary debate on the concession of urban services. In this process, many of the principles that had sustained the origin and development of technical networks were questioned; among them, the belief in a state operator as the only way to guarantee universal access to basic urban services. Furthermore, the concessions incorporated new actors to the management of the technical networks – the differentiation between the concessionaire company and the regulatory bodies – and large international groups, with the implications of belonging to a global market (Catenazzi, 2011).

Because of these measures, the urban issue as such was displaced from the political scene and had no place in the public debate. Officially, the responsibility was in the Ministry of Housing and Urban Development, whose performance was very low and within the scope of the Ministry of Social Development. In addition, the National Land Commission – originally created at the beginning of the 1990s – was in charge of land ownership regularization.

The approval of the Economic Emergency Law and Reform of the Exchange System (2002) – that is to say, the abandonment of the convertibility regime – had, among other consequences, the renegotiation of the concession contracts and was the first step to return to the entrepreneurial state.

During the second cycle, the growing centrality of the state in the political scene gave greater importance to territorial planning as a public policy tool for development. In this process, the Under-Secretariat of Territorial Planning for Public Investment (SSPTIP) (2004) was created under the newly created Ministry of Federal Planning, Public Investment, and Services. Four years later, the National Council for Territorial and Land-Use Planning (COFEPLAN) was set up. The creation of the Secretariat of Access to Habitat (2014) at the federal level extended the institutionalization of sociospatial inclusion policies.

The SSPTIP prepared the first Strategic Land-Use Plan (PET) (2008) that, together with its different updates, broadened the territorial planning agenda. The second PET (2011) summarized the inclusion of urban topics in the national agenda and strengthened the activities aimed at promoting territorial planning in the public sphere. The third PET (2015) lay down as its main challenges the strengthening of the legal-normative framework of territorial planning and the systematic production of information and knowledge about the territory.

The federal involvement in various actions of the SSPTIP contributed to reinstalling territorial planning in the country. The creation of COFEPLAN strengthened the dialogue between the nation and the provinces through joint work processes – among them, the formulation of the Strategic Projects Identification and Weighting System and the construction of the Territorial Indicators System (SIDET) and its web platform, the ATLAS ID. Likewise, technical and financial support was given to 21 pilot projects for local, regional, and provincial land-use planning in 16 provinces.

Within the framework of COFEPLAN, the SSPTIP prepared a draft bill for the national land-use plan, which the government did not prioritize and therefore never reached the National Congress for its approval.

Despite this growing institutionalization of urban policy on the national agenda, these measures have only incorporated some specific instruments to regulate land markets and have not managed to permeate a sectorial scheme of resource allocation. The challenge of ensuring that decisions on the allocation of budgetary resources agree with the territorial planning of public investment remains a pending issue. This situation increases the risk of undermining such

processes, a common issue in planning processes unconnected from the allocation of budgetary resources.

At the provincial level, land-use planning and regulation are very weak, and
only three districts currently have a land-use planning regulation:

• The autonomous city of Buenos Aires approved the Urban Environmental
Plan (PUA) in 2008, after a long debate and serious questioning. Until
now, its impact on public decisions has had little relevance. Additionally,
the city has an Urban Planning Code (CPU), approved in 1977, that does
not respond to the PUA's proposals.[3]

• The province of Mendoza sanctioned the Law on Land-Use Planning in
2009. Although it defines a complete and complex planning process, the
managing instruments that would allow a strong public action are only
outlined.

• Lastly, in November 2012, the province of Buenos Aires approved Law
14,449 on Fair Access to Habitat, after four years of intense debate in
several social forums and continuous advocacy work by a vast group of
social organizations. The norm regulates the right of all inhabitants of
the province to have a decent place to live in conditions that favor their
full integration. To achieve this, it strengthens with new instruments the
state's capacity to intervene – together with other social and economic
actors – in the alteration of urban dynamics and the land market to combat
the exclusion of large middle and poor sectors. The new norm partially
modified the 1977 Law 8912 of Land-Use Planning, sanctioned during the
civic–military dictatorship. That law remains in force, with a technocratic
and elitist conception of urbanism (typical of the time of its approval) that
ignores the way popular sectors operate in the production of urban space
and therefore hinders the production of social interest housing solutions.

Innovation and discontinuity in local experiences

A distinctive trait of Argentina is the heterogeneity of its local governments,
both within each province and between provinces.[4] There are approximately
2,260 local governments, belonging to 23 provinces, and the autonomous city
of Buenos Aires. As an example, the disparity in size is evident in that 46 percent of the population of the country lives in only 2.4 percent of the municipalities that have more than 100,000 inhabitants.

During the 20 years analyzed, local governments showed a greater dynamism
than the provincial ones in terms of their capacity to face urban and housing
problems. Some municipalities became laboratories to examine changes in the
local agenda regarding the inclusion of the land markets regulation and the territorial integration of sectoral policies.

However, the dynamism of the municipal governments in Argentina is conditioned by their limited financial autonomy,[5] even though – during the period
studied – consolidated public expenditure increased from 31.6 to 50.2 percent

in percentages of the gross domestic product (GDP) and the participation of municipalities increased slightly from 2.6 to 3.4 percent (Figure 7.1).

Due to their low financial autonomy, the local governments usually prioritize the problems derived from the national and provincial agendas on which their access to additional resources depends (Clemente, 2012). In this sense, innovative experiences depend on the possibility of adapting centralized policies to the local context.

During the first cycle, and within the framework of the state reform, decentralization and focalization processes established the municipal territory as a privileged area of public action. The decentralization promise indicated that when approaching the community, the objective of achieving a better quality of life for the population could be achieved thanks to the proximity and daily life shared between the authorities and beneficiaries. In truth, decentralization was also expected to contribute to austerity policies and, at the same time, to dilute distributive conflicts by avoiding their channeling to the central state.

Faced with an increase in their responsibilities, the municipalities resorted to strategic planning as a revaluation of the local space and as an instrument to identify the competitive advantages of their cities. Urban projects were the main type of intervention, focused on the revaluation of public space and the recovery of the so-called opportunity territories (territories that emerged from the privatization and deregulation of the state). The large urban projects (GPU) carried out by the local governments with the largest populations were located on the coastal fronts, the ports, the railway maneuvering yards, and former productive

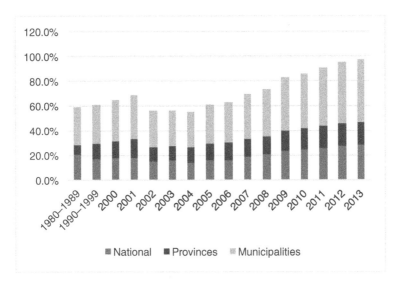

Figure 7.1 Consolidated public expenditures in percentages of GDP

Source: Capello et al. (2013). Based on data from the Ministry of the Treasury.

establishments. During the first cycle, Córdoba and Rosario continued and extended their emblematic projects to recover their shores in the Suquía and Paraná rivers, and Buenos Aires began the elitist project of Puerto Madero.

The strategic planning processes improved the management capabilities in different municipalities of Argentina and contributed to an integral territorial approach in the municipal administrations. However, according to a study by the International Institute for Environment and Development of Latin America (IIED-AL), the first generation of Strategic Local Development Plans (1995–2000) limitedly problematized the relationship between poverty and development (Bertolotto and Clemente, 2008). This would later become part of its weakness and subsequent loss of prestige, attributed – among other things – to its incapacity to anticipate the severity of the 2001–2002 crisis.

During the second cycle, because of a change in the national economic policies, local governments strengthened their role in the design and execution of territorial policies. The main concerns of the technical teams shifted from local development (focused on counteracting the effects of the national socioeconomic policies during the 1990s) to facing the negative effects of economic growth on urban and environmental development. Some municipalities (Morón, Trenque Lauquen, Rosario, San Fernando, etc.) implemented various regulatory and management reforms that introduced changes in urban and tax legislation and included tools for the recovery of real estate valuation produced by public action. The aim of all this ranged from the improvement of the local fiscal situation to the financing of sociourban programs with redistribution criteria. Many of these experiences are linked as well to the construction of GPUs with a great capacity for territorial transformation and seeking – at the same time and despite all the controversies involved – greater territorial equity. Some examples are the Puerto Norte project in Rosario, the expansion of the city of Trenque Lauquen, the urban reorganization of San Fernando (until 2012), and the transformation of the central area of Morón (Reese and others, 2014).[6]

These initiatives, innovative in Argentina, have enjoyed weak legal backing and varying degrees of success, both in their capacity to influence the urban development processes and in their possibility of improving public financing. In short, the scarcity of resources and the discontinuity of financing programs discouraged a more active role of municipalities (especially the medium and small ones) in territorial development.

Collective actions and bringing together the demands for fair access to habitat

During the first cycle of the period, the increase in unemployment and underemployment, as well as poverty and indigence, displaced the matter of access to land and housing as the main driving force for the mobilization of the popular sectors. Thus, whereas housing conditions had been a key element of social organization during the import substitution model (until the mid-1970s), work replaced it after the neoliberal boom (Cerrutti and Grimson, 2004).

The implementation of targeted assistance plans and the increase in public–private partnerships to access basic services turned social organizations into mediators between households needing assistance, the state, nongovernmental organizations, and private actors (mostly concession companies). These experiences contributed to holding the most vulnerable families responsible for their own housing.

During the 2001–2002 crisis, Argentina witnessed new forms of collective action in the resistance to neoliberal policies – the mobilizations of the unemployed (*piqueteros*), the emergence of neighborhood assemblies, the recovery of bankrupt factories and service companies by their employees, and the multiplication of cultural collectives (Svampa, 2008).

In a context of high social participation, the public policies implemented since 2003 promoted the formation and consolidation, respectively, of new and old social collectives. The main point of the struggles was the social economy as a way out from unemployment and/or the social production of habitat as an answer to the housing emergency. Examples of this revaluation process of social mobilization were the creation of the Forum of Land, Infrastructure and Housing Organizations of the Province of Buenos Aires (FOTIVBA) in 2004, gathering more than 60 technical and grassroots organizations; the growth of the Tupac Amaru Neighborhood Organization (which, since its origin in Jujuy in 1999, expanded to 16 Argentine provinces); and the establishment of the Non-Governmental Entities Network of Córdoba, with organizations that have more than 30 years of experience in the field of popular housing.

The experience of FOTIVBA is especially relevant because, together with public universities, it promoted the participatory drafting and approval of the aforementioned Fair Access to Habitat Law. The strong opposition the law suffered during the four years of discussion and the central controversies of the legislative debate are still present and expressed in the resistance of some provincial and municipal officials, as well as real estate agents, to guaranteeing its full implementation. The obstacles focus on the application of principles based on an expansion of rights and the use of the instruments contained in the regulation, which impose a transformation of the bureaucratic and elitist practices that are commonly applied in urban planning and in housing policies.

As part of the process of bringing together the social claims for fair access to habitat, some 50 organizations from all over the country (including FOTIVBA) formed in 2009 the collective Habitar Argentina[7] (HA) with the manifest intention of influencing the public debate through a complex agenda, which combined the discussion of new national legislative proposals related to the formulation of urban housing programs. The group designed projects aimed at the regularization of rural and urban land, the social production of housing, inclusive urbanism, residential social rent, and access to basic services for the popular sectors.

Based on the accumulated experience, HA launched a campaign to establish a position and influence the political debate based on a set of proposals gathered in a document called the National Consensus for a Decent Habitat (2014). The text summarizes nine proactive proposals with two priority strategies: implementing the rights approach in urban policies and addressing the situation of rural and urban housing as specific problems, but without losing sight of the interrelationships and continuities that link them. The nine basic proposals cover the following aspects: a) guiding principles for the design and implementation of comprehensive territorial policies; b) public policies for regulation and redistribution of income in land markets; c) regulation of the rental market; d) social production of housing; e) security of tenure and regularization of urban and rural land; f) democratic procedures in cases of evictions; g) democratic security for decent housing; h) participation and access to information; and i) access to social facilities and basic services.

Additionally, in the consensus document, social organizations promote a turn in the debate by focusing their claim on access to decent housing. Thus, the document addresses the problem from a more comprehensive approach:

> Decent habitat includes universal access to land and housing, together with infrastructure networks, social facilities, services, and work and production spaces, respecting the cultural and symbolic components of the community and its environmental qualities, according to the particularities of the urban and rural environment.

The consensus document has served as a tool for social, academic, and political organizations in the country to bring about a profound debate to improve the local urban policies in each town, city, and province.

Sustainability and environmental management

The Habitat program has among its main objectives to promote the development of sustainable and healthy human settlements. To this end, it encourages the adoption of the principles and strategies of Agenda 21 and the 1992 Rio Declaration on Environment and Development.

The implementation strategies require an integrated approach to the provision of services and environmental policies that protect fragile ecosystems and ecologically vulnerable zones from the harmful effects of a world in the process of urbanization. The strategies also point out the risks of the current dependence of most urban centers on nonrenewable energy sources, which increases air pollution and thereby contributes to and exacerbates climate change. Finally, they promote urban and rural planning and the need for solutions that encourage an efficient use of energy and pay due attention to the end users and their attitudes and practices.

Reactive environmental policies

In general, the main topics of the environmental debate during the 20 years examined could be classified as a) the tension between the protection of natural resources and extractive economic activities and b) urban problems, especially those related to pollution and the risks of disasters. In this framework, what stands out is that the main environmental policies were developed in response to emergencies, social conflicts, or international pressure.

The Argentinean constitutional reform of 1994 expressly established the protection of the environment, and a large number of international treaties were incorporated into the regulatory framework during the period under study. This and the sanctioning of some relevant national laws – which generated great debates (such as the minimum budget for the protection of native forests and the preservation of glaciers) – complemented and strengthened domestic legislation. However, the main political parties do not have clear positions. This contributes to generating, on the one hand, the conditions for a reactive environmental policy and, on the other, a political weakness to face the obstacles and resistance posed by the economic sectors affected by environmental regulations (Ryan, 2014).

Beyond these continuities, it is possible to point out differences between the two cycles.

During the first cycle, the political and environmental management responsibilities were concentrated in a single national agency, whose priority followed international environmental agreements. The aforementioned constitutional reform had caused a profound change in the exploitation of natural resources. It established that the state had the responsibility of dictating the rules regarding the "minimum budgets for environmental protection" and transferred its implementation to the provinces (gas, oil, and mining), giving way to a compulsory privatization by excluding the state (provincial or national) from any exploitation activity.

In practice, Argentina developed a policy aimed at environmental protection, rather than a strategic approach to favor sustainable development (Clichevsky, 2002). In general, a defensive attitude was adopted, trying to legalize the care of the environment as an economic externality and transferring the burden of environmental remediation costs to society. In fact, the main changes in environmental legal issues were based on the need to provide internationally acceptable conditions to foreign capitals that intended to invest in Argentina and to trade. The exporters had to start addressing the environmental issue; otherwise, they would be excluded from international trade (Acuña, 1999).

During the second cycle, the "development with inclusion" model entails a set of tensions and limitations expressed in political contradictions in different levels (which will be further explained in the next section). Its most visible manifestation is the conflicts in which social, cultural, and environmental rights clash with the productivity focus of the model – that had been the core of the developmental and neoliberal models.

In addition, the environmental policy aimed at promoting disaster risk reduction in development policies and land-use planning at all levels. In this process, climate risk reduction strategies were outlined at different scales and through intersectorial work among state agencies. Some provinces – such as the Neuquén – enacted laws that incorporate the risk approach in land-use planning and developed the Provincial Program for Risk Reduction and

Adaptation to Climate Change. Among the measures taken was the creation of a Provincial Risk Network to coordinate actions between provincial and local planning areas.

The issue of a total supply of energy provided by renewable sources – including solar energy, wind power, hydropower, tidal power, geothermal, and biomass (agricultural and urban waste and firewood) – was the subject of government plans and programs, both in the area of commercial electricity generation and in the production of biofuels (Secretaría de Ambiente y Desarrollo Sustentable de la Nación, 2015). However, all this was barely applied.

Finally, the fragmentation of the organisms dedicated to environmental issues was a recurrent feature of both cycles. As an example, to solve problems related to floods or watershed management, more than 10 agencies can be responsible. This makes it difficult to operate, because there is a need for lots of coordination that usually is lacking or works intermittently. The creation of the Matanza Riachuelo Basin Authority (2006), which is the highest authority on environmental matters in one of the most polluted basins in the metropolitan area of Buenos Aires, could be an improvement, but there are still many doubts regarding its operation.

The increasing judicialization[8] of environmental issues

The most important case of judicialization of an environmental problem was that of the Matanza Riachuelo river basin (CMR), one of the most extensive in the metropolitan area of Buenos Aires and one of the most polluted in the country.

The conflict was taken to the judicial authorities by a group of neighbors, who filed a claim demanding the rehabilitation of the environment and the creation of a fund to finance its sanitation (2004). This process originated a legal action[9] that held the state, the province of Buenos Aires, the autonomous city of Buenos Aires, and 44 companies were responsible for damages. Subsequently, the demand was extended to the 14 municipalities of the Province of Buenos Aires located in the CMR.

The lawsuit gave rise in 2006 to the creation of the Matanza Riachuelo Basin Authority (ACUMAR)[10] that is now the highest authority in environmental matters – an autonomous, self-governing, and interjurisdictional entity that, with great difficulties and shortcomings, has tried to fulfill its role. In 2008, the Supreme Court of Justice (CSJN) issued a ruling that forced ACUMAR to carry out a program to improve the quality of life of the inhabitants of the basin, recompose the environment in all its components (water, air, and soil), and prevent further damages. The creation of ACUMAR and the deployment of public policies, driven by the ruling of the CSJN, represent a turning point not only in the basin but also in Argentina's environmental policies. The decisions of the judiciary regarding the socioenvironmental problem of the basin has had the undeniable virtue of placing the issue on the public agenda and promoting a set of policies aimed at improving the quality of life of the inhabitants.

It should be noted that the environmental and urban liability of the basin is the result of a secular process of polluting industrial growth and scarcely regulated territorial development that entrusted the market with the construction of the territory. However, the involvement of the court shook the existing inertia, placed the issue on the political agenda, and forced the governments at all levels to take a stance in relation to socioenvironmental problems and formulate policies (Merlinsky, 2013; Ryan and Napoli, 2013).

The Riachuelo lawsuit had a great influence on matters of environmental jurisprudence. From it, many other large demands were filed in the country based on the collective effects of environmental pollution. Among them stand out the ones lodged in the federal jurisdiction of San Isidro (regarding the environmental damage caused by the construction of 102 closed neighborhoods in the northern area of Buenos Aires); in the federal court of Campana (related to the same situations as the previous one, in the Luján River basin); the one that halted the establishment of the Monsanto company in Malvinas Argentinas, in the province of Córdoba; and that of the Chamber of Crime of the Cordovan capital against two soy producers and a fumigator for spraying fields with agrotoxics at a distance of less than 500 meters from populated neighborhoods.[11]

Social mobilization against the diverse forms of extractivism

Among the main commitments of Habitat II to achieve the sustainability of human settlements is the efficient use of resources in order to guarantee economic and social development, as well as environmental protection. However, Argentina has historically based the expansion of its economy on the exploitation of its natural resources. It has adopted a neo-extractive development style, marked by the general introduction of agribusiness (a spread of single-crop farming and use of transgenic seeds through direct seeding) and a significant growth of mining and oil activities – all of which generate serious pollution problems and loss of biodiversity. The situation has not changed: the country is going through a period characterized by the primacy of an export model based on those characteristics and functional to the interests of the most developed countries.

During the studied period, this gave rise to intense and growing tensions that led to the organization and mobilization of different groups in defense of sustainable development and ways of life. Thus, the main existing tensions can be summarized as follows:

- Those originated by the promotion of different mining or oil activities conflicting with the environmental protection and the rights, styles, and quality of life of the communities in different areas of the country.
- Those linked to the expansion of the agricultural frontier and the concentration of production dominated by monoculture, in conflict with the productive capacities and rights of indigenous peoples and small peasant producers.
- Those linked to environmental deterioration caused by the setting up of potentially polluting factories.

These tensions focused on the overexploitation and deterioration of natural resources reached the urban debate, as policies stimulated real estate dynamics – characterized by the concentration of supply in luxury products – to the detriment of areas fulfilling important environmental services – such as water basins, wetlands, and mountains.

Various social mobilizations arose in opposition to large-scale open-pit mining. The "Esquel effect" (2003)[12] – resulting from a significant neighborhood movement organized under the motto "no to the mine" – had a mushroom effect, awakening other regions of the country where self-summoned assemblies were organized (Svampa et al., 2009). Thus, at present, there are 26 mining conflicts registered in the country in which the mobilization of the population is decisive. Faced with this resistance, seven Argentine provinces recently sanctioned laws that prohibited mining with toxic substances. However, in many cases, these laws have not stopped exploration projects or the advancement of mining investments.

It is no coincidence that in this new economic scenario – characterized by the presence of large transnational corporations – the ancestral struggles for the land have become stronger, hand-in-hand with the indigenous and peasant movements, while new forms of mobilization and citizen participation emerge, centered on the defense of natural resources, biodiversity, and the environment – all of which created a new cartography of resistances (Svampa, 2008). Thus, during the period under study, there were countless conflicts with small peasants and indigenous communities regarding both land tenure and environmental problems. In 2010, the Chaco Argentina Agroforestry Network had identified 259 cases just in the province of Chaco (REDAF, 2010, 2011).

Popular mobilizations also faced the construction of important industrial plants that posed risks of environmental contamination and could affect the health of the population. The most important of these was the resistance of the city of Gualeguaychú – in the province of Entre Ríos – against the authorization of the Uruguayan government to build two pulp mills on the eastern bank of the Uruguay River (near the city of Fray Bentos) and led to an important international dispute. The conflict lasted for about six years, involved large and numerous popular mobilizations, and managed to prevent one of the companies from constructing its plant.[13] Also significant is the aforementioned conflict in which, since 2012, the resistance of the small town of Malvinas Argentinas (located in the center of the province of Córdoba), led by the Assembly of Neighbors "Malvinas Fight for Life", managed to stop the construction of the largest transgenic corn seed plant in Latin America by the multinational company Monsanto (the largest producer of genetically modified seeds in the world and one of the leading manufacturers of agrochemicals).

Access to housing and urban infrastructures

The Habitat program defines how to guarantee progressively the full exercise of the right to adequate housing and proposes three main strategies. First, it proposes decentralizing housing policies and managing them at the subnational and local levels. Second, it highlights the relevance of promoting the legal security of tenure and equal access to land for all. Finally, it mentions the advantages offered by nontraditional financial arrangements and encourages communities to establish housing and community development cooperatives of all kinds, especially for the provision of housing.

Description of the housing situation

The main transformations are seen in precarious households and in the evolution of the coverage of water and sewage services.

In the country as a whole, the percentage of precarious households decreased during the studied period. According to data from the last three national censuses, in 1991, the percentage of these households was 37.3 percent; in 2001, 29.9 percent; and in 2010, it fell slightly to 29.5 percent (Table 7.1 and Figure 7.2).

Table 7.1 Evolution of the precarious housing situation, 1991, 2001, and 2010

	1991		2001		2010	
	Abs	%	Abs	%	Abs	%
Total Households	8.927.289	100%	10.073.625	100%	12.171.675	100%
Households in irreparable housing ([1])	752.357	8.4%	560.477	5.6%	476.894	3.9%
Overcrowded households in housing of good condition ([4])	348.413	3.9%	346.771	3.4%	824.010	6.8%
Quantitative deficit	**1.100.770**	**12.3%**	**907.248**	**9.0%**	**1.300.904**	**10.7%**
Households in fixable housing ([2])	1.662.676	18.6%	1.646.371	16.3%	1.668.330	13.7%
Overcrowded households per room in housing of cood conition ([3])	569.899	6.4%	456.238	4.5%	616.767	5.1%
Qualitative deficit	**2.232.575**	**25.0%**	**2.102.609**	**20.9%**	**2.285.097**	**18.8%**
Total precarious households	**3.333.345**	**37.3%**	**3.009.857**	**29.9%**	**3.586.001**	**29.5%**
Total households in housing in good condition and not overcrowded	**5.593.945**	**62.7%**	**7.063.769**	**70.1%**	**8.585.675**	**70.5%**

Source: Prepared by the author based on the 1991, 2001, and 2010 censuses.

([1]) Households living in "*ranchos*," "huts," "premises not built for housing purposes", and "mobile homes".
([2]) Households living as subtenants and in "tenement house rooms".
([3]) Households living as principal tenants and in "apartments", having a ratio of more than 2.00 people per room, leading to overcrowding and other related issues.
([4]) Households living as principal tenants and in "apartments" and sharing them with other households.

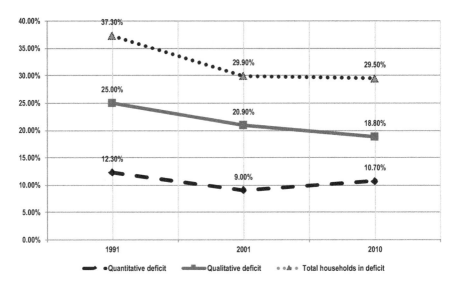

Figure 7.2 Evolution of the housing deficit in 1991, 2001, and 2010

Source: Prepared by the author based on the 1991, 2001, and 2010 censuses.

Table 7.2 Relative variation of population, households, and occupied dwellings, 1991, 2001, and 2010

	Relative Variation 1991–2001	*Relative Variation 2001–2010*
Population	13.9%	9.1%
Households	12.8%	20.8%
Occupied dwellings	14.1%	16.5%

Source: Prepared by the author based on the 1991, 2001, and 2010 censuses.

Interpreting the evolution of the precarious housing situation requires contextualizing these results according to the demographic changes of the period (Table 7.2).

The analysis of the registered data shows the following results:

- The evolution of the registered housing deficit is related to demographic changes. As shown in Table 7.2, in the last period between 2001 and 2010 there was an important difference between population growth (9.1 percent) and that of households (20.8 percent). Even though the growth of occupied housing was higher than in the previous decade (16.5 percent and 14.1 percent, respectively), this growth did not compensate for the higher demand generated by the creation of new households.
- The changes in composition and the reduction in household size clearly affected the indicator "Overcrowded conditions in good housing", which

shows a 100 percent growth in the period 2001–2010. In absolute terms, this means that between 2001 and 2010 more than 450,000 households could not buy or rent housing and therefore shared a good-quality house.

• The construction quality of the Argentine housing stock shows a clear improvement throughout the period. Both the unrecoverable and recoverable houses decrease their participation in the total, in favor of good-quality housing.

Of the total of households in precarious housing situations, the relationship between quantitative and qualitative deficit remains the same. Approximately one-third of the total precarious households require a new house. In order to confirm the evolution of the variables after the crisis of 2001–2002, the data from the census were compared with the results of the Permanent Household Survey (EPH) corresponding to the fourth quarter of 2003 compared to the same period of 2014 (for the main urban agglomerates of the country).

This comparison shows an important improvement in the material conditions of life in the second cycle. For example, households with adequate flooring went from 79.8 to 85.6 percent, those with an exclusive bathroom went from 94.5 to 96.8 percent, and critical overcrowding had a significant drop from 4.6 to 3.1 percent.[14]

The slight decrease in the precariousness situation (0.4 percent in the intercensus period 2001–2010) shows an unequal regional distribution. The territorial distribution of precarious housing shows that they are still concentrated in the provinces of northern Argentina (Map 7.1).

To complete the panorama of the housing situation, it is important to point out that the Argentine housing stock shows a large percentage of uninhabited units. As shown in Table 7.3, after a high growth from 15.4 to 19.3 percent between 1991 and 2001, it decreases and its participation in the total drops to 18.1 percent in 2010. Relative variation in the number of uninhabited dwellings decreased significantly during the period, from 50.5 percent between 1991 and 2001 to 7.1 percent between 2001 and 2010 (Table 7.4).

These figures must be analyzed in detail because the censuses report eight different causes for the uninhabited houses on the day of the survey.[15] Therefore, it is possible to estimate globally that close to 50 percent of the houses found uninhabited can be considered unoccupied units awaiting speculative valuation.

Likewise, it is necessary to analyze briefly the behavior of the residential rental market. The evolution of tenant households during the period shows the following changes (Table 7.5 and Figure 7.3):

• Owner occupancy is the biggest category, but, in the last period between censuses, its participation in the total decreased from 70.6 to 68.7 percent.
• In turn, the tenant category is the second largest but the fastest growing (74.7 percent) between 2001 and 2010, after long decades in which their participation had reduced. Between 2001 and 2010, close to 840,000

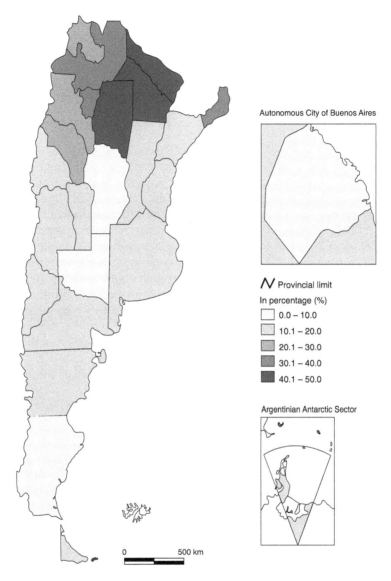

Map 7.1 Percentage of precarious households by province – 2010

Source: 2010 Census. Final results. Series B, No. 2, Volume 1.

Table 7.3 Uninhabited housing, 1991, 2001, and 2010

	1991		2001		2010	
Total Housing	10.062.731	100%	12.041.584	100%	13.812.125	100%
Uninhabited housing	1.547.290	15.4%	2.328.923	19.3%	2.494.618	18.1%

Source: Prepared by the author based on the 1991, 2001, and 2010 censuses.

Table 7.4 Relative variation in the number of uninhabited housing, 1991–2001 and 2001–2010

Relative Variation 1991–2001	Relative Variation 2001–2010
50.5%	7.1%

Source: Prepared by the author based on the 1991, 2001, and 2010 censuses.

Table 7.5 Evolution of housing tenure, 1991, 2001, and 2010

Census	Owner occupancy		Tenant		Other*	
	Total	%	Total	%	Total	%
1991	5.486.831	61.5	1.101.575	12.3	2.338.883	26.2
2001	7.115.508	70.6	1.122.208	11.1	1.835.909	18.2
2010	7.774.540	68.7	1.795.906	15.9	1.747.061	15.4

Source: Prepared by the author based on the Urban Development and Housing Under-Secretariat (2010) and the 2010 census.

* Includes all situations of informal tenure and tenure by dependency relationship.

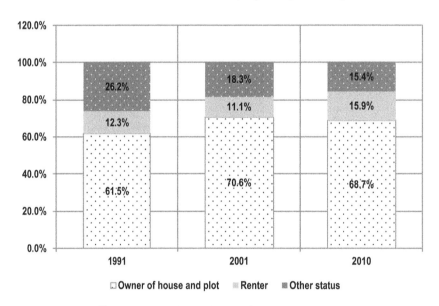

Figure 7.3 Types of housing tenure, 1991, 2001, and 2010

Source: Prepared by the author based on the Urban Development and Housing Under-secretariat (2010) and the 2010 census.

households joined the residential rental market – an average of just over 93,000 homes per year.

- Whereas in 2001, tenants accounted for 11.1 percent, in 2010, this increased to almost 16 percent. This increase occurred mainly at the expense of the formal owners.

As seen, during the second cycle, there is a strong change, and residential rental assumes a greater role. When comparing the results of the Permanent Household Survey for the fourth quarter of 2003 with the same period of 2014, urban tenant households grew from 15 to 19.1 percent.

The residential rental market in Argentina is not controlled and depends solely on supply and demand. Thus, there is no official agency in charge of registering the housing units offered or under a rental contract, the housing conditions of the units offered are not controlled or inspected, and the prices are not fixed or categorized. This explains the vast number of abuses registered with the rights of nonowner households. In a recent paper, Reese et al. (2013) note that

> both the representatives of the supply and the demand in the residential rental market agree that in the face of secure tenure or property, renting represents an unstable and weak condition that worsens with the lower income of the households and the greater precariousness of working condition. [. . .] The lease is very rarely perceived, both by supply and by demand, as a stable long-term relationship that forms part of the safe and permanent options to access decent housing.
>
> (102)

During the second cycle, access to mortgages was difficult. As shown in Figure 7.4 for the city of Buenos Aires, the evolution of mortgage loans for housing registered a break in 2002, since the "pesificación" (conversion of foreign currency debt contracts to peso denominations) of the loans originally agreed in dollars, falling from 10,000,000 to 2,000,000 dollars.

For the middle- or lower-middle-income sectors – that had some savings capacity and sought credit – this became a major limitation for access to housing.

To close the description of the housing situation, the evolution of the coverage of public water supply and sewerage is presented as a paradigmatic example of urban infrastructures closely related to health. The population with public water services increased from 66.2 percent in 1991 to 81.8 percent in 2010. The population with public sewerage also grew from 34.3 percent in 1991 to 48.9 percent in 2010, as shown in Table 7.6. Therefore, the imbalance between both networks has been stable during the period.

The examination of the EPH data shows that in the fourth quarter of 2003, 81 percent of households had public water in the house; this increased to 87.9 percent in the same period of 2014.

The increase in the public water and sewerage service coverage shows an unequal regional distribution. The households with the lowest public water service availability are in the northeast and in the province of Buenos Aires (Map 7.2). The houses with the lowest availability of sewerage are located in the center and south of the country (Map 7.3).

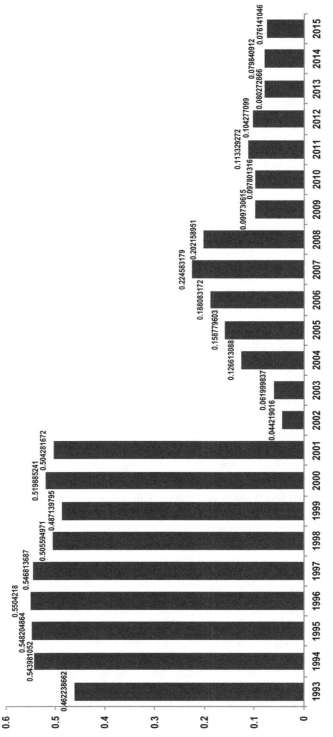

Figure 7.4 Participation of mortgages in the purchase and sale operations of the city of Buenos Aires between 1993 and 2015

Source: Prepared by the author based on the General Directorate of Statistics and Censuses (Ministry of Finance GCBA) with data from the Notaries Association of the City of Buenos Aires.

Table 7.6 Evolution of the population with public water and sewerage coverage, 1991, 2001, and 2010

	1991		2001		2010	
	Abs	*%*	*Abs*	*%*	*Abs*	*%*
Total population in private households	32.245.467	100	35.923.907	100	39.672.520	100
Water Supply						
By public network with pipes inside or outside the house but within the land	21.335.278	66.2%	27.672.749	77.0%	32.442.606	81.8%
By public network with off-site pipes	682.320	2.1%	490.355	1.4%	335.213	0.8%
Other forms of provision and water sources	10.227.869	31.7%	7.760.803	21.6%	6.894.701	17.4%
Sewerage						
Transported to public network	11.065.713	34.3%	15.268.987	42.5%	19.381.029	48.9%
Other	21.179.754	65.7%	20.654.920	57.5%	20.291.491	51.1%

Source: Prepared by the author based on the 1991, 2001, and 2010 censuses.

Program changes and persistence of the deficit

During the first cycle, as part of the reform of the state, the transformations in housing policy were reflected in a readjustment of the national administrative apparatus through two particularly significant processes. On the one hand, the resources of the National Housing Fund (FONAVI) were transferred to the Federal Co-Participation Fund (August 1992). A few years later, the Federal Housing System Law (1995) was passed, and a resource distribution-coefficient was established to allow a reorientation of these resources and greater control by the provinces (Cuenya, 2000). On the other hand, the Banco Hipotecario Nacional (BHN) transformed from retail banking to wholesale banking (March 1990); years later, it was privatized (1997). Now it operates as a limited company[16] with a majority state participation, also engaging in other financial activities. Both processes modified the bureaucratic dynamics of the organisms and marked a new position of the state towards the housing and habitat problems. The state strategies related to the housing issue tended to focus on "facilitating" the development of solutions through the market and launching programs to alleviate poverty (Cravino et al., 2002).

FONAVI, created at the beginning of the 1970s, was the main fund devoted to financing housing. FONAVI had as its main housing offer the so-called "turnkey" housing projects. That is, new homes in low- or medium-density projects located in the suburbs of cities. Since the decentralization, the programs carried out by the provincial autarchic institutes developed a greater diversity of options, which were a more adequate response to the complex

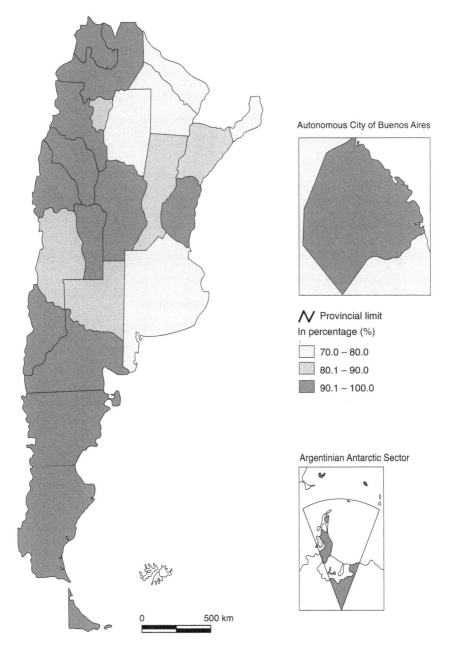

Autonomous City of Buenos Aires

N Provincial limit

In percentage (%)

▢ 70.0 – 80.0

▢ 80.1 – 90.0

▢ 90.1 – 100.0

Argentinian Antarctic Sector

0   500 km

Map 7.2 Population in private homes with public water service by province, as a percentage, 2010

Source: Census 2010. Final Results. Series B, N° 2, Vol. 1.

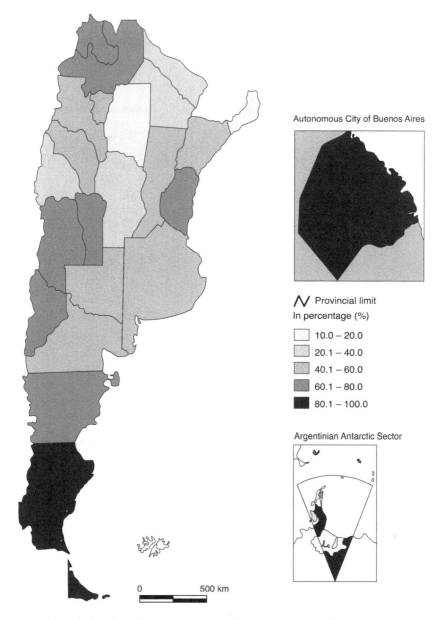

Autonomous City of Buenos Aires

N Provincial limit
In percentage (%)

	10.0 – 20.0
	20.1 – 40.0
	40.1 – 60.0
	60.1 – 80.0
	80.1 – 100.0

Argentinian Antarctic Sector

0   500 km

Map 7.3 Population in private homes with public sewerage service by province, as a percentage, 2010

Source: 2010 Census. Final results. Series B, No. 2, Vol. 1.

housing demands. In that process, plots with services and land ownership regularization were offered in most provinces, with interventions that were generally ex-post. According to the report "Istanbul + 5" – prepared by the National Directorate of Housing Policies of the Under-Secretariat of Housing and Urban Development (2000) – "the FONAVI was oriented to the low and medium income population. And, although it partially covered the requirements of the poorest population, in Argentina there were no high-impact actions or a sustained policy directed at this sector".

The BHN led the ranking of mortgage lender banks. The validity of the aforementioned convertibility regime (which consisted in setting the equivalence of a peso and a dollar) produced a significant increase in the total loan portfolio of the financial system and, in particular, of the lines for housing acquisition. However, this increase did not contribute to increasing the participation of low-income sectors in housing finance. On the contrary, it only represented a partial solution for the middle- and high-income sectors, without solving the structural deficit problems. At the same time, the high rate of unemployment coexisting with the convertibility regime had two devastating consequences. On the one hand, it led to defaulting by those who had managed to access financing. On the other, it displaced potential buyers, reducing the access possibilities to this mechanism (Banzas and Fernández, 2007).

During the second cycle, the orientation of public spending was redefined and investment in housing construction was prioritized to promote economic growth and construction activity. A significant feature was FONAVI's loss of prominence. In effect, public investment based on budgetary and extra-budgetary funds tripled the distribution base of the Federal Housing System. This process partially reversed the decentralization initiated in the previous period, because the national government assumed a preponderant role – through the Federal Housing Programs (PFV) – in determining the use of public resources allocated to this sector. The concentration of resources at the national level relied on the Federal Housing System and its advisory body, the National Housing Council (CONAVI), in order to legitimize decisions among national, provincial, and local governments.

Since 2003 – within the framework of the Federal Housing Program, the FONAVI, and other housing programs – public investment in housing grew significantly. However, the relative growth verified in the variation of production costs affected by rising inflation eroded the capacity of the PFV, made it difficult to sustain production goals, and led to a slowdown in production processes (Figure 7.5) (Rodulfo and Boselli, 2014).

Housing production, based on the 2012 data of CONAVI, reached 657,007 housing solutions (SH) (351,217 new homes and 305,790 housing improvements) between 2003 and 2011, with an average close to 70,000 SH/year, the highest until that date. In nominal terms, the comparison between the periods 1993–2001 and 2003–2011 shows that the number of new housing units completed (VN) registered a slight decrease, whereas housing improvements (MH) have multiplied by more than five since the implementation of the PFV,

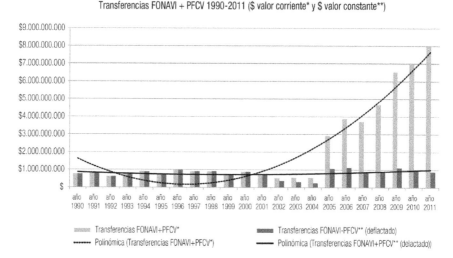

Figure 7.5 Evolution of public investment in housing (1990–2011)

Source: Rodulfo and Boselli (2014). Graph based on data from the National Housing Council (2012).

which represents 46.5 percent of the total production (Figure 7.6) (Rodulfo and Boselli, 2014)

The distribution of improvements versus completed new homes in the different jurisdictions of the country is variable. Whereas in Misiones, the improvements represent 80 percent of the total production, in the city of Buenos Aires, they are only 2 percent.

Decisions regarding the location of new housing units created problems related to urban expansion and the growing requirements of infrastructure and urban mobility, which were not properly addressed and were poorly evaluated in their scope (Del Río, 2012). The demand for land increased the expectations of capturing speculative valuations originated by the state. The extent of public investment made even more evident the absence of a comprehensive policy to accompany and ensure access to land (Catenazzi and Reese, 2010).

The implementation of the PFV also promoted the participation of nongovernmental actors, organizations, and social movements in programs that led to the establishment of worker cooperatives and the promotion of various production methods. This mobilization gave rise to a proactive action that managed to incorporate its proposals in the governmental agenda – some of which became institutional regulation. Such is the case of the Techo y Trabajo (Roof and Work) and Mejor Vivir (Better Living) programs, which will be explained in depth later in this chapter.

Additionally, 2012 saw the creation of a credit line called the Argentine Credit Program (PRO.CRE.AR). Its aim was to expand the opportunities for the middle-income sectors with co-financing capacity, which, as noted in the

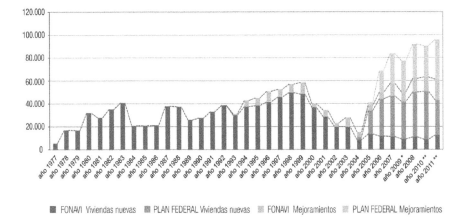

FONAVI Viviendas nuevas ■ PLAN FEDERAL Viviendas nuevas ▧ FONAVI Mejoramientos ▧ PLAN FEDERAL Mejoramientos

Figure 7.6 Evolution of housing production (1977–2011)

Source: Rodulfo and Boselli (2014). Graph based on data from the National Housing Council (2012).

previous characterization, had had no public support for more than a decade. This expansion was achieved by bringing together two lines of state action. On the one hand, the construction of housing projects and, on the other, the mobilization of public resources for a mortgage loan program. For this purpose, it put together trusts funds, including public (state lands and interest rate subsidies) and private resources (contributions to the pension system and private lands) applied through the PRO.CRE.AR.

The mobilization of joint financing contributions through mortgage loans involved the Banco Hipotecario and the National Social Security Administration (ANSES) in the application of resources to beneficiary households, as well as the related business sector and medium and small companies.

Neighborhood upgrading policies

Although Argentina has low rates of urban informality compared to other countries in Latin America, it has been a long-standing problem and a difficult social conflict. The forms adopted by urban informality are usually classified into two types: the *villas* (or *villas miseria*), with an irregular urban structure and located in consolidated areas of the formal city, and the informal settlements with planned urban structures, located in the peripheries of the cities. Both are characterized by the precariousness of the constructions, by the lack of basic services and public spaces, and by the environmental vulnerability of their locations.

Since the return of democracy (1983), there have been significant transformations in the approaches and policies related to urban informality. Although the approaches did not change the remedial bias they always had, the policies went from the eradication of "illegal" neighborhoods (present in the civic–military dictatorship) to the logic of integrating them into the city. In this context, the programs and actions for land ownership and urban legalization were progressively broadened – and gradually became the shared responsibility of all state levels (nation, provinces, and municipalities). The effects of the new neighborhood legalization policies are reflected in the results of the 2001 census.

The other side of these land ownership regularization processes in informal neighborhoods is the amount of time they demand, depending on the urban characteristics and the particular legal situation of each neighborhood at the beginning of the legalization project. The processes are extremely long and partly explain the minor reductions registered in the census data, despite the significant effort made, especially in the last decade. In addition, the intermediate (security of tenure) and final products of the process (proper deed) can only be carried out in successive and chained stages. Thus, the formalization of the deed is the final stage or step of a long list of formalities and procedures.

During the first cycle, a series of national and provincial land ownership legalization programs were launched in Argentina with the enactment of Law 23,967 (1991), which enabled the transfer of land owned by the state to its occupants. This law was complemented by the creation of the National Public Land Commission "Programa Arraigo," from the presidency of the nation. In addition, Law 24,374 was passed in 1994, creating a system of land ownership regularization in favor of occupants who could prove the public, peaceful, and continuous possession for three years of the urban real estate whose main destination is the only and permanent home. As can be seen, the policy of the sector in the 1990s was strongly focused on the regularization of property.

The move towards a more focused approach to comprehensive neighborhood upgrading began in 1997, when the Argentinian government signed the loan agreement with the Inter-American Development Bank (IDB) to finance the Neighborhood Upgrading Program (PROMEBA), originally developed by the Ministry of Social Development. The aim of the program was to improve in a sustainable way the quality of life and the habitat of the populations living in informal neighborhoods and, in such way, contribute to the urban and social integration of the poorest sectors of the population. In order to fulfill this purpose, it developed three lines of action: a) the provision of urban infrastructure, community equipment, and environmental sanitation; b) the regularization of land ownership; and c) the strengthening of human and social capital. In this way, PROMEBA became a program for onsite redevelopment of neighborhoods that started from the efforts of the inhabitants and finances new works and actions, expanding the total of the resources invested in that area of the city.

During the second cycle, PROMEBA fell under the scope of the Under-Secretariat of Urban Development and Housing of the Ministry of Federal Planning, Public Investment and Services (Ministerio de Planificación Federal, Inversión Pública y Servicios), and a series of gradual reforms were set in motion. PROMEBA became a model of comprehensive intervention and, in recent years, had an important performance at the national level. It worked together with various programs, such as Provision of Drinking Water

(PROPASA); Social Development in Border Areas NEA-NOA (PROSOFA); and the Federal Programs for Housing Construction and Improvement, Housing Emergency, Urbanization of Villas, and Settlements in Greater Buenos Aires.

According to IDB information, the first PROMEBA operation benefited 60,569 families. The second stage, completed in 2012, benefited 71,888 families living in 105 villas and settlements, and the third, currently under execution, plans to benefit 67,087 families in 91 settlements.

The experiences of recent years have shown PROMEBA's high capacity to adapt to the different realities of the country and the different operating structures of local governments. It is important to highlight also the experience of the Rosario Hábitat program, implemented locally until 2012 by the municipality of Rosario in the province of Santa Fe.

Finally, it is worth highlighting the incipient complementarity that the neighborhood upgrading programs and actions are having with some urban policy tools that facilitate the progressive attainment of several basic urban planning standards. Such is the case of the aforementioned Fair Access to Habitat Law of the province of Buenos Aires that, through the creation of "social habitat promotion zones", promotes the definition of urban parameters, administrative regulations, incentives, and specific financing mechanisms for the execution of neighborhood upgrading programs.

At the same time, Argentina shows some important setbacks in terms of addressing the problem of precarious neighborhoods. The most important and recent case is the massive transfer of inhabitants of *villas miseria* in the city of Córdoba (plan "Mi Casa, Mi Vida" – "My House, My Life" plan) to the so-called "city neighborhoods", located in the urban periphery and other localities of the metropolitan region.

The productivity of urban economic activities

The Istanbul Declaration points out the importance of promoting the development of more balanced and sustainable human settlements through the promotion of productive investments, the creation of jobs, and the promotion of social infrastructure in small and medium-sized cities and towns. It also recommends stimulating national and local economies through the promotion of economic development, social development, and environmental protection in order to attract national and international financial resources and private investments, generate employment, and increase income, guaranteeing a stronger financial base for the development of housing and human settlements.

From competition between territories to neo–developmentalism

The different stages of development in Argentina show – as in the rest of Latin America – strong and periodic fluctuations derived from the economic cycles of growth and stagnation (Figure 7.7), alternation (according to the

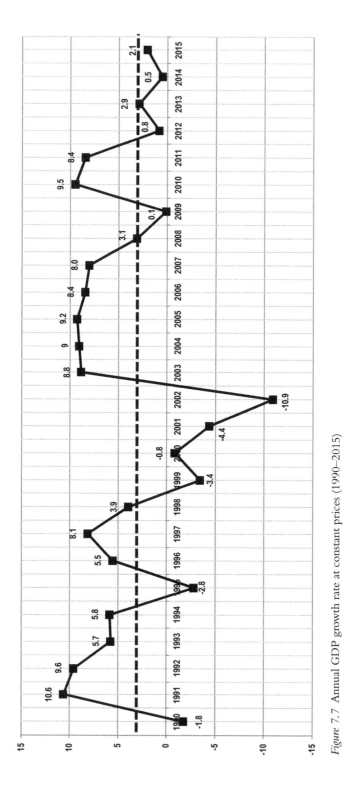

Figure 7.7 Annual GDP growth rate at constant prices (1990–2015)

Source: Prepared by the author with data from the UN Economic Commission for Latin America and the Caribbean (ECLAC) and the National Institute of Statistics and Censuses. (Retrieved on June 1, 2016, at: http://bit.ly/1Moihxq.)

United Nations Economic Commission for Latin America and the Caribbean (ECLAC) scheme) between "outward growth models" and "inward growth models", asymmetries between regions, and weaknesses due to the high concentration of income and the power of privileged groups, among other reasons.

The deepening of the neo-liberal cycle initiated during the civic–military dictatorship involved the implementation of a set of measures that ensured macroeconomic stability over any other aspect. At the same time, the prevailing idea was that development would come from the economic growth associated with the opening of markets, labor relaxation, and the reduction of the state's intervention and regulatory capacities. As has been thoroughly demonstrated (Coraggio, 2008; Barbeito and Lo Vuolo, 1992; Nochteff, 1995, among others), the argument that this economic growth model would be equivalent to integral development was useful to the interests of local economic sectors and to global financial and commercial flows. However, it increased public indebtedness, the disintegration of the national productive fabric, poverty, unemployment, and inequality, all of which, in the case of Argentina, resulted in the aforementioned 2001–2002 crisis (CELS, 2015).

In this context, and as mentioned in the first part of this chapter, during the first cycle analyzed, the internal logic of production and reproduction of the cities in Argentina underwent significant changes. The predominant type of management of the majority of urban collective consumption strengthened its links with the market, and the result was the privatization of services, with its differentiating potential over the structuring of urban territories. This privatization process was not simply a change in the property regime, but the transfer of coordination and government functions to the private sector.

In this way, the economic transformations and the changes in state intervention provoked strong inequalities among the different social groups. These material and symbolic inequalities and distances – social, economic, and politically constructed – were reflected in the cities through social fragmentation processes and residential segregation. Among the most important effects of neo-liberal urbanization are:

- The pressures in the real estate markets induced by the expansion of the demand for new high-quality products and the existence of capital aimed at real estate investment whose profitability had (and still has) as its basic condition the location in areas of opportunity;
- The deterioration of "traditional" sectors of the city due to the appearance of other areas of interest and the changes in the commercialization and consumption patterns;
- An accentuation of the urban space fragmentation coinciding with a worsening of socioeconomic inequalities; and
- A transformation in the patterns of production due to tertiarization processes in economic activities.

Although these changes had a strong territorial impact – mainly in the metropolitan region of Buenos Aires and the main cities of the Argentinian urban system – the intermediate centers were not exempt from them. On the contrary, this process gave rise to new opportunities and limitations in relation to their relative location, together with an accelerated transformation of their urban economic base. We refer to the effects that the medium-sized cities suffered according to the more or less territorial differences in relation to the most dynamic territorial nodes.

Since 2003, the economic growth driven by the change in state policies focused on the gradual reconstitution of productive networks, the expansion of the domestic market and services, the increase in formal employment, and poverty reduction. Thus, the country went through a strong economic growth process that lessened since 2009 due, among other reasons, to the limitations of the model and the global economic crisis. The latest official statistics revealed a GDP growth of 2.1 percent in 2015 (Figure 7.7).

Not all regions or all the social sectors benefited in the same way from this process, but there is a broad consensus on the relationship between the so-called "growth model with inclusion", which was also accompanied by an important effort in social spending, and the highly positive effects in terms of the recovery of territorial and social cohesion.

From the point of view of regional development, the Argentinian economic model followed the historical pattern of marginalizing the regions – that, like the northeast and the northwest, were marginal to the dominant accumulation in a dependent economy (Map 7.4). Faced with this, during the second cycle, several public works plans were launched to reduce territorial asymmetries. The economic and social indicators in the different regions improved, and the expectation about their possible impact on the historic migration to the big cities grew.

However, the contradictions of the model limited the capacity to transform these traditional regional asymmetries. Several studies show a gap between the expansion of economic activities promoted by the national public policies and the impact of this process on local communities (Rofman, 1999). For example, the recent Strategic Development Plan of Chaco (2014) shows that in multiple localities of the province, the available capacities (business, human, technological, and economic-financial) to launch a proper cycle of productive expansion with social redistribution continue to be very limited. The limitations are largely due to the inequality in the degrees of productive interrelation and labor insertion of the resident populations in the different regions.

This limited articulation and territorial cohesion are evident, above all, in the northern region of the country and in some areas of the south. The territories with the highest levels of activity and productivity are in the central Argentine strip. In this way, there are different incorporation "speeds" into the territorial development process, and even if the general growth of the economy continued in the coming years, the gaps between the mobilization of the productive apparatuses and the use of the commercial and local development opportunities could deepen (CELS, 2015).

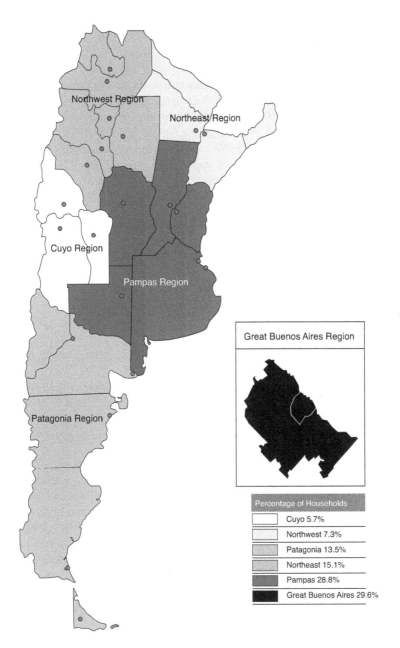

Northwest Region

Northeast Region

Cuyo Region

Pampas Region

Patagonia Region

Great Buenos Aires Region

Percentage of Households

	Cuyo 5.7%
	Northwest 7.3%
	Patagonia 13.5%
	Northeast 15.1%
	Pampas 28.8%
	Great Buenos Aires 29.6%

Map 7.4 Regions defined for the statistics of the National Institute of Statistics and Census (INDEC)

The functioning of the real estate market

Despite the strong changes in macroeconomic policy during the 20 years studied, the real estate market's main features remained unchanged: generalized speculative practices by its actors, artificial rise in prices, concentration of the supply for high-income sectors, very high tax informality, and a strong pressure on the state to favor deregulation.

During the first cycle, the aforementioned convertibility regime was in effect, imposing the freezing of the exchange rate as a mechanism for drastically reducing inflation. In that context, there was a reactivation of private construction leveraged by an increase in the supply of long-term real estate loans in dollars. This process was accompanied by relatively low-interest rates due to the abundant inflow of speculative capital and external debt. This consolidates some changes in the real estate market, changes that had been incipient due to the economic instability of the previous decade:

- There is a new type of real estate developers: more professional, with greater investment capacity, and with links to external capital.
- As a consequence, there is product innovation (residential, commercial, and recreational). The offer now becomes increasingly exclusive, becomes sumptuous, and generates greater territorial impact.
- The process of changing the location pattern of the high-income sectors is consolidated through a strong acceleration of the peripheralization of the new ventures.
- Environmental conflicts intensify and multiply in different cities due to the impact of urbanization projects.
- The state (in its different levels) stimulates this process through the sale of assets well located and without conditions (such as Puerto Madero) to the most concentrated real estate capital, contributing to aggravate the segregation processes. Concurrently, investment in private transport infrastructure is privileged and basic services are privatized.

The rise in land prices derived from these changes promoted a greater retention of vacant land open for speculation that, together with a very low production of equipped land, accentuated the supply shortage and bottleneck problems, especially in high-demand Argentinian cities. This process reduced the options of the low- and middle-income sectors to gain access to real estate products. Furthermore, there was no correlation in the tax policy at any of the state levels to compensate for these effects through redistributive measures.

After the 2001–2002 crisis, the real estate market kept the strong dynamism of the previous decade, due to causes that can be summarized as follows:

- The changes in public policies produced an important economic reactivation and a gradual resurgence of productive sectors. The high levels of national economic growth affected the demand for urbanized land in most urban centers of the country – for all sorts of activities and all categories.

- The increased investment in public works resulted in a high valuation of urban land and significant rents for private landowners. This also produced a significant increase in speculative expectations and prices.
- Real estate in Argentina was always a source of value, both for families and investors. Faced with the uncertainty caused by the recurring economic changes, this trend became widespread and strengthened since the international financial crisis in 2009. Thus, it is important to highlight the strong patrimonial bias of Argentine society, which has turned the real estate market into one of the main investments, accentuating the rentier tendency of the urban economy.
- The improvement of the purchasing power of the population reflected in investments in real estate, which became the privileged mechanism of the upper- and upper-middle-income sectors for saving and preserving the value. As a result, the real estate supply of high-quality products deepened. For instance, an independent survey carried out by Clarin newspaper revealed that 60.8 percent of 16,807 respondents would buy a house (rather than do another type of investment) if they had savings (Clarín, 2007).
- The real estate concentration in the higher-income sectors is partly explained by the very limited supply of mortgage financing, which affected the middle and lower-middle-income sectors with some savings capacity.

The analyzed processes explain not only the high concentration of the market in higher-income sectors but also the increase of urban informality through land occupation as the only option for the poor in search for a place to live. Different factors – both political and related to real estate interests – have so far prevented the prospect of defining criteria and implementing common and minimum public policies oriented towards sustainable urban development. In the two decades being studied, the real estate market has become one of the main factors significantly deteriorating the productivity and competitiveness of economic agents in the cities of Argentina.

Urban poverty, intra-urban inequality, and social exclusion

The signatory countries in the Habitat II summit committed themselves to improve the quality of life in human settlements, facing "the deterioration of conditions that, in most cases and especially in developing countries, have reached critical proportions". The central issues defined were the increase in poverty, unemployment, inequality, and social exclusion. Among the measures directed to face these challenges, priority was given to those that would stimulate employment opportunities that generate enough income to achieve an adequate standard of living and guarantee quality jobs. Linked to this, the countries committed to ensuring that people living in poverty have access to productive resources, such as credit, land, education, training, technology, knowledge, and information.

From growth to reducing poverty and inequality

Historically, poverty, inequality, and informality occupy a central place in the socioeconomic problems of Argentina, given that the country resorted to – with the exception of certain periods – a free market model with an unequal distribution of resources that benefited a minority with high incomes and with enough capacity to guarantee their reproduction.

The 1990s were characterized by increasing job instability and loss of jobs, as well as an unfavorable distribution of income to workers (especially the less skilled), which also affected the middle strata. The labor market crisis and the increase in inequality affected strongly the living conditions of vast sectors of the middle class. This process was correlated with the emergence of a new poverty, linked to the lack of financial resources. In parallel, the driving idea of the social policies was the focus of the programs on the "structural poor".

The dismantling of the national productive system and the weakening of the state in its role as guarantor of rights led to increasing levels of unemployment, precariousness, and social exclusion. As shown in Figure 7.8, in 2002 the Argentinian labor market presented a high level of open unemployment. This situation was aggravated by a greater labor uncertainty because of the growing prevalence of unregistered remunerated positions (informal employment) and the low structuring of independent occupations. As stated by Beccaria and Maurizio (2003), both phenomena influenced each other: on the one hand, the growing uncertainty was explained by the existence of a large group of people who, in the absence of full and stable employment, were willing to accept low-quality jobs. On the other hand, the greater availability of unstable positions caused the unemployment rate to increase. A large section of the labor force regularly moved between precarious jobs, short-term jobs, and brief periods of unemployment. In this way, unregistered employment in the country – after a long upward trajectory – came to affect one in every two workers in 2003.

Faced with this serious social deterioration, the policies applied since 2003 launched a broad set of actions that, together with the reactivation of the productive apparatus and domestic consumption, had a clear redistributive intention. The improvement of salaries, the diffusion of associative forms of small-scale production, and the great expansion of social protection programs were measures that allowed a positive change in the indicators of poverty, indigence, occupation, and inequality.

From the beginning of the cycle, there was an increase in job formality. Because of this process, in 2010, the number of formal workers was 43 percent higher than at the best time during the previous decade under the convertibility regime. Among the factors that seem to explain the reduction in informality is the increase in activity levels. In particular, there is a clear relationship between the reduction of informality and the growth of GDP.

As shown in Figure 7.9, these processes had a significant impact on poverty and indigence.[17]

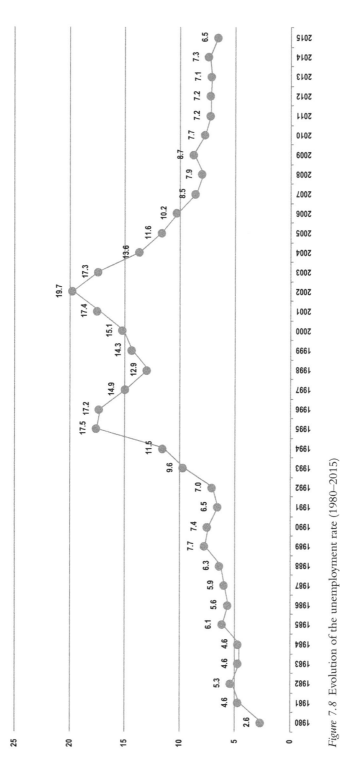

Figure 7.8 Evolution of the unemployment rate (1980–2015)

Source: Prepared by the authors based on data from the Economic Commission for Latin America and the Caribbean (ECLAC). Data retrieved on June 1, 2016, from: http://bit.ly/2cRFWut.

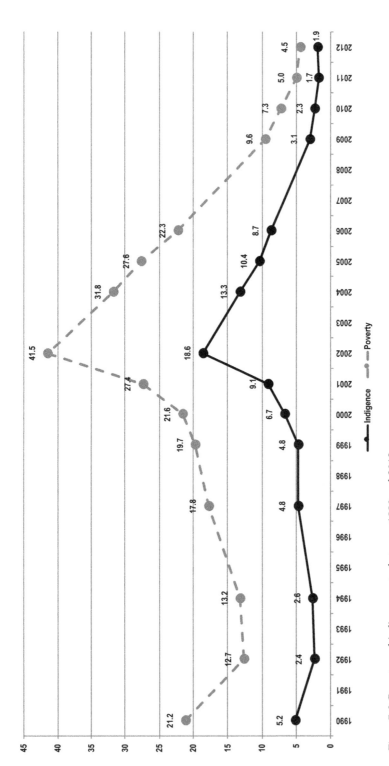

Figure 7.9 Poverty and indigence rates between 1990 and 2012

Source: Prepared by the authors based on data from the Economic Commission for Latin America and the Caribbean (ECLAC). Data retrieved on June 1, 2016, available at: http://bit.ly/2cRFWut.

According to ECLAC data, at the beginning of the cycle, 41.5 percent of the country's population did not have the necessary resources to cover the basic expenses of their households, whereas almost 19 percent of the population did not have enough income to cover the basic food expenses (Figure 7.9). In 2012, these percentages had significantly reduced: 4.5 percent of the population was below the poverty line, whereas almost 2 percent was below the indigence line. It should be noted that these figures are controversial. This debate has been the result of the scant credibility of the data provided by the INDEC, intervened by the executive branch and under suspicion of hiding or manipulating information to disguise inflation rates. Thus, measuring poverty became an object of dispute between the INDEC and other public and private sources of information. In any case, other indicators confirm that poverty decreased in the country as a result of income transfer policies to the most vulnerable sectors and other actions that improved the provision of goods and services, contributing not only to provide more financial and materials resources to families but also to an extension of their rights.

In the past decade, different social protection programs were created, but the most important measure was the Universal Child Allowance and the Universal Allowance for Pregnancy, social insurance for children whose parents had a precarious job, were unemployed, or had low wages. This measure implied not only an important step in the recognition of children's rights but also meant recognizing the critical problem of the labor market – the high proportion of informal employment, with no rights or access to social security.

In turn, the evolution of the indicator of unsatisfied basic needs (NBI)[18] shows a substantial improvement, particularly in recent years. Between 1980 and 1991, the percentage of households with NBI fell by almost 6 percentage points, whereas in the following intercensus period it fell by 2.2 points, and between 2001 and 2010, it showed a strong downward rate with 5.2 points (Figure 7.10). However, it is worth noting that in these periods the absolute number of households with NBI did not behave in the same way. Between 1980 and 1991, the absolute number fell by 12.5 percent (from 1,586,967 to 1,410,876 households with NBI); between 1991 and 2001, it increased by 2.1 percent (from 1,410,876 to 1,442,934); and between 2001 and 2010, it decreased by 29.8 percent (from 1,442,934 to 1,111,622).

Figure 7.10 illustrates the evolution of households with NBI between censuses, and Maps 7.6 and 7.7 show the percentages of households with NBI by province in 2001 and 2010.

Finally, it is important to point out that redistributive policies had an impact on the reduction of inequality. A careful analysis of the official data shows the following changes:

- Argentina presents some differences in inequality in the distribution of income between provinces. However, these are not significant, as their Gini coefficient varies in a range of approximately 0.37% to 0.53%.

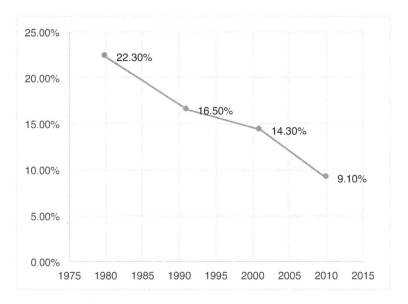

Figure 7.10 Percentage of households with unsatisfied basic needs, 1980, 1991, 2001, and 2010 in Argentina

Source: Prepared by the author based on national censuses.

- In almost all provinces, there is a tendency to improve the distribution of income in the period studied, although it is important to note that this improvement is somewhat small compared to other economic indicators of growth at the national level.

The expansion of popular urbanization

Argentina is a country in which, historically, lower-income sectors have had to face structural limitations to access legally a decent living space, through the market, social production, or public policies. The two main causes of this situation are, on the one hand, the speculative nature of the real estate market, which explains the constant price increases,[19] and on the other, the fragmentary, weak, and inadequate state policies in terms of territorial intervention and regulation.

Expansive growth through the grid plan has been the traditional way of constructing Argentinian cities. Historically, the model was based on the mechanism of the low-priced popular subdivision[20] with low infrastructure coverage and, in certain historical periods, low transport fares for users. For this, the production of urban land responded almost exclusively to the market and the predominance of largely speculative interests. This process resulted in a low occupation of the territory, with gross densities in vast sectors of the

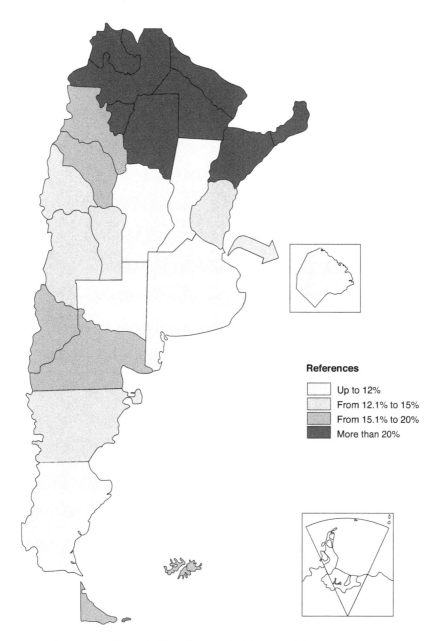

Map 7.5 Percentage of households with unsatisfied basic needs by province, 2001
Source: 2001 census, INDEC.

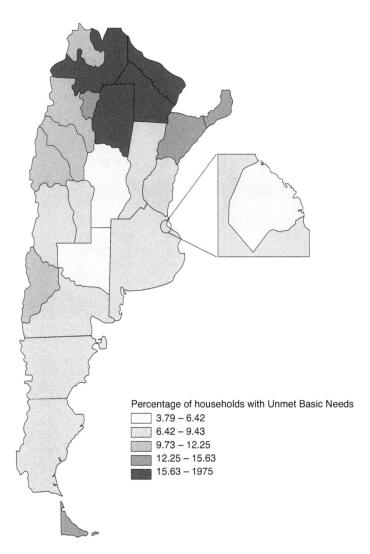

Map 7.6 Percentage of households with unsatisfied basic needs by province, 2010

Source: Dirección Nacional de Relaciones Económicas con las Provincias (DINREP).

peripheries that vary between 10 and 30 inhabitants per hectare, substantially increasing the costs of urbanization.

Informal self-urbanization includes a variety of tenure statuses, as well as extralegal localization and construction characteristics, which do not conform to the land or housing regulations. At the same time, it leads to very diverse association and co-management habitational strategies in the face of need. Housing precariousness and the risk of eviction determine both the conflicts among dwellers and the interventions of the public authorities, which range from repressive actions based on the protection of private property to the construction of new housing units aimed at reducing the quantitative deficit without giving too much attention to the quality of their urban impact.

Thus, the characteristic process of urban expansion in Argentina implies the occupation of the land before its complete urbanization. The exceptions are the social housing districts created by the public sector and those destined for the upper segments of the market.

In this context, during the first cycle, new urbanization patterns consolidated and extended, and there was a deterioration of the fragmentation of the urban space, coinciding with the worsening of socioeconomic inequalities. The dynamics of urbanization expressed in the isolation of the poor (in *villas* and slums) and the self-segregation of the sectors with higher-income levels (in closed neighborhoods). The localization guidelines of the new ventures generated a juxtaposition of two types of growth: one continuous and the other one discontinuous. In turn, this process happened as well in the popular urbanization through the completion of suburban subdivisions, the densification of the old intra-urban *villas*, and the creation of new settlements with land occupation in the peripheries. These were the most relevant forms of access to land for the popular sectors during the years covered by this study, which explains the high rates of urban informality.

However, the census data does not seem to confirm it. As can be seen in Table 7.7, the households in informal tenure grow proportionally up to 1991, and during the 1980s, they show an important hike due to the socioeconomic policies of the dictatorship, imposed since the middle of the previous decade. In this way, the figures reflect the sociourban situation of those years, in which the organized land occupations – since 1981 and 1982 (the so-called settlements) – were one of its most dramatic expressions. As of 1991, the censuses show a gradual reduction.

Given that the processes of segregation and sociospatial exclusion produced by the problematic functioning of the land market during the 20 years covered by this study did not vary significantly, the figures deserve some explanatory comments.

Table 7.7 Evolution of the percentage of households in an irregular tenure situation (1960–2010), with country totals

Census	% of households in an irregular tenure situation
1960	10.0%
1970	12.7%
1980	12.7%
1991	17.6%
2001	15.7%
2010	14.2%

Source: Prepared by the author based on the Under-Secretariat of Urban Development and Housing (2010) and the 2010 census.

In the first place, it is important to point out that the reduced participation of households with informal tenure in the total number of households does not imply that informality has decreased in the last 20 years. On the contrary, an increase in the number of households was registered in almost all the districts of the country (with the exception of the autonomous city of Buenos Aires) but was less than the sum of the owner and tenant households. Indeed, census data show that nationally, between 2001 and 2010, informality increased by 9.2 percent, which means that 146,000 families (16,220 per year) had to occupy land or live in occupations or farms without legal titles. The most dramatic case occurred in the capital city, where informality among censuses increased by 69 percent; that is, close to 54,700 families were added to the *villas*, etc. (6,077 families per year).

Second, census figures undercount informality because in the many neighborhoods that were in the process of land ownership regularization, people claimed to be owners even when they only had a precarious tenure document, delivered by the provincial or municipal governments as part of the long processes.

The appearance of associative forms for the social production of habitat

As seen in the previous paragraphs, a substantial part of the housing stock, the equipment, and enabling of urban land in Argentina (which is impossible to measure accurately) was built through very different self-managed forms, mostly without state support, in long processes known as the social production of habitat. Thus, historically, there has been a huge cultural heritage and rich experience in individual, family, or organized production of habitat, especially in low-income social sectors in Argentina.

From this accumulated knowledge, towards the end of the 1960s and beginning of the 1970s, different neighborhoods' construction experiences (small scale and in different cities) – with technical assistance and systematized methodologies – are put into practice. The main idea of these experiences was that the participation of the beneficiaries in the construction and improvement of housing significantly expand the degree of satisfaction and the quality of the units in the precarious and poor neighborhoods.

These initiatives, mainly promoted by civil society organizations, had little public support and, in general, were financed with funds from international cooperation. These experiences tested prototypes of core housing and evolutionary housing (Vivienda semilla y evolutiva), with rationalized technologies suitable for self-construction and incorporating reduced maintenance facilities. Participatory methodologies were at the center of the proposals, seeking to promote the strengthening of popular organizations and self-management. All cases included social accompaniment to solve the most urgent problems and legal advice to ensure the security of tenure.[21]

In the following decades, very diverse methodologies of social production of habitat spread, thanks to the creation and strengthening of multiple social organizations. During the first cycle, these were the basis of a broad set of experiences based on mechanisms of social and solidary economy, forms of organization for self-management, and appropriate constructive practices.

The change of policies and priorities in the debate during the second cycle allowed the promotion of important advances to extend the forms of social production of habitat.

As discussed earlier, the national government launched the Federal Programs, among which were the Emergencia Habitacional Techo y Trabajo (Emergency Housing – Roof and Work) and Mejor Vivir (Better Living). In the first case, the objective was to generate access to work through the cooperative model, solving labor problems (through an adequate training and the future transformation of the groups into social enterprises), and, at the same time, providing an alternative solution to the housing deficit. The program achieved a broad participation of social organizations (and especially of the movements of the unemployed) and took advantage of the previous experiences of the different habitat organizations but did not become a sustainable tool, which in time meant the closing of many of the cooperatives. The transition of the members of cooperatives into the formal labor market is highly difficult, and a set of limitations and uncertainties prevented the possibility of such transference.

Regarding Mejor Vivir, aimed at finishing and upgrading housing, its final implementation was the result of the proposals from social organizations, such as the aforementioned FOTIVBA and the NGO network Red Encuentro de ONG (Organizaciones No Gubernamentales, in Spanish), among others.

Grassroots organizations also succeeded in promoting important local regulations. An example of this is the Land and Housing Fund, created in the municipality of Quilmes, with a percentage of the resources collected for construction rights and assets alienated by the municipality. It had an enforcement body, the Land and Housing Community Council, whose members included representatives of community organizations, the University of Quilmes, and the Vicaría de la Pastoral Social (Vicariate of the Social Pastoral) of the Bishopric.

Social organizations also acquired experience in the judicial procurement of their claims, managing to stop evictions by means of the constitutional right to protection or – as in the case of the organizations of La Cava in San Isidro – to prevent the municipality and province from transferring to private owners the lands destined to the redevelopment of the neighborhood (Varela, 2012).

Another important example was the passing of Law 341 in the autonomous city of Buenos Aires in 2000, with the purpose of financing – with soft mortgage loans – housing cooperatives for the purchase of real estate, refurbishment, or construction of new houses. Beyond the valuable experiences that the law helped launch, over the years, its application has been discontinuous and fragmentary, which prevented the achievement of its objectives.

Finally, it is important to mention once again the Fair Access to Habitat law of the province of Buenos Aires, which includes a set of instruments (social development program, microcredit program with technical assistance, the creation of a specific trust fund, etc.) aimed at promoting different associative forms of popular habitat production. According to the information released, the programs are applied in different municipalities, although it has not reached the necessary scale to represent a powerful policy of social production of the city.

Urban morphology

The Habitat program gives relevance to making exhaustive use of the existing infrastructure in urban areas. In order to achieve adequate housing for all and the sustainable development of urban settlements, the World Plan of Action proposes the promotion of an optimum occupation density of the available lands – in accordance with their capacity – and to ensure access to parks, recreational areas, and common spaces and services.

The Istanbul Declaration mentions the fact that many cities are unduly using peripheral lands for urban activities, while existing land and infrastructures are not fully developed or used. To avoid unsustainable urban growth, it is necessary to encourage land-use patterns that minimize the demand for transportation, save energy, and protect open spaces and green areas. At this point, the strategies for the implementation of the World Plan of Action point out the importance of warranting an adequate urban density, together with the definition of guidelines for the mixed use of lands.

Argentina: an urban and unequal country

Although Argentina is one of the most urbanized countries in Latin America, the urbanization rate varies among the different regions of the country. For example, in the northeastern region, the urban population reaches 76 percent. This regional disparity shows the possibility of further deepening the urbanization process. In this context and as proposed in *Argentina Urbana* (2011), by the SSPTIP, the question of the dynamics of the urbanization process remains relevant, particularly regarding rural productive development and migration to cities.

The distribution of the population in the country is notoriously unequal. From the agro-exporting stage in the late nineteenth century to the import substitution, the spatial configuration of Argentina increased the urban primacy of Buenos Aires. However, in the last decades, the census data register a slow evolution towards a better distribution. In the last intercensus periods, the cities that grew the most are those between 50,000 and 500,000 inhabitants, which are the same intermediate cities that fulfill the role of provincial and departmental capitals (Map 7.7).

During the first cycle, these problems were not subject to debate or policy formulation, given that the country was governed by the free functioning of the market forces and the conviction that these should be the ones structuring the territory.

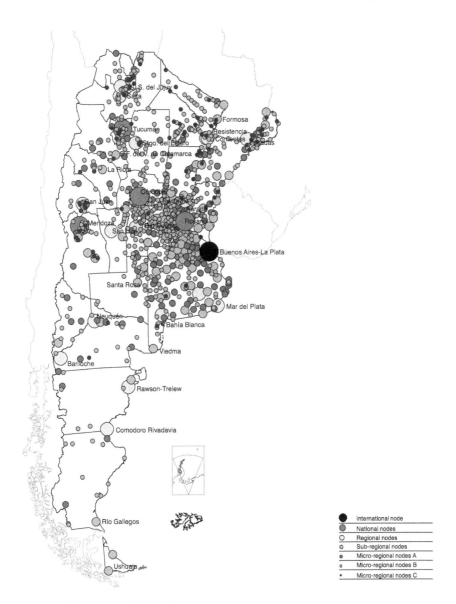

Map 7.7 Urban system classifications

Source: SSPTIP. Based on data from CIMOP and the Under-Secretariat of Rail Transport.

As discussed in the first paragraph, during the second cycle, the Under-Secretariat of Territorial Planning of Public Investment prepared the Strategic Plan, which in its updates focused on the notion of territorial development:

Territorial development is the process by which the capabilities of a given territory are increased in order to make it available for social use. Its dynamics are in the process of implementing public policies, concurrent with the evolution of social and economic trends that characterize each historical period. The socio-economic activities and physical facilities necessary for their deployment are linked to the resources of the territory, and thus form the territorial organization.

(Under-Secretariat of Territorial Planning of Public Investment, 2008)

As can be seen, the definition is based on the need for a strong public intervention that guarantees a certain course of action and the sustainability of the process. The adopted strategy has three intervention lines:

- It defines three types of intervention areas: those to be developed, those to be improved, and those to be upgraded.
- It promotes the strengthening of a polycentric system of urban centers in the national territory.
- It prioritizes the interventions based on identifying connectivity corridors, understanding these as linking and development centers.

Map 7.8 shows the territorial model that the plan proposed in 2011.

Low density and fragmented urban expansion

During the period studied, there are three predominant trends in the urban growth model of Argentinian cities: a) the reduction of population density, b) the fragmentation of peri-urban spaces, and c) the growing dimensions of urban expansion. Historical urban growth has been characterized by a discontinuous expansion, which leaves large vacant spaces that are subject to real estate speculation. This growth is of two types: a) large urban areas with informal patterns of land use and b) a diffuse growth, with residential areas for high- and medium-high-income groups, which usually incorporate commercial and recreational equipment and connectivity based on networks of avenues and highways that privilege the use of private cars. Although it still occupies a small space in relation to the total area of the country, the concern derives from the fact that urbanized land grows at a much higher rate than the urban population (Argentina Urbana, 2011).

These features of urban growth demand increasing areas of urbanized land and pose one of the main questions about the sustainability of the current trends, because they involve high costs of infrastructure and public transport.

The dispersed production of urban land – leaving large interstitial gaps – implied an increase in costs, both economic and socioenvironmental. This type of expansion raises the cost of laying basic infrastructure networks (water, sewers, pavements, gas, electric power, street lighting); stresses the public budget for its maintenance; complicates the mobility of residents; and, with it, complicates the possibility of accessing urban goods and services, because the length of the routes is proportional to the efficiency of public transport services. Therefore,

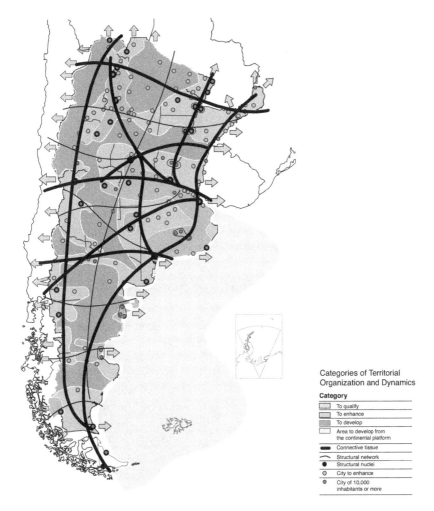

Map 7.8 Preferred territorial model of the Territorial Strategic Plan, 2011

Source: SSPTIP (2011).

it makes the integration between neighborhoods more difficult, given the lack of an articulating public space system (Argentina Urbana, 2011).

The logic of urban land production, which deals with the dynamics of urbanization in different-sized cities, is guided by the behavior of the land market demand and associated with speculative practices of land retention in the expectation of its revaluation without genuine investment. The demand for land in cities leads to an exponential increase in its price, and this has progressively increased expulsions and evictions under the figure of urban renewals – groups that for years inhabited strategic areas for their social benefit.

The trend of the new organization of Argentinian cities, along with the lines of what several authors called a "multifragmented city", is the location of social sectors of high and low resources in increasingly delimited geographical spaces. This type of urban growth implied a greater visibility of internal borders in order to maintain a material and symbolic distance. The juxtaposition of ways of life not only reinforced urban fragmentation but also fueled conflicts over the use of the territory.

With this same logic, and during the last 20 years, the real estate market also generated new products for the denser urban areas, reinforcing the concentration of supply in high-income households. The goods with the greatest impact were the "towers with amenities", which have as a condition (to cushion the costs of common spaces and services) the overdensification of the plots and, consequently, taller buildings.

Both situations generated numerous and intense conflicts – partly discussed earlier – with neighborhood groups opposed to the unsustainable forms that the real estate dynamic adopted during the period.

Conclusions, recommendations, and new issues of the urban agenda

Habitat III offers a worldwide public scenario to catch up on the pending subjects and outline the new issues of the urban agenda, based on the assessment of what has been done during the last 20 years. As stated at the beginning of the chapter, in Argentina during this period, two economic development styles have alternated since the end of the Second World War: one that we could call "neo-liberal or outward growth" and another of "inward growth". These conclusions have a double purpose: on the one hand, to systematize the way these cycles affected the dimensions analyzed and what were the achievements and pending subjects and, on the other hand, to present the keys aspects that explain the urban housing problem in Argentina in the face of the new agenda

Regarding urban policies and governance, in Argentina territorial problems have low political visibility at the national and provincial levels. This situation moved towards a greater – but incipient – institutional strengthening of urban policy. Although the effort made by the national government during the second cycle was reflected in different plans and projects, their impact on decision-making processes is still scarce. In fact, urban policy has not managed to permeate a sectorial scheme of resource allocation. The challenge of ensuring that public investment has territorial integration and equality as priorities remains a pending issue.

The public debate on the right to a decent habitat has managed to mobilize different social groups, but their pressure has yet to be reflected in the policies and legal norms on land-use management. The Law of Fair Access to Habitat of the province of Buenos Aires is a key example because it gathered the associative experiences in social management of the habitat and, from a comprehensive perspective, gave a normative and institutional response to social and urban inclusion. So far, the instruments to regulate land markets promoted by the law were implemented in various innovative experiences by local governments but face great difficulties in sustaining their continuity.

Regarding sustainability and environmental management, the last two decades were characterized by the imposition and validity of different forms of extractivism. During the second cycle, governments failed to overcome the contradictions between extractivism and the industrialist emphasis of the "inward" development style. The impact was a dangerous expansion of the agricultural frontiers and the mining and oil ventures, which affected entire towns and indigenous communities. The growing social conflict and the rising judicialization of issues are related to a greater environmental awareness of the population regarding issues of environmental quality and natural resource management, which also have a strong importance in local and regional cultural patterns. The resistance to the different forms of extractivism (in particular, mining) brings face to face the tensions between both types of development.

Regarding access to housing and urban infrastructure, the percentage of households in deficit housing situations decreased during the period and the coverage of water and sewerage services increased. The composition of the housing deficit showed a slight decrease in the qualitative deficit, although the need for new housing for a third of the households with housing problems persists and the historical regional differences remain. The stagnation of the relative weight of unoccupied dwellings between 2001 and 2010 is closely linked to the increase in the percentage of tenants. In short, a large number of units were built between private real estate ventures and public investment; this did not reduce the deficit, but rather fueled the phenomenon of "tenancy", especially in the middle-income sectors with no access to mortgage loans.

The housing panorama does not register great changes; nevertheless, the housing policies did change and the changes were relevant. First, public investment increased substantially in the second cycle as a promoter of economic growth and construction activity, although the increase in production costs due to inflation affected the results. Second, the housing policy was centralized (PFV), and, in recent years, mortgage credits have broadened with the participation of contributions from the social security system (PRO.CRE. AR). In third place, the housing solutions related to housing and neighborhood upgrades (PRO.ME.BA and others) increased.

So, how can we explain the link between a constant housing deficit despite sustained public investment and qualitative changes in the housing policies? Beyond demographic changes – such as the increase in the number of households – that affected the housing deficit, housing policies still have a sectoral vision and therefore are independent from the workings of the real estate market.

Regarding productivity and competitiveness of the economic agents in the cities of Argentina, a set of factors explain their low levels, but also, in the two decades under study, the real estate market has been at its highest rate due to the multiple speculative practices and the excessive increase in land prices. The real estate market in Argentina has become a privileged instrument of financial

income, which led the urban land to undergo a process of differential appreciation in relation to other goods and the average income of the population.

In relation to urban poverty, inequality, and social exclusion, poverty drastically decreased during the period – but without discussing its magnitude,
which is controversial due to the low reliability of the INDEC data. During the
second cycle, social programs of income transfers to the most vulnerable sectors
contributed to an expansion of rights and helped reduce inequality. However,
urban informality remained. There was an increase in households with informal tenure (although their participation in the total number of households
decreased), in addition to the problems of under-registration, widely recognized by social organizations.

Regarding morphology, low-density urban expansion – with high social,
environmental, and economic costs – is the result of the "peripheralization" of
poverty (in *villas* and slums), together with the self-segregation of households
with higher-income levels (in closed neighborhoods). In addition, housing
plans and neighborhood upgrading programs contributed to this unsustainable
urbanization dynamic.

Now, beyond the differences between both cycles, urban and housing policies have in common structural guidelines that are the product of the inertia
of a conservative and traditional conception of territorial problems and of the
centralized and sectoral ways of responding.

The magnitude and persistence of the housing deficit have been explained
historically, not only in Argentina but also throughout Latin America, through
poverty. However, during the two decades analyzed, poverty decreased much
more than the housing deficit.

In this sense, a first observation is that Argentina – a country whose urban
population exceeds 90 percent – has not managed to have housing and urban
policies that associate urbanization with the democratization of social relations
achieved with the implementation of the new generation of public policies. On
the contrary, during the second cycle, there was a simultaneous and contradictory process of expansion of citizenship with persistent sociospatial exclusion.

Therefore, the current situation reveals the inadequacy of conceiving the
housing problem only as a problem of poverty – that is, of precarious working
conditions, insufficient salaries, and weak social capital – because this conception ignores a series of factors linked to the real estate market and the actions
of the state, which together generate the conditions for the reproduction of
territorial inequality.

The dynamics of exclusive urbanization, resulting from a discontinuous urban
growth that leaves large spaces without urbanization and, therefore, subject to
real estate speculation and inefficient or weak state regulation, represent two
sides of the process of reproduction of the high levels of informality – regardless
of the increase in employment or a greater dynamism of the economy. Thus,
housing and urban informality are the only possible refuge for thousands of
families in our cities and, at the same time, their worst option because the violation of their rights becomes the usual answer to their needs.

Access to adequate housing for all and the sustainable development of human settlements are widely recognized human rights, both nationally and in the different provinces of Argentina. However, there is no consensus on how these rights are violated or on the public policies necessary to guarantee them. The main actors of urbanization and access to urban land do not take part in the formulation of housing policies, and the behavior of the real estate market is far from transparent. The problem acquires political visibility and creates social conflicts because, despite the increase in public investment, the housing deficit remains stable and land occupations are recurrent.

Regarding the validity of a sectorial and centralized management of the housing policy, it is important to bear in mind that the response to the problem in Argentina (as in almost all of Latin America) has been historically restricted to the mere provision of "a roof" – without considering the location and strongly divorced from urban and environmental policies – as well as land management. Thus, during the 20 years analyzed, the housing policies aimed at the lower-income sectors were generally focused on two main lines of action: the construction of new housing units and the urban and land ownership regularization of the popular urbanization. In this context, the response in Argentina has segmented the fields of action. Whereas housing construction contributes mainly to the improvement of the economic activity and the creation of employment in the construction sector, regularization policies contribute to the alleged social and urban integration through the granting of property titles. Yet both lines of action tend to reinforce low-density urbanization, distanced from the centrality areas in cities that have a large number of idle urban plots, with an excellent location in terms of access to urban goods and services and therefore with high valuation expectations.

In this framework, achieving the availability of enough urban land and adequate conditions is a necessary condition to ensure the efficient and effective management of urbanization and social housing programs and projects. The management and intervention instruments on land markets have an extraordinary potential for social redistribution insofar as they have the capacity to affect one of the main mechanisms of reproduction of urban inequality. Thus, urban housing policies can have a direct impact on improving the quality and living conditions of the population, but they must include the structural aspects of the city's production process – such as the unfair distribution of the costs and benefits of public investment and the consequently restricted access to urban benefits and services, as well as the unequal appropriation of real estate valuations generated by public decisions. The only way housing policies, programs, and projects will overcome the stage of compensatory and remedial actions (as they have traditionally been conceived) and become a privileged instrument of social equalization is by intervening on these dynamics. From this perspective, Argentina has had some important advances in the last 10 years, both in terms of policies and local experiences and in the approval of the Law of Fair Access to Habitat of the province of Buenos Aires. The institutional fragility of some achievements refers to the importance of collective actions through strategic alliances between different social actors, such as public universities, social organizations, and human rights organizations.

The current situation in Argentina is bleak. The orientation of public policies and programs since the end of 2015 is clearly aligned with the interests of the most powerful political and economic sectors, regardless of social, housing, or environmental matters. The reduction in recent months of public policy to market criteria violates the principle of recognition and enforcement of citizenship rights. In this sense, and despite the official rhetoric, important contradictions appear between the orientation of the current official measures and the objectives aimed at equity and territorial sustainability, as seen in the documents of the Habitat II and III summits, as well as those of the 2030 Agenda for Sustainable Development.

As previously stated, the commitments and policy recommendations resulting from Habitat II had little presence in the formulation of public policies in Argentina. Undoubtedly, the existing distance between the "should be" laid out in international documents and the urgency of social demands in our countries plays against their capacity to exert influence. In that sense, it seems essential that both governments and civil society organizations can produce a translation of the main guidelines of the Habitat III summit in a register that accounts for the tensions and contradictions inherent in the local processes of territorial development.

Notes

1 The term neo-developmentalism alludes to alternatives to the Washington Consensus doctrines merging structuralist and Keynesian ideologies (Bresser-Pereira et al., 2014; Khan et al., 2010, and others). (Note from the editors.)

2 A foreignization of the economy entails an increase in the predominance of foreign capital in the business ownership and leadership. (Note from the editors.)

3 Since its approval almost 40 years ago, the CPU suffered multiple modifications of all sorts that tried to correct the rigidities of the original standard and account for particular situations. The most important was made in 1989. Additionally, there were an important number of exceptions and dubious normative interpretations, resulting from the pressure of groups linked to the real estate business and to situations of proven corruption.

4 Argentinian local governments do not have a similar institutional political structure, nor comparable faculties or competencies among the provinces. The constitutional reform of 1994 establishes that each province must dictate its own constitution, ensuring municipal autonomy and regulating its scope and content in the institutional, political, administrative, and financial fields.

5 The current Argentinian system of tax co-participation foresees the distribution of the product of a set of taxes only between the central government and the provinces, whereas the latter also implement co-participation regimes with their respective municipalities. Even so, the central governments have always set in motion different programs that relate them directly with the local ones.

6 In all four cases, the valuation of land produced by public action is the main factor in negotiating with private investors to finance the urban transformation of the sites and to carry out actions in other sectors of the city.

7 Habitar Argentina is a multisectorial space made up of grassroots organizations, academic institutions, social movements, and national and provincial legislators working

together to generate a political and normative framework that guarantees the right to housing, land, and habitat (ttp: //habitarargentina.blogspot.com.ar/).

8 Judicialization refers to an overreliance on courts and judicial means for addressing public policy questions and political controversies or moral issues. (Note from the editors.)

9 This is the case "Mendoza, Beatriz Silvia and others vs. National State and others for damages (damages arising from environmental pollution of the Matanza River – Riachuelo)".

10 Law 26,168 of 2006.

11 Additionally, a large number of environmental organizations recently brought a lawsuit against the National Service of Food Health and Quality (SENASA) demanding a risk analysis of the 400 registered herbicides containing glyphosate in order to proceed to the subsequent prohibition of their use and commercialization.

12 The municipality of Esquel has a population of around 30,000 inhabitants. It is located in the province of Chubut, in the Patagonian region of Argentina.

13 The enterprise belonged to the Spanish company ENCE.

14 We express our gratitude to Dr. Verónica Maceira for her help in processing the EPH data included in this work.

15 1. Everyone was temporarily absent; 2. The dwelling is for rent or sale; 3. The dwelling is under construction; 4. The dwelling is used as a shop/office/clinic; 5. The dwelling is used for holidays or weekends; 6. The house is closed for unknown reasons; 7. The house is abandoned; and 8. Not specified.

16 Since its privatization, the bank's management (with more than 20 percent of the share package) is in the hands of Inversiones y Representaciones Sociedad Anónima (IRSA), which controls the largest real estate group in Argentina, owns the main shopping centers, and develops the most important and controversial real estate projects.

17 According to INDEC, poor households are those in which the sum of the income received by all members is less than the poverty line, which represents the value of all goods and services necessary for the household to meet its basic needs. Indigent households are those whose total income does not reach the indigence line, which represents only the consumption of food necessary to ensure the physical reproduction of the members of the household.

18 The indicator of unsatisfied basic needs accounts for the structural poverty situations through aspects such as the existence of children of school age not attending any educational institution, inadequate (precarious housing, hotel or pension rooms) or insufficient conditions (three people or more per room) in housing and health (no toilet), or serious limitations to produce an income according to the needs of the family group (four or more dependents of a member with a low educational level).

19 The dynamics of the real estate market are analyzed more exhaustively in the section "The functioning of the real estate market".

20 Popular subdivision is understood as the fractioning, minimum urbanization, and sale in monthly installments – promoted by private agents – of parcels of land destined for housing of the low-income sectors. The division into lots has been a central element in the sociospatial organization of the territory.

21 Some examples are the actions developed by AVE-CEVE (Association of Economic Housing – Experimental Center for Economic Housing) in the province of Córdoba, the IIDVI (Housing Research and Development Institute) in Chaco and the northeast of the country, and the pioneering experience of Barrio Justo Suárez in the autonomous city of Buenos Aires (CABA).

Bibliography

Acuña, G., (1999), *Marcos regulatorios e institucionales de América Latina y el Caribe en el contexto del proceso de reformas macroeconómicas: 1980–1990*, United Nations Economic Commission for Latin America and the Caribbean ECLAC, Environment and Development Series Nº 20, Santiago de Chile.

Azpiazu, D. and Basualdo, E., (2004), *Las privatizaciones en la Argentina. Génesis, desarrollo y principales impactos estructurales*, Facultad Latinoamericana de Ciencias Sociales FLACSO-Argentina, Buenos Aires.

Azpiazu, D., Catenazzi, A., and Forcinito, K., (2004), "Recursos públicos, negocios privados: agua potable y saneamiento ambiental en el Área Metropolitana de Buenos Aires", Working Paper Nº 19, Universidad Nacional de General Sarmiento, Los Polvorines Buenos Aires.

Banzas, A., and Fernández, A., (2007), "El financiamiento a la vivienda en Argentina. Historia reciente, situación actual y desafíos", Working Paper Nº 18, Centro de Economía y Finanzas para el desarrollo de la Argentina, Buenos Aires.

Barbeito, A., and Lo Vuolo, R., (1992), *La modernización excluyente: transformación económica y estado de bienestar en Argentina*, CIEPP-UNICEF, Lozada, Buenos Aires.

Beccaria, L., and Maurizio, R., (2003), *Movilidad ocupacional en Argentina*, Sciences Institute, Universidad Nacional de General Sarmiento, Los Polvorines Buenos Aires.

Bertolotto, M., and Clemente, A., (2008), "Deuda y haber en los procesos de Planificación Participativa", In Heras, A. and Burin D, (eds.), *Trabajo, Desarrollo y Diversidad*, Editorial Ciccus, Buenos Aires.

Bresser-Pereira, L. C., Oreiro, J. L., and Marconi, N., (2014), *Developmental Macroeconomics New Developmentalism as a Growth Strategy*, Routledge, London.

Capello, M., Grión, N., and Valsagna, L., (2013), "Anatomía del Gasto Público Argentino: Expansión en la última década y desafíos a futuro", Working Paper Nº 39, Edition 135, Fundación IERAL – Fundación Mediterránea, Córdoba.

Catenazzi, A., (2011), "Las redes de agua y saneamiento en la agenda urbana: encuentros y desencuentros", In *Infraestructuras Urbanas en América Latina: gestión y construcción de servicios y obra pública*, Editorial IAEN, Quito.

Catenazzi, A., and Reese, E., (2010), "Derecho a la ciudad. La dinámica de crecimiento urbano, el déficit habitacional y las asignaturas pendientes", *Journal Voces en el Fénix*, 1, School of Economic Sciences, Universidad de Buenos Aires. Buenos Aires.

Centro de Estudios Legales y Sociales (CELS), (2015), "Una perspectiva de derechos sobre las políticas de desarrollo y de acceso justo al hábitat", In *Derechos Humanos en la Argentina. Informe 2015*, Centro de Estudios Legales y Sociales, Siglo Veintiuno Editores, Buenos Aires.

Centro de Estudios Legales y Sociales (CELS), (2016), "Vulneraciones de derechos en tomas de tierra y asentamientos. Entre la necesidad, el mercado y el Estado", In *Derechos Humanos en la Argentina. Informe 2016*, Centro de Estudios Legales y Sociales, Siglo Veintiuno Editores, Buenos Aires.

Cerrutti, M., and Grimson, A., (2004), "Buenos Aires, neoliberalismo y después. Cambios socioeconómicos y respuestas populares", *Cuadernos del IDES*, Nº 5, October, Buenos Aires.

Clarín, (2007), "If You Had Money Saved, What Would You Do with It?", *Survey, Digital Clarin*, April 2, 2007.

Clemente, A., (2012), "Descentralización y planificación del desarrollo local", In Álvarez, M. and Catenazzi, A. (eds.), *Gestión municipal y ciudad. Dilemas y oportunidades*, Program to Enhance Municipal Management, Buenos Aires.

Clichevsky, N., (2002), *Pobreza y políticas urbano-ambientales en Argentina*, Environment and Development Series Nº 49, ECLAC, Santiago de Chile.

Coraggio, J. L., (2008), *Economía social, acción pública y política (hay vida después del neoliberal-ismo)*, Ediciones CICCUS, Buenos Aires.

Cravino, M. C., Fernández, R., and Varela, O., (2002), "Notas sobre la política habitacional en el área metropolitana de Buenos Aires en los '90'", Instituto del Conurbano, Universidad Nacional de General Sarmiento, Working Paper, Buenos Aires.

Cuenya, B., (2000), "Cambios, logros y conflictos en la política de vivienda en Argentina hacia fines del siglo XX", In *Ciudades para un futuro más sostenible (29/30): notas para entender el mercado inmobiliario*, Bulletin, Buenos Aires.

Del Río, J. P., (2012), "El lugar de la vivienda social en la ciudad: Un análisis de la política habitacional desde el mercado de localizaciones intra-urbanas y las trayectorias residenciales de los habitantes", Doctoral Theses, School of Humanities and Educational Sciences, Universidad Nacional de La Plata, La Plata.

Government of Chaco Province, (2014), *Plan de desarrollo territorial de la Provincia del Chaco*, Government of Chavo, Resistencia.

Khan, S. R., and Christiansen, J., (2011), *Towards New Developmentalism: Market as Means Rather Than Master, Routledge Studies in Development Economics*, Routledge, New York.

Lazarte, F., Naidicz, L., and Ruiz, L., (2012), "La distribución del ingreso en Tucumán y en otros aglomerados de Argentina. Su evolución en los últimos años", conference presentation, X Conference of Latin American Statistics Associations, October 16–19, Córdoba, Argentina.

Merlinsky, M. G., (2013), *Política, derechos y justicia ambiental: el conflicto del Riachuelo*, Fondo de Cultura Económica, Buenos Aires.

Nochteff, H., (1995), "Los senderos perdidos del desarrollo. Elite económica y restricciones al desarrollo en la Argentina", In Azpiazu, D. and Nochteff, H. (eds.), *El Desarrollo ausente*, Tesis-Norma-FLACSO, Buenos Aires.

Pírez, P., (2001), "Cuestión metropolitana y gobernabilidad urbana en la Argentina", In Madoery, O. and Vázquez, A. (eds.), *Transformaciones globales, instituciones y políticas de desarrollo local*, Homo Sapiens, Buenos Aires.

Red Agroforestal Chaco Argentina (REDAF), (2010), *Conflictos sobre tenencia de la tierra y ambientales en la Región del Chaco Argentino*, Second Report, Santa Fe, Argentina.

Red Agroforestal Chaco Argentina (REDAF), (2011), *Conflictos sobre tenencia de la tierra y ambientales en la Región del Chaco Argentino*, Third Report, Santa Fe, Argentina.

Reese, E., Almansi, E., and Del Valle, J., et al., (2013), "Políticas habitacionales y la regulación del alquiler en Argentina", In Blanco A. G., Fretes V., and Muñoz, A (eds) *Busco casa en arriendo: Promover alquiler tiene sentido*, Inter American Development Bank, Washington.

Reese, E., Baer, L., Cuenya, B., Duarte, J., Esteban, A., and Itzcovich, P., (2014), *Análisis comparativo de la implementación de mecanismos de captura de plusvalía en 4 ciudades argentinas*, Fiscal Management Division, Inter American Development Bank (IDB), Washington, DC.

Report of the United Nations Conference on Human Settlements (HABITAT II), (1996), *Istambul Declaration on Human Settlements*, United Nations General Assembly, Istanbul, 3–14 June.

Rodulfo, M. B., and Boselli, T., (2014), "Dilemas y desafíos de la política habitacional argentina desde un enfoque de derechos", *Cuadernos de Vivienda y Urbanismo*, 7:14, Universidad Javeriana, Bogota.

Rofman, A., (1999), "Economías regionales. Modernización productiva y exclusión social en las economías regionales", *Realidad económica Journal*, 162, Buenos Aires.

Ryan, D., (2014), "Política y ambiente en la Argentina: ¿Un caso de baja politización? Análisis de la aprobación de las leyes de bosques nativos y protección de glaciares", *Revista*

Estado y Políticas Públicas, 2:3, Facultad Latinoamericana de Ciencias Sociales FLACSO, Buenos Aires.

Ryan, D., and Napoli, A., (2013), "Legal Mobilization and the Politics of Water Pollution: The case of the Matanza-Riachuelo Basin in Argentina", In *Politics of Fresh Water*, Taylor and Francis, London.

Secretaría de Ambiente y Desarrollo Sustentable de la Nación, (2011), *Vulnerabilidad y adaptación al cambio climático para la gestión y planificación local*, Government of Argentina, Buenos Aires.

Secretaría de Ambiente y Desarrollo Sustentable de la Nación, (2015), *Sistema de Indicadores de Desarrollo Sostenible*, Eighth edition, Government of Argentina, Buenos Aires.

Subsecretaria de Planificación Territorial de la Inversión Pública, (2008), *Plan Estratégico Territorial*, Ministry of Federal Planning, Public Investment, and Services, Government of Argentina, Buenos Aires.

Subsecretaria de Planificación Territorial de la Inversión Pública, (2011), *Argentina Urbana*, Ministry of Federal Planning, Public Investment, and Services, Government of Argentina, Buenos Aires.

Svampa, M., (2008), Argentina: una cartografía de las resistencias (2003–2008), *Revista Osal*, 9:24, October, CLACSO, Buenos Aires.

Svampa, M., Álvarez, M. S., and Bottaro, L., (2009), "Los movimientos contra la minería metalífera a cielo abierto: escenarios y conflictos. Entre el 'efecto Esquel' y el 'efecto La Alumbrera'", In Svampa, M. and Antonelli, M. (eds.), *Minería transnacional, narrativas del desarrollo y resistencias sociales*, Editorial Biblos, Buenos Aires.

Varela, O., (2012), "Del barrio al Congreso. Organizaciones barriales, participación y derecho a la ciudad", Conference presentation at: X Jornadas de Investigación urbana y regional:"Políticas de vivienda y derechos habitacionales. Reflexiones sobre la justicia Espacial en la Ciudad Latinoamericana", Instituto Javeriano de Vivienda y Urbanismo, Facultad de Arquitectura y Diseño, de la Pontificia Universidad Javeriana de Bogotá, Colombia.

8   Ecuador

From Istanbul to Quito

Fernando Carrión and Alexandra Velasco

Introduction

To conduct a periodic evaluation of public policies, particularly in housing and urban development, it is very important to understand the function, quality and impact of these policies. Even more so if one considers that there has been a tendency since 1976 to reformulate international goals every 20 years, without recognizing the great differences that exist between the cities of the world and without considering that cities themselves change rapidly. This forces cities not only to assess performance but also to demand accountability more frequently. One might ask the following questions: What is the point of proposing long-term policies when cities change every day? In these diverse and long-term contexts, is it feasible to build urban agendas that are unique to each reality rather than have one agenda for all? How can we understand a new urban agenda if it is not clearly defined? What was the previous agenda? How does it relate to the new one?

This chapter seeks to understand what has happened in the 20-year span from 1996 (Habitat II, Istanbul) to 2016 (Habitat III, Quito) with respect to urban policies designed globally but implemented in Ecuadorian cities. This approach will be developed under an evaluation of the fulfillment of the main commitments of Habitat II (global), assumed by the government of Ecuador at the local level of cities.

Internationalization of urban politics: its moments

There is no doubt that cities take on more importance in the current context of globalization. This has become evident when certain instances of internationalization of urban policy are materialized at the national and local levels. In this perspective, there have been two key moments, discussed in the following sections.

Internationalization from the International Congresses of Modern Architecture

The first arises in the first third of the 20th century under the influence of modern architecture and urbanism, driven by a group of European specialists led by the figure of Le Corbusier. The International Congress of Modern Architecture (CIAM) – founded in 1928 and dissolved 30 years later – was the space where a set of proposals were formulated that had great influence and international impact, especially in Latin America. Definitions about cities and housing were set within a functionalist lens, through the spatial segregation of the functions of residence, circulation, work and recreation, with a priority given to housing against other uses, with good hygienic conditions and multifloor construction.

Without a doubt, such a proposal put into question the traditional city, and could well be interpreted as the formulation of a new urban agenda. The global influence of CIAM was very strong, and perhaps the most significant in Latin America was the construction of Brasilia, later declared by United Nations Educational, Scientific and Cultural Organization (UNESCO) as a world heritage site, as a faithful reflection of this current characteristic of a moment of world urbanism. But the CIAM also influenced the first proposals of urban planning that were present in several cities of the region, including Quito.

UN recognition of the problems of cities: the creation of UN Habitat

The second moment arises from the institutionalization of the UN Habitat and not from certain personalities of urbanism. On January 1, 1975, the UN General Assembly established the United Nations Human Settlements Program (UN Habitat), an entity designed to convene global meetings of national governments to discuss and agree every 20 years on planetary policies on two themes: habitat and human settlements, concepts imported from the natural sciences that were used to define the city. The creation of the organization was undoubtedly a step forward, because the member countries of the international organization recognized the importance of cities as a problem requiring specialized international treatment.

The first United Nations Conference on Human Settlements took place in 1976, organized by UN-Habitat and held in Vancouver, whereby the mission and institution were legitimized within the UN and globally. On that occasion, the debates revolved around the rapid process of urbanization that was being experienced on a world scale as a result of the vigorous rural/urban migration and the natural growth of the population, which produced a significant growth of "human settlements", called *favelas* in Brazil, *villas miseras* in Argentina, *pueblos jovenes* in Peru, *rancho* neighborhoods in Venezuela, popular colonies in Mexico or *callampas* in Chile.

The emergence of this problem ended up in the development of a "dual city": informal/formal, legal/illegal. In other words, Habitat I sought to manage not to reduce the rapid and uncontrolled growth of cities. Latin America in 1951 had 41 percent of the population concentrated in cities, but by the beginning of the 21st century it had already doubled, showing that the agreed objectives had not been fulfilled.

Twenty years later, the United Nations Conference met again in Istanbul in 1996, as the world continued to experience uncontrollable urbanization and its consequences were seen in the cities. At the time, the general debate was about the significance of globalization (the global city) and neoliberal theses, framed in the processes of the so-called "Washington Consensus", which promoted deregulation of markets and the decentralization of responsibility for urban development, as well as repositioning of international bodies for financial and technical cooperation in urban and local matters. The search for efficiency in the management of urbanization, for which quantitative techniques of measurement of results were used, later led to the formulation of the "Millennium Development Goals", born at the world summit of the year 2000 held at the UN headquarters in New York.

In 2016 the third world summit of cities organized by UN-Habitat was held in Quito, 20 years after the second and 40 after the first. This meeting took place at a time when cities had gained a significant weight in the world, in two senses: On the one hand, it must be recognized that today the world is urban. By 2007, according to UN-Habitat, the urban population exceeded the rural population, with both the populations of Europe and the Americas concentrated in cities at a rate above 80 percent. Moreover, at the global level, politics are essentially urban, as is the economy. On the other hand, a new global order emerged through three key international actors: a) declining states, b) the market represented by large transnational corporations and c) cities that have achieved a unique role. Today, cities have an international presence as a metropolis (New York, London, Tokyo), as a cluster (of salmon in Chile, of technology in Silicon Valley) and as joint communities (48 municipalities on the Ecuador–Peru border). Cities also have achieved institutional recognition through the creation of the United Cities and Local Governments (UCLG), whose purpose is "[t]o be the united voice and global representation of autonomous and democratic local governments, promoting their values, goals and Interests, through cooperation between local and regional governments and the vast international community".

International cooperation (including UNHabitat) strongly promoted the decentralization of the state so that cities can have self-government. However, this framework is not consistent with its own objectives for cities. For example, when local governments ask for credits directly from international institutions, their requests are immediately denied because these institutions only grant funds to national governments or. So, when a city requires a loan, it does so under the quotas, guarantees and national priorities. Similarly, these international organizations formulate urban policy proposals without regard to cities, so that when they organize city summits, cities are not represented through their democratically elected authorities.

At the Habitat III summit, debates were held about what must be done in the city, without their city governments having a voice and vote. That is, the city had become an object without a subject or an arena without government. In other words, an unacceptable ventriloquism occurred: others speak and decide for the city. It is as if, since the first summit of Habitat I in 1976, nothing has changed: national governments and their international organizations decide for cities without them being present.

Commitments acquired in Habitat II

In June 1996 in Istanbul, more than 150 countries met to define actions, plans and strategies aimed at, first, achieving adequate housing for all and, second, pursuing the sustainable development of urban settlements in an urbanized world (Habitat II, 1996: 12). The assembly of countries recognized that more than 1 billion people in the world did not have decent living conditions in urban and rural areas. There was also a growing concern about the sustainability of development, understood as a balance between economic development and environmental protection, without neglecting the recognition of fundamental human rights, including the right to development.

The commitments made in 1996 were aimed at providing decent, safe, healthy, accessible and affordable housing; sustainable human settlements; participation and empowerment: gender equity; financing of housing and human settlements; and international cooperation.

From Istanbul to Quito: a historic issue

The 20 years that have passed since Istanbul (Habitat II, 1996) cannot be measured chronologically, because in this period there have been at least three key events in Ecuador: dollarization in 2000, the Citizens' Revolution in 2007 and the economic crisis that begun in 2014, which has had significant impacts on urban development and housing policies in Ecuador.

Urban consequences of the dollarization of the Ecuadorian economy

At the end of the previous century and at the beginning of this century, Ecuador went through one of its worst economic, financial and fiscal crises. Its public debt exceeded the total value of the gross domestic product (GDP); inflation had grown up to 95 percent; and unemployment and underemployment reached 16 percent and 50 percent, respectively. The devaluation of the Sucre was around 500 percent in the last two years, and between 1998 and 1999 some 30 banks and financial institutions had collapsed. Poverty and extreme poverty rates among the population increased rapidly, widening the gap between the poor and the rich, further concentrating incomes on the richest decile.

Several factors determined the crisis, but two had great influence. The first had to do with the price reduction of a barrel of oil below $10, which was the primary revenue of government, and the other was the bankruptcy of a large part of the private financial sector. In the first case, the drop in the price of a barrel of oil was an exogenous factor caused by the Asian crisis and the loss of confidence in emerging countries, among which was Ecuador. In the second case, the bankruptcy of the private financial sector had to do with endogenous factors associated with the structural adjustment policies that promoted the reduction of the state and its expenditure, and the principle that the economy is better regulated by the natural market.

In 1994 Ecuador adopted economic policies to liberalize its financial market with unregulated interest rates, supposedly to attract foreign capital and thereby improve the economy. One of the most deregulated sectors was the financial sector, where regulatory entities such as Superintendency of Banks did little to prevent that deposits and remittances from Ecuadorians were returned to the countries from which they had been sent.

The mechanism adopted by the bankers was the creation of companies that only existed on paper, which requested "linked credits" from banks that, once granted, expatriated those resources. In those years this was a common practice adopted by many private banks and financial institutions. The state entities in charge of exercising control over the financial sector did not take notice and did nothing to prevent it. This led to a great distrust of the system, massive withdrawals of money and, consequently, the bankruptcy of many banks – indeed, a domino effect. Other endogenous measures were the adoption of a currency band exchange rate system, which produced a steep rise in the value of the dollar in relation to the national currency. This was compounded by the serious effect of the "El Niño" meteorological phenomenon of 1998–1999.

Under these conditions, the bankruptcy of the financial sector led the state to partially assume what was called the "bank bailout" to alleviate the massive impoverishment of millions of Ecuadorians who had entrusted their savings to banks. It is estimated that the bank bailout cost the government of Ecuador more than US$5 billion. An additional US$3.8 billion, deposited by customers in banks, were frozen and only returned in part, without considering interest nor the loss of profit.

These events led to an accelerated increase in poverty, which forced many families to take their children out of school and skip health examinations. There was then an accelerated loss of human capital. Poverty due to structural factors in the Ecuadorian society, was aggravated by a crisis of significant magnitude,[1] resulting in emergency policies that became permanent programs.

One of the economic policy measures adopted because of this crisis was dollarization, which meant the replacement of the national currency, the Sucre, by a solid currency, the US dollar.[2] The objective of that policy was to eliminate the devaluation of the Sucre and the accelerated loss of its purchasing power, an objective that was achieved, but with the loss of monetary policy. This required the country to develop more competitive capacities, since from the end of the year the country's income – and therefore its revenue – depended no longer on the issuance of banknotes by the Central Bank, but rather on the capacity of the country to raise external resources via exports and financing. Other economic measures in this period were an increase in the prices of basic services, oil products and gas, as well as the restructuring of Brady and Euro-bond debt by Global Bonds (CONAM, 2010: 12).

The magnitude of the crisis and the accelerated growth of poverty signifi-cantly restrained employment and income opportunities for hundreds of thou-sands of Ecuadorians, who were forced to emigrate mainly to Spain and the United States. A few years later they began to send remittances of financial resources to their relatives residing in the country. Remittances became the sec-ond most important currency income in Ecuador,[3] after oil exports.

These and other factors enabled the country to enter into a process of rela-tively rapid economic recovery,[4] of notable expansion of the domestic market, improvement of the living conditions of broad sectors of the population and poverty reduction. Dollarization had made it possible to recover economic stabil-ity and also allowed for the reappearance of long-term credit and the reduction of inflation, which has since remained in single digits, always below 5 percent, thereby recovering the purchasing power of the citizen. The change of the cur-rency from the Sucre to the dollar gave confidence to the national productive sectors. But dollarization also had negative effects, such as the loss of sovereignty in monetary matters and an excessive growth of expensive imports and a decrease in consumption of a part of the local production. Nonetheless, the benefits obtained by Ecuador have been greater than the weaknesses of the system.

The 2007 Citizens' Revolution: the return of the public

The turn of the 21st century produced not only a very acute economic crisis, which led to dollarization, but also a political one. Proof of this was the great instability that existed between 1996 and 2006, when there were nine presi-dents of the republic. In addition, the political system of representation initi-ated with the return to democracy collapsed and new political parties (PRIAN, SP, AP) were born, leaving behind the traditional ones (ID, DP, PRE). With this process new ways of doing politics emerged.

In 2007 President Rafael Correa Delgado won the presidency of the repub-lic and began a process of important change that could be defined in the eco-nomic realm as post-neoliberal (not post-capitalist) and in the political realm as opposed to "*partidocracia*". This process is called the Citizens' Revolution. In his government a return of the public was perceived, going from the approval of a new constitution in 2008 by means of a plebiscite to the application of new public policies linked to a process of change to create the socialism of Buen Vivir or Sumak Kawsay.

Three fundamental elements outline Correa's program: the defense of sov-ereignty, the reduction of socioeconomic inequalities and the change of the productive matrix in a context of economic stability born of dollarization and a substantial increase in revenues from the exploitation of natural resources by the national oil company. By 2016, in a period of economic crisis, this cycle seemed to be ending prior to the general elections.

The crisis of the model: closing a cycle?

The 2016 economic crisis that Ecuador experienced had its main explanations in three external factors: the deceleration of the Chinese economy, which reduced the demand for exports; the decline in commodity prices, mainly oil; and the appreciation of the dollar in a context in which the country had no monetary policy. This had two negative consequences: loss or competitiveness of Ecuadorian exports and a budgetary shortfall. Ecuadorian exports lost competitiveness because they became more expensive, whereas non-dollarized countries devalued their currencies to keep their export prices competitive (Colombia and Peru, among others). The high oil revenues during 2008 and 2014 had allowed the state to have a significant weight in the economy and in all areas of social life to the extent that investment and public spending were the main drivers of growth. Between 2002 and 2006 public expenditure accounted for 20.9 percent of GDP, whereas in the period 2007–2015 it rose to 32.6 percent of GDP, which accounted for the expansion of the state. During the years 2013–2014, the state budget reached more than 40 percent of GDP, with a current expenditure of 28 percent. In 2015, the International Monetary Fund (IMF) estimated that the Ecuadorian economy would shrink by −4.5 percent in 2016 and by −4.3 percent by 2017 (by 2015, +0.3 percent).[5] In addition the country was shaken in 2016 by an earthquake of magnitude 7.8 on the Richter scale, which would increase this negative estimate. According to the President of the republic, the earthquake resulted in a loss of 3 percent of GDP, as well as devastating human and material losses.

In the nearly 10 years of the Citizens' Revolution, public investment was favored over domestic and foreign private investment, to the point that economic dynamism depended almost exclusively on the state. When the state saw its revenues reduced, mainly as a result of the fall in oil prices in 2014, investment in general fell apart and could not be sustained. Many sources of national private capital had already migrated to other latitudes in previous years as a consequence of an environment of uncertainty and mistrust – among other things – of 11 tax reforms. Another important part of the expenditure went to subsidies, mainly of fuels, which generated serious distortions in the economy: before the crisis, the amount of the subsidies represented about 20 percent of the general state budget (PGE).

Ecuador has not been able to overcome its poorly diversified production structure, with an excessive weight of primary goods and, as a consequence, a limited supply of export goods, where the sale of oil remains the main source of income. In addition, despite the expansion of trade relations with China and other countries, the United States remains the main trading partner, unlike countries such as Chile, Peru, Brazil, Uruguay or Argentina, which have diversified their markets.

In Ecuador, a large part of the public investment and expenditures went to expand and strengthen state productive and social infrastructure with important rehabilitation projects and construction of roads, bridges, refineries, ports, airports, reservoirs for irrigation systems, hospitals and educational units, among others. The investment came not only from oil revenues but also from foreign loans, mainly from China, estimated to be about US$30 billion. In energy matters, several hydroelectric plants were built, some of them already completed, which has allowed the replacement of the energy supplied by oil-dependent thermoelectric plants.

The fact that Ecuador is a dollarized country generated economic stability until 2014, but since then, the appreciation of the dollar (according to the Inter-American Development Bank greater than 20 percent) and the continuous devaluations of countries with a similar supply of export products, such as Colombia and Peru, among others, have brought many problems in terms of foreign trade. The government budget for 2016 was US$29,835,000, and the budget deficit – which is beginning to be constant – was estimated to exceed US$7 billion. In addition to past due debts with contractors, suppliers, services, local governments, etc., the figure exceeds US$10 billion.

Correa's government believed that the price of oil would stay high for a long time and forgot that the economy has a cyclical behavior. At the time, it did not create any contingency fund, despite the fact that during the period of the oil boom, the state was estimated to have received about US$300 billion, in addition to having increased tax collections. The Correa government argued that the best saving was investment, but beyond that discussion, the fact is that the government lacked funds to mitigate the economic downturn. Ecuador therefore had serious liquidity problems by 2016 as a result of falling revenue and had problems not only in sustaining public investment but also in covering current and capital expenditures. To finance the huge fiscal deficit, the Correa government favored three sources of financing: increased taxes, the sale of state assets and internal and external public indebtedness. The administration carried out 11 tax reform (up to the last ones approved following the earthquake of April 2016).

By 2016, the government sent the Assembly a budget close to US$30 billion, lower than that of 2015, establishing a price per barrel of oil of US$35, much lower than the US$79 that it set in 2015, and that led to two budget reductions. The fiscal deficit for the current year was estimated at US$10 billion, which the government expected to cover with US$1 billion of domestic debt, US$4.8 billion of external debt and about US$700 million from anticipated sale of oil, but would still leave a deficit of US$3.5 billion.

The crisis was so deep that it is not so far-fetched to ask whether the national government, identified as post-developmental or 21st-century socialist, was closing a cycle. In that sense, there was a deep uncertainty about the future, although there was a sense that the economic crisis would continue and would probably be longer than expected.

In more recent years, the increase in the price of oil on the international market allowed the state to expand infrastructure and social investment, all of which helped the country reduce poverty levels and achieve better social indicators. Despite the achievements since 2007, there were still some deficits, mainly in child malnutrition. Unemployment and poverty are beginning to suffer significant increases.

Urbanization and cities in Ecuador

The Ecuadorian urbanization process responds mainly to a double demographic behavior: natural growth of the population and migration, which has led to an increase of density in some territories over others, change in the rural/urban relationship and modification of the weights and counterweights of certain regions and the number of cities. In 1950 Ecuador had 3.2 million inhabitants, almost 2 percent of the total population of Latin America, being the ninth country with the largest number of inhabitants in the region, preceded by Bolivia with 5 million inhabitants and followed by Haiti with 3.4 million. In the last 20 years, there has been a structural change in the pattern of urbanization in Ecuador and its cities, compared to what happens in other Latin American countries: the country climbed to the eighth position with 16.3 million, after Chile with 17.9 million and followed by Guatemala with 16.2 million (CITE – FLACSO, 2015: 11).

From the 1980s onwards urbanization became widespread, leaving very few empty spaces within the national territory. Ecuador became a very dense country, so much so that it became the densest country of South America. In this double condition lies a large part of the increasing demands for a new territorial organization of the state, for better forms of political representation of the national spaces and for greater public investment.

The population growth rate has tended to decrease, having a steeper decline in 2000 due to the emigration of people– a product of the economic crisis of those years – although from 2003 it tended to stabilize. This trend will have to be confirmed in the coming years, as can be seen in Figure 8.1.

The Ecuadorian urbanization: from rural to urban

In the last 30 years, Ecuador has stopped being a predominantly rural and peasant country to become an urban and citizen nation. The urban population has had unprecedented growth, from 28 percent in 1950 to 49.6 percent in 1982. This means, according to the census trends from 1982, that in 1983 Ecuador became a country with a predominantly urban population. Today, more than 70 percent of the population lives in cities, a situation that is in line with the general trend of urbanization in Latin America, albeit late in comparison to other countries.

These data show three undeniable facts: the conversion of Ecuador into a country with a predominantly urban population, the gradual reduction of the population in the countryside[6] and the reduction of urbanization rates, both across the country and in certain cities in a differentiated manner. In this way, it said that growth of the cities is reaching its limit, because the rural population with the capacity to migrate to the city is no

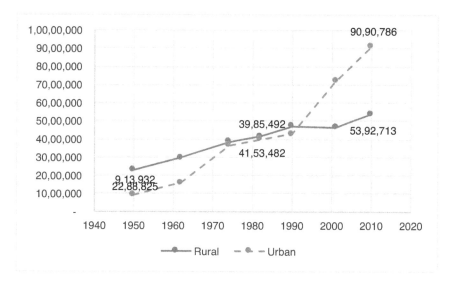

Figure 8.1 Evolution of urban and rural population (1950–2010)

Source: National Report Ecuador 2016, INEC Data, Population and Housing Censuses 1950, 1962, 1974, 1982, 1990, 2001, and 2010.

longer so significant. In fact, it is very difficult for Ecuador to ever have one or two cities that can count on a population such as Lima or Bogota, much less Buenos Aires or Mexico City.[7] There is a significant reduction in the migration of the population from the countryside to the cities, which means that the cities are de-accelerating their growth. If in 1982 51 percent of the national population lived in the countryside and therefore could potentially migrate to the city, by 2010 this percentage was reduced to 33 percent. To this must be added a reduction in the fertility rate: between 2001 and 2010, the figure dropped from 2.8 to 2.4 children per woman. In turn, there is a redirection of migratory flows within the country, mainly outward, reducing the speed of growth of the main cities of Ecuador and establishing new forms of interurban relations.

There is also a reduction of urbanization rates: in 1950, the country had an overall urbanization rate of 4.7 percent; in 1990, it reached 3.8; in 2000, it declined to 1.9; and in 2010, declined to 1.3. In other words, the more urban the country becomes, the less cities grow. In the last two intercensus periods, the rate was cut in half.

This is why it can be said that the cycle of migration from the countryside to the city is over and that of international emigration has opened up, triggered in 2000 as a result of the financial and banking crises of 1999 and 2000, producing very important changes in national urbanization patterns. This process tended to be stopped and even partially reversed from 2011 to 2013, when there was a negative balance between arrivals and departures of Ecuadorians. There are more Ecuadorians who return to the country in relation to those who leave, as shown in Figure 8.2. It is very probable that this change in the trend is also due to the repatriation policies promoted in the government of the Citizens' Revolution, an issue that stabilized in the years 2010 and 2013, because in 2014 there was a new emigration rebound, also linked to the economic crisis in the country.

At the same time, urbanization was unequal and exclusive, which was expressed in high levels of urban primacy.[8] There is an evident bicentralism, composed of two large cities at the apex of the pyramid and a strong dispersion of the population in small cities. In other words, urbanization developed from the outset and so far in a polarized fashion. Today two large cities, Quito and Guayaquil, have 41 percent and 219 small/medium cities, and 49 percent of the total population. The formation of these two large urban agglomerations is explained by structural factors: some natural regions and others related to the organization of production. Guayaquil is the regional axis of the economy of agro-export (port, coast), Quito, of the internal market and the seat of state centralism (capital, sierra). While the urban primacy of Quito and Guayaquil is maintained in this century, it should be noted that there is a slight decrease: in 2001, the two cities accounted for 43 percent of the population; for 2010, it is 41 percent (INEC, national census carried out in 2001 and in 2010). That is, in 10 years the relative concentration of the population decreased by two points, and in return, we see a relative growth of medium and small cities. Does this mean a change in the trend towards territorial concentration of the population in the country? These data can be corroborated in Table 8.1 by size of cities; that is, according to the existing hierarchy.

Both cities have had a change in their relative weights within the country, across different the time periods. For example, in the 1970s, when the state became a national actor in the exploitation and commercialization of oil, Quito became important. This changed in the 1990s, when the state contracted with private firms through deregulation and Guayaquil became more important. Then, since 2007, when the Citizens' Revolution came to power, Quito that managed to position itself strongly, thanks to the prevailing policy of public revenue.

It cannot be ignored that new poles of regional development have arisen in the last 15 years, as a result of the local population increase, and greater regional trade with strategic locations. A network of intermediate cities has been formed, which is consolidated: Cuenca, thanks to the Peace Accords in 1997, the Declaration of World Heritage and the remittances of migrants; Santo Domingo de los Colorados as an intermediate city between Quito and Guayaquil and between Sierra and Costa, with its own regional influence; Duran with the link with the port of Guayaquil, as happened with Machala, with Puerto Bolivar; and the growth of the port cities of Manta and Esmeraldas, as

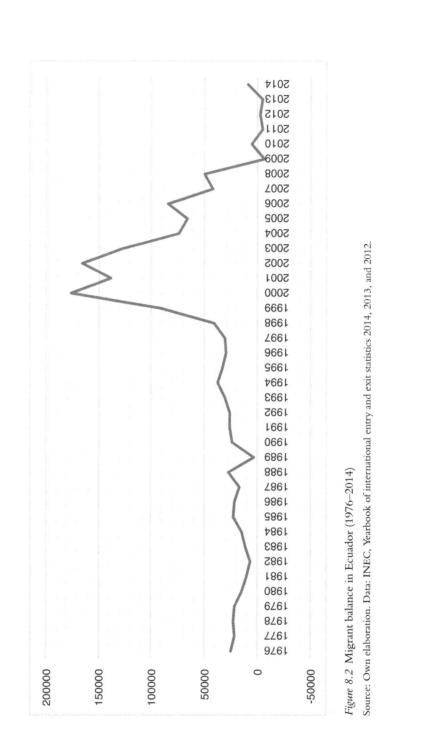

Figure 8.2 Migrant balance in Ecuador (1976–2014)

Source: Own elaboration. Data: INEC, Yearbook of international entry and exit statistics 2014, 2013, and 2012.

Table 8.1 Categorization of city size by population

Category	Population distribution			
	2001		2010	
Metropolitan City1	43%	Guayaquil and Quito	41%	Guayaquil and Quito
Big City2	57%	Cuenca, Machala, Portoviejo, Manta, Ambato and Santo Domingo	59%	Cuenca, Machala, Portoviejo, Manta, Durán, Santo Domingo
Middle City3		Riobamba, Esmeraldas, Milagro, Ibarra, Loja, Babahoyo, Quevedo, Durán, Latacunga, La Libertad and Santa Elena		Riobamba, Esmeraldas, Milagro, Ibarra, Loja, Babahoyo, Quevedo, Ruminahui, Ambato, Santa Elena, La Libertad
Small City4		Top 10 in terms of population: Otavalo, Tulcán, Chone, Pasaje, Santa Rosa, Jipijapa, Daule, Lago Agrio, Huaquillas, Quinindé		Top 10 in terms of population: Otavalo, Latacunga, Daule, Salinas, Pasaje, Tulcán, Chone, Montecristi, Quinindé, Santa Rosa

(1) Cities with the largest population (Quito, Guayaquil). (2) 25 percent of the population not located in large cities. (3) 25 percent of the population not located in medium-sized cities. (4) 50 percent of the population not located in small cities (fewer than 100,000 inhabitants).

Source: INEC, Population and Housing Censuses 2001–2010.

well as Portoviejo, Loja, Ibarra Riobamba, Milagro, Babahoyo and Quevedo as cities with more than 100,000 inhabitants. Other cities that show a very slow growth are: Ambato or Latacunga, and Lago Agrio, Huaquillas and Jipijapa.

When one looks at the demographics across to the scale of cities, what is observed is that the great metropolis and the big cities present a greater percentage of adult populations in relation to the medium and small cities, which are composed mainly of populations at both ends of the age range: children, adolescents and older adults (MIDUVI, 2015: 12).

Analyzing migratory balances by cantons, a new reality appears: the places with the highest balances are those where illegal markets – particularly drug trafficking – have settled. The cities that suffer the most from this phenomenon are the ports like Esmeraldas, Manta, Guayaquil and Puerto Bolivar as places of export of narcotics; Sucumbíos on the border with Colombia, which is an import zone of cocaine; and Santo Domingo and Machala, cities of internal intermediation.

The city: from the periphery to cosmopolitan introspection

The fact that cities now grow with a rate of urbanization significantly lower than they had 20 years ago[9] and that the international arena has a greater weight on the city (globalization), poses a significant change in the pattern of Ecuadorian urbanization. Since the 1990s, what could be called a dynamic of "cosmopolitan introspection" that has come to life as a result of the articulation, on the one hand, of the return to the built city and, on the other, of the formation of a trans-territorial city in the context of the overall process of global urbanization.

Return to the built city: new centrality, new periphery

The city that grew in the past on the basis of demographic pressure on the periphery (suburban invasions) and an industrial development model of import substitution (metropolitan areas), started to be produced in a context of high internationalization. This gave rise to what could be considered a logic of cosmopolitan introspection, that is, a pattern of urbanization "inward" in a context of globalization. In addition, there is a change in the pattern of urbanization, because for the first time there is the possibility of producing city on qualitative terms, not just quantitative. Not more but better quality of services, not more but better infrastructures, equipment, roads, transportation and so on.

Regarding the reduction of urban growth, there are clear manifestations: a change in the direction of the urbanization pattern that transits from the urban centrifugal development – that generated the peripheral city – towards a centripetal form that puts in the foreground the return to the constructed city and with that the "inversion of investments" from the periphery to the central zones. There was a historic change: the elimination of demographic pressure in the construction of public policies and the emergence of pressure from the real estate sector for the redirection of urban growth at a time when the neoliberal city model was being promoted.

Hence, most of the major investments made in different Ecuadorian cities are located in the interior of the city more than in its peripheries (as was the case in the previous urban conjuncture). As an example, we have in Quito the large investment in the historical center, the Bus Rapid Transit (trolleybus, *ecovía* and *metrobus* – BRT) and the next subway of Quito; in Guayaquil, the Malecon 2000 and urban regeneration; and in Cuenca, the historic center, the Barranco and the tram, among other cities and projects. The paradox of this process is that this "urbanization of the city" happens along an acute process of depopulation of the central parts of the cities. This invites us to think of a phenomenon of an "emptied society", where mobility becomes more important; the central areas begin to lose residential populations; gentrification, renewal and accessibility/mobility arise; and where new centralities are also emerging, among them the so-called globalization artefacts:[10] shopping and conventions centers, theme parks, a world trade center and large hotels and airports, among others.

This pattern has produced a related change in the urban peripheries: urban expansion, diffuse integration of the territories and natural growth of the urban footprint in the form of a conurbation of the surrounding areas, such as the phenomenon of valleys near Quito (Tumbaco, Los Chillos) or Guayaquil (Samborondón or Daule), and even more so by the integration into the global networks of cities – increasingly distant and apart from the requirement of spatial continuity. This situation has produced a city structured as a constellation of discontinuous spaces that lead to new forms of urban segregation: territorial fragmentation and social foreign character.[11] The growth of the peripheries acquires a new expression: its growth no longer comes from demographic pressure but from land speculation. It should be highlighted that urban land in "peripheral" areas has a growth that is well above population growth, estimated at a ratio of 4 to 1; that is, its urban area grows four times faster than the population. In addition, there is a relocation of the population with higher incomes in these places in the form of gated communities (Caldeira, 2000), which drives urbanization (Carrión, 2014: 80).

Cities of outsiders: the territorial outskirts of the city

The migration patterns have transformed on the basis of new dynamics of relations of origin/destination: the interurban links are enhanced over rural/urban – that is, the migrant has a previous life in the city and not in the countryside. In addition, the relationship origin – destination is not broken, as happened in the past. In these new relationships, economic and cultural remittances play a role, as well as the development of the technology that allows people to maintain links, thanks to cellphones, Skype, WhatsApp, Facebook, internet cafes and many other modalities that exist today.

Remittances are directly related to the international emigration of the population and how the migrant stabilizes at the destination. For that reason, the expulsion of the population that took place in the country from 1999 to 2000 began to be felt strongly five years later, that is, in 2007, with a peak amidst the context of the Citizens' Revolution. After 2007, remittances begin to fall, but never to the level of 2004, as can be observed in Figure 8.3. The paradox of

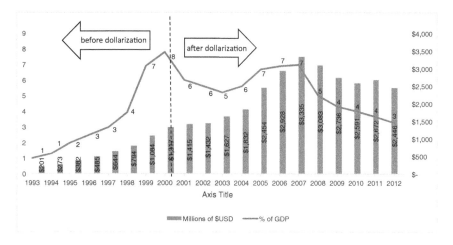

Figure 8.3 Remittances received in dollars and in percentage of GDP per year

Source: Central Bank of Ecuador, 2013.

this behavior is that the crisis that pushed out so many began to change when the migrants themselves sent their remittances, which became the country's second source of foreign exchange.

If in the earlier period Roberts (1978) had described the "town of peasants" emerging from rural/urban migration now we can talk of the "city of outsiders" from interurban/international migration, without breaking the umbilical cord between the people who live here with those who live there, producing significant changes in the two poles, thanks to the integration of the territories from the urban economies and the development of new communication technologies. Increased capital flows, people mobility, new communication technologies and illegal markets[12] – inscribed in the context of the new global economy – give new forms to urbanization and *metropolization*.[13] They are not isolated cities, but rather cities integrated into urban systems according to territorial areas: local, regional, national or international. Similarly, cities stop growing exclusively by the extension of their physical limits (urban expansion) and by the articulation of several cities under conurbation processes, as well as by urban systems and binational cities where space continuity loses relevance as opposed to a distant, discontinuous, and different integration of territories.

In many cases, such articulations are expressed in two ways: according to Sassen (Sassen, 1991: 34), "the north of the cities of the South integrates to the cities of the North", establishing new forms of segregation in interurban terms; or, in terms of Beck (1998: 71), the formation of cities that operate as "symbolic communities", but shaped in "transnational social spaces". That is, distant cities are geographically integrated through economy and technology, and each one develops nodes within it that specialize and connect with other nodes in other parts of the world, generating in turn foreign elements within its immediate urban context because they are adapted to transnational requirements and not to local norms or parameters.

International migration born of the financial crisis of the beginning of the century allows us to understand the conformation of "new cities", as a result of the articulation of national urban territories with those that are mainly located in the United States or Europe. A new problem arises that is difficult to understand: cities that lack space continuity but which are strongly linked by the new technologies of communication, culture and economy. And, in turn, the reverse phenomenon has also intensified: important migratory flows from the United States to Ecuador, producing a similar process: the cities of Cotacachi, Vilcabamba, Cuenca and, to a lesser extent, Quito (Viteri, 2016: 6).

The basic question is how to understand cities that are span territories of different countries or continents but which are highly articulated. That is to say, transnational cities that are integrated through two modalities: high-standard markets located in the new centralities and international migrations that integrate the regions of origin with those of destination, through cultural and economic remittances and technology.[14] This reality has led to cities located simultaneously in national territories but articulated with external territories, breaking with the logic of the spatial continuity of urban development.

In the last 20 years growth in the big cities – Quito, Guayaquil and Cuenca – has occurred from these premises and from different approaches, independent of the scale and geographical location of the cities. Yet some cities and their governments have undergone significant transformations through important enterprises, which could be defined as the so-called large urban projects (GPUs), substitutes for urban planning. We have a group of cities that have made a significant leap in their development, but others, unfortunately, that live a sustained state of crisis.

Among the first are Guayaquil, the most populous city in the country, which has been experiencing the modernization of its municipality since the 1990s.[15] It has undergone profound institutional reengineering and strong personalized leadership. Up to that time, there was an institutional dispersion composed of multiple local powers that disputed hegemony (municipality, government and ministerial offices) that finally ended up being subordinated to the municipality and its mayor, Leon Febres Cordero (president of Ecuador between 1984 and 1988). From this moment, a public instance like the municipality takes the baton to impel the development of the city, creating a set of private foundations that develop significant urban projects under a private/public/local logic.

The legitimacy that the municipality attained was so large that it captured important economic resources to support its action and obtain unprecedented social support to build a dominant project of the city that was maintained until recently. In order to carry out the proposal, an anchor project was designed: the Malecón 2000, which recovers and enhances its geographical location as the "main port"; claims the identity issue in which communicative programs have been of vital importance;[16] and for called urban regeneration of emblematic sites such as Cerro Santa Ana, Malecón del Salado, Av. 9 de Octubre and the airport (former Simón Bolívar) José Joaquín Olmedo. To this must be added two elements: the road works (multiple overpasses and roads) and transportation (Metrovía) that have facilitated the intraurban connection and the city with the rest of the country. And, on the other hand, an extensive program of legalization of urban property and the construction of popular housing projects (Lot 1 and 2 with more than 10,000 housing units) was carried out.

Since 2007 this model of urban development has been strongly questioned by the national government, because it did not direct its actions towards the suburbs where the lowest-income population is located. After this critique, a model of city management was established with two projects and two heads: the one presided over by the mayor and the other by the president in permanent conflict. The central government carried out works and programs within the urban perimeter to improve the living conditions of the poorest sectors of Guayaquil, located mainly in the south of that city, thus modifying the logic of local power.

Quito, the country's political-administrative capital, claimed its "metropolitan" status in 1993 with the promulgation of the Metropolitan Regime Law, which gave it new powers and a decentralized and participative municipal administration.[17] From the beginning of this century, with a change in public logic, it promoted an institutional reengineering aimed at introducing entrepreneurial and private management criteria, based on a corporatized logic by sector (environment, pollution, tourism and historical center, among others).

One of the emblematic projects of the city has been the recovery and empowerment of the Historic Center, which has allowed the government to structure a discourse and a proposal of linking the city to the tourist circuits of the world and of integrating the population to the whole of the city through a renewed identity it generates. Its designation as a Cultural Heritage of Humanity allowed Ecuador to define a proposal for the planning of the Historic Center of Quito (master plan) with sufficient resources[18] and with an institutional framework to carry it out (ECH Historic Center, Central Zone Administration).

Of the most important innovations of the city is the constitution of an extended public transport system that has as a central axis the "trolebus", or electric bus. Its branches, through BRT systems, turned into an important alternative to prioritize public over private transportation joining similar proposals in Latin America (Bogotá, México, Santiago). To this proposal can be added the construction of the new metro in Quito, which is co-financed with the central government for an amount of more than US$2 billion, which will link the south of the city with the north through 22 km and 15 stops. This project has been questioned because it left unconnected important nodes of origin and destination of travel, because of 46 percent increase over the price approved by the city council and because it is serving only 15 percent of the city's trips, among other issues.

Cuenca, the third largest Ecuadorian city, also declared a World Heritage Site, achieved an international position that validates its status as capital of the southern region of the country. To this must be added the benefits obtained from the peace agreements with Peru and the presence of remittances sent by the emigrant population from outside the country. The city has been able to maintain a highly redistributive social economy, to the extent that it is one of the cities with the best quality of life in the country and has less social and economic polarization. There is a generalized and adequate provision of basic services, and its central project of development has been the recovery of the historical center of the city. At the same time, the city has become a magnet to attract hundreds of foreigners who have come to the city to retire, which has led to a surge in new goods and services (bars, restaurants, new real estate projects).

Other cities of smaller scale have become suitable referents of local management, among them stands out Manta, which has managed to take advantage of a military base, tourism and fishing to get ahead. Loja has promoted innovative environmental projects, especially in the field of solid waste. In turn, Cotacachi has become an international model in terms of participatory management.

In several of the cities mentioned, the role of real estate capital has been key, developing housing for low-income sectors in the peripheries, shopping centers and high-standard housing buildings and urban business centers. There are the cases of Ciudad del Río in Guayaquil, González Suárez/October 12 in Quito and Plaza del Sol in Manta.

It is also worth mentioning the significant increase in coverage of urban services in Ecuadorian cities, which now supply 95 percent of the population, including electricity, potable water, telephone and sewerage.[19]

The rising protagonism of the Ecuadorian city – operating over the last 20 years – is part of a global trend that recognizes cities as entities that, while reorganizing national territorial structures, can contribute to the incorporation of citizens through better governance and proper use of natural resources as alternatives to improve the quality of life for its inhabitants. However, these processes end up overwhelming the local governments because they do not have the skills or resources to face this new reality. Neither can the national government assume the problem because it is very distant. Hence, two interconnected proposals have emerged simultaneously: decentralization and privatization, which eventually led local governments to be stronger vis-à-vis the national government, but weaker towards local society.

Decentralization of the state

With the spread of urbanization throughout the national territory, there were greater local demands for autonomy, as well as greater prominence of cities in the context of the national government. But there was also an international trend that advocated for strengthening local governments under a different perspective, so there is not only one project of decentralization, but several that have been debated. Indigenous peoples and nationalities advocate a plurinational state. The provincial councils, want to increase their capacity for intermediation, rich regions, autonomy and privatization, poor areas greater investment and better representation and international cooperation also influence this debate.

The establishment of autonomy

In the 1990s, a process of state decentralization began. In 1997, the "Special Transfer Law of 15 Percent of the National Budget for Sectional Governments" was passed, transferring 15 percent of the net current revenues of the budget. Also, the "Special Law on Decentralization and Social Participation" was passed, which structures political, fiscal and administrative autonomy. This proposal to reform the state through decentralization also generated a substantial change in the institutions of governance, passing from a service-providing municipality to the constitution of a local government. Subsequently, at the beginning of the 21st century in a context of state modernization, the national government transferred resources and competences to subnational governments and began a wave of privatization in which local governments acquired more power facing the national government, but they became weaker vis-à-vis local society.

Therefore, seeking to strengthen local capacities, redefine relations between the executive and sectional governments and avoid overlapping functions. The dismantling of the planning system was promoted so that the municipalities could supposedly increase their autonomy. But what was implemented instead was the deregulation of local markets and the liberation of public action for the benefit of the market. The next legal instrument approved in 1998 was the new constitution, where there are two lines that seek to strengthen local governments and therefore the territories: a) on the one hand, the strengthening of administrative decentralization with new functions and powers, and on the other, b) fiscal decentralization. The constitution granted the municipalities transfers of resources, but this did not mean an increase of financial autonomy because the central governments transferred the resources within a logic of patronage. It would have been different if the tax base had been decentralized to expand the sources of income. In terms of new authority and responsibilities, little progress was made, because those new ones that appeared, such as environment, already existed. It was also very difficult to achieve the transfer of powers because a centralized institution was established, called the National Competence Council, which was responsible for determining the level of competence required and the budgets to be transferred with each type of responsibility.

In 2008 and with Alianza País in power, a new constitution was approved, defining a new legal order of the state, namely, plurinational and decentralized. It established a complex division of territory: provinces, metropolitan areas (more than one and a half million inhabitants, i.e. Quito and Guayaquil), cantons, parishes (urban and rural) and special territories (indigenous territorial districts, insular, border areas). In terms of competencies, there was a substantial change: types of competencies are established by level, exclusive or concurrent. The financing model is similar to that adopted in 1998.

The process of decentralization of the state that begun in 2001 responds to the fact that the economy, politics and population are predominantly urban. One clear expression of this is that the state budget tends to urbanize. In 1997, the resources of the autonomous sectional system did not reach 5 percent of the national budget, whereas a few years later they reached 20 percent.

In 2000, the central government, in terms of net current income, transferred 9.9 percent (US$295.4 million) to subnational governments (provincial councils and municipalities). Since that date, participation increased significantly to

20.9 percent in 2004 (US$896.5 million), 18.8 percent (US$1053.4 million) in 2006, 19.3 percent (US$1847.3 million) in 2008, 18.9 percent (US$1720.8 million) in 2009 and in 2011 23.9 percent of the PGE. In other words, there was growth in percentage terms and also in absolute numbers; in one case, by regulatory changes and in others, by the rise in oil prices, respectively. However, an economic crisis begun in 2014, which significantly affects the resources allocated to the decentralized autonomous governments (GAD).

For example, capital expenditures, that is to say those destined to the fixed assets and equity increases of the GAD (social programs or institutional public work projects) have increased ostensibly since 2008, given the modifications in the law: 15 percent of permanent income and 5 percent of nonpermanent income). Later in the Organic Code of Territorial Ordering Autonomy and Decentralization (COOTAD) Act, determined 31 percent participation (21 percent of permanent income and 10 percent of nonpermanent income of the PGE), must be earmarked for capital investments (Pérez, 2015: 44).

This set of situations led to an increase of the assertiveness of the city and its significance as a political actor, because it has a specific weight in the national scenario. In addition, its institutional role has been strengthened by the presence of more competencies, which suggests that the city is moving towards the constitution of a new form of institutional arrangement local governments. Ecuadorian cities have undertaken political-administrative reforms aimed at changing the functions of their administrations, traditionally providing basic services and managers of urban activities, to become instances of promoting social, economic and territorial development and prioritizing issues such as productivity and competitiveness, equitable human development and environmental sustainability through the expansion of democracy, governance and the promotion of citizen participation.

However, this multilevel development of the state structure is at a crossroads with what could be called a counter-reform since the National Assembly approved the COOTAD in 2016, and the central government began to exercise the leadership, execution and control in key areas such as housing, health and education, whereas territorial planning, food security and productive development are part of the decentralized powers. In other words, the regionalization disappears and some competencies are re-centralized, due to the economic crisis in the region. In Ecuador this was due to the reduction of exports in China, the fall in the price of oil and commodities and the appreciation of the dollar against other currencies. Crises show many things, unlike bonanzas. In structural terms, the urban primacy expressed in Quito/Guayaquil bicentralism was not modified, although there was a change in the local/national relationship. In other words, the new regulatory framework produced some interesting changes in terms of vertical decentralization, that is, between levels of the state with the transfer of resources and competition. In terms of horizontal decentralization, the weight of executives increased over other functions of the state, such as the presidency, and in terms of territorial decentralization it remained virtually unchanged.

Territorial smallholding

An important change has occurred in the national territory in terms of a process of aggressive division linked on the one hand with the criterion of "divide and conquer" born of state centralism, as well as clientelism as a dominant practice in politics and, on the other hand, to the very demands of the territories for access to the budget, infrastructure and representation. Thus, from 1974 to the date, four new provinces and 111 additional cantons have been created, particularly since 1982 corresponding to the return to democracy, as seen in Figure 8.4.

In 1982 Ecuador had 20 provinces, 126 cantons and 947 parishes, whereas now it has 24 provinces, 224 cantons and 1,299 parishes. Thus, we have an important process of *territorial smallholding*, to the degree that the provinces increase by 20 percent, parishes by 37 percent and cantons by 78 percent. This means that the greatest atomization occurred in the cantonal area, thanks to the emphasis on municipal decentralization, the demands of local groups and the protagonist role of urban societies.

In contrast to this territorial structure of the autonomous regime, the National Secretariat for Planning and Development (SENPLADES) generated a different proposal for the dependent regime, composed of zones, circuits and districts as administrative levels of planning that serve "for a better identification of needs and effective solutions for the provision of public services" (SENPLADES, 2016), as shown in Figure 8.5.

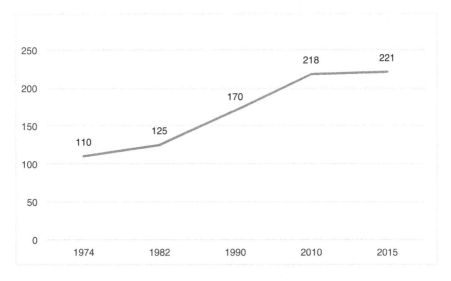

Figure 8.4 Creation of cantons in Ecuador (1974–2016)

Source: Own elaboration. Data: (Villavicencio, 2010).

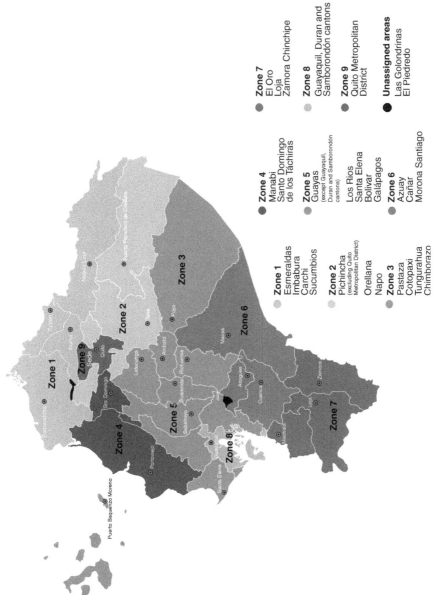

Figure 8.5 SENPLADES planning areas

Source: (SENPLADES, 2016).

Zone 1
Esmeraldas
Imbabura
Carchi
Sucumbíos

Zone 2
Pichincha
(excluding Quito
Metropolitan District)
Orellana
Napo

Zone 3
Pastaza
Cotopaxi
Tungurahua
Chimborazo

Zone 4
Manabí
Santo Domingo
de los Táchiras

Zone 5
Guayas
(except Guayaquil,
Duran and Samborondón
cantons)
Los Ríos
Santa Elena
Bolívar
Galápagos

Zone 6
Azuay
Cañar
Morona Santiago

Zone 7
El Oro
Loja
Zamora Chinchipe

Zone 8
Guayaquil, Duran and
Samborondón cantons

Zone 9
Quito Metropolitan
District

Unassigned areas
Las Golondrinas
El Piedredo

Nine planning zones, born of the neighboring provinces, were formed according to geographic, cultural and economic proximity. Each zone is divided into several districts composed of circuits. The district is the basic unit of planning and provision of public services. It coincides with the canton or union of cantons. One hundred and forty districts have been formed in the country. Each district has an average of 90,000 inhabitants. However, for cantons whose population is very high, such as Quito, Guayaquil, Cuenca, Ambato and Santo Domingo de los Tsáchilas, districts were established within them. Finally, the circuit is the locality where a set of quality public services are within the reach of citizens and is made up several establishments in a territory within a district. It corresponds to a parish or set of parishes. There are 1,134 circuits with an average of 11,000 inhabitants each (SENPLADES, 2016). Curiously, the political-administrative division on which decentralization is based has little to do with SENPLADES' proposed de-concentration.

Urban infrastructure and access to housing

Public investment in infrastructure

If a comparison of public investment between 1998 and 2013 is made, there are clearly two periods: one from 1998 to 2006, when US$5.796 million in the eight years are invested, and the other from 2007 to 2013, with US$33,339 in six years. This reveals two important issues: first, the immense amount of resources that the country received as a result of the increase in the price of oil, and second, the strengthening of the public logic of state investment, that is, the return of the public. In this context, public investment in infrastructure grows significantly until 2013, when the economic crisis begins to have a presence, as can be seen in Figure 8.6.

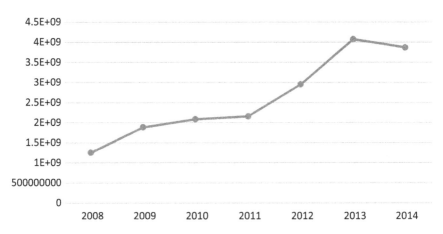

Figure 8.6 Public investment in infrastructure in Ecuador (2008–2014)

Source: Authors. Data: (SENPLADES, 2014).

On the other hand, the areas that have had the greatest public investment since 2008 are transportation and energy (energy matrix change). Both areas are linked to the promotion of productivity and tourism, as well as to the connection of the city with the countryside and the regions, and the country with the world (ports and airports).

The investment in infrastructure was the most visible action of the government of Rafael Correa. It started with US$480 million in 2008 and amounted to US$1.5 billion in 2013, as shown in Figure 8.7. Ports, airports and land terminals grew everywhere (some were already in disuse due to the absence of internal travel demand, such as the airports in Tena or Santa Rosa in Machala), as well as for large investments in urban transport projects, such as the Quito metro and the Cuenca tram.

In the case of energy and electricity, it is the second largest item in terms of infrastructure, with hydroelectric power being the bulk of the investment made. Investment in energy and electricity was US$1,371,276,438 between 2008 and 2014, which is destined to change the country's energy matrix. Urban electrification is the fourth item in terms of investment.

The third is the area of urban development and housing, although with great difference in monetary terms in relation to previous investments, as summarized in Figure 8.8. Although the investment has been significant in urban-marginal areas of several cities of the Ecuadorian coast and to a lesser extent of the Sierra, it cannot be denied that it is considerably inferior to the indicated infrastructure investments and smaller than the realized ones in 2008. However, this investment has not maintained a regular pattern over time: from 2007 to 2008 a significant reduction remained until 2011. Investment in public spaces was made on land owned by the central government within the urban perimeter and in counter-proposal to local works led by opposition mayors such as Samanes Park and Santay Island in Guayaquil or Guápulo Park in Quito.

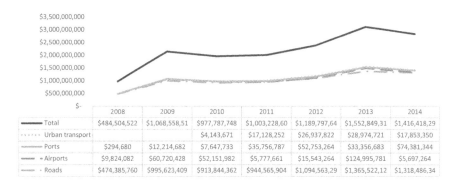

	2008	2009	2010	2011	2012	2013	2014
Total	$484,504,522	$1,068,558,51	$977,787,748	$1,003,228,60	$1,189,797,64	$1,552,849,31	$1,416,418,29
Urban transport			$4,143,671	$17,128,252	$26,937,822	$28,974,721	$17,853,350
Ports	$294,680	$12,214,682	$7,647,733	$35,756,787	$52,753,264	$33,356,683	$74,381,344
Airports	$9,824,082	$60,720,428	$52,151,982	$5,777,661	$15,543,264	$124,995,781	$5,697,264
Roads	$474,385,760	$995,623,409	$913,844,362	$944,565,904	$1,094,563,29	$1,365,522,12	$1,318,486,34

Figure 8.7 Public investment in the transportation sector in Ecuador (2008–2014)

Source: Authors. Data: (SENPLADES, 2014).

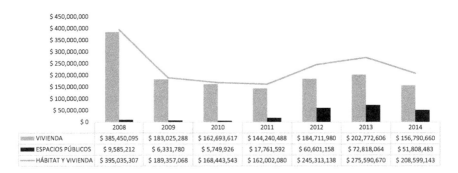

	2008	2009	2010	2011	2012	2013	2014
VIVIENDA	$ 385,450,095	$ 183,025,288	$ 162,693,617	$ 144,240,488	$ 184,711,980	$ 202,772,606	$ 156,790,660
ESPACIOS PÚBLICOS	$ 9,585,212	$ 6,331,780	$ 5,749,926	$ 17,761,592	$ 60,601,158	$ 72,818,064	$ 51,808,483
HÁBITAT Y VIVIENDA	$ 395,035,307	$ 189,357,068	$ 168,443,543	$ 162,002,080	$ 245,313,138	$ 275,590,670	$ 208,599,143

Figure 8.8 Public investment in the habitat and housing sector in Ecuador (2008–2014)
Source: Authors. Data: (SENPLADES, 2014).

The situation of housing in Ecuador

According to the Ecuador National Report 2015 for Habitat III presented by the Ministry of Urban Development and Housing (MIDUVI), approximately 2.8 million Ecuadorians (18 percent of the total population) live in precarious and informal settlements. Although it is true that the percentage of housing in inadequate conditions has declined from 70 percent in 1990 to 45 percent in 2010, a high percentage of dwellings with inadequate materials are still present in floors, ceilings and walls in relation to total housing in Ecuador (see Table 8.2). In addition, account should be taken of the great difference that exists across the territory. In the countryside, the conditions are much more precarious than in the city, with 73 percent of inadequate housing in the countryside and 29 percent in urban areas (MIDUVI, 2015).

This is expressed in the qualitative housing deficit, measured by the number of dwellings whose living conditions are considered unrecoverable, from the combination of predominant materials of the floor, wall and ceiling. In 2010, the country had a 33 percent deficit, being slightly higher in the rural areas, with 35 percent rural compared to 31 percent urban (www.sni.gob.ec). Overcrowding, considered when more than three people live in a bedroom, is also an indicator that has been declining ostensibly in the last 20 years. In 1990, 32 percent of households in the country lived in these conditions, whereas in 2010 that figure fell to 17 percent.

The access rate for basic services[20] increased from 32 percent in 1990 to 49 percent in 2010 (see Table 8.3). However, the differences between provinces are large, with those of the coast being the least favored, followed by the Amazonian provinces. For example, in the province of Los Ríos, 16 percent of homes have access to basic services, whereas Pichincha, located in the Ecuadorian Sierra, has the highest percentage (85 percent) of the country.

In most cities of the country there is a shortage of green areas and recreation space, with the Urban Green IVU Index of 4.7 m^2 per inhabitant, well below the 10 m^2 to 15 m^2 per person recommended by international standards. This

Table 8.2 Indicators of housing conditions in Ecuador, 1990, 2001, and 2010

	1990			2001			2010		
	Total	Urban	Rural	Total	Urban	Rural	Total	Urban	Rural
Households living in own homes	#######	#######	#######	#######	#######	#######	#######	#######	#######
% of households living in own homes	68%	58%	80%	67%	69%	79%	64%	59%	73%
Overcrowded homes	691,821	#######	#######	778,667	414,041	#######	668,280	378,238	#######
Homes in inadequate housing	#######	#######	#######	########	728,244	#######	########	719,360	#######
% of inadequate housing	70%	51,73%	94,53%	56,3%	40%	84%	45%	29,4%	73%
% of overcrowded households	34%	7%	4%	27%	22%	4%	17%	15%	1%
Public Services Access Index	32%	5.3%	3.50%	41%	59%	9,4%	49%	66%	18%

Source: Authors, with data from: www.sni.gob.ec.

Table 8.3 Housing ownership and access to basic services by province – 2010

Region	Province	% households in own house and fully payed	% housing with basic public services
Coast	Esmeraldas	49	28
	Manabí	48	28
	Santa Elena	41	29
	Guayas	51	45
	Los Ríos	52	16
	El Oro	45	58
	Santo Domingo de los Tsáchilas	37	40
Mountains (Sierra)	Carchi	45	64
	Imbabura	47	63
	Pichincha	34	85
	Cotopaxi	57	29
	Tungurahua	52	52
	Bolívar	59	30
	Chimborazo	59	40
	Cañar	55	36
	Azuay	46	57
	Loja	49	48
East	Sucumbíos	48	25
	Napo	49	39
	Orellana	50	22
	Pastaza	41	46
	Morona Santiago	51	34
	Zamora Chinchipe	52	44
Insular Region	Galápagos	38	25

Source: Authors. Data: www.sni.gob.ec.

means that there is a per capita deficit of at least 6.3 m². Among the 221 municipalities of Ecuador, only 10 comply with this recommendation (INEC, 2010), that is, 2 percent, and the problem is more acute in cities with populations between 1,000 and 10,000.

At the same time, there is a shortage of land and affordable housing for the lower-income population, who must resort to illegal practices: invasion, disregard of standards and irregular provision of services. Urban growth has been uncontrolled outside the urban boundary, causing social and territorial fragmentation and placing great anthropic pressure on ecologically sensitive and agroproductive territories. Facing this reality, municipal governments have shown a weak fiscal capacity to mobilize resources aimed at improving the provision of services, reducing the deficit of formal housing, improving public transportation and generating quality public space (see Table 8.4) (MIDUVI, 2015: 19).

Housing tenure in Ecuador takes different forms. The first one is fully paid for and represents 47 percent, followed by those that are those donated, with 10 percent, and the one that is being paid for, with 6.5 percent. The result is that 84.5 percent of the homes are owned, which is a significant amount, as can be seen in Table 8.5.

Table 8.4 Ecuadorian cities meeting the Urban Green Index

City	Province	Green Urban Index	City	Province	Green Urban Index
Mera	Pastaza	23.82 m²/hab	Pablo Sexto	Morona Santiago	13.93 m²/hab
Quito	Pichincha	20.40 m²/hab	Sigchos	Cotopaxi	13.41 m²/hab
Huamboya	Morona Santiago	15.98 m²/hab	Paute	Azuay	12.60 m²/hab
Mocha	Tungurahua	14.97 m²/hab	Quero	Tungurahua	12.06 m²/hab
El Pan	Azuay	14.43 m²/hab	Saquisilí	Cotopaxi	11.05 m²/hab

Source: INEC, Population and Housing Censuses 2010.

Table 8.5 Types of housing tenure by households

Housing Tenure Type	Households	%
Own and totally paid	1,786,005	47%
Leased	816,664	21%
Borrowed or assigned (not paid)	489,213	13%
Own (Donated, inherited or by possession)	409,281	10%
Own in process of payment	249,160	6.50%
By services	59,145	1.60%
Antichresis	7,470	0.90%
Total	3,810,548	100%

Source: MIDUVI, Ecuador's National Report, 2015.

Housing policies

There have been four explicit housing policies in Ecuador during the last hundred years. The first appeared during the 1920s from an isolated and unconnected institutional framework in which municipal government and social security each acted alone. In this context, policies were aimed at "residential programs or new housing projects". The second one originated in the 1960s thanks to the policy goals and resources coming from the Alliance for Progress: financing of savings through the private, cooperative and mutual system, as well as the public sector (the emerging Housing Bank and the Ecuadorian Institute of Social Security). It was a policy proposal in which the state intervened directly through the production and promotion of residential units, for which the National Housing Board was created. The third emerged in the 1990s, when there was a shift in the design of policies to reduce the quantitative deficit under the influence of neoliberal policies: the state ceases to be a real estate builder and final lender, and the private sector creates new institutions integrated to the capital market, to capture domestic savings and distribute resources. The state goes from being a builder and a promoter to being a regulator. It replaces the "one purpose" state bank (Ecuadorean Housing Bank) with the multipurpose commercial private bank, following the Chilean model.

Starting in 2007, a new policy of repositioning housing appeared on the public agenda, after an absence of 10 years. The government of Rafael Correa and the Citizens' Revolution posed the return of the public agenda and the strengthening of the state as a regulatory body. In this context, the housing policy found a new space and created part of a diversified housing supply by sectors: a) for the middle and upper sectors (private banking), b) for the middle and low sectors (creation of the Bank of the Ecuadorian Social Security Institute and Banco del Pacífico, a public bank) and c) for low-income sectors (supply subsidies).

Added to this was the government agency for real estate management,[21] which became one more entity in the real estate market "because of the need of the Central State to organize public sector properties since there was a dispersion of institutions that did not have legalized or identified assets, or institutions such as the Central Bank with properties that they did not use" (Inmobiliar.gob.ec, 2016). In other words, the state resumed social housing programs, became a lender and entered the real estate market as one more actor in the real estate market.

In general, there have been two significant policy moments in these 20 years. One was based on the need to solve the problem of the homeless through regularization, plots with services, auto-construction and some investment. This policy was faced by the state through two axes: the creation of the Ministry of Urban Development and Housing and the National Board of Housing, whose main policy was what could be called the "effect of the place" or, incorrectly, "human settlement", which should be granted infrastructure and localization services: transportation, water, energy, education and health. The second policy was defined by the quantitative deficit of housing, which is faced with a policy of financing under the rules of the market by granting the subsidy to demand (actually to the supply), which brought many unprecedented situations. For example, the social compensations directed to the private world and not to the public domain and housing was built in places distant from the cities and on their peripheries, leading to dwellings isolated from the city, as happened with the Ciudad Bicentenario project in Quito.

Environment and urban sustainability in Ecuador (1996–2016)

Environmental management has been one of the most complex issues in the last decade, mainly due to two events that have had an impact on public opinion and public policy. 1) the emblematic case of Chevron/Texaco, with the historical judgment that the Ecuadorian state filed before national and international courts due to the environmental disaster caused by the oil company during its operation in the 1970s and that today Ecuador pays for the arbitration award; and 2) the Yasuní ITT Initiative (Ishpingo Tiputini Tambococha), developed by environmental nongovernmental organizations (NGOs) and environmental movements, and later championed by the Correa government in 2007, in order to "sell oil underground", that is, to propose to the international community the sale of oil that would not get extracted, deducting the revenues that would have been generated by its exploitation, and investing in conservation projects. Both events generated great sympathy and adherents, mainly young people and those in the academic and scientific community and the media, both national and international.

The government promoted an environmental agenda based on the rights of nature, which was approved in the constitution of 2008. However, after six years of meetings, lobbies, travels and a great media apparatus, the Yasuní initiative failed and in June 2015 oil exploitation began in the heart of one of the most mega-diverse areas of the world (Araujo, 2014). This situation generated a very interesting urban precedent. When the government decided to leave the project a campaign was initiated to ask the Ecuadorian people whether to drop it or not. Although the initiative was located in the "Amazonian rurality" (actually virgin jungle), the campaign was mainly concentrated in the cities in terms of the collection of signatures, dissemination of the proposal, awareness, communication and so on. It was the young people who pushed the struggle because the project was restarted, which generated a process of national socialization where young people positioned themselves as one of the key players in the environmental arena, raising their demands regarding urban environmental issues: pollution, use of the bicycle, reduction of environmental impacts and improvement of urban infrastructure.

In this way, the campaigns developed around Yasuní and Chevron/Texaco, generated a critical urban mass capable of collecting signatures for environmental causes, placing pressure on and denunciation of social networks of any environmental violation and causing stoppage of work. Therefore, it can be affirmed that in the 1980s and 1990s the environmental struggles were more rural, whereas today – with the appearance of information technologies – these demands are urbanized.

New economic interests, contrary to environmental protection, appeared with the reprimarization of the economy (mining, large hydroelectric) and frustrated the hopes of thousands of Ecuadorians raising socioenvironmental struggles of hundreds of indigenous and peasant communities, including the deaths and imprisonment of environmental leaders. Added to this is the fact that the oil crisis and the fall in GDP create more extreme pressures on natural resources, while the government promotes a development model based on an empty discourse of content and promotes a decentralized policy towards subnational governments that assume the conflict of the environmental management without its own agenda.

To understand this urban/environmental dynamic of the last two decades, it is necessary to recognize the evolution of the legal framework in the country. In 2004, the Ecuadorian government issued the Environmental Management Law (LGA), which established the Decentralized Environmental Management System (LGA, 2004, Art. 5), subject to the guidelines of the National Council for Sustainable Development (2004, Chapter 10). In this system, the Ministry of the Environment became the National Environmental Authority, and municipalities, NGOs and private companies become the executors of these policies.

Subsequently, with the COOTAD, the autonomous decentralized governments have among their exclusive competences the provision of solid waste management services, potable water, sewage treatment, wastewater treatment and environmental sanitation, regulation, prevention and control of environmental pollution (Art. 54 and 55. COOTAD, 2010). However, there are no regulations or codes that could specify the level of environmental crime or how to address it at the local level.

Water and sewerage

Water is the most important natural resource in the economic and social life of cities and countries. The availability or lack therefore depends on the development of many activities of urban and rural populations, as well as their survival. In the water, as well, serious environmental problems that a city or region are facing are exposed. According to the Concesiones database of the National Secretary of Water (SENAGUA) in 2011, sectoral demands for water use in the country are predominant (80 percent of the flow used), followed by domestic use (13 percent) and industry (7 percent), as shown in Figure 8.9.

According to ECLAC, the treatment of urban and industrial liquid wastes is almost nonexistent in the country (only 7 percent), and the few treatment plants that they have are located in the south of the country. The sewage disposal system leads directly to the rivers and other bodies of water. The growth of cities produces waste that, due to the inefficient management of solid waste, accumulates in dumps, streams and water courses, causing serious deterioration of the environment and human health, without applying established norms (ECLAC, 2014: 16).

Regarding water quality, the Water Law of 1972 and Art. 22 of codified law No. 2004–016 currently govern the current SENAGUA, together with the Ministry of Health and other state entities, responsible for implementing the policy to prohibit any contamination of waters that affects the development of flora or fauna. The applicability of this and other laws related to water resources has not been efficient in the country due to the lack of determined policies of sanction, monitoring of polluters and the assignment of functions for water management to an excessive number of institutions without seeking interinstitutional coordination or cooperation. At the same time, the Ministry of the Environment is the highest environmental authority, whose guiding function allows it to establish environmental standards for the control of water pollution. However, these standards do not apply. The same situation happens with SENAGUA, which should manage water conservation and management policies. However, it, too, does not have a structure that allows it to effectively control water quality (ECLAC, 2014: 19).

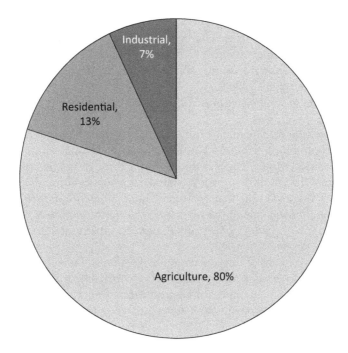

Figure 8.9 Distribution of water consumption in Ecuador
Source: Concesiones Database (SENAGUA, 2012).

In practice, a number of agencies conduct quality sampling, such as munici-palities, provincial councils, MIDUVI and others, but not in a planned and coordinated manner. To see how critical this situation is, Quito, the capital of Ecuador, does not have any system of wastewater treatment of importance, despite a study carried out in 2010 that recommended the construction of two large treatment plants to the north and south of the city. The current treatment systems are either very small or are found inside some industries. As a conse-quence, the deterioration of water quality is reflected in the high pollution rates recorded in the Machángara, Guayllabamba and Monjas rivers. Efforts to solve this problem in Quito have not been fruitful, and despite years of studies, millions of dollars of investment and study updates, it is estimated that only by 2018 could Quito have its first wastewater treatment systems.

This situation is not exclusive to the city of Quito. Almost all medium and large cities in Ecuador, with the exception of Cuenca and some sectors of Guayaquil, lack water treatment systems. The consequences of water pollution are reflected in the high levels of parasitic diseases, diarrheal diseases and loss of aquatic biodiversity. Similarly, in many rivers, despite having water running along its channel, it cannot be used for irrigation, livestock or electricity gener-ation. This has important consequences for the management of water resources because the lack of water in the low zones increases pressure on the *páramos* and higher ecosystems to supply good-quality water to the local populations.

Ecuador is one of the richest countries in terms of water resources in South America: 43,500 m^3 per person per year (2.5 times the world average), and yet it is the most backward country in the Andean region regarding water and sewer service coverage (Table 8.6).

The situation of wastewater in Ecuador in 2000 by size of city is summarized in Table 8.7.

In Ecuador, the management of solid waste has three characteristics: a) it is a public responsibility: 8 out of 10 cities manage it through units or departments of the GAD itself, whereas the rest do it through public companies or joint ventures (INEC, 2014); b) it is a fundamentally local municipal activity (see Figure 8.10); and c) the joint management of competition begins to be felt in some cases. Perhaps one of the most striking cases is the one of the municipalities of Tulcán (Ecuador) and Ipiales (Colombia) that united to binationally administer the service.

However, 60 percent of Ecuadorian municipalities still maintain a rudimentary form of management (open pit, controlled or cell) of their solid waste, which represents a great source of environmental pollution. In addition, 50 percent of municipalities maintain a differentiated management of hazardous wastes generated by health centers (INEC, 2014). This is a very complex urban

Table 8.6 Coverage of drinking water and sewerage in the Andean area

Country	Coverage of drinking water %			Coverage of sewerage %		
	Total	Urban	Rural	Total	Urban	Rural
Bolivia	73,5	93	44	63,5	82,3	35,3
Colombia	90,6	98	73	83,4	97	51
Ecuador	70,3	81,5	51,4	58	70	37
Perú	75,4	86	50,7	73,7	89	39

Source: Pan American Health Organization, Health Situation of the Americas, 2005.

Table 8.7 Water, sanitation and water treatment by category of cities

City Category	Population size (thousands of inhabitants)	Number of cities	Urban Population (thousands of inhabitants)	Potable Water Supply (Lts/ person/day)	Population with sewerage (%)	Treated residual water (%)
Very small	From 2 to 10	98	789,560	243	4.6	0.5
Small	From 10 to 100	73	3,606,306	231	14.9	3.1
Intermediate	From 100 to 1,000	13	4,100,425	225	19.9	5.8
Big	More than 1,000	2	5,643,498	530	33.6	17.2

Source: (Cabrera et al., 2012).

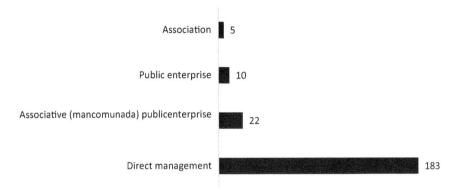

Figure 8.10 Type of waste management in Ecuadorian municipalities
Source: (Cabrera et al., 2012).

subject that compromises the quality of urban life. In no case are there recycling processes that can be used for electricity generation, biogas, composting or local economic development.

In 2015, at the national level, 39 percent of Ecuadorian households separated waste, 14 percentage points more than in 2010. Despite this, almost 60 percent of the Ecuadorian population does not classify their garbage, mainly due to the lack of containers and collection centers at the national level (INEC, 2014). In urban areas, each inhabitant produces 0.57 kg/day, on average, which rises to 0.72 kg/day in the island region (Figure 8.11).

In short, the issue of garbage has not yet been resolved in a technical and generalized way. Rudimentary practices in solid waste management, collection and treatment service subsidies and lack of technical and operational capacity sharpen this problem at the national level. Comprehensive management responses have occurred in isolated cases, thanks to international cooperation. Such was the case of Loja and Bahía de Caráquez, a city south of the Ecuadorian Sierra, and the other on the coast. Both cities started with separation processes at the source. However, the lack of continuity of public policies with the change of mayors and the lack of funding undermined these interesting initiatives. In the case of Quito, there are garbage separation containers called green dots in certain neighborhoods and public buildings in the capital. However, their extent and incidence are minimal.

Air quality

The management of air quality in the country presents deep gaps, from the technical to the institutional aspects. There is no follow-up to signed agreements. There is legislative dispersion, little clarity regarding jurisdiction and

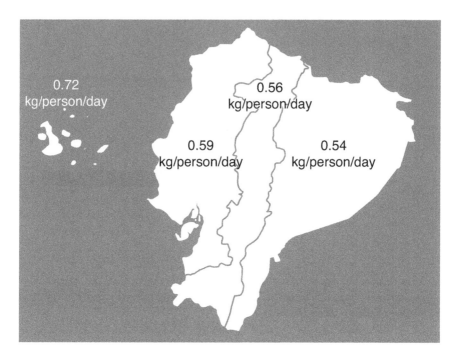

Figure 8.11 Per capita production of solid waste by geographic region in Ecuador
Source: AME – (INEC, 2014).

competencies and institutional and budgetary weakness of the Ministry of Environment (MAE). The only reference in terms of management is the city of Quito, whose problem of environmental pollution led to the creation of the Corporation for the Improvement of Air (CORPAIRE) in 2004. CORPAIRE began its activities with three major projects: 1) the Vehicle Technical Review, 2) the Metropolitan Atmospheric Monitoring Network (REMMAQ) and 3) the Air Quality Index. In 2009, CORPAIRE was liquidated by order of the incoming mayor, Augusto Barrera, as part of its "municipalization" agenda, passing its activities, plans and projects to the MAE. Today air monitoring is scarce and there are no statistics, just like the review vehicle technique that was exceeded by the amount of motor vehicles that were added during the last five years.

In the case of Guayaquil, there is no monitoring network for air quality, so the level of air pollution cannot be established. In Cuenca, monitoring is carried out by Telecommunication, Drinking Water and Sewerage Company (ETAPA). In seven additional cities there is only one station, and only the particulate material (PM10) is measured. Air pollution is caused by the mixing of many pollutants, including particulate matter. These particles are able to penetrate the respiratory tract and pose a health risk by increasing mortality from respiratory diseases, lung cancer and some cardiovascular diseases (WHO, 2016).

The average annual concentration of fine particles in suspension of less than 10 or 2.5 microns in diameter is a common measure of air pollution. According to the World Health Organization (WHO), the particulate matter limits in suspension for cities are 20 μg/m³ for PM10 and 10 μg/m³ for PM2.5. In the case of Ecuador, several cities exceed the limit established by three and even six times. Clear examples of this situation are Santo Domingo, Quito, Milagro and Portoviejo. However, many other cities do not have air quality monitoring stations, so the situation may be worse in several regions of the country.

For its part, the MAE in 2010 drew up a National Air Quality Plan in order to generate an adequate framework for regulation, control, monitoring and coordination of the actors involved in air quality management. However, to date the document, its projects, programs and financing plans are insubstantial.

Environmental awareness

Environmental awareness has been increasing in the country in the last 10 years. It can be said that three factors influence this statistic: on the one hand, greater access to information on different environmental issues, such as climate change, river or air pollution, etc., thanks to information technologies, especially among youth and students; 2) the direct impact faced by thousands of Ecuadorian families due to an environmental problem – one out of two households are affected in their neighborhoods by visual pollution, contaminated water, excessive noise, accumulation of garbage or air pollution; and 3) at least half of Ecuadorian households are aware of some environmental campaign or project at both the public and private levels (INEC, 2014). However, according to the 2010 census only 38 percent of the urban population knows good environmental practices, 21 percent have environmental training and 24 percent recycle.

It could be said that the young people and the indigenous population have the highest level of environmental awareness in Ecuador. This is verified in the different environmental campaigns that have come together in the country. Yasunidos is an example of this, because it is a movement that managed to gather more than 1 million signatures to propose the popular consultation of whether the Yasuní National Park should be exploited or not. Another example is indigenous resistance to mining projects that affect their water basins and irrigation systems.

Productivity and the urban economy in Ecuador

Between 1980 and 2000 Ecuador's GDP recorded low growth rates – only 2 percent between 1980 and 2001 and decreasing by half a point per year between 1980 and 1990. The macroeconomic crisis of 1998–1999, the worst in more than two decades, had a devastating effect on the rural areas of the coast, due to the *El Niño* phenomenon, and on the urban middle class, affected by the closure of banks. The increase in GDP began to occur in 2000, when the country adopted the US dollar as the national currency, thus renouncing the option of using monetary policy to generate greater competitiveness and growth. However, this measure improved stability and increased investment and thus the economy's ability to generate employment and reduce poverty (World Bank, 2005: 15).

Twenty years ago, Ecuador presented a clear bicephalic structure in terms of economic and development centers and poles. Today, in Quito and Guayaquil, without taking away their predominance in the national GDP, have joined other cities whose economic activity attracts and generates jobs, new migration poles and new lines of development. This is how Cuenca, Machala, Santo Domingo, Durán, Milagro, Manta and other medium-sized cities have joined new markets and emerging and consolidating economies, as a result of the processes of globalization and regional and transnational trade. Of this, 94 percent of the population is located in the Sierra and Costa regions, of which 56 percent is concentrated in the provinces of Guayas, Manabí and Pichincha.

Urban poverty and social exclusion

In 2001 the national poverty rate was around 45 percent, whereas in 1990 it was 40 percent. During the same period, people living in poverty increased from 3.5 million to 5.2 million. This increase was unequally distributed in the national territory, being strongest in the urban areas of the coast and the Sierras, where the poverty rate increased by more than 80 percent between 1990 and 2001.

This was reflected in the level of urban poverty in 2001, when the urban poverty rate was higher than in rural areas (from 1.1 million to 3.5 million), leading to poverty. The urban poor were employed in the informal sector, whereas in rural areas they were linked to agricultural activities. The causes of this process were due to three situations: 1) migration from the countryside to the city of people with low purchasing power and low educational level; 2) the 1999 crisis, especially affecting the urban middle class; and 3) changes in the level and composition of employment from one area to another.

Similarly, changes in the territoriality of poverty varied in time and space. In 1990, the rural Sierras housed the largest proportion of the poor (37 percent), followed by the rural coast (28 percent). In 2001, the poor were concentrated in urban areas (20 percent and 26 percent in the Sierras and the coast, respectively). In absolute terms, the poor increased by 300 percent on the urban coast and by 500 percent in the urban Sierras, with Guayaquil and Quito being the ones with the highest increase.

In the 1990s internal and external migration reflected this critical situation. Thousands of Ecuadorians decided to look for better opportunities in other countries such as Spain, Italy and the United States, as well as in the urban areas of the country. In the case of urban migration, this posed great challenges for the mayors of the receiving cities, starting with the low capacity to generate employment and income and the provision of basic services.

As can be seen in Table 8.8, the employment rate remained almost constant in 2000 and 2002, and in addition, women had the fewest job opportunities in times of crisis (World Bank, 2005: 76). In the case of the cantons, 44 of the 200 cantons increased their poverty rate. The highest increases were recorded in the provinces of Azuay, Bolívar, Cotopaxi, Guayas, Loja, Manabí and Pichincha. On the other hand, there was a phenomenon that persists to this day: the large cities are home to the poorest and the richest in the country. This can mask important welfare differences of a specific population group in one neighborhood relative to another.

As is evident from census data, the differences between neighborhoods of the same city are significant. Turumbamba-Quito and Ayacucho-Guayaquil have five times more poor people than in Iñaquito and Febres Cordero, respectively, whereas in Loja the differences are not greater (El Sagrario has 23 percent versus Sucre with 35 percent).

Population and urban employment as of 2007

The urban employment rate has had an important rebound in the last 10 years, along with the increase in the national GDP. For example, urban employment in 2014 alone accounted for 54 percent of the economically active population (EAP), an increase of 3.5 points from 50.5 percent in 2013. The urban underemployment rate fell from 42.7 percent in 2013 to 40.8 percent in 2014, and the urban unemployment rate in that same year was 4.6 percent of the EAP, as seen in Figure 8.12. On the other hand, the working age population (PET) at the national level amounted to 11.3 million people in 2014: 7.8 million in

Table 8.8 Employment, unemployment and income per hour rates in Ecuador (1999–2002)

	1997	1998	1999	2000	2001	2002
Rate of activity	56.80	58.50	60.20	57.50	63.90	58.50
Male	71.10	71.80	73.20	70.40	74.50	70.30
Female	43.30	46.20	48.00	45.20	53.00	46.90
Employment rate	90.80	88.50	85.60	91.00	89.10	90.80
Male	90.30	92.10	89.70	94.40	93.20	94.70
Female	87.60	84.40	80.70	87.20	84.10	87.00
Unemployment rate	9.20	11.50	14.40	9.00	10.90	9.20
Male	6.60	7.80	10.20	5.90	6.70	5.20
Female	12.40	15.50	19.20	12.70	15.80	12.90
Labor income per hour (2000, US$)	1.06	0.72	0.48	0.55	0.70	0.83
Male	1.08	0.74	0.52	0.59	0.77	0.95
Female	1.03	0.68	0.44	0.48	0.60	0.64

Source: Survey on Employment, Unemployment and Underemployment, (INEC), 1997–2002.

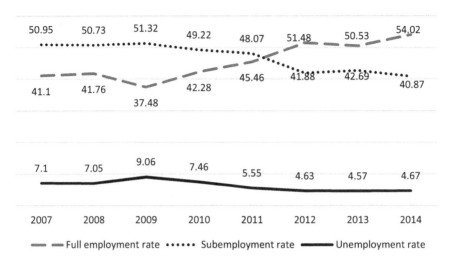

Figure 8.12 Full employment, underemployment and urban unemployment rate (2007–2014)

Note: Annual measures from September

Source: National Survey of Employment, Unemployment and Underemployment, INEC, 2014.

the urban area (69 percent of the total PET) and 3.5 million in rural areas. The economically active population (PEA) was 7.1 million people, of which 4.9 million (68 percent of the total EAP) were in the cities and 2.3 million in the countryside (32 percent). Gender distribution establishes that 2.8 million women and 4.3 million men are of working age.

Regarding the full employment rate, there were significant annual increases in Quito and Guayaquil (9 percent and 5 percent, respectively). In addition, Quito presented the largest full employment rate in relation to the other cities (67 percent), followed by Cuenca with 65 percent. Ambato presented the lowest rate of full occupation: 49 percent (Table 8.9).

With regard to unemployment, the city with the highest rate was Quito, with 4.9 percent of the EAP, followed by Ambato, with 4.8 percent, and Cuenca, with 4.2 percent (Table 8.9). Machala recorded the lowest unemployment rate (2.7 percent) in 2014.

On the other hand, women are still at a disadvantage compared to men with regard to job opportunities in cities. Although it is true that their employability has improved in the last 10 years, female employment is still a minority in several economic branches. Figure 8.13 shows this situation.

Regarding the type of employer, it was observed that the main one is the private sector, with a ratio of eight to two employers in the private versus the public sector. However, recently there has been a growth (not significant) of full employment in the public sector. In terms of underemployment, women

Table 8.9 Full employment rates by cities (2007–2014)

Year	Quito	Guayaquil	Cuenca	Machala	Ambato
2007	7.5%	7%	6%	5.9%	3.7%
2008	6.2%	8%	5.8%	8%	4%
2009	6%	13%	6%	9.6%	3.7%
2010	5.8%	10%	4%	6%	3.7%
2011	4%	6%	4.1%	4.9%	4.7%
2012	3.4%	6.5%	4.4%	4.8%	4.2%
2013	4.7%	5.5%	4.3%	3%	3.6%
2014	4.9%	4%	4.2%	2.7%	4.9%

Source: National Survey of Employment, Unemployment and Underemployment, 2014-INEC.

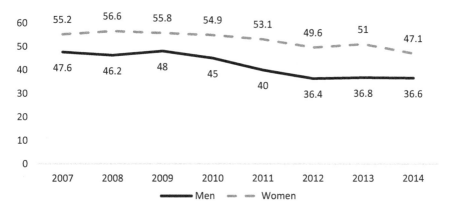

Figure 8.13 Underemployment rate by gender (2007–2014)

Note: Annual measures from September

Source: National Survey of Employment, Unemployment and Underemployment, 2014-INEC.

are in greater proportion to men, although this has gradually decreased in the last five years.

As for labor income, women's situation again makes them vulnerable because they receive a lower salary than men for doing a similar job. This gap has been gradually shortened in the last three years.

Conclusions and recommendations

In official documents, such as the National Report for Habitat III, there is no reference to the commitments made by the Ecuadorian state in 1996 and, therefore, they do not contain a general evaluation of what happened from Istanbul in 1996 to Quito in 2016. The 20 years between the two world summits cannot be understood chronologically, but rather historically. In that period three distinct junctures in the commitments can be clearly identified: the crisis that led to dollarization and that stabilizes the economy, the change of political content since 2007 with the Citizens' Revolution, and the economic crisis that has been present since 2014. It should be added that there have been two different housing policies in the period: one based on the Chilean experience and inspired by Habitat II, and another that arose with the return of the public, which will have to see if it survives whose survival to the current economic crisis in still unclear.

Holding these conferences within a period of 20 years seems to have disconnected them from reality. City dynamics of growth and innovation that force them rethink policies on an ongoing basis. Perhaps a period of no more than 10 years may be more realistic, in addition to having a permanent monitoring commission per region. Instability has been the tone which leads to the question: Does it make sense to have an interval of two decades between world summits about cities given such a changing reality? In 2008, a new constitution was approved in the country, which recognizes the right to the city in Article 31, which was later included in the National Plan for Good Living 2009–2013. What does this mean? If such commitments are enshrined in the supreme charter of a state or in a national plan, this does not guarantee they are fulfilled. Consider the cases of the municipalities governed by Alianza País: how they distance themselves from the proposal and how they later claim this right at the world summits.

Ecuador has enjoyed an economic boom in this century, first with dollarization and then with the substantial increase in oil prices. Although it has not been a long time, two observations can be made: economic growth does not guarantee that agreements are met, and the crisis that has been going on since 2014 suggests that the little way traveled can be lost.

If the earthquake in the areas of Manabí and Esmeraldas (2016), which revealed the country's vulnerability to the risks that come from nature, is added to the economic crisis. It can be inferred that the urban sustainability in the country has these two dimensions: economic and environmental. Moreover, it can be said that vulnerability is a consequence of the development of a country or a region. Hence it is necessary to think about producing development (growth, equity) for sustainability to be achieved.

To pose a "new urban agenda" is to know what remains from previous agendas. In the case of Ecuador, there is no connection between the old agenda of Habitat II and the new one that will replace it in Habitat III. If the starting point was not clear, the arrival will not be either. Moreover, if the final document has no action points what does the new urban agenda in Ecuador mean?

Is the "new urban agenda" advocated by Habitat III actually aware of what kind of city is to be avoided and what kind of city is to be achieved? That is, how will it be different from the one that exists now? In short, what is the starting point to get to something new? These temporal milestones rarely work. For example: the statement "since October 20, 2016 you will enter a new reality", makes little sense. In this context, it is already mentioned that the new city must be participatory and inclusive for all, but in the agenda capital and labor are not in a condition of equilibrium. The new urban agenda will end up being a list of good intentions that will guide the international cooperation agencies as a mandate and the national governments as a suggestion. Citizenship will operate as an object and not as a subject of the process of urban development, in the same way it is increasingly operating as a consumer or taxpayer, rather than as a political actor. These international agendas change very little in time, although the cities change constantly, according to the political forces that govern them.[22]

Notes

1 "Between 1998 and 1999, Ecuador experienced a drop of approximately 10 percent in per capita income" (Larrea, 2012).
2 On March 13, 2000, Ecuador approved the Economic Transformation Law, which modified the monetary regime, legalizing dollarization.
3 According to a FLACSO (Facultad Latinoamericana de Ciencias Sociales, that is, the Latin American Social Sciences Institute) study in the decade from 1998 to 2007, 1,001,848 Ecuadorians migrated.
4 According to ECLAC (the United Nations Economic Commission for Latin America and the Caribbean), Ecuador was one of the countries with the highest economic growth in the region between 2002 and 2006.
5 The Correa government said before the earthquake that the Ecuadorian economy would grow by +0.3 percent and after the earthquake that would decrease by −0.3 percent.
6 According to the Census of Population and Housing of Ecuador, in 2010 Ecuador had an urban population of 9,090,786, whereas the rural population was 5,392,713 inhabitants.
7 A similar phenomenon occurs when large cities of the region are compared with Asia: Canton has 43 million inhabitants, Tokyo 40 million and Shanghai 31 million. Mexico today is in tenth place and San Pablo in thirteenth of the largest cities in the world, when not long ago they were among the largest cities. They will not grow anymore because the migration from the countryside to the city has ended, because there are no more rural inhabitants willing to migrate, nor is there the magnitude of potential migrants that exists in Asia.
8 The larger city establishes very particular relations with the rest of the urban network to which it belongs. These relationships are expressed through changes in the relative weight of the first city in varied dimensions such as population; employment; wealth generation; power distribution; and the capacity for cultural, social and productive innovation.
9 In 1950 the average rate of urbanization was 4.6 percent, whereas now it is 2.2 percent; this is because in 1950 the potential disposition of the migratory mass was around 60 percent, whereas in 2010 it does not reach 20 percent.
10 The cities of Loja, Manta, Machala, Cotacachi, Ambato, Puyo and Riobamba, among others, do not escape this logic.
11 This foreign character exists in the sense that our cities have become spaces to build foreigners: to enter a building or urban structure, identification (passport) and prior authorization (visa) are required.
12 Another form of integration into the global economy comes from illegal drug markets, international migration and human trafficking, as well as from the sale of arms and smuggling. Notably, in 2014 there was as much money laundering as there was foreign investment in the region.

13 Metropolitanization will not depend, as in the previous period, on the development and strengthening of the state, located in capital cities, but on the territorial displacement of the economy, which will not only push the growth of other metropolis (Brazil has 29 metropolitan regions, Mexico 59, Colombia 22) but also the emergence of new research themes: intermediate cities, intangible historical heritage, city clusters (of salmon in Chile or tourism in Peru, for example) and strengthening of municipalism (national and international), among others.

14 This is a substantial difference regarding rural/urban migrations: whereas the international ones at this moment do not break the ties of relations, in the former it did occur and with an additional fact: the peasant economy and culture were reproduced in the urban peripheries, in the manner of peasant cities.

15 Traditionally the municipality of Guayaquil was managed by populist administrations.

16 "Guayaquil more citizenship" and the "great Guayaquil" are the slogans promoted by the municipality and the provincial council.

17 "Quito more citizenship" is an expression used by the current administration to demonstrate the achievements of citizen participation in neighborhood, sectoral or thematic *cabildo*s and corporations.

18 The main financing was born with the creation of the cultural heritage protection fund FONSAL (Fondo de Salvamento del Patrimonio Cultural) in 1988, the achievement of a pioneering credit with the IDB in 1992 and the important support of international cooperation.

19 Water is at 96 percent, electricity 99.5 percent, sewage 90.9 percent and garbage collection service 98 percent (VII Population Census and VI Housing 2010, available at: www.inec.gob.ec).

20 The number of homes that have access to public services (water, sewage, garbage collection and electricity), expressed as a percentage of total housing.

21 "INMOBILIAR provides a service to public sector institutions for real estate management, which means: providing public institutions such as educational units, UPC's and CIVBs with spaces (land or infrastructure); administer the assets of the Central State; carry out renovations or readjustments in buildings of the Public Service; generate an information base or cadaster on real estate of the state; in addition, it has in charge emblematic projects like the administration of the Citizen Care Centers, the Governmental Platforms, the integral urbanistic projects called Millennium Campus. Currently, one of the central axes of INMOBILIAR's work focuses on the sale of goods that are not going to be used by the state, based on the institutional objective of giving them the best use or destination" (Inmobiliaria Publica, 2016).

22 In Latin America, the devolution cycle to local authorities is only 15 years old, which means that local powers are very young, and that citizen participation and representation have a short history (Carrión, 2016).

Bibliography

Araujo, A., (2014), "Perforaciones en el ITT arrancarán en el 2015", *Diario El Comercio*, August 17. Available at: http://bit.ly/1w0WV5i

Banco Central del Ecuador (BCE), (2013), *Estadísticas Macroeconómicas: Presentación estructural 2013*, Division of Economic Statistics, BCE – Ecuador. Available at: http://bit.ly/2dpdVk9

Beck, U. (ed.), (1998), *¿Qué es la globalización? Falacias del globalismo, respuestas a la globalización*, Paidos, Barcelona. Available at: http://bit.ly/2dpdTJ3

Cabrera, H., Garcés, M., and Paredes, P., (2012), *Producción de aguas servidas, tratamiento y uso en el Ecuador. Proyecto de Desarrollo de Capacidades para el Uso Seguro de Aguas Servidas en Agricultura*, FAO, WHO, UNEP, UNU-INWEH, UNW-DPC, IWMI, and ICID. Available at: http://bit.ly/2dHrINW

Caldeira, Teresa, (2000). *City of Walls: Crime, Segregation, and Citizenship in São Paulo*. University of California Press, Berkeley.

Carrión, F., (2003), "El problema de la vivienda en el Ecuador", *Diario Hoy Newspaper*, January. Available at: www.flacso.org.ec/docs/provivieec.pdf

Carrión, F., (2014), "El urbicidio o la producción del olvido", *Observatorio Cultural*, No. 25, Santiago de Chile. Available at: https://works.bepress.com/fernando_carrion/684/

Carrión, F. (2016), "La ventriloquía de Hábitat III", Seres Urbanos, *Diario El País Web*, blog post. Available at: http://bit.ly/2I6nb93

Centro de Investigaciones de Políticas Públicas y Territorio (CITE) and Facultad Latinoamericana de Ciencias Sociales (FLACSO), "Transformaciones demográficas y procesos de urbanización en Ecuador", *Quito*. Available at: http://bit.ly/2blKJrQ/

Consejo Nacional de Modernización del Estado (CONAM), (2010), *Informe Nacional de Modernización*, Government of Ecuador, Quito.

Centro de Investigaciones de Políticas Públicas y Territorio (CITE) and Facultad Latinoamericana de Ciencias Sociales (FLACSO), (2015), "Transformaciones demográficas y proceso de urbanización en Ecuador", white paper by CITE-FLACSO, May 15, Web, Quito.

El Telégrafo, (2016), "Comisión legislativa inicia el estudio de reformas al Cootad", *El Telégrafo Newspaper*, February 10. Available at: http://bit.ly/2dYWy87

Granda, C., and Zambonino, D., (2014), "Reporte de Economía Laboral", *Direction of Labor and Economic Studies*, Instituto Nacional de Estadística y Censos (INEC). Available at: http://bit.ly/2dchdla

Inmobiliaria Publica, (2016), *Inmobiliaria Publica, Preguntas Frecuentes*, Web. Available at: www.inmobiliariapublica.ec/preguntas_frecuentes/, Last accessed: March 19 2016.

Instituto Nacional de Estadística y Censos (INEC), (2010), *Índice de Verde Urbano*, Web. Available at: http://bit.ly/2dchjcw, Last accessed: March 19 2016.

Instituto Nacional de Estadística y Censos (INEC), (2014), *Anuario de estadísticas de entradas y salidas internacionales 2014*, Direction of Sociodemographic Statistics, INEC, Available at: http://bit.ly/1MSjp10, Last accessed: March 15 2016.

Larrea, A. M., (2012), *Modo de desarrollo, organización territorial y cambio constituyente en el Ecuador*, Second edition, Secretaría Nacional de Planificación y Desarrollo (SENPLADES), Quito.

Lattes, A. E., (2001), "Población urbana y urbanización en América Latina", *Facultad Latinoamericana de Ciencias Sociales (FLACSO)*. Available at: www.flacso.org.ec/docs/sfcclates.pdf, Last accessed: March 22 2016.

Ministerio de Desarrollo Urbano y Vivienda de Ecuador (MIDUVI), (2015), *Informe Nacional del Ecuador*, Ministry of Urban Development and Housing, Sub-Secretariat of Habitat and Human Settlements, Government of Ecuador, Quito. Available at: http://bit.ly/2dQ0OE0, Last accessed: March 22 2016.

Pérez, R. and Cantuña, F., (2015), *Estadísticas de los gobiernos seccionales y provinciales en el Ecuador: 2004–2013*, Apuntes de Economía No. 62, Dirección Nacional de Síntesis Macroeconómica, Banco Central del Ecuador, Quito. Available at: http://bit.ly/2dci9pP, Last accessed: April 4 2016.

Report of the United Nations Conference on Human Settlements (HABITAT II), (1996), *Istambul Declaration on Human Settlements*, United Nations General Assembly, Istanbul, 3–14 June.

Sassen, S., (1991), *The Global City*, Princeton University Press, Princeton, NJ.

Secretaría Nacional de Agua (SENAGUA), (2012), *Diagnóstico de la información estadística del agua en Ecuador*, ECLAC, Final Report, Web. Available at: http://bit.ly/2F1YOHD, April 4 2016.

Secretaría Nacional de Planificación y Desarrollo (SENPLADES), (2014), *Proyectos emblemáticos en Guayas*, Secretaría Nacional de Planificación y Desarrollo, Subsecretaría Zona 8 Guayaquil, Durán y Samborondón. Available at: http://bit.ly/2dciQzw, Last accessed: April 10 2016.

Secretaría Nacional de Planificación y Desarrollo (SENPLADES), (2016), *Sección Zonas Administrativas*, Government of Ecuador. Available at: http://bit.ly/2dGxRtc, Last Accessed: April 10 2016.

United Nations Economic Commission for Latin America and the Caribbean (ECLAC), (2014), *Diagnóstico de las Estadísticas de Agua en el Ecuador*, Santiago de Chile. Available at: http://bit.ly/2dC23sT

United Nations Population Fund (UNFPA) and Facultad Latinoamericana de Ciencias Sociales (FLACSO), (2008), *Ecuador: La migración internacional en cifras*, FLACSO Ecuador, Quito. Available at: www.flacsoandes.edu.ec/libros/digital/43598.pdf, Last Accessed: March 14 2016.

Villavicencio, G., (2010), "Gobiernos seccionales en Ecuador: estatismo y estatalidad en crisis (1998–2009)", *Universitas*, 13, July–December, pp. 41–67. Available at: http://bit.ly/2dGyaE7, Last Accessed: March 9 2016.

Viteri, A., (2016), *U.S. Immigration to Ecuador*, Interview, Telesur English. Available at: http://bit.ly/2dtdtO6

World Bank, (2005), *Ecuador: Evaluación de la Pobreza*, Poverty Reduction and Economic Management Unit for Latin America and the Caribbean, World Bank, Alfaomega Colombiana, SA. Available at: http://bit.ly/1ZBzFJM

World Health Organization (WHO), (2016), *Base de datos de contaminación ambiental del aire por ciudad y por país*. Available at: www.who.int/phe/health_topics/outdoorair/databases/cities/en/, Last Accessed: April 24 2016.

9 A global quantitative perspective

The Habitat Commitment Index

Martha Susana Jaimes

The analysis presented in previous chapters is complemented with a quantitative evaluation of the implementation of the Habitat II Agenda in Latin America and the Caribbean, through the Habitat Commitment Index (HCI). The HCI is an instrument that was elaborated in 2015–2016 by the Global Urban Futures Project (GUF) at The New School of New York. This chapter presents the results of this index using national-level data, and the following chapter focuses on the availability of data at the city level to allow rigorous monitoring of city performance.

The Habitat Commitment Index: an instrument to measure performance[1]

As UN member states prepared to meet in Quito in October 2016 to agree on a New Urban Agenda (NUA) at Habitat III, the GUF team recognized the importance of scrutinizing the previous urban agenda and assessing how effective it has been. Unfortunately, there has been little effort so far to thoroughly gauge the progress made toward meeting the objectives agreed upon in the previous agenda from the 1996 Habitat II conference in Istanbul. Given the economic growth of the past two decades, how well have countries used their resources to meet the commitments of the Habitat II agenda?

To answer this question, the GUF developed the HCI, a way of measuring country performance on a set of indicators that takes per capita income levels into account to gauge progress over time. The HCI assesses each country's degree of compliance with the commitments established in the Habitat II Urban Agenda, according to a set of indicators related to urban performance. Although some socioeconomic indicators such as poverty, access to basic services and access to education can provide a characterization of people's well-being, the objective of the HCI is to measure not only the well-being of urban households but also the degree of commitment by national governments to meet the goals and objectives established in Habitat II.

An important objective of the HCI is to allow for a comparison of each country's performance on a global scale. In this way, the fulfillment of the commitments between countries and between regions is traced, while the index also helps identify the level of progress between Habitat II and Habitat III, and the challenges each country faces today. The results of this analysis pose important questions to the NUA that was approved in Quito during Habitat III and provides important feedback on the performance of national governments in relation to urban commitments.

The HCI's measurement recognizes that, at the time of accepting the Habitat II commitments, countries had different starting points in terms of urban development and had widely differing levels of available resources. Distinct levels of urban development between countries created major challenges in terms of comparability throughout the 20 years between Habitat II and Habitat III. In this sense, the HCI also considers that during the period, some countries have experienced faster economic growth, whereas others have faced slower growth rates or even some degree of economic stagnation. It was then that the team recognized the importance of measuring the degree of compliance of countries according to their own performance and initial conditions and their capacity to achieve the proposed goals according to each country's available resources. Following the main objective of comparability across countries and across time, the index was adjusted in order to capture the different possibilities of compliance identified in the sample of countries.

The HCI is an index that accounts for the level of progress in the indicators that measure Habitat II commitments, according to resource availability for each country. Country capacity according to available resources is measured through gross domestic product (GDP) per capita. In addition, this index seeks to evaluate the performance of each country, not by the absolute level of its achievements, but against the maximum level reached historically by countries with similar resource capacity. Country comparisons following these parameters were based on the methodology developed by Fukuda-Parr et al. (2015)[2] for the SERF Index (Social and Economic Rights Fulfillment, or SERF) to measure the performance of states in fulfilling social and economic rights. An important aspect of this methodology is that by using an achievement possibilities frontier (FPL), which determines the highest possible level of performance in terms of urban indicators at any given level of resource availability, a score is assigned to each country based on the achievement possibilities of all countries with the same level of resources. Following this methodology, the HCI established predicted performance levels by income for six categories: Residential Infrastructure, Employment, Poverty, Sustainability, Gender, and Institutional Capacity.

The country-adjusted scores offer a new perspective on urban development. For example, in 1996 only 37 percent of Burundi's urban population had Urban Access to Electricity, whereas in Belize over 96 percent had Urban Access to Electricity. However, Belize's per capita GDP at that time was almost ten times that of Burundi. Using the HCI's scoring based on historical data, Burundi was actually performing at around 96 percent of what was possible. Although the raw numbers put Belize and Burundi at opposite ends of the spectrum in terms of urban electricity provision in 1996, their HCI scores are nearly equivalent – meaning that based on their resources, Burundi was performing about as well as could have been expected in terms of urban electricity access.

Likewise, the level of Urban Access to Improved Sanitation was roughly the same for Peru and Vietnam in 1996, at 73.3 percent and 72 percent, respectively. However, at that time Vietnam had a per capita GDP (purchasing power parity, or PPP, 2011 international dollars) of $2,197, whereas Peru's was significantly higher, at $6,240. Based on the HCI's analysis using the APF derived from historical data, Vietnam received a score of 92.6 out of 100 in terms of its achievement for Urban Access to Improved Sanitation relative to its capacity. Meanwhile, Peru's capacity-adjusted achievement on the indicator was more modest, at 80.6 out of 100.

Identifying commitments and selecting indicators

Based on a detailed review of the Istanbul Declaration and related documents from Habitat II, the GUF identified seven commitment categories and several goals that had been agreed upon and that would form the basis for the HCI evaluation:[3]

> Adequate shelter for all
> Sustainable human settlements
> Enablement and participation
> Gender equality
> Financing shelter and human settlements
> International cooperation
> Assessing progress

The HCI seeks to analyze the progress made on the commitments, goals and principles of the 1996 Habitat Agenda by dividing them into six broad categories, referred to as dimensions throughout the study.

Choosing indicators: challenges in data collection

Moving from identifying the commitments of Habitat II to creating a list of indicators that were useful for the HCI presented several challenges. The first, and greatest, challenge was the lack of urban data at the national level. For many of the indicators we looked at – access to adequate housing, for example – data have simply not been collected in a rigorous manner across countries. For other indicators, data are available at the national level but are not disaggregated between urban and rural. For example, since Habitat II, no European country collected data on poverty at the urban level. While recognizing that using combined urban and rural data is not ideal, the importance of including some indicators, such as Exposure to Environmental Risk, in the assessment outweighed the problems of using aggregated national-level data. For other indicators, data have not been collected consistently in the period between Habitat II and the present. The initial HCI analysis focuses on assessing progress on individual indicators during the period between 1996 and 2014, plus or minus one year depending on data availability.

The SERF methodology, used to calculate the HCI, posed constraints in choosing indicators. The SERF methodology relies on an underlying assumption of a positive correlation between an indicator and economic growth. For many of the data sets, this was not the case, and therefore they could not be used. For example, measurements of inequality using World Bank data showed no correlation with income, despite research suggesting otherwise, such as Kuznet's curve hypothesis. Gender-related indicators, which will be discussed in depth in a later section, also frequently showed no correlation with income. Some environmental measurements, such as reduced per capita carbon emissions, showed the reverse – as wealth increased, carbon emissions also increased. After testing 116 data sets, only 15 satisfied HCI requirements. Table 9.1 shows the final 15 indicators chosen across the six HCI dimensions.

Latin America and the Caribbean according to the HCI

According to the HCI, Latin America and the Caribbean improved its average score in the provision of public services and Urban Poverty Headcount, while still facing significant challenges in relation to governance and quality of employment. Latin America and the Caribbean is the second most urbanized region in the world, with a growing population now living in urban areas.[4] In 2014, according to World Bank data, 79.6 percent of the total population in the region lived in urban areas, and in the period between 1996 and 2014, urban population increased by 40.5 percent at an average annual rate of 1.2 percent. The region's growing urbanization came with positive economic performance for the whole period, with an average GDP growth of 3.1 percent between 1996 and 2014.[5] However, economic growth has slowed when compared to the average rate of growth of previous decades, where it grew at rates above 5 percent, especially in the 1970s and 1980s. Similarly, despite having gained share in world GDP during these two decades, from 1990 on, the region has been losing its share in spite of a good level of participation in world trade and attracting high capital flows (Ocampo, 2012).

The economic structure of cities in the region has undergone important transformations stemming from changes in the orientation of economic policy, especially the transition from a period of state-led industrialization[6] to a period of high trade liberalization. In the period analyzed by the HCI, between 1996 and 2014, a common denominator is the profound transformation of the nature of urban economies. The modernization process in cities has been determined by the substitution of an industrialization model that guaranteed stable employment and better wages and working conditions with a model led by the expansion of the tertiary sector within a framework of labor market flexibility (Ziccardi, 2008). This shift has had a significant impact on employment vulnerability and informality, as well as income inequality. These two

Table 9.1 Selected HCI indicators

TOTAL INDICATORS TRIED FOR HCI 116			TOTAL INDICATORS USED FOR HCI 15 (12.93%)		
INDICATORS TRIED: 7 USED: 2	INDICATORS TRIED: 46 USED: 3	INDICATORS TRIED: 24 USED: 4	INDICATORS TRIED: 15 USED: 2	INDICATORS TRIED: 10 USED: 2	INDICATORS TRIED: 14 USED: 2
INSTITUTIONAL CAPACITY	GENDER	RESIDENTIAL INFRASTRUCTURE	POVERTY	EMPLOYMENT	SUSTAINABILITY
Quality of Government	Female Tertiary Enrollment	Urban Piped Water on Premises	Infant Mortality	Vulnerable Employment	Exposure to Environmental Risk
International Country Risk Guide	World Bank	World Bank	World Bank	World Bank	Yale University
Government Effectiveness	Maternal Mortality	Urban Access to Electricity	Urban Poverty Headcount	Formal Employment	Electricity Production from Renewable Resources
World Bank	World Bank	World Bank	World Bank	ILO/OECD	World Bank
	Female Employment in Non-Agricultural Sector	Urban Access to Improved Sanitation			
	World Bank	World Bank			
		Water Safety			
		Yale University			

aspects, employment and inequality, pose great challenges for both economic and social policy, especially at a time when growth prospects are uncertain as GDP growth rate continue to slow down, passing from almost 6 percent in the year 2000 to 0.8 percent in 2014 (Vakis et al., 2015).

While the economy was thriving, social progress accompanied GDP growth and urbanization. In the period between 1996 and 2014, the region improved both poverty and inequality. Poverty declined by half, from 42 percent of the region's population in 2002 to about 24 percent in 2013. Paradoxically, in the global context, Latin America and the Caribbean is the only region that has managed to reduce income inequality, while remaining the most unequal in the world. The regional Gini coefficient, according to per capita income, fell 5 percent, from 0.57 in 2000 to 0.52 in 2012 (UNDP, 2016). This break-through came after a period of growing inequality between 1980 and 1990. After this period, countries in the region identified income distribution as a main policy target and implemented a wide range of social policies, effectively reducing inequality amid the 2000 decade. Since the second half of the 1990s, as part of the structural reforms packages, countries fostered policy improve-ments promoting higher social security benefits and greater investments in public services, increased investment in education, and higher efficiency in social spending. These efforts translated into improved income distribution, lower incidence of poverty, and better income levels for the population (UN Habitat, 2014: 3).

However, as UN Habitat and the Corporación Andina de Fomento (CAF) point out:

> Latin America and the Caribbean is the only region in the world whose Gini coefficient, on average, is around 0.5, placing it in the category of "Very High Inequality". In 2008, five of the 10 most unequal countries on the planet – Brazil, Colombia, Dominican Republic, Guatemala, Chile – were in this region. Even in the last decade, Latin American countries classi-fied as less unequal – Costa Rica, Peru and Uruguay – were less equitable than the most unequal in Europe. Therefore, it is possible to consider that inequality is the most distinctive feature of the Latin American region.
>
> (UN Habitat, 2014: 40)

The role of cities in changes in the trend of inequality has been emphasized, acknowledging that it is thanks to a greater coordination between national and local governments that the urban income gap has been reduced. However, efforts should concentrate on designing public policy instruments that allow for "income derived from urban dynamics to be shared by society as a whole" (UN Habitat, 2014: 3). Designing these instruments is one of the main chal-lenges for urban policy and its key contribution to improving the quality of life of its citizens.

The assessment of urban policy according to social indicators' performance requires an adequate impact evaluation that depends on the availability of urban data. Some of the indicators included in the HCI – for example, Urban Poverty Headcount – allow for differentiated analysis between urban and rural areas. Other indicators, such as those in the Residential Infrastructure dimension: "Access to Safe Water", "Improved Urban Sanitation", "Urban Electricity", and "Piped Water on Premises", are also a measure of improvements in the quality of life in urban areas, especially in cities with rapid urbanization. However, most indicators are based on national measures and do not allow this distinction. The fact that urban data are negligible highlights the importance of constructing good baseline indicators to have an adequate assessment of urban performance and, in this case, evaluating the level of the implementation of the commitments assumed in Habitat II, as well as the new goals determined by the New Urban Agenda.

Monitoring and evaluating results based on quality information that allows researchers and policy analysts to capture the particularities of the urban areas will provide better tools to understand relevant urban dynamics. The quantitative and analytical exercise described in the following section is a proposal for the monitoring of the Habitat commitments and represents a work in progress that can be further improved once quality urban indicators become more common.

HCI scores for the region

The HCI allows for a long-term analysis of country performance according to the commitments of the Habitat II agenda. In case of Latin America and the Caribbean, a total of 29 countries were included in the index – out of 41 that make up the region.[7] The HCI allows an evaluation of the level of fulfillment of the commitments assumed by these countries in 1996. Based on the capacity of each country to implement policies that target the main goals of the Habitat II agenda, the index measures each country's performance according to the performance of other countries with a similar GDP per capita.

In the period between Habitat II and the present, Latin America and the Caribbean's regional per capita GDP (PPP, USD constant at 2011 international prices) went from \$8,994 in 1996 to \$13,220 in 2014, a total variation of 46.98 percent. Meanwhile, the average HCI score for all countries included in the index fell slightly, −0.11 points, from 71.96 points in 1996 to 71.86 points in 2014.[8] The negative variation in the HCI score indicates that although economic growth was positive, the region did not reach its potential performance according to the outcome indicators included in the index. Figure 9.1 shows the performance for each country in the region during the period of study.

A second important result is that the region showed a high variation between the countries analyzed. For example, Uruguay had the best performance according to the change in scores between the base year and the final year. Uruguay's score went from 70.1 to 76.75 points, which represents an improvement equivalent to 6.64 points in the HCI score. El Salvador came second, with an increase of 5.75 points, and Argentina, with an increase of 5.57 points,

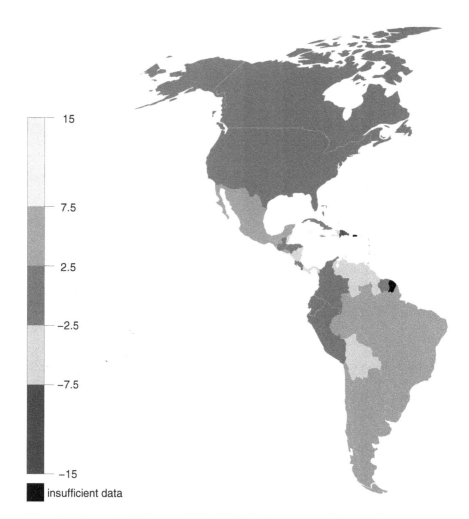

Figure 9.1 Change in HCI scores (1996–2014), Latin America and the Caribbean
Source: The Habitat Commitment Project. 2016.

between the base year and the final year. The Dominican Republic, on the other hand, had the poorest performance with a negative variation of −11.25 points, with a base year score of 65.49 and a score of 54.24 points in the most recent year. Venezuela also showed a poor performance, with a change of −6.64 points, going from 74.2 to 67.56 between the base year and the final year. Belize went from 81.23 points in the base year to 75.47 in the final year, a change of −5.75 points. Figure 9.2 shows the composite index scores for each country in the base year, the final year, and the change between these scores.

In terms of the greatest increases and decreases by country, rather than delve into the cases, we want to illustrate how the HCI results effectively correspond

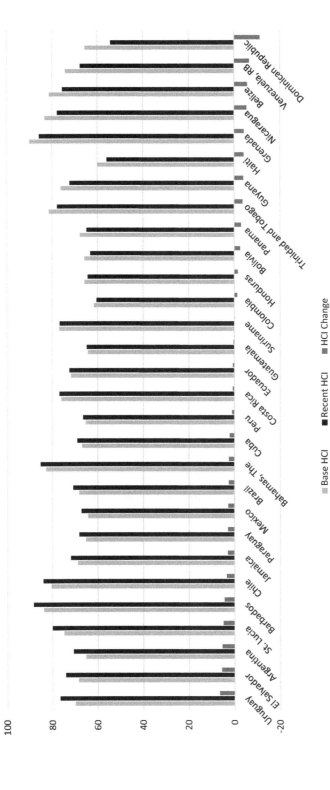

Figure 9.2 HCI results for Latin America and the Caribbean (1996–2014)

Source: The Habitat Commitment Project. 2016.

with the socioeconomic realities of most countries. In the case of Uruguay, the overall performance in the HCI shows the country's progress in economic, social and political matters, which is consistent with its performance in other indexes, such as the HDI, where it occupied the 3rd place among the countries of the region and the 55th place in the world in 2015. According to the HCI, Uruguay's best performance was in the Urban Poverty Headcount indicator, which improved by 40.45 points between the base year and the final year. For its part, Female Tertiary Enrollment also presented outstanding performance, with a change in the score of 31.14 points between the base year and the final year.

Uruguay was the only country in the region to reach 100 points in the Water Safety indicator, not only in the base year but also in the final year, which resulted in zero change along the period of analysis. This score reflects a continuous commitment to improve the quality of water and basic sanitation in the country.[9] Uruguay's good performance in the composite HCI is a result of high scores in the Residential Infrastructure category and also reflects the country's effort to maintain good macroeconomic stability, while promoting innovative social policies that benefit its relatively small population.[10]

Uruguay's HCI score is consistent with the country's recent recognition as one of the most equitable in the region as a result of an ongoing effort to guarantee the continuity of its policies oriented towards social inclusion, mitigation of poverty and good quality of life. As a result of this set of policies, Uruguay is one of the countries with the best pension coverage as well as other social benefits. In 2014, 87 percent of the population over 65 years old had pension coverage, a figure slightly higher than the results for Argentina and Brazil. This type of policy has contributed to extreme poverty reduction – from 2.5 percent in 2006 to 0.3 percent in 2014 – and increased the percentage of the population defined as middle class.[11] Uruguay is an excellent example of how a country can translate good economic performance into actions that improve relevant areas that contribute to the fulfillment of the commitments of Habitat II.

On the other hand, despite its excellent economic performance, the Dominican Republic had the lowest scores in the region in most of its indicators. The Dominican Republic was the country with the lowest performance, measured by the change in the HCI score, which dropped −11.25 points. The country went from 65.49 points in the base year to 54.24 points in the final year. Of the total of 14 indicators included in the composite HCI for the Dominican Republic (the country did not have information available for the calculation of the Formal Employment indicator), only four indicators showed a positive change between the base year and the final year.

Good performance indicators such as Female Tertiary Enrollment, which had a change of 33.39 points (above the regional average of 24.18 points), were not enough to improve the Dominican Republic's overall score. Other indicators were determinant in the fall of the composite index. Among the indicators of greatest deterioration for the country we can find Female Employment in Non-Agricultural Sector, which showed a change of −58.46 points. This change is explained by the recession experienced by the country in 2004, which pushed women into lower-paying, less qualified jobs, in contrast with high female employment in the 1990s (ILO, 2013: 10). Other indicators, such as Quality of Government also presented a negative change of −48.73; Urban Poverty Headcount had a change of −20.87 points and access to Urban Piped Water on Premises had a change of −21.15 points. However, the country's poor performance in these indicators is a matter of concern once we identified its high deviation from the regional average.

HCI scores are also a reflection of the political and social challenges the Dominican Republic has struggled with in the past 20 years, despite its excellent economic performance. The country has had one of the strongest economic growth rates in Latin America and the Caribbean, with an average growth rate between 1996 and 2014 of 5.3 percent, thanks to which the Dominican Republic was classified as the fourth fastest-growing economy in the region (after Panama, Argentina and Peru) (Carneiro et al., 2015: 6). However, the country's economic performance has not translated into better social or infrastructure outcomes, and the results of the HCI are consistent with findings described in other studies on the Dominican Republic, which also point to the paradox of strong economic growth coupled with increasing poverty, poor income distribution and limited government capacity (ILO, 2013: 16).[12]

The Dominican Republic's urban population classified as poor doubled between 2000 and 2014, from a total of 1.2 million to 2.4 million.[13] The structural transformation of the economy, determined by growth of the service sector, especially tourism, and a decline in the share of manufacturing and agriculture in total production have contributed to productivity growth but not to wage growth or improved employment conditions (Carneiro et al., 2015: 7). The stagnation of real wages prevents lower-income populations from escaping poverty, a fact that often comes with growing informality in the labor market. Informal labor went from 54 percent of total employment in 2004 to 56 percent in 2013. This explains HCI scores for indicators such as Non-Vulnerable Employment and Urban Poverty Headcount. In addition, poor government capacity has allowed for inefficient infrastructure and rising costs that pose high burdens to the national budget and has created a consequent loss of competitiveness. The institutional turmoil has had a negative impact on public perception of government capacity, a fact that reflected on the performance of HCI's Quality of Government and Government Effectiveness indicators. Although recent efforts to combat poverty and inequality, increase investment in education and health and improve the provision of basic infrastructure services have increased, the Dominican Republic's performance in the HCI reflects how rapid economic growth does not necessarily mean improved overall socioeconomic conditions.

Interpreting the HCI indicators

The HCI allows us to describe the joint effects of urbanization, economic growth and outcomes related to the commitments from Habitat II. Each of the components of the index allows for an approximation to the most important categories expressed in these commitments. Taking this into consideration, we find it important to analyze the region's progress according to each of the indicators that make up the HCI dimensions. The dimensions with the best performance for Latin America and the Caribbean were, in order, Poverty, with a positive variation of 6.65 points between the base year and the final year; Gender, with a variation of 4.5 points; Sustainability, with a variation of 2.96 points; and finally Residential Infrastructure was in the fourth place, with a 2.9-point increase in the final year score with respect to the base year.

The Employment and Institutional Capacity dimensions experienced a decline explained by lower scores between the base year and the final year. The negative change in scores indicates that potential improvements in these dimensions did not take place. The Employment dimension, for example, had a negative variation of −7.04 points, whereas Institutional Capacity had a negative variation of −13.16 points, as shown in Figure 9.3. A more detailed analysis of each indicator allows a better understanding of the countries' compliance with the commitments defined at Habitat II.

From a general perspective, the indicator with the best average performance for the group of countries in the region was Urban Poverty Headcount,[14] which presented a variation of 24.41 points between the base year and the final year. Female Tertiary Enrollment came second, with an increase of 24.19 points from the base year to the final year. The average regional performance of these two indicators is outstanding, as shown in Figure 9.4.

Other indicators such as Formal Employment, Non-Vulnerable Employment, Government Effectiveness and Quality of Government are the main drivers of the region's low overall performance between Habitat II and Habitat III. The indicators contained in the Institutional Capacity dimension, both the Government Effectiveness and the Quality of Government, had a negative change of −8.15 and −8.31, respectively, indicating a deterioration in citizen perception of government performance in the region.

Poverty in Latin America and the Caribbean: great improvements and growing challenges

The main finding emerging from the HCI for Latin America and the Caribbean is how great progress in the Poverty dimension is a result of the region's effort to diversify its social policies in the past 20 years. The average regional score for the Poverty dimension improved by 6.65 points, going from 81.65 to 88.30 points between the base year and the final year. This dimension, which includes indicators of Urban Poverty Headcount as a percentage of the total population and Infant Mortality, condenses one of the most significant social achievements in the region's recent history. The positive change in this dimension was driven by the Poverty indicator score, which had an outstanding variation of 24.41 points in the region's average score. Infant Mortality for its part had a change of 3.61 points. The result in the Urban Poverty Headcount indicator follows the positive results also described by other poverty indicators, mainly chronic

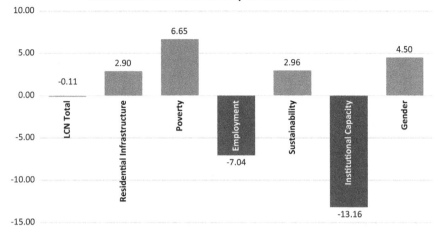

Figure 9.3 Latin America and the Caribbean: HCI variation by dimension (1996–2014)

Source: The Habitat Commitment Project. 2016.

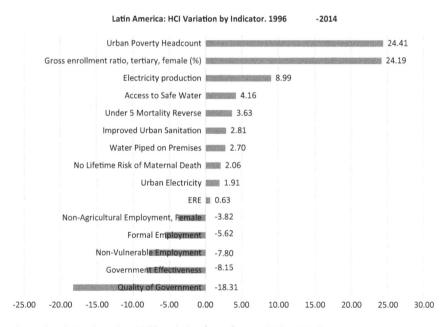

Figure 9.4 Latin America: HCI variation by indicator (1996–2014)

Source: The Habitat Commitment Project. 2016.

and multidimensional poverty. However, when considering these two measures, there is a greater poverty risk for households located in urban areas due to a greater dependence on labor income. This fact highlights the importance of identifying qualitative differences between urban and rural poverty to define better policies that can target specific needs associated with urban quality of life.

Poverty reduction in Latin America and the Caribbean is widely acknowledged by various international agencies. The UN, through the United Nations Development Program (UNDP), points out that "since 2003, thanks to the adoption of innovative social policies and inclusive economic growth, more than 72 million people have emerged from poverty and 94 million have been incorporated into the middle class" (Gray et al., 2016: 4).[15] The population living under income poverty fell from 42 percent in 2002 to 23 percent in 2013. In this way, during the past decade, the region managed to translate economic growth into income growth, especially for the poorest and the urban poor who depend on labor income.

The population living in extreme poverty (less than $2.5 per day) went from 26.6 percent in 1993 to 11.5 percent in 2013; the population in moderate poverty (between $2.5 and $4 per day), 8 percent to 12.9 percent; and the population in vulnerability ($4 to $10 dollars a day) went from 34.3 percent to 38.4 percent in the same period between 1993 and 2013. About 45 million people increased their income, overcoming moderate poverty and extreme poverty by passing the threshold into the vulnerability category. Today, the vulnerable population represents the highest proportion within the three categories in the region. The most notable increase, however, is the middle class (from $10 to $50 per day), which went from 20.6 percent in 1993 to 34.6 percent in 2013, improving levels of inequality and bringing the regional Gini coefficient to one of the lowest historical levels, 0.493, in the region's history (Gray et al., 2016: 7).[16]

Despite positive achievements in relation to income, Latin America and the Caribbean cannot be classified as a middle-class region. Most of the population that emerged from poverty today are still vulnerable to poverty, which implies that there is a substantial risk that they will return to the levels of moderate poverty and extreme poverty they came from, especially on the verge of drastic changes in the economic growth trend. The GDP went from a growth rate of over 6 in 2010 to 0.8 in 2014, a fact that has already generated significant impact on the labor market and begins to have an impact on the population's income levels. Other poverty measures, such as chronic poverty,[17] seek to measure the impact of the environment on the determinants of poverty and to understand the persistence of poverty even under favorable income conditions. This means that although mobility was given by the improvement in income levels, additional factors may have contributed to such mobility, and it is important to reinforce them before a shift in the economic cycle.

The institutional framework, the quality of social services provided by the state and local governments and market dynamics are factors that contribute either to upward mobility or to poverty incidence.[18] Therefore, the role of social policy is preponderant, as demonstrated by the Latin American case. Innovative social policies aimed at improving social protection have accompanied the benefits of positive economic growth in the region in the last two decades. Cash transfers, childcare and care for the old and education and human capital development programs are some of the main areas towards which different government programs have been directed from a national perspective. Yet an analysis of the role of urban policy in poverty reduction and inequality requires a deeper discussion on the impact of urban policies on local labor markets, income distribution, consumption possibilities and access to formal and good-quality jobs, which are all topics that go beyond the HCI's capacity to comparatively evaluate them, given the current availability of data at the city level.

Nevertheless, cities have played an important role in changes in the urban quality of life in Latin America, thanks to improvements in the provision of urban infrastructure such as mass transportation, access to healthcare providers (hospitals, clinics, ambulances), access to schools and childcare, access to parks and recreational spaces and residential infrastructure, all of which affect the urban population's access to economic agglomerations and more dynamic labor markets and improve their health and well-being. Strengthening local policies that aim to provide this type of service by local governments is very important to protect the vulnerable population and guarantee the permanence of recent achievements in relation to poverty.

According to the information analyzed for the period 1996–2014, Argentina was the country with the best performance in the Poverty dimension, with a change in the score between the final year and the base year of 31.43. This high change in the score is explained by an outstanding performance of the indicator of Urban Poverty Headcount, which showed a change of 60.29 points between the base year and the final year, and is the highest change in the countries of the region (for its part, the other complement indicator within the Poverty indicator, Infant Mortality, had modest behavior, with a change of 2.57 points). Progress in the Urban Poverty Headcount indicator is explained by a significant improvement in the percentage of the urban population classified as poor, from 35.9 percent of the urban population in 2001 to 4.7 percent in 2014.

This means that the urban population considered poor according to the national poverty line for Argentina decreased by 31.2 percent in that period, whereas the per capita GDP (PPP, constant international prices of 2011) in the country increased from $ 3,285 in 2002 – the lowest level in the entire review period – to $ 14,715 in 2013, according to data from the World Bank's WDI. The combination of the improvement in the Poverty indicator in relation to the economic performance of the country allowed for an HCI score showing significant improvement. The result for Argentina[19] is greater than the average for the region, a fact that has been recognized in various analyses of the regional context where the country stands out with respect to Chile, Peru and Bolivia.

The Dominican Republic, as previously mentioned, had the lowest performance in the Poverty dimension within the region, with a change of −9.67 points. This behavior is explained by a very low performance in the indicator of Urban Poverty Headcount, which varied by −21.87 points. The Dominican Republic was one of the few countries in the region that presented an increase in Urban Poverty Headcount rates. In 2000, the country had 23.7 percent of the urban population classified as poor, and this figure grew to 31.8 percent in 2014. In the same period, per capita GDP (PPP, constant international prices, 2013) grew from $2,233 in 1996 to $5,879 in 2013. Despite having improved per capita income levels and having one of the most dynamic economies in the region, the country had a poor performance in the HCI score. The HCI score in the Urban Poverty Headcount indicator went from 57.11 points for the base year to 35.24 in the final year.

The second indicator included in the poverty dimension, Infant Mortality, represents the infant mortality rate for children under five years per 1,000 births. In the regional context, the indicator performed well according to the HCI score and presented a positive change equivalent to 3.63 points between the final year and the base year. Overall, the indicator shows how the region has improved the provision of services to the poorest in the period between 1996 and 2014, reducing the Infant Mortality rate by 69 percent between 1990 and 2015, from 54 deaths per 1,000 births in 1990 to 17 per 1,000 in 2015.

Bolivia was the highest achiever according to the performance of the Infant Mortality indicator, presenting a change in its HCI score of 9.59 points between the base year and the final year. Infant mortality went from a total of 88 deaths per 1,000 births in 1994 to 44 per 1,000 in 2014. According to the World Health Organization, Bolivia has performed well in different health indicators, thanks to better conditions and increased health services supply in urban areas (WHO, 2015). There is, however, a large difference in the distribution of improved health services. Urban areas have benefited the most from government efforts, which is why these areas have been the main drivers of improving indicators.

Although we outlined results that correspond to the general features regarding poverty in the region, it is important to recognize that poverty reduction has different patterns in each country, and the type of protection systems and social policies adopted also vary across the region. However, the main trend in Latin America and the Caribbean was an improvement rather than a reduction of social protection systems and poverty alleviation programs, a fact that marks a significant difference from other regions in the world (Ocampo and Gómez-Arteaga, 2016: 14). The same can be said of the provision of urban infrastructure – the Residential Infrastructure dimension for Latin America had a positive variation in the HCI score between 1996 and 2014 of 2.9 points – and urban transportation in the region, which accounts for better access to basic services and has steadily grown, together with GDP, but still lags behind urbanization growth trends.

The region now faces an important challenge due to slowing economic growth and even higher urbanization trends. Despite the improvement in the provision of basic services during the period analyzed by the HCI, Latin American cities still face important challenges linked to informal housing and the spatial segregation of the urban poor. Ongoing disequilibria of housing supply and demand that lead to high levels of informal housing, a very high proportion of the urban population – 77 percent – that does not have access to safe sanitation and high rural–urban migration, which puts pressure on labor markets, prove how relevant and adequate an urban agenda is for the region (Muggah, 2018).

The great advance in poverty in Latin America and the Caribbean was mainly due to an appropriate approach to social policy from a national perspective:

> In addition to favorable external conditions (high commodity prices and broad access to External funding), progress during this "golden social decade" can be attributed to the creation of stronger and more innovative Welfare States. New forms of social protection have emerged in the region, including universal basic pensions with a non-contributory component such as the ones in Argentina, Bolivia, Brazil and Chile; a universal health system such as the one in Colombia; the expansion of contributory social security in Ecuador and Uruguay; the mono-tributary schemes in Uruguay for microenterprises and self-employed workers; and the growing popularity of cash transfer programs that began in Brazil and Mexico as small focalized programs, a model further expanded to include universal transfers such as the benefits and allowances for each child in Argentina.
>
> (Ocampo and Gómez-Arteaga, 2016: 1)

Despite these important achievements at the national level, governments still need to address the discussion on the role of cities in preserving socioeconomic sustainability and their fiscal responsibility and independence in order to implement social programs that are targeted to specific needy populations and communities.

Gender: one of the areas of greatest progress

The second-best performing dimension for Latin American and the Caribbean, according to the HCI, was Gender. This dimension showed a positive change in the average score for the final year of 4.5 points. The result is due to an outstanding performance in the indicator of Female Tertiary Enrollment, an indicator that showed a change of 24.19 points between 1996 and 2014 according to the HCI. The region also had a positive performance in the Maternal Mortality indicator, which improved 2.06 points in the average HCI for the region. Finally, the Female Employment in Non-Agricultural Sector indicator had a negative performance, with a change in the score of −3.82 points.

Barbados had the best performance of the region in the Gender dimension, with a change in the score of 22.19 points. The island has been characterized by a high performance in the Human Development Index in comparative terms within the region and recently stood out with position of 24 in the Global Gender Gap Index of 2015. Within the HCI Gender dimension, the country had an excellent performance in the indicator of Maternal Mortality, from 98.64 points in the base year to 99.11 in the final year. The Female Tertiary Enrollment also showed a remarkable performance. According to the indicator, the proportion of women between the ages of 19 and 24 enrolled in tertiary education increased from 49 percent in 1999 to 90 percent in 2011, which translated into an HCI score that changed from 55.97 to 98.51 points, an outstanding variation of 42.54 points. Finally, the Female Employment in Non-Agricultural Sector indicator also showed a positive change and the highest for the region, with a variation in the score from 74.65 in 1996 to 98.4 in 2013, an increase of 23.56 points.

Education is one of the leading areas towards gender equality in Barbados. There is a higher educational performance of women compared to men, and since 1993 there has been a higher admission of women than men to higher education institutions. Although there are slightly more men than women who complete formal education at the secondary level, on average, women and girls are reaching higher levels within the educational system (mainly university) than boys and men.

The outstanding result in the indicator of Female Employment in Non-Agricultural Sector for Barbados can be explained by the improvement in the educational level of women, which allowed for changes in the distribution of occupations between men and women. The country is an excellent example of how continuity in gender policies can lead to good performance in relevant indicators. Although there is a high gender differentiation in occupations, women have gained greater participation in technical occupations. The male/female ratio in these occupations declined from 2.1 to 1.08 between 1996 and 2012. This ratio has also fallen among legislative and administrative occupations, going from 1.49 to 1.08 between 1996 and 2002[20] (Ibid:10). The results described here highlight the scores for this indicator within the HCI and show how in Barbados the participation of women in non-agricultural jobs, usually located in urban areas, has increased.

Chile, for its part, had the best performance in Female Tertiary Enrollment. This indicator showed a variation of 56.07 points between 1996 and 2014. In 1996, 23 percent of the female population between 19 and 24 years old was enrolled in tertiary education. By 2013 this proportion had risen to 88 percent. This change in the proportion of women registered in higher education programs determined a score, according to the level of GDP per capita for the country, of 31.93 points in 1996 and of 88 points in 2014. The indicator shows how an increasing number of women entered higher education in the period of analysis, demonstrating a positive impact of the government policies focused on expanding the coverage. Although policies were defined without a specific differential approach, the results have been marked mainly by greater coverage and participation of women within that educational level.

According to the Organisation for Economic Co-operation and Development (OECD), a high reduction in the educational gap is observed in Chile over the generations. In Chile, like in most of the countries that belong to this organization, among the older generations (55 to 64 years), tertiary education is higher in men, reaching 23 percent, whereas women reached 20 percent. In younger generations (between 25 and 34 years), however, the gap was reduced to only one percentage point among those with tertiary education, with 42 percent of men reaching this level and 41 percent of women (OECD, 2013).

Bolivia had the lowest performance in the Gender dimension, with a declining HCI score of −12.84. The country performed positively in the Maternal Mortality indicator, a result that reflects the efforts to improve health coverage as described before for the case of Infant Mortality. This indicator showed had a change of 8.27 points. However, *Female Employment in Non-Agricultural Sector* had a remarkably low performance due to a change of −33.97 points between the final and the initial scores. The most recent low score is a result of a significant fall in the level of female employment in the non-agricultural sectors, which mainly measures employment levels in the manufacturing and service sectors, commonly located in urban areas. In 1996 95.9 percent of the total level of female employment was outside the agricultural sector, but by 2008 this level of employment fell to 65.2 percent, indicating a strong shift in the female labor force between the non-agricultural and agricultural sectors.

The persistent inequality in access to employment in Bolivia has been recognized by both nongovernmental organizations and official entities in charge of measuring employment. The government recently implemented several programs aimed at reducing discriminatory practices in the labor market, while recognizing that certain cultural patterns make it difficult for women to enter the labor market.[21]

Decent employment in the face of economic slowdown

The indicators that make up the Employment dimension for Latin America and the Caribbean present a behavior that reflects the constant tension between policies that seek to improve the quality of employment and the cyclical effects of the economy. On the one hand, the indicator of Formal Employment showed a change in the score between the base year and the final year of −5.62 points, and on the other *Non-Vulnerable Employment* showed a change of −7.8. The low performance of the two indicators shows that despite the progress made in terms of poverty and inequality, a great challenge persists in the region regarding the quality of employment and stable working conditions.

According to the International Labor Organization (ILO), the effects of the recent economic slowdown on labor markets are evident. According to the "Panorama Laboral 2015" report for Latin America and the Caribbean, the unemployment rate in the region has increased (they estimate that it will increase from 6.2 percent to 6.7 percent between 2014 and 2015) and the trend in wage growth has reversed, with important implications for household incomes in the region (ILO, 2015: 29). Similarly, employment quality measures have deteriorated, explaining the performance of employment indicators within the HCI. After a period of growth in salaried work, mainly between 2008 and 2012 (ILO, 2015: 45), self-employment (nonsalaried) grew faster than salaried employment in 2014, which interrupted the trend observed in previous years (ILO, 2015: 47). At the same time, there has been an increase in the rates of informality in the region because of less access to jobs with social protection coverage, while the growth of real average wages has also fallen significantly: in 2013 grew 1.1 percent and in 2014 only 0.3 percent (ILO, 2015: 41).

In this way, the results in the HCI Employment dimension for the region represent an important call to protect the sources of employment and income of households and sources of insurance, such as social protection and health systems.

Institutional capacity: the main challenge in the region

For Latin America and the Caribbean, the Institutional Capacity dimension incorporated in the HCI, which was the lowest-performing dimension according to the change in the average score between the base year and the final year, was −13.16 points. The inclusion of the Institutional Capacity dimension within the composite index seeks to capture, through its indicators Government Effectiveness and Quality of Government, civil society's perception of government performance in terms of the formulation and implementation of public policies. These two measures were incorporated in the index in order to follow up on the level of compliance with the commitments and degree of development of an institutional framework that would guide the implementation of the NUA defined in Habitat II.

The Latin American and Caribbean region performed poorly on the average score of these two indicators, especially in the Quality of Government indicator. The Government Effectiveness indicator changed from −8.15 points, from an average score of 66.73 points in the base year, to 58.57 points in the final year. For its part, the score in the Quality of Government indicator went from 60.81 points in the average score for the base year to 42.5 points in the final year, which led to a change of −18.3 points. This shows a high deterioration in performance. By analyzing countries' scores one by one, we found that some countries in particular had a negative impact on the average score of the region, as they obtained high negative changes in their scores, whereas the countries with a positive performance presented changes of smaller magnitude.

In the case of the Quality of Government indicator, Belize was the country with the lowest performance. The change in the score for this Central American country was −39.82 points, going from 89.55 points in the base year to 49.72 points in the final year. The performance in the indicator reflects a poor perception about the effectiveness of the government, possibly as a consequence of the low levels of investment in infrastructure and provision of basic services derived from the high rates of corruption. The World Bank's Doing Business Index, which measures the perception of businessmen and investors on the country's business climate, also has a low score attributed to institutional barriers, high levels of corruption and unnecessary bureaucratic procedures imposed on employers. These results were indicated in the most recent Doing Business Report of 2016, in which the country ranked 120th out of 183 according to this index.

Venezuela was the country with the highest deterioration in the performance in the indicator of Quality of Government according to the change in the score between the base year and the final year. In 1996, according to the HCI, the country had a score of 58.23 points in the indicator; in 2012, the year of the last available information, the score was 7.47 points. The total change in the Quality of Government score was −50.76 points, indicating a deep deterioration in the indicator.

Finally, it is important to highlight those countries with outstanding performance within the Institutional Capacity dimension. Santa Lucia was the country with the best performance in the dimension, in which it presented a variation of 7.59 points in the HCI. El Salvador presented the best performance in the indicator of Government Effectiveness, with a change of 17.87 points, and Panama was the country with the best performance in the Quality of Government indicator, with a change of 5.81 points between the final year and the base year.

Conclusions

According to the composite HCI results, the Latin American and Caribbean region did not achieve the expected performance followed by the commitments established in the NUA of Habitat II. Although some countries made important progress, as in the case of Uruguay, El Salvador and Argentina, most of the countries performed very poorly, and even a high proportion had a significant setback.

In 1996, during the Habitat II conference, the region was facing a very different political, social and economic reality than that in 2016, before Habitat III. Twenty years ago, Latin America and the Caribbean faced major social challenges and was the second poorest region in the world after sub-Saharan Africa. Urban Poverty Headcount was framed by important levels of informality. The states faced limited capacity to meet the needs of the population in terms of public services, health and social protection, among others. A more conscious approach to the role of the state in the impact on the quality of life of the population, as well as the guarantee of adequate access to some of the most pressing social services, have been decisive for the region's advancement in the most relevant social indicators. Yet there is still a lack of coordination between national and urban policy, and cities still face most of the challenges without having enough policy instruments to directly address them. Today Latin America faces a different reality in terms of progress in the urban development agenda. However, these advances are the result of a set of policies defined from the national level for the entire population and do not come from an understanding of the dynamics of urban areas or from instruments derived from the commitments assumed within the Habitat II agenda.

As we pointed out in this quantitative survey, social progress does not depend only on good economic performance – economic growth for the last 20 years was not the highest – but on institutional arrangements as well. Good economic performance must be accompanied by a high degree of political commitment to fulfill the proposed goals and a clear understanding of its long-term effects. The region performed better than expected given its level of income in indicators related to poverty, gender, sustainability and residential infrastructure, areas where there is an incremental pattern of policies, but still faces major challenges in terms of employment and institutional capacity. Both advances and challenges were analyzed here from a general national perspective, but we still have to consider that their effects in rural and urban areas still need to be seen in a differentiated way. In this sense, saying we are still in debt with an adequate urban policy is as valid as saying that we still lack an adequate measurement and evaluation of urban practice.

Although the results indicated by the HCI reflect a number of observations on the development patterns of the region over the last 20 years, it should be emphasized that the greatest concern, and for which the index was implemented, is given by the countries' capacity to follow through with the commitments defined in the urban agendas. In that sense, the HCI is a means of drawing attention to the need for more appropriate instruments to follow up on the commitments derived from these agreements. For the most part, the measurements presented here derive from data at national level that do not conform to the diversity and specificity of Latin American cities. The results of the quantitative analysis described here demonstrate that the effective reach of such commitments is low and that adequate measurement and monitoring instruments are still required at the urban level, the subject of the next chapter. This situation is due to a poor definition of the urban agenda as an instrument of policy, which should be one of the main challenges of the Habitat III NUA.

Notes

1 This section, which describes the HCI and its methodology, is based on the chapter "The Habitat Commitment Index", included in the book "The Habitat Commitment Project: Assessing the Past for a Better Urban Future", published in July 2016 by The New School and the Global Urban Futures Project and whose authors are Michael Cohen (GUFP Director), Lena Simet (GUFP Coordinator) and Bart Orr (lead author), with the collaboration of Crista Carter, Melissa De la Cruz, Martha Susana Jaimes, Younghyun Kim, David López García and Justin Roberts. The launch and official presentation of the book were made during the third preparatory conference in Surabaya, Indonesia, in July 2016. The full book is available in English at www.globalurban futures.org/#!habitat-commitment- Project-booklet / kzh9m.

2 The methodology used for the construction of the HCI is described in the second chapter of the book entitled "Measuring Social and Economic Rights: The SERF Index Approach". Following this methodology, to measure the degree to which countries are meeting their commitments, the degree of fulfillment for each indicator was scored according to each given level of resource availability – resource levels are measured through per capita GDP as an approximation to economic capacity. Benchmarks should reflect what is feasible when a country allocates the maximum resources available to meet commitments and uses the most effective means to do so. Based on the long-term "production frontiers" framework used in economics, achievement possibilities frontiers (APFs) were built, representing the value of a given indicator versus available resources for all countries and then identifying the outer boundary of the set. Just as a frontier of production possibilities shows the maximum possible production of a good for any level of investment of a given resource, the APF reveals how well a country can perform in accordance with the commitments of the urban agenda, given a level of resources. A specific description of the HCI methodology can be found at www.globalurbanfutures. org/#!habitat-commitment-index/hs5a2.

3 This is the actual text for each of the commitments described in the Habitat Agenda contained in the declaration. The full version of the Istanbul Declaration can be found at the following link (accessed on May 16, 2017): www.un.org/ga/Istanbul+5/declaration.htm

4 The most urbanized region in the world is North America, with 81.47 percent of its population concentrated in urban areas. Latin America and the Caribbean is second

(79.61 percent), followed in order, according to World Bank data for 2014, Europe and Central Asia (70.66 percent), Middle East and North Africa (63.74 percent), East Asia and the Pacific (55.72 percent), sub-Saharan Africa (37.23 percent) and South Asia (32.6 percent). These calculations are based on information from the World Development Indicators (WDI) of the World Bank.

5 Author's calculations based on regional GDP growth data from the WDI of the World Bank.

6 State-led industrialization is a term proposed by Ocampo (2012) in exchange for "import substitution".

7 Of the 41 countries that make up the region, 29 were included in the index according to data availability. The minimum cut was 7 indicators out of a total of 15. Most of the Caribbean islands were excluded because they did not have enough information. The countries included in the analysis for Latin America and the Caribbean are Argentina, Bahamas, Barbados, Belize, Bolivia, Brazil, Chile, Colombia, Costa Rica, Cuba, Ecuador, El Salvador, Grenada, Guatemala, Guyana, Haiti, Jamaica, Mexico, Nicaragua, Panama, Paraguay, Peru, Dominican Republic, St. Lucia, Suriname, Trinidad and Tobago, Uruguay and Venezuela.

8 The HCI was calculated for the base year (1996) and the final year (2014) for all countries in the world, with a total sample of 169 countries out of the 217 that make up the WDI from the World Bank. Within the study, the main analyses are made according to the change between the final year and the base year of the indicator, whose score is derived from the methodology defined for the HCI (this methodology was described in the initial part of this chapter). The change between the base year and the final year is used as a measure of progress in the indicators.

9 For more information on the projects focused on water and sanitation in Uruguay, access the following link where you will find investment projects and technical assistance, as well as the specificities of the agreement with the World Bank (consulted on 02 August 2016): http://web.worldbank.org/WBSITE/EXTERNAL/NEWS/0,,cont entMDK:22497464~pagePK:64257043~piPK:437376~theSitePK:4607,00.html

10 According to figures from the World Bank, in 2014 Uruguay's total population was 3.4 million.

11 In a recent World Bank country report, the authors point out that Uruguay has the highest percentage of population classified as middle class within the region. The report also highlights the excellent performance in other indexes such as the Human Development Index, the Human Opportunity Index and the Index of Economic Freedom. For more information see (accessed August 2, 2016): www.worldbank.org/en/country/ uruguay/overview

12 According to the International Monetary Fund (IMF), "the little impact of economic growth on poverty levels in the Dominican Republic is worrying. According to official estimates and using the Bank's methodology, poverty levels in 2010 were the same as in 1990. According to the most recent report on the Millennium Development Goals (MDGs) prepared by the national government in collaboration with UNDP, it is estimated that the country will not be able to meet MDG 1 – to reduce by half, between 1990 and 2015, the proportion of people whose income is less than a dollar a day – as well as MDG2 – to achieve universal primary education by the year 2015".

13 This information comes from the Millennium Development Indicators – World Bank. The data were consulted in May 2016.

14 In Latin America, only nine countries had appropriate information for this indicator. This means that of the total of 29 countries that were included in the HCI, only 9 had information for the Urban Poverty indicator. These countries were Argentina, Bolivia, Colombia, Dominican Republic, Ecuador, Guatemala, Paraguay, Peru and Uruguay.

15 The UNDP report includes an assessment of the social achievements in the region in terms of the expected performance according to the per capita gross national income level. This is an exercise similar to that proposed by HCI, in the sense that the performance for the indicators taken by each index is controlled by the level of income as a

measure of the potential for progress. In the case of the HCI, the per capita GDP per country was used. The two indexes present similar results for indicators such as improved sanitation, improved water (water security), maternal mortality and infant mortality, which perform well or better than expected according to the category defined in the UNDP index. The indexes also coincide in the result for the indicator of vulnerable employment, which had an expected performance according to the category UNDP and a negative change, according to the valuation given by HCI.

16 The information presented shows the reduction in the incidence of poverty in the last decade and expresses how the concentration of the regional population advances towards the middle part of the income pyramid. Each monetary segment is expressed in terms of the amount of daily dollars per person. On the Gini coefficient the authors note that it is the lowest since the years prior to the industrialization of the region. Before the industrialization of 1880, the Gini coefficient stood at 0.464, and after the arrival of industrialization it reached even 0.6 in 1920 and remained at levels close to it until recent years, when it began to decline.

17 Chronic poverty is a relevant concept when it comes to understanding the factors that affect mobility. Although cyclical elements such as higher incomes have a high incidence in such mobility, other structural factors are very relevant when defining the permanence of mobility in time, as well as its process, especially when facing a change in the economic cycle. Vakis et al. consider three important determinants of chronic poverty: endowments, which include the individual's physical abilities and assets; the context, which includes markets, services in the environment, risk levels and the institutional framework; and the mental disposition of the individual, which includes aspirations and psychological well-being (Vakis et al., 2015: 10).

18 According to the definition of chronic poverty of the report referenced, it is found that in the region there is a high incidence in both rural and urban areas. The authors note that in five countries, Chile, Brazil, Mexico, Colombia and the Dominican Republic, the number of people in chronic poverty in urban areas surpasses the number in rural areas. In Brazil, there is a one-to-one relationship (Vakis et al., 2015: 15).

19 Argentina has been recognized for its excellent results in terms of poverty reduction in the region. The data for the urban poverty used in the HCI are derived from the WDIs that base this indicator on the data collected through the Permanent Household Survey (EPH) of Argentina. The EPH contains information on the variation of the prices of goods and services included in the consumer basket used to define the Consumer Price Index that measures inflation. The recent debate on the methodology implemented for the calculation of inflation in the country has led to the need to review the information collected through this survey. It is important to clarify that, if the data used to calculate the Consumer Price Index do not measure price variation accurately, indicators measuring poverty could be overestimated, given that poverty is measured by the purchasing power of a household income in accordance with the prices of consumer goods contained in the basket. In February 2016 the Argentine government declared a "statistical emergency" and the need to review some of the official indicators that measure the social and economic conditions of the population, suspending the publication of statistical data. For more information see (document consulted on June 30, 2016): https://aldiaargentina.microjuris.com/2016/01/08/decreto-552016-administracion-publica-declaran-en-estamento-de-emergencia-al -indec-y-al-sen /

20 Gender differentiation is more persistent among low-skilled occupations. There are 4.5 times more men than women in jobs related to crafts and heavy jobs, such as plant operators and machinery, and skilled agricultural workers. The gap between men and women in these occupations has even increased.

21 The information described here comes from the analysis from the official information on Bolivian labor market statistics. The calculations and further analysis are available at the following link (accessed August 31, 2016): www.ceicdata.com/en/blog/high-gender-discrimination-bolivia%E2%80%99s- labor market

Bibliography

Allen, C., and Maughan, J., (2016), *Country Gender Assessment (CGA): Barbados*, Caribbean Development Bank, Kingston.

Carneiro, F., Iwulska, A., Reyes, J., and Sánchez-Martín, M., (2015), *Resilient Growth, Persisting Inequality: Identifying Potential Factors Limiting Shared Prosperity in the Dominican Republic*, Caribbean Knowledge Series, World Bank, Washington.

Fukuda Parr, S., Lawson-Remer, T., and Randolph, S., (2015), *Fulfilling Social and Economic Rights*, Oxford University Press, Oxford.

Gray Molina, G., et al., (2016), *Multidimensional Progress: Welfare Beyond Income*, United Nations Development Program, New York.

International Labor Organization (ILO), (2013), *Growth, Employment and Social Cohesion in the Dominican Republic*, ILO, Geneva.

International Labor Organization (ILO), (2015), *Labor Overview 2015: Latin America and the Caribbean*, International Labor Organization, Lima. Available at: http://bit.ly/1M6CsxQ, Last accessed: February 8, 2016.

Muggah, R., (2018), "Latin America's Cities Are Ready to Take Off. But Their Infrastructure Is Failing Them", *World Urban Forum Blog*, Web. Available at: http://bit.ly/2Wxv0gZ

Ocampo, J. A., (2012), *The History and Challenges of Latin American Development*, United Nations Economic Commission for Latin America and the Caribbean-ECLAC, Santiago de Chile.

Ocampo, J. A. and Gómez-Arteaga, N., (2016), "Social Protection Systems in Latin America: An Assessment", ESS-Working Paper No. 52, ILO, Geneva.

Organization for Economic Cooperation and Development (OECD), (2013), *Country Note: Chile, Education at a Glance*, Web.

United Nations Development Program (UNDP), (2016), *Multidimensional Progress: Welfare Beyond Income*, Regional Human Development Report for Latin America and the Caribbean, UNDP, New York.

United Nations Human Settlements Program (UN Habitat), (2014), "Building More Equitable Cities: Public Policies for Inclusion in Latin America", *UN Habitat and Corporación Andina de Fomento CAF*, Web.

United Nations Secretariat, (2015), *The Millennium Development Goals Report*. Available at: www.un.org/millenniumgoals/2015_MDG_Report/pdf/MDG%202015%20rev%20 (July%201).pdf, Last accessed: February 8 2016.

Vakis, R., Rigolini, J., and Luchetti, L., (2015), *Left Behind: Chronic Poverty in Latin America and the Caribbean*, International Bank for Reconstruction and Development and The World Bank, Washington, DC.

World Health Organization (WHO), (2015), *Urban Health Profile: Bolivia*. Available at: http://bit.ly/2dpgUJh, Last Accessed: August 8 2016.

Ziccardi, A., (2008), *Processes of Urbanization of Poverty and New Forms of Social Exclusion*, Siglo XXI Editores, Bogotá.

10 From tiers to tears

Measuring city performance using the Habitat Commitment Index

Lena Simet

Introduction[1]

We live in a world of cities. According to the United Nations, the year 2007 was the turning point when for the first time more people were counted to live in cities than in rural areas (UN-Habitat, 2006). Following this "demographic milestone", the literature on the topic grew exponentially, and the historian Mike Davis (2006) from the University of California compared this event with the industrial revolution.

The rapid population increase in the 20th century and the urban growth since the 1950s are indisputably important phenomena. Numbers from the UN Population Division (2018) show that in 1950 30% of the world population lived in cities, in 2007 half did, and in 2060 this number is estimated to reach 68%. It is interesting to look at the annexes of such reports, which describe the data sources. These show that all data originate from national statistical offices of member states, which the UN is bound to use. This raises some important questions about the definition of cities. Are cities defined the same everywhere? Who is counted as an urban dweller and who as a rural dweller?

Despite attempts to set universal standards, countries have different definitions of cities. Some countries define cities by minimum population numbers; others use population density or administrative boundaries. In Kenya, for example, a city is defined as a place with more than 2,000 inhabitants. This threshold is 5,000 in India – with the qualification that half of the men must work in nonagricultural activities (Schmid-Kallert, 2017). China and Germany use population density to define cities. Based on these contrasting thresholds, many of the cities in Kenya and Germany would be classified as rural in China and India.

To complicate matters, who is counted as part of a city's population? Are inhabitants of the slums in Mumbai, Cape Town, or Nairobi included? What about people sleeping alongside train tracks in Jakarta, unregistered (non-*hukou*) migrant workers in Shenzhen, or those living in fenced and video-surveilled gated communities? Annexes of UN reports do not provide answers to these questions but raise concerns about misreporting and the completeness of information – with potentially significant consequences. Satterthwaite (2007) finds that skewed urban data have problematic ramifications in policy debates related to urban poverty, public health, and greenhouse gas emissions. Brenner and Schmid (2014) caution a misunderstanding of the "urban age" story, which they refer to as a statistical artifact, distorting labor markets, housing, education, and infrastructure development.

To address these imbalances and establish universal standards for development, UN member states adopted the 2030 Agenda in 2015. To stress the relevance of cities in implementing the agenda and to set a new vision for cities for the next 20 years, the New Urban Agenda (NUA) was adopted at the Habitat III conference in October 2016. The Global Taskforce of Local and Regional Governments (2017) calls the NUA "an indispensable framework for the achievement of the 2030 Agenda". However, in contrast to the Sustainable Development Goals (SDGs), the NUA provides little guidance on how to turn commitments into concrete actions or how to measure progress.

In preparation for Habitat III, the Global Urban Futures Project at The New School created the Habitat Commitment Index (HCI), a quantitative tool to assess the performance of countries and cities in global agendas to understand whether cities are likely to reach set targets and where they currently stand. The HCI also sought an answer to the question whether economically thriving places are more apt to achieve commitments and, if not, what factors improve urban well-being.

Most monitoring initiatives establish rankings based on absolute performance in a given indicator (see SDSN, 2017; or ODI, 2016). The results of such rankings are hardly surprising. The highest performers are often located in Europe or North America, followed by Asia or Latin America, with sub-Saharan Africa at the tail end. Further, such rankings do not give insight into *effort*. In 2016, Norway's coverage of improved infrastructure was three times that of Mali. Although this is interesting, it hides the effort Mali has made in the last decade in improving its coverage, especially in the light of the country's resources (Cohen et al., 2016). We argue that performance rankings are only meaningful when they include a qualifier that considers local capacity. Doing so, we find very different performance results than ordinary rankings do. We also find that economic growth does not automatically result in improved urban indicators. Urban India and China are prime examples of this.

The city-level HCI was not only confronted with conceptual questions such as "what defines a city". An even greater challenge was the lack of city-level data. Most global urban databases, including those of the UN or the World Bank, present urban data at the country level but not at the disaggregated, city scale. There are only a handful of city databases, generally part of political initiatives or centered on a particular topic such as transport or health (see Salud Urbana en America Latina (SALURBAL), Urban Health in Latin America, is a five-year project launched in April 2017 by Drexel University) or showcase processed data without an option to access the raw data due to confidentiality concerns (see the World Council on City Data or Siemens' Green City Index).

Ultimately, the HCI shows that at the current state of data, the SDGs and the NUA cannot be monitored across cities.

These reflections do not intend to question the trend of urbanization or the utility of global reports and statistics. Instead, this chapter demonstrates that indicators and measurement tools are often fuzzy. It is a call for more and better city data and a more careful use of statistics. After all, how do we know whether countries meet their commitments without having information?

This chapter is structured as follows. The second section briefly reviews the HCI, its methodology and data collection process. The third section focuses on city performance in four HCI indicators and examines city-level trends in inequality and greenhouse gas emissions. The fourth section returns to the question of urban data and implications for future global city-level analyses. The fifth section concludes the chapter.

The Habitat Commitment Index 2.0

The HCI is part of a larger research project to measure urban performance since the Habitat II conference in 1996.[2] This study was motivated by the belief that an NUA should be built on an analysis of what worked and what has not worked so that past mistakes would not be repeated. In the run-up to Habitat III, no such evaluation had been done, and many argued that to do so would be too time and resource intensive. The HCI showed that not only was such an assessment possible but that the results were in many ways unexpected. Other than anticipated, urban indicators did not improve at the same speed as economies grew, and there had been little urban progress since 1996, on average.[3]

The HCI is relevant because commitments are made at the country level. However, urban averages disregard the differences within a country. An urban average for the United States, for example, is not very telling about New York City's performance in the SDGs or Baltimore's advancements in meeting NUA commitments. To address this issue, post–Habitat III we shifted the focus from the country level to a city-level analysis, developing the "HCI 2.0". In doing so, we hope to tell a more complete story of urban progress and to contribute to SDG monitoring.

The HCI methodology: measuring performance, not outcomes

The HCI is a composite score of indicators relevant to urban well-being. It draws on the SERF methodology developed by Fukuda-Parr et al. (2015), which weights performance by GDP per capita.[4] The rationale of this methodology is that it makes little sense to compare countries at vastly different resource levels, such as Sweden and Togo, in providing access to improved sanitation, because Sweden's GDP per capita in 2016 was, with 44,004 USD about 30 times that of Togo, which amounted to just 1,363 USD in 2016 (World Bank Open Data, 2016). Instead, this methodology considers the historical achievement of countries at similar GDP levels, as, for example, Belize and Guatemala, countries with very different achievement levels despite similar GDP per capita of about 7,000 USD in 2016. Belize achieved an overall HCI score of 75.5, whereas Guatemala achieved a score of 64.8, with very little improvement since 1996.

The HCI is calculated using the Achievement Possibility Frontier (APF), which is created for each indicator, using all available historical data. Figure 10.1 is a graphic presentation of the APF, where each dot represents a country/city. The spread of the dots shows that at each resource level, the outcome indicator values vary greatly. The APF curve is constructed with the highest performer at each resource level. The HCI score is then calculated using the distance from the APF.[5]

In order for this methodology to work, a correlation between a given indicator and available resources is required. There is certainly a range of factors influencing available resources and the capacity of a city. Yet to this day there is a) very little research on how to measure local capacity and b) hardly any city data available for comparative purposes. Consequently, the city-level HCI uses city GDP per capita as a proxy for available resources.

HCI scores use a scale of 0 to 100. A score of 100 does not necessarily indicate 100% fulfillment of an indicator, but 100% of the maximum score is historically possible for a given per capita GDP.

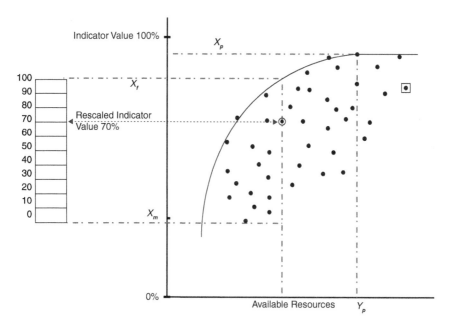

Rescaling Indicator Values
Source: Randolph, Prairie, and Stewart 2012, Figure 2.

Figure 10.1 The achievement possibility frontier

HCI 2.0 indicators, data sources, and a global city sample

Because the HCI 2.0 is set to assess city performance in the SDGs and the NUA, HCI indicators are based on the commitments and targets of both agendas. This resulted in a "wish-list" of 47 indicators across 11 dimensions, shown in Figure 10.2.

The country-level HCI study, presented in Chapter 8, mostly used indicators from development agencies (e.g. the United Nations and the World Bank), data that have already been collected and harmonized to allow for cross-country comparison. However, such data do not exist at the city level, at least not in a comprehensive fashion. The GUF therefore had to construct its own database for the HCI 2.0, surveying 53 data sources for a sample of 178 cities, for the years 2000–2016. Due to differences in the measurement of indicators across cities, 201 indicators and 38,000 data points were collected to meet the wish list.[6] Figure 10.3 shows the 178 cities included in the HCI 2.0 database.

Forty-eight percent of the collected data came from national governments, 23% from private institutions, 21% from intergovernmental institutions, 6% directly from local governments, and 1% from nongovernmental organizations (NGOs). Throughout this process, it became clear that cities across countries often use incomparable data collection methods. Moreover, many indicators did not correlate with GDP per capita. Of the 47 indicators included in the wish list, only 4 could be included in the HCI analysis. This stresses the need for future research for better proxies to measure local capacity. Of the four indicators, two are related to basic services (access to safe water and electricity) and two are socioeconomic indicators (infant/under-five mortality and employment rate).

Findings: how are cities doing?

This section is organized in two subsections. First, HCI scores on the indicators *access to electricity*, *access to safe water*, *under-five mortality*, and *employment* are presented, with a focus on cities in sub-Saharan Africa, a region often understudied and the region that has made the most notable advances since 2000 in all indicators except employment. The second section provides insight into ongoing research on intraurban inequality and the relationship between climate change and economic growth and urban density.

HCI scores for electricity, safe water, infant mortality, and employment

The compliance of the indicators *access to electricity*, *access to safe water*, *under-five mortality*, and *employment* with the HCI methodology indicates that, on average, cities with a higher GDP have greater access to electricity and safe water, have a higher employment rate, and have a lower under-five mortality. Although African cities have progressed the most in these four indicators since 2000, six

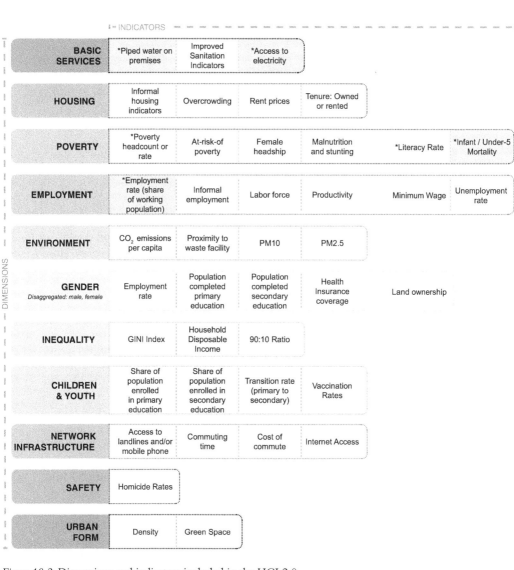

Figure 10.2 Dimensions and indicators included in the HCI 2.0

Figure 10.3 Map of HCI 2.0 city sample

of the seven cities with the highest scores in 2016 are located in Latin America. Belo Horizonte, Bogotá, Curitiba, and Medellín all had HCI scores of close to 100.

Kigali, Rwanda, is a positive example of a city that successfully translated economic growth into improved urban infrastructure and services. The city's GDP per capita grew from USD 1,900 in 2000 to USD 6,000 in 2015. Over the same time, access to electricity improved by 26 HCI scores, reaching 76 HCI points in 2015. This indicates that Kigali is currently performing at about 76% of what is achievable considering its GDP per capita. Kigali's scores in infant mortality have improved too, by more than 25 HCI points, reaching an HCI score of 84 in 2015.

Monrovia (Liberia) and Harare (Zimbabwe) performed less well than Kigali. Particularly alarming are the cities' declining HCI scores in electricity and safe water. Since 2000, electricity HCI scores declined by −6.5 and −26.8, respectively. During Liberia's 14-year civil war, which ended in 2003, the country's energy sector was the primary target for warlords. This left the capital Monrovia with scars still visible today (Lupick, 2012). Declines in safe water were even starker, with HCI scores decreasing by −56 in Monrovia and −71 in Harare. Harare's decline in performance can be attributed to a number of factors, including poor maintenance of the water infrastructure and Operation Murambatsvina, which displaced many residents, leading to overcrowding and a lack of access to water. The economic decline experienced between 2000 and 2009 further resulted in government mismanagement, corruption, and a disinvestment in infrastructure (Tibaijuka, 2005). The lack of access to safe water caused a cholera outbreak, described by The Zimbabwean (2009) as the worst in Africa in the past 15 years. Despite this worrisome decline, Harare was not the lowest performer in safe water in 2016. Lagos, Dodoma, and Bandung all had significantly lower water HCI scores, of less than 10.

In terms of employment, four African cities and one Southeast Asian city showed the largest improvements since 2000 (see Figure 10.4).[7] At the same time, African cities ranked among those with the largest drop in the employment HCI score, where despite increases in a city's GDP per capita employment levels declined.

Lusaka stands out as the city with the largest increase in the employment HCI since 2000. The city has been recognized as one of the fastest-developing cities in southern Africa, thanks to improving infrastructure and recent economic reforms, doubling its GDP per capita between 2000 and 2016. The city's employment rate increased from 30.6% in 2000 to 66.6% in 2016, which is reflected in an increase of the employment HCI score by 65 points. Antananarivo, in contrast, has slowly shifted from a labor-intensive agricultural, manufacturing, and textile industry to a less intensive, more technical production pattern, which has generated greater economic growth but lower employment. The city's employment rate declined from about 57.3% to 41.9% between 2000 and 2016, and GDP per capita increased from USD 4,948 to USD 5,419. Antananarivo's case is a classic example of jobless economic growth, where the economy grows while its level of employment decreases.

Other city trends: inequality and climate change[8]

The Gini coefficient, the most commonly used measure of inequality, and carbon dioxide emissions, one of the primary greenhouse gases associated with climate change, did not form a suitable APF to calculate the HCI. In the case of the Gini coefficient, there was no statistically significant correlation with GDP per capita, and in the case of the CO_2 emissions, there was an insufficient number of data points. Instead of presenting HCI scores, this subsection reflects on indicator-specific analyses, such as controlling performance by region or analyzing relationships with other urban and socioeconomic indicators. Although the findings in this section should not be considered conclusive, they intend to provide insight for future research.

Intraurban inequality

Cities are places of opportunity, as people can benefit from work and training, proximity to other people, and physical access to quality services that are important for well-being. Yet cities are often divided, producing exclusionary spaces and concentrating disadvantage. Crime rates are higher in cities that are more unequal, people in unequal cities are more likely to consider themselves unhappy, and inequality can impede local economic growth (Glaeser et al., 2009; Hsieh and Moretti, 2015). Furthermore, intergenerational mobility highly depends on local factors and could potentially be enhanced using place-based policies (Kline and Moretti, 2014; Chetty et al., 2014).

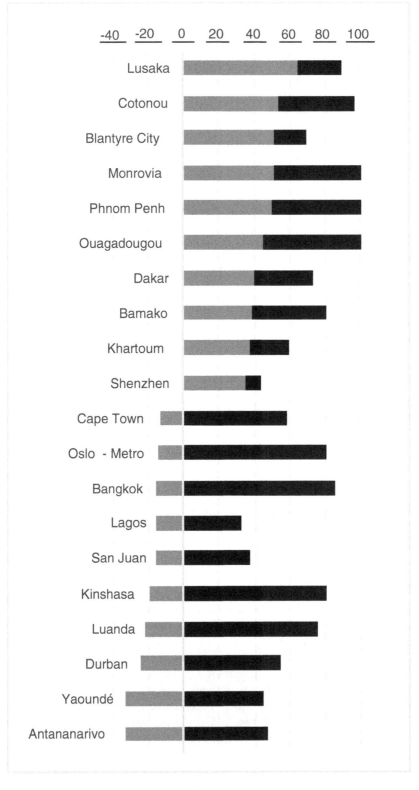

Figure 10.4 Change in the employment HCI score (2000–2016)

Although the missing correlation between GDP per capita and the Gini coefficient may seem surprising, it reflects a long-standing debate about the relationship between economic performance and inequality. Different theories reflect the diverging perceptions about economic systems, linked to political, social, and ideological perspectives. Conventional theories suggest that increases in inequality are correlated to higher growth (see Smith, 1937; Lewis, 1954; Kuznets, 1963) due to the savings and the incentives effects. Heterodox theories, on the contrary, emphasize that inequality may lead to credit constraints, which may result in poverty traps, harming growth (Easterly and Rebelo, 1993).

As Figure 10.5 shows, no city in our sample with GDP higher than USD 25,000 had a Gini coefficient larger than 0.5. Despite a missing correlation, this suggests an inverse relationship between GDP and the Gini. The great variation of inequality across African cities could be one explanatory factor for the lacking correlation. Consider the capital cities of Zimbabwe and Tanzania, for instance. Although both cities have similar income levels, Dodoma ranks among the cities with the lowest inequality (with a Gini of 0.3 – similar to Gothenburg or Helsinki), whereas Harare is the most unequal city in our sample (0.66).

In 2016, Astana (0.23) was the least unequal city in the sample. In Asia, Mumbai was the most unequal (0.58). In Europe, Belgrade had the highest inequality (0.46), Reykjavik the lowest (0.28). In the Americas,

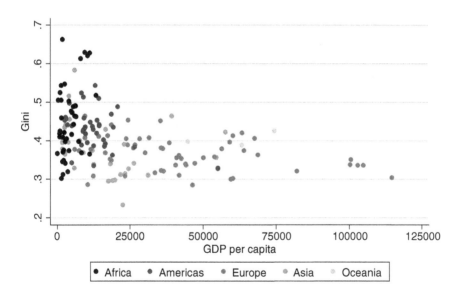

Figure 10.5 Intraurban inequality and GDP per capita, 2016

Source: Own graphic using Oxford Global Cities 2030 database.

Bogotá had the highest inequality levels (0.54), Vancouver the lowest (0.32). Five of the six most unequal cities were South African (with a Gini of about 0.62).

We also noticed that inequality patterns have shifted since 2000, as depicted in Figure 10.6. Although inequality increased slightly in European cities, it remained the region with the lowest inequality in 2016, with an average Gini of 0.37. The most surprising change was the decline in inequality across cities in the Americas. Although inequality in African cities declined too, the rate of decline was much faster in America's cities than in Africa, making Africa the region with the highest urban inequality in 2016.

Of the 178 cities included in the Gini analysis, 41% experienced declining inequality between 2000 and 2016, 31% had no significant change, and 28% reported increasing inequality. The cities with the largest increase are Bangui, Central African Republic (+0.15); Delhi, India (+14); Lomé, Togo (+0.12); Sofia, Bulgaria (+0.11); Tirana, Albania (+0.10); and Bhilai Nagar, India (+0.10). On the contrary, Ouagadougou, Burkina Faso, had the most notable decline in inequality, with a drop of 0.28 Gini points. Moscow, Russia; Bamako, Mali; Freetown, Sierra Leone; Luanda, Angola; and La Paz, Bolivia, also had large declines, ranging between 0.12 and 0.17 Gini points.

The stark differences of income inequality in cities within regions and countries reaffirms the importance of local leadership, urban policy, and practice. It further suggests the importance of studying and analyzing inequality, not only national inequality but at the local scale too.

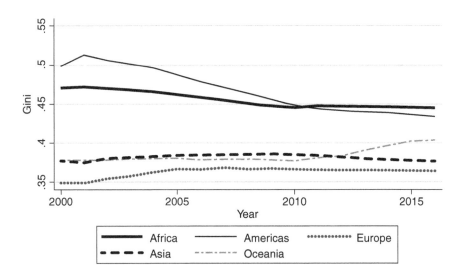

Figure 10.6 Intraurban inequality across regions over time (2000–2016)

Source: Own graphic using Oxford Global Cities 2030 database.

Climate change[9]

Carbon dioxide (CO_2), one of the primary greenhouse gases associated with climate change, has been rising since pre-industrial times (IPCC, 2014). In 2016, measurements of atmospheric CO_2 concentrations reached 400 ppm, the highest level that has ever been recorded. CO_2 levels are projected to increase further, potentially raising temperatures above 3° C by 2050 – endangering food supplies and causing significant loss of life and damage to property (Jones, 2017). CO_2 emissions are particularly relevant to assessing urban performance, as cities are both the primary producers of CO_2, accounting for 70% of global emissions, and are often most at risk, with around 90% of urban areas located on coastlines (C40, 2018).

Our data indicate that richer cities tend to have higher CO_2 emissions. This mirrors known national-level trends for emissions to increase as countries industrialize and urbanize. According to Oxfam (Gore, 2015), an average person among the richest 1% of the global population emits 175 times more carbon than the average person in the poorest 10% of the global population.

Although our data are limited in both number of cities and time span, they show no indication of what has been referred to as an "environmental Kuznets curve" – the hypothesis that environmental indicators decline along with economic development until a certain point, at which the relationship reverses. Such a relationship has been shown related to other pollutants, such as sulfur dioxide, which rose sharply in industrialized countries prior to declining after regulatory changes (Jaunky, 2011). Although some authors have reported evidence of a CO_2 Kuznets curve at the national level, our analysis seems to support findings indicating that, thus far, CO_2 emissions have not declined with economic development, but may instead stabilize.

The relationship between CO_2 and economic development seems logical – the higher productivity of urban areas requires more energy, as does the resulting high consumption. It is also reasonable to expect that urban density reduces transportation needs, resulting in less emissions. This is true, although the relationship between CO_2 and urban density is weaker than that between CO_2 and income. The low levels of per capita carbon emissions in Marrakech (low density) and Dar Es Salaam (high density) suggest that the level of economic development is more important in determining the level of carbon emissions of a city than density, but that density becomes an increasingly more influential factor as cities become wealthier. It may therefore be considered an important strategy for mitigating rising emissions with economic development. Our data also suggest that compact cities emit less CO_2 than sprawling cities.

In conclusion, economic growth is positively correlated with rising CO_2 emissions – a finding that is troublesome for the prospects of long-term climate change mitigation. Although an important factor, the level of economic development of a city does not in and of itself predict environmental outcomes, and factors such as urban form can be influential. Also, as the cities with the highest levels of emissions are also the wealthiest with the most resources to invest in carbon reduction and mitigation strategies, one can remain hopeful.

Urban data and difficulties in monitoring the SDGs

Perhaps the most significant finding of the HCI 2.0 is the inadequacy and lack of city-level data. Using concrete examples, this section highlights data problems we identified, concluding that with the existing data, a global assessment and monitoring of the SDGs at the city level cannot be done. Monitoring the SDGs in cities will require improvements in the capacity to produce, organize, coordinate, and analyze data. Nontraditional or unofficial sources of data (e.g. produced by communities or big data) could be useful to fill gaps. A key challenge ahead is how to incorporate these diverse sources of data into a SDGs' performance monitoring framework.

Matching city boundaries

Each country has its own method of defining a city and its boundaries. Criteria for defining cities range from population size and density, functional or historic norms such as urban functions, to being a recipient of national urban policy funds or having received city rights through a charter. This is problematic, as it undermines the comparability, and thus the credibility, of comparative city analyses. More importantly, it will affect the monitoring of the SDGs and the NUA. To overcome the limitations of comparing national statistics, the European Commission (Kotzeva and Brandmüller, 2016) launched a study measuring urban areas using geospatial technology. The results suggest that our world is much more urban than the UN Population Division estimates. According to this methodology, the world is already 84% urban, and Africa and Asia are not 40% and 50% urban, but closer to 80% and 90%, respectively. This new approach, however, was received with skepticism (see Angel et al., 2018). The low population density threshold used may have mistaken areas that are agricultural or small villages in proximity to cities as urban.

As disputes about the most accurate definition of urban areas and their thresholds continue, about two-thirds of all countries use an administrative definition to classify urban areas, often with an additional element such as population size, density, or economic function. Bhutan, for example, requires a particularly long list of criteria to be met; four of the five following conditions must be fulfilled for a settlement to be considered urban: a) it must have a minimum of 1,500 inhabitants, b) a minimum population density of 1,000 persons per km^2, c) >50% of the population should be employed in nonprimary economic activities, d) the spatial expansion should surpass 1.5 km^2, and e) it should have economic potential for future growth. Other countries are less stringent (UN-Habitat, 2018). In Denmark or Iceland, any settlement with more than 200 inhabitants is classified as urban. Although this low population threshold makes sense in Iceland (with a total population of 334,000), it is less applicable in highly populated countries such as Nigeria or Japan, where cities start at 20,000 or 50,000 inhabitants, respectively.[10] Other countries use population density to differentiate between urban and rural. Here, too, stark differences can be noted. Whereas in Germany settlements with more than 150 persons per km^2 are defined as urban, China sets the threshold at 1,500 persons (ibid). According to estimates by New York University's Urban Expansion Project, 387 cities of more than 100,000 people are not officially classified as such by the Chinese government.

Urban data are also shaped by different concepts of city boundaries. Whereas some countries measure the city proper, others collect data for urban agglomerations or metropolitan areas. Although each concept has its merits, they could not be more different in the method of analysis and territorial scale. The city proper is associated with the political and administrative or historical part of a city, whereas urban agglomerations regard the contiguous territory inhabited at urban density levels without considering administrative boundaries. Metropolitan areas are usually associated with conurbation, representing a densely populated urban core and less populated surrounding territories, encompassing multiple jurisdictions, municipalities, and even satellite towns.

Nairobi demonstrates these different concepts particularly well. As depicted in Figure 10.7, Nairobi's urban extent (medium gray outline), has long

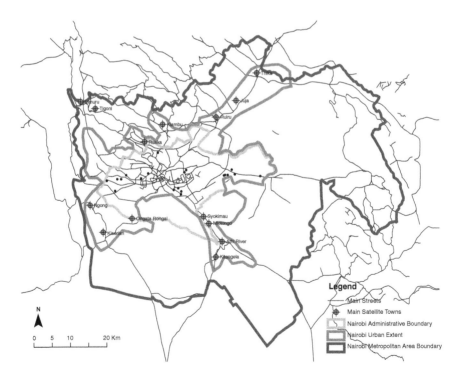

Figure 10.7 Defining Nairobi City using different concepts

surpassed the administrative boundary (light gray) of the city, expanding over several satellite towns. However, the urban extent has not (yet) reached the boundaries of the metropolitan area (dark gray). Hence, if we analyze Nairobi using data for the administrative or the metropolitan area, it would distort the city's actual population.

Matching conflicting criteria and concepts were part of the constant battle in the HCI 2.0 data collection process. It reminded us of puzzle solving, where the data points collected from different sources were supposed to be pieced together in a logical way – sometimes without success. We started with a list of 780 cities, for which we had gathered GDP data from the Oxford Economics Global Cities databank.[11] As we collected outcome, output, and process indicators for this sample, the list was eventually reduced by four times to 178 cities. This drop was driven by different reasons. In low-income countries and sub-Saharan Africa, data were often only available for capital or primary cities. Information on smaller urban areas and secondary cities, where an important share of the projected urban population growth will take place, is particularly scarce. As we aimed for a representative global sample, with a similar sample size across regions, we reduced the number of cities in Europe and the Americas accordingly.

The matching process itself required research and local expertise about a city's boundary and data collection criteria. It may not be evident to an "outsider" that Cebu City's GDP per capita, which is calculated by region and adjusted to the city boundary, matches provincial outcome data. Or that metropolitan Belo Horizonte, which includes 48 municipalities, has a statistical agency that collects data not only for each municipality but also the entire metro area. However, despite local expertise, the matching process failed in many cases. In San Salvador and Kingston, for example, outcome data was only available for the city proper, whereas GDP was measured at the metropolitan scale.

The fact that data are collected by several agencies and departments, using different city boundaries, presents a major challenge for monitoring the SDGs and the NUA at the city level. It also raises a conceptual question of the geographical unit that should be used for monitoring. Consider the case of Greater Jakarta, one of the largest urban agglomerations in the world, with more than 31 million inhabitants, spread across nine municipalities. The HCI 2.0 finds that official statistics are only available for DKI Jakarta, the center district, which is home to about 11 million people. How appropriate is a Jakarta score if we only measure the center district? What about the surrounding districts? As major businesses and high-income neighborhoods are located in the center, the score may be beautifying Jakarta by excluding information on poorer and struggling municipalities. This raises doubts concerning the validity of a partial, administrative score and suggests that the entire urban extent should be subject to a unified and overarching monitoring system.

Lacking universally comparable standards

Beyond the difficulty in establishing a shared definition of what is urban, target indicators differ across countries and cities too. Of course, it is important to allow for contextual difference. However, cross-city comparisons can be flawed if indicators are not comparable. Take the example of slums and informal settlements included in SDG indicator 11.1.1. Definitions vary by country, and data are hardly available beyond the national level, often because sample sizes are not big enough to be representative of informal settlements. Due to the lacking standards, the accuracy of global estimates on slum populations are highly contested. The population of Kibera, for example, Nairobi's largest slum, varies from 170,000 to 2.5 million, depending on the source (Kallergis, 2018). Due to these methodological challenges, the HCI 2.0 does not include an indicator on slums.

The difference in collecting and processing local data was also very apparent in the educational variables collected in the HCI. Most European cities collect data on educational attainment, which measures the highest level of education that individuals have completed. Asian and African cities, in contrast, collect information on completion and enrollment rates. Although all three indicators are relevant and provide interesting insights in educational attainment, they are not comparable.

The lack of universally comparable standards also appears in the classification of SDG indicators by the UN Statistical Commission. In 2016, the commission endorsed a global framework of 223 indicators to monitor progress in the SDGs, grouped in three tiers based on their level of methodological development and data availability (UN Statistics Commission, 2018).[12] Of the indicators perceived as relevant to cities (18 indicators), *only 4* are categorized as Tier I, as having a clear concept, methodology, and with data currently being collected.[13] Seven of the indicators, that is 39%, are currently not collected by half of the countries, and another seven indicators (39%) have no clear methodology and concept. As if this wasn't troublesome enough, the highly contested slum indicator 11.1.1 is among the four Tier I indicators.

Alternatives to official data

The lack of comparable data is in part due to the difficulty and cost of creating and implementing standardized assessments. New data systems can be cost-prohibitive for municipalities, especially those that are small in terms of population and economic resources. However, there are two promising sources that can complement official data: a) local community groups and b) big data.

Data produced by nongovernmental sources can play a crucial role in addressing data gaps at low cost or validating the quality of official statistics. Kallergis (2018) shows that Shack/Slum Dwellers International's (SDI's) Know Your City Campaign, for example, provides citywide slum data for more than 100 cities, tracking living conditions in slums through community conducted household surveys.[14] Community collected information is important for monitoring; moreover, it enhances accountability and opens the possibility for collaborative planning and development that creates alternatives to evictions.

There is also increased interest in leveraging big data for meeting the demands of SDG indicators (see Kharazi et al., 2016). Big data does not only refer to the volume, variety, and velocity of data; it also refers to how data are used and information is diffused. By means of big data and predictive analytics, local governments can track key indicators of neighborhood change in order to develop and implement place-based investments and policies. Urban big data can be generated from the Internet of Things (IoT), administrative records, individual or household-level survey data, geospatial imagery, commercial information, citizen science, and social media.

Conclusion

Three years after the adoption of the SDGs and two years after the agreement on the NUA, how to monitor and assess the performance of cities in achieving the SDGs and the NUA remains a debate rather than a concrete line of action. Although there is broad consensus on the need for targets and indicators, their exact definitions continue to be unclear and contested.

What is less debated is the methodology that should be used for monitoring these indicators and the utility of ordinary rankings. How insightful is a global ranking where European and North American cities are filling the positions of "high performers" while African cities are located in the lower ranks? The HCI offers an alternative approach, as it assesses performance in light of local capacity. Instead of comparing New York City with Accra, the HCI compares cities at similar resource levels to identify what is realistically attainable, considering what has been historically achieved at different levels of available resources. The question thus is not who performs better, but who uses its economic resources to further the common interest most.

As part of the city-level HCI, we created a database for 178 cities, with the objective of measuring the progress of cities in meeting SDG targets and NUA commitments. The HCI scores presented in this chapter show that African cities have made important progress in providing safe water and electricity, yet they still have a far way to go to reach full coverage. Our data also show that African cities have the greatest variations in inequality, with Harare being the most unequal and Dodoma ranking among the least unequal cities. In regard to climate change, we find that richer cities emit more CO_2 and that GDP per capita is a greater predictor of carbon emissions than density levels are. Although this may be a pessimistic prospect, it raises hope that rich cities will repurpose their wealth to mitigate future emissions, investing in green growth instead of furthering the prevailing trade-off between environmental protection and economic growth.

Unlike the country-level HCI, the city-level HCI could not rank cities by their performance in fulfilling global targets. Instead, we came to the dissatisfying and sobering conclusion that at the current state of data, a global comparative assessment of cities cannot be done. Data are often produced using different methods, criteria, and concepts that yield to incomparable results. Two further conclusions can be drawn from the HCI study: a) city-level data need to be better defined and improved and b) local government capacities in producing, collecting, and analyzing data will need to be strengthened. Big data or information generated by private firms could complement information from public sources. Community generated information has proven as an important addition too, as the case of SDI's Know Your City Campaign has demonstrated.

The HCI findings presented in this chapter should not be considered absolute or exhaustive. They offer a glimpse of an immense work that lies ahead, in harmonizing and growing local databases. These data are not only important for research purposes. One should not underestimate their effects on decisions at the local, regional, and international levels. The importance and urgency of better city-level databases can therefore not be stressed enough.

Notes

1 The findings presented in this chapter are based on research conducted over the course of two years by the Global Urban Futures Project: Bart Orr, Martha Susana Jaimes, Beryl Oranga, David Lopez Garcia, Melissa De la Cruz, Justin Roberts, Younghyun Kim, Juan Pablo Ripamonti, Fernando Bercovich, Ayesha Issadeen, and Belen Fodde. Special thanks to Michael Cohen for directing and continuously inspiring this wonderful team.

2 The Observatory on Latin America (OLA) and the Global Urban Futures Project (GUF) jointly designed the research project "The Habitat Commitment Project" in 2015.

3 Chapter 10 of this book describes the results of the country-level HCI study, with a focus on Latin America.

4 SERF stands for the Social and Economic Rights Fulfillment Index, which measures the performance of countries and subnational units on the fulfillment of economic and social rights obligations.

5 For details on how to calculate the city-level HCI see: (GUFP, 2018)

6 A data point refers to information on an indicator and a city for a particular point in time.

7 The employment rate is measured as the ratio of total employed (across six broad industries) to a country's working age population (ages 15 to 64).

8 The Global Urban Futures Project "HCI 2.0 Progress Report" (GUFP, 2018) presents further assessments of city-level indicators.

9 Special thanks to Bart Orr for his research and expertise on the topic of climate change and cities.

10 Nigeria's population was about 186 million in 2016, Japan's was 127 million (World Bank, 2016).

11 www.oxfordeconomics.com/microsites/databank

12 Tier I: Indicator is conceptually clear, has an internationally established methodology and standards are available, and data are regularly produced by at least 50% of the countries. Tier II: Concept and methodology are available, but data are not regularly produced by countries. Tier III: No internationally established methodology is available or methodology is being (or will be) developed or tested.

13 UN-Habitat identified these 18 indicators as relevant to measure city progress. Of these, 15 appear in SDG 11, 2 in SDG 1, and 1 in SDG 6. (SDG 1: End poverty in all its forms everywhere, SDG 6: Clean water and sanitation for all, and SDG11: Make cities and human settlements inclusive, safe, resilient and sustainable.)

14 In Monrovia, Liberia, for example, SDI complements official statistics on electricity. SDI surveys inquire access to electricity and the main source and type of connection. The HCI 2.0 database includes this information.

Bibliography

Angel, S., Lamson-Hall, P., Guerra, B., Liu, Y., Galarza, N., and Blei, A., (2018), "Our Not-So-Urban World", Working Paper No. 42, The Marron Institute of Urban Management, New York University.

Brenner, N. and Schmid, C., (2014), "The 'Urban Age' in Question", *International Journal of Urban and Regional Research*, 38:3, pp. 731–755.

C 40 Cities, (2018), *Why Cities? Cities Have the Power to Change the World*, Available at www. c40.org/why_cities, Last Accessed: September 11 2018.

Chetty, R., Hendren, N., Kline, P., and Saez, E., (2014), "Where Is the Land of Opportunity? The Geography of Intergenerational Mobility in the United States", *The Quarterly Journal of Economics*, 129:4, pp. 1553–1623.

Cohen, M., Orr, B., and Simet, L., (2016), *The Habitat Commitment Project*, The New School, New York.

Davis, M., (2006), "Planet of Slums", *New Perspectives Quarterly*, 23:2, pp. 6–11.

Easterly, W. and Rebelo, S., (1993), "Fiscal Policy and Economic Growth", *Journal of Monetary Economics*, 32:3, pp. 417–458.

Fukuda-Parr, S., Lawson-Remer, T., and Randolph, S., (2015), *Fulfilling Social and Economic Rights*, Oxford University Press, Oxford, USA.

Glaeser, E. L., Resseger, M., and Tobio, K., (2009), "Inequality in Cities", *Journal of Regional Science*, 49:4, pp. 617–646.

Global Taskforce of Local and Regional Governments, (2017), *The New Urban Agenda as an Indispensable Framework for the Achievement of the 2030 Agenda*, Available at: www.global-taskforce.org/new-urban-agenda-indispensable-framework-achievement-2030-agenda, Last Accessed: September 1 2018.

Global Urban Futures Project, (2018), *The Habitat Commitment Index 2.0: A Progress Report*, The New School, New York.

Gore, T., (2015), *Extreme Carbon Inequality: Why the Paris Climate Deal Must Put the Poorest, Lowest Emitting and Most Vulnerable People First*, OxFam Report.

Hsieh, C. T. and Moretti, E., (2015), "Why Do Cities Matter? Local Growth and Aggregate Growth", Kreisman Working Paper Series in Housing Law and Policy, 36.

IPCC, (2014), "Climate Change 2014: Synthesis Report", Contribution of Working Groups I, II and III to the Fifth Assessment Report of the Intergovernmental Panel on Climate Change.

Jaunky, V. C., (2011), "The CO2 Emissions-Income Nexus: Evidence from Rich Countries", *Energy Policy*, 39:3, pp. 1228–1240.

Jones, N., (2017), *How the World Passed a Carbon Threshold and Why It Matters*, Published at the Yale School of Forestry and Environmental Studies, New Haven.

Kallergis, A., (2018), *From Slums to Neighborhoods: Towards an Analytical Framework for Informal Settlements*, The New School, New York.

Kharrazi, A., Qin, H., and Zhang, Y., (2016), "Urban Big Data and Sustainable Development Goals: Challenges and Opportunities", *Sustainability*, 8:12, p. 1293.

Kline, P. and Moretti, E., (2014), "People, Places, and Public Policy: Some Simple Welfare Economics of Local Economic Development Programs", *Annual Review of Economics*, 6:1, pp. 629–662.

Kotzeva, M. M. and Brandmüller, T., (eds.), (2016), *Urban Europe: Statistics on Cities, Towns and Suburbs"* Publications Office of the European Union, Luxembourg.

Kuznets, S., (1963), "Quantitative Aspects of the Economic Growth of Nations: VIII. Distribution of Income by Size", *Economic Development and Cultural Change*, 11:2 (Part 2), pp. 1–80.

Lewis, W. A., (1954), "Economic Development with Unlimited Supplies of Labour", *The Manchester School*, 22:2, pp. 139–191.

Lucci, P., Khan, A., Hoy, C., and Bhatkal, T., (2016), *Projecting Progress: Are Cities on Track to Achieve the SDGs by 2030*, ODI, London.

Lupick, T., (2012), "Liberia's Long Wait to Turn on the Lights", *Al Jazeera*. Available at: www.aljazeera.com/indepth/features/2012/06/201261912122040806.html

OECD, (2018), *Divided Cities: Understanding Intra-Urban Inequalities*, OECD Publishing, Paris, https://doi.org/10.1787/9789264300385-en

Satterthwaite, D., (2007), *The Transition to a Predominantly Urban World and Its Underpinnings*, (No. 4), International Institute for Environment and Development (IIED), London.

Schmid-Kallert, E., (2017), *Magnet Stadt: Urbanisierung im Global Süden*, Bundeszentrale for Politische Bildung, Bonn.

SDSN, (2017), *SDG Index and Dashboard Report 2017: Global Responsibilities*, Bertelsmann Stiftung and Sustainable Development Solutions Network, New York.

Smith, A., (1937), "The Wealth of Nations: Modern Library", *New York*, 423.

Tibaijuka, A. K., (2005), *Report of the Fact-Finding Mission to Zimbabwe to Assess the Scope and Impact of Operation Murambatsvina*. United Nations Special Envoy on Human Settlements Issues in Zimbabwe, New York.

United Nations Human Settlement Program (UN-Habitat), (2006), *State of the World's Cities 2006/2007*, Earthscan, London.

United Nations Human Settlement Program (UN-Habitat), (2018), SDG Indicator Workshop during the HLPF at The New School, New York.

United Nation Population Division, (2018), *2018 Revision of World Urbanization Prospects*, UN Department of Economic and Social Affairs, New York.

United Nations Statistics Commission, (2018), *Tier Classification for Global SDG Indicators*. Available at: https://unstats.un.org/sdgs/iaeg-sdgs/tier-classification/

World Bank Open Data. Available at: https://data.worldbank.org/, Accessed 2016.

The Zimbabwean, (2009), "Cholera Outbreak in Zimbabwe, the Worst in Africa", *The Zimbabwean [Harare]*, 27 May 2009, Print.

11 Six countries and twenty years

A transversal reading of Latin American urban policy

María Carrizosa

This chapter puts forward "an implied look and a transversal reading" (Barbero, 2007) across six countries of the subcontinent, which amass a third of the Latin American population. The text groups in major themes the most relevant critiques repeated in the country chapters of this book. The central issues include the contradiction between housing policy and urban policy, the unchecked power of real estate developers, the fragility of the achievements of the Habitat agenda, and legal achievements that lack sufficient implementation. It also includes reflections on the acute weaknesses of the broad decentralization trend in Latin America, the growing inequality in the region, and the relative irrelevance of United Nations Habitat declarations. The chapter concludes with brief comments on what should be new forms of urban practice in the coming decades.

This is a broad but necessarily limited perspective. Any transversal reading runs the risk of losing sight of the critical specificity of each case, thus sacrificing precision in order to broaden the horizon. The effort here is to provide a qualitative second-level analysis that strives to find a common ground across the six country studies and to analytically comment on their assessments. The objective is to highlight ideas that help recognize achievements and setbacks and inform principles based on lessons from "worst practices" – rather than "best practices" – that may contribute to the elaboration of future regional work plans. We believe that better urban futures depend on acute, responsible, and independent critiques, which is precisely what we want to contribute to.

Housing policy against urban policy

The first alarming reflection that this book offers is that housing policy has supplanted urban policy. Instead of being a component of urban policy, housing policy has not only neglected urban policy but has run against its primary intention: to promote sustainable territorial development and to improve the living conditions of the population. A paradigmatic case of this situation is Chile, where for thirteen years there was no national policy for urban development (Rodríguez and Rodríguez, this volume). What existed was a "successful" housing construction policy, which between Habitat II and Habitat III managed to produce more than 3.2 million units, reducing the quantitative deficit to a single digit.

Nonetheless, over the years Chile realized that this "triumph" came at a very high cost. What good is it for the poor to have new homes in places so peripheral that it is too expensive to live in them? What good is it to build housing projects without complementary urban services, without schools, parks, or public transportation? Very little. This is the genesis of the "houses without people" phenomenon, where people eloquently denounce failures in public policy by "voting with their feet." The turning point from success to the failure of the housing policy was the year 2013, when the national government began a government-led demolition program to tear down thousands of social housing units that, because of their poor quality, were uninhabitable (Rodríguez and Rodríguez, this volume). The televised demolition of Pruitt-Igoe had already taught this lesson to American housing experts thirty years ago. One can only hope that learning this experience from a sister country can make it easier for other countries in Latin America to learn this lesson.

Unfortunately, the Chilean history is far from being an atypical case. As Ziccardi pointedly states, although there is much of housing policy in Mexico (or financing policy for the construction of new homes to be more precise), there has been no real federal urban policy in the last forty years. In Mexico, the Chilean phenomenon of "people without houses and houses without people" (Rodríguez and Rodríguez, this volume) and the case of "lots of housing and little city" (Ziccardi, this volume) is repeating itself on an even larger scale. If in Chile there are 1 million unoccupied subsidized housing units, in Mexico there are 5 million. Estimates for Brazil are starker, mentioning 6 million vacant units. Indeed, the massive construction of cheap housing is the result of ambitious national policies. But the lesson that these governments are learning is that housing policy cannot dictate urban policy, but rather vice versa. When housing policy supplants urban policy, it betrays its potential to serve as social policy. Housing can be a vehicle of social development for low-income populations, but not any type of housing can help; it must be of good quality – it must be *adequate* housing.

Over the last twenty years Latin America has suffered from the fact that without a functioning urban policy, government action can worsen the existing patterns of urbanization (Fernandes, this volume). It is indeed perverse that government action does not help create a better quality of life for all citizens, but on the contrary works to amplify territorial inequalities. Hence, it is urgent to reverse such a perverse pattern (Ziccardi, this volume). The contradiction between housing policy and urban policy reveals the weakened role of the public – the commons – in urban governance and a tendency for the general public to be subordinated to the interests of private developers, as discussed next.

The power of private developers

The bold policies of mass construction of social housing described earlier are, to a large extent, based on a financing model that combines credit, savings, and subsidies; where the role of the state is reduced to that of a facilitator of the housing market. In this sense, it is important to draw attention to the role that not only the market but also subsidies have on urbanization. Under the prevailing model, the state, by targeting subsidies to demand, does nothing other than subsidize supply. Indeed, governments demonstrate their commitment to the poor with generous public subsidies for housing. But these subsidies are wrongly called "subsidies to the demand" for they benefit developers much more than the inhabitants themselves. Beyond an inconsistency of language, this reveals a paradox in housing policy, which, being exclusively oriented to new housing, reduces its potential contribution to alleviate poverty, as Torres eloquently articulates (Torres, this volume).

A simple inspection of the composition of the housing deficit, comparing the quantitative versus qualitative housing deficits, is illuminating. In all cases analyzed, there is a mismatch between the demands revealed by each deficit and the efforts made by the housing policy to meet them. The qualitative deficit is always higher than the quantitative deficit, but it receives less policy attention. Moreover, the relationship between the two types of deficits is not addressed properly. Despite the potential to curb the quantitative deficit by means of addressing the qualitative deficit via subdivision, expansion, or adding additional floors, what has been happening is quite the opposite: solutions to the quantitative deficit, (i.e. new homes) immediately become part of the qualitative deficit that the government must meet. By disregarding quality, government action *produces* qualitative deficit precisely when it provides solutions to meet the quantitative deficit. The result is not only public disinvestment, which is serious problem on its own, but worse still, the use of workers' funds to subsidize these operations (Ziccardi, this volume) deepens the paradoxes of housing policy, making it perversely unfair.

Furthermore, fueled by the injection of subsidies, the housing supply market seems to be blind to the real housing needs. The current housing policy model does not promote enough diversity in the housing supply. Instead, the focus is almost exclusive on new single-family dwellings, ignoring other housing alternatives and tenure options that could better match the composition of the actual deficit. In fact, the current social housing supply does not adjust well to changes in population. The chapters of both Mexico and Argentina explain that currently single-family households are decreasing, whereas expanded, composite families, as well as one-person households, are increasing. However, the public–private machinery for mass production of single-family housing remains inflexible to these demographic changes. And as mentioned before, neither do the public funds adjust to the composition of the deficit. For instance, Torres notes that although in Colombia two-thirds of the housing deficit is qualitative, only 16% of the resources are earmarked for upgrading programs. Notwithstanding important efforts in upgrading programs in Argentina (130,000 units starting in 1997), Brazil (as part of the noteworthy Growth Acceleration Plan, PAC), and Chile (250,000 units since 2006), the financial imbalance between housing construction versus upgrading is dominant in the region, despite the prevalence of the qualitative over the quantitative deficit.

The sustained emphasis of the housing policy in construction reveals the unrestrained power of the actors who promote it, which is reinforced by the comfort that it represents for governments to shield themselves in their role of mere market facilitators. Private developers are the main promoters of what Moloch and Logan (1976) called the "growth coalition": a group composed of real estate developers, land-owning elites, and local officials, who reproduce the idea that urban growth is intrinsically good. Authors in this volume see this same idea being repeated across the region, and they claim the need to react to it faster and better. Private developers aptly obtain building permits and subsidies to carry out projects fitting their needs, but these do not necessarily connect with the real necessities in the ground and do not necessarily create viable urban neighborhoods.

A careful reading of the assessments presented in this book, and in particular the chapter on Brazil, shows that private–public partnerships have worked as a privatization mechanism where the state cedes power to private urban developers. Fernandes deepens this criticism by claiming that even flagship urban initiatives praised at the international level, such as the Ministry of Cities or the Minha Casa Minha Vida program (a part of which supported "social production of habitat"[1] processes), are the first to be dismantled as deregulated private interests enter into play. In this sense, Fernandes explains that the Ministry of Cities lent itself more than others to be transformed into little more than a "clientelist desk" (Fernandes, this volume). To see such a weakened urban governance in one of the most paradigmatic success stories of the Habitat II agenda should serve as a wakeup call to take with caution the celebratory mood towards the public–private partnerships actively promoted by the Habitat III agenda.

Fragile and short-lived nature of achievements

One common conclusion derived from the six country chapters is the acknowledgment that progressive political and institutional reforms tend to be weak and, when successful, they are often fragile and short-lived. Although accomplishments in inclusive urban reforms are achieved through long, sustained, and concerted efforts from actors across different sectors and classes, results can easily be reversed by new political leaders. Significant urban policy reforms in Argentina, Mexico, and Brazil have been undermined by changes in political ideology that favor more deregulated urban markets.

Catenazzi and Reese highlight in this book the Habitar Argentina initiative, which from 2001 to 2005 and with developments until 2009, triggered new forms of collective action linking grassroots organizations, academic institutions, social movements, and national and provincial legislators to articulate jointly their demands for a fair access to habitat. These are important achievements that could not reach the necessary scale before facing an adverse political environment. In Mexico, despite the enormous efforts of civil society organizations to position the urban agenda, in these twenty years of ideological oscillation, "there has been a gradual weakening of the institutional capacity of the federal government to govern urban development processes" (Ziccardi, this volume). Furthermore, while the Spanish edition of this book was in process, Brazil suffered an abrupt political process that led to the impeachment of President Dilma Rousseff. The crisis had been brewing since 2015 amidst an environment of economic recession that then transformed into a political crisis, all of which undoubtedly affects negatively federal policies in the urban sector (Fernandes, this volume). Even beyond the current situation, Fernandes notes that

> in spite of the substantial financial investments and innovative national programs . . . from the perspective of the urban reform agenda . . . [in] the last 15 years . . . there has been a gradual, notable backlash at all governmental levels insofar as the articulated processes of urban development, policy, planning, and management are concerned.
>
> (Fernandes, this volume)

The fragility of the achievements is already beginning to be felt in Ecuador, where an environment of political imbalance, originated in an economic crisis, has been brewing. This environment is weakening the drive of the citizens' revolution project that the Correa government led for a decade (Carrión and Velasco, this volume). In the Colombian case, it is worth remembering how the move to the "demand-driven" subsidy model crushed one of the most interesting institutional and financial structures devised to support the Social Production of Habitat processes, that is, popular housing organizations (OPV by its name in Spanish). OPVs were legally recognized in the previous policy model as providers of social housing projects and therefore subsidy operators. The shift to the "subsidies to the demand" model dissolved a housing movement in Colombia that had developed over twenty years and that was already inspiring reforms in other countries across the region.

What we are seeing are economic and political waves, successive trends of re-democratization and de-democratization, which although perhaps historically unavoidable, highlight the fragility of the achievements of the urban reform agenda. The point in fact is that to terminate is easier and much faster than to construct. It should be noted that despite the historical ups and downs, it is only after a country has effectively accomplished certain targets that it becomes possible to refine its policy objectives and set more refined ones. This process is most evident in the Chilean case, where the effective satisfaction of the quantitative housing deficit led to a more judicious scrutiny of the housing policy outcomes in qualitative terms.

Legal structures, but little implementation

Latin America has had, for a long time, a clear inclination to raise urban democratic principles at the level of laws or constitutional rulings in order to ensure that the "right to the city" is less vulnerable to economic and political fluctuations. Undoubtedly, Brazil and Colombia are the most celebrated cases of this trend in the region and beyond. Both countries achieved judicial recognition of the right to adequate housing, as well as of the ecological and social function of property and of the city itself. These countries were regional pioneers in the introduction of land-use plans mandating municipalities to plan their own territories. For instance, it can be said that Brazil is one of the best pupils of UN Habitat guidelines: "urban policy in Brazil reflects, either deliberately or coincidentally, the agenda of Habitat II" (Fernandes, this volume). Even international financial institutions and the Cities Alliance argued Brazil was a model to follow worldwide. Hence, this is why it is so revealing that Brazil, even having the 2001 City Statute and the 2003 Ministry of Cities, has had such difficulties in effectively regulating urban development.

The fragility of these achievements is explained by the fact that "federal policies on cities were and remain sectorial, isolated, and fragmented, reflecting the same institutional fragmentation that exists between different ministries, and even internally within the four secretariats of the Ministry of Cities" (Fernandes, this volume). To this Fernandes adds "the Ministry has never been able to achieve a proper degree of recognition vis-à-vis other federal ministries, it has failed to promote inter-ministerial articulation, and has repeatedly lost vital budgetary resources. No national urban policy has been formulated, let alone implemented" (Fernandes, this volume). We are bound to conclude from this account that the lack of implementation of urban policies cannot be blamed on the lack of laws or of resources. The sanctioning of norms and the development of legal frameworks, urban regulations, and plans does not guarantee their effective implementation.

Colombia is also experiencing similar implementation problems. The deployment of instruments to make operational the normative achievements of the political constitution of 1991 and of the Law of Territorial Development of 1997 was lengthy and complicated. And even today there are many challenges to implement them at a national level. Curiously, just when in the legal realm the most laudable objectives were achieved, on the ground, violations to the newly expanded rights intensified. In spite of this imbalance, as summarized by Lemaitre in her concept of "legal fetishism," constitutional romanticism prevails, and normative success becomes a mere gesture about which only symbolic efficacy is expected (Lemaitre, 2007). This situation is far from ignored and in fact informed the strong position held by the Colombian government during the preparatory process towards Habitat III. In agreement with other countries, such as the United States and Argentina, these member states argued against including the right to the city in the final text of the New Urban Agenda, arguing it would be contradictory to included it if countries were not capable of enforcing in full.

The chapter on Mexico offers interesting insights on this phenomenon of normative conquests going alongside implementation deficiencies. Success in this case was

> the explicit and compulsory requirement of engaging in citizen participation processes for all public decisions linked to life in cities . . . however,

these spaces turned out to be instances to legitimize the implementation of urban policies designed exclusively by the government apparatus.

(Ziccardi, this volume)

As participation gains narrative value, apparent (not genuine) participation becomes more common, that is, instances where consultation is presented as participation. Nevertheless, Ziccardi highlights a few cases of genuine citizen participation at the local level, which have managed to assert their voice by exercising veto power over ongoing urban projects.

Artificial decentralization

The authors of the country chapters in this volume agree that one fundamental cause for the shortcomings in the implementation of urban regulations and plans in the region is the intense process of administrative decentralization. Ziccardi explains that after thirty years fostering decentralization, progress has been made in transferring greater responsibilities for urban management and administration to local governments. However, their institutional capacity has not been strengthened correspondingly. These authors explain that decentralization has not met its high expectations and that it remains more nominal than real. Greater administrative decentralization does not necessarily imply fiscal decentralization, or local democracy, or appropriate and effective social policies to meet the needs of the poor. In sum, in spite of its promises, decentralization has not meant democratization.

Some authors go further and suggest that perhaps the decentralization trend has been excessive because it safeguards an autonomy that is sacred but weak, incapable of taking the actions that proper urban management entails. Consider for instance Brazil, a country with more than 5,500 municipalities, all of which hold the same constitutional entitlements, although their economic, political, and territorial realities are radically different. The electoral system worsens this state of affairs as it gives rise to an over-representation of underpopulated rural areas in the National Congress (Fernandes, this volume). Or, what is worse still, it is common to find an important number of small municipalities that prefer to maintain their dependence on federal transfers, because they are fearful of antagonizing local elites when using their legal powers to collect capital gains charges.

Similarly, in Colombia, the benefit of having 99% of 1,100 municipalities with their territorial development plans issued is not so clear. An evaluation of these documents showed that most plans are but de-contextualized copies of plans from other localities. Among the technical failures identified, it is worth mentioning that more than half of the municipalities inadequately delimited the urban perimeter, do not have clear urban expansion criteria, do not consider agricultural or forestry uses, and that only 12% captured land valorization taxes (Torres, this volume). The chapter on Ecuador also denounces problems of inefficiency in decentralization, because "excessive territorial smallholding" ends up producing "local governments that are powerful vis-a-vis the national government but weak vis-à-vis its local society" (Carrión and Velasco, this volume). As decentralization progresses, tensions tend to grow between different levels of government. Ecuador is undoubtedly an extreme case of this situation. There, for example, both the president's office itself and the Guayaquil city government are advancing large urban projects on the same territory. These projects are not only disconnected but furthermore they are incompatible to such a degree that inconsistencies are promoting a legal limbo originating from the state itself.

Another aspect related to decentralization that is increasingly relevant in the region, mainly because of its absence, is metropolitanization. In Argentina, for example, "the metropolitan phenomenon was never really considered in national or provincial legislation" (Pírez, 2002 in Catenazzi and Reese, this volume). The lack of metropolitan institutionality is a problem because it prevents the development of a shared regional vision "to the point that municipalities, rather than neighbors with common goals, become rivals" (Torres, this volume). Although there are few isolated success stories, such as the metropolitan area of the Valley of Aburrá where Medellín is located, there is still much to be done in this regard. For instance, in Brazil, the thirty metropolitan regions existing countrywide lack an adequate institutional and normative scaffolding so they currently operate in a sort of gray legal environment (Fernandes, this volume).

Throughout these accounts there is much disenchantment with the promises of decentralization. One can even point out some voices encouraging processes of re-centralization in the configuration of urban policies. The authors in this volume make a generalized call to truly national, cross-sectoral, and more efficiently articulated urban policies.

Continuing inequality and exclusion

The overall balance of these qualitative evaluations is not positive. In spite of undeniable progress in the provision of urban infrastructure and services, in the reduction of the quantitative housing deficit, and the laudable legal achievements, the efforts to curb poverty and to mainstream community participation, as well as other institutional and programmatic innovations, have not succeeded. Inequality and exclusion in Latin American cities have worsened. Latin America is the second most urbanized region in the world, and it remains one of the most unequal and violent regions in the world.

Over the last twenty years, inequality has intensified. The relationship between those with the highest and lowest incomes is so extreme that experts are beginning to question the usefulness of traditional indicators to measure inequality. Recent studies in Chile exploring the "lion's share" in detail, that is, studies of the richest tiers of the population, conclude that it is necessary to revise the conventional estimates based on quintiles of income and the Gini coefficient. Between 2005 and 2012 in Chile, the richest 1% earned 30.5%

of the total income, whereas the 0.1% richest received 17.6%, and the 0.01% earned 10.1% (López et al., 2013 in Rodríguez and Rodríguez, this volume). Beyond the need to refine the indicators in order to better reflect this reality, these numbers also urge a reformulation of the objectives and strategies in the region to combat such extreme inequality.

Of course, participatory urban planning and inclusive urban policies have some potential to reverse this situation. However, this is not the norm. The role of government, either by direct action or by inaction (letting the market dictate urban form) has reinforced patterns of sociospatial segregation in the territory. "There may be some social mobility, but this is not expressed in the territory," as Rodríguez and Rodríguez note in this volume. The spatial result of the urban political powers at play is one of increasing inequality: "cities in Brazil are the socio-spatial expression of an exclusionary and perverse socio-political pact. A gigantic housing deficit coexists with an equally gigantic stock of vacant built properties and serviced urban land, as well as tens of thousands of informal settlements" (Fernandes, this volume). Intra-urban imbalances are a priority for public action in Latin America, not only because they must be addressed in themselves but also because they set off a chain of negative effects that affect many other areas such as safety, health, and even productivity.

In this sense, the point this book draws attention to is that it is not a question of urban problems becoming increasingly difficult or that governments are becoming less equipped solve them. On the contrary, resources and capacity have steadily increased in the region in the last two decades, and social, political, and economic achievements are undeniable. As mentioned earlier, poverty has declined and basic needs' indicators are showing important progress. The region also has a commendable corpus of statistical data, as well as a remarkable tradition of urban research. But Latin America must live up to its performance potential, rather than sink below what it is actually capable of.

It is important not to lose sight of the global perspective when studying the exacerbation of intra-urban inequality. What is reasonable to expect from a country given its circumstances? What does the trajectory of other countries facing similar objectives and with similar resources tell us? This is precisely the reflection that The New School proposes with the Habitat Commitment Index (HCI) described in chapter 9. This index highlights the relative lack of effort that the region has devoted to certain issues, not in absolute terms, but in light of its current economic capacity. Compared with other regions of the world, Latin America has both the best performance in poverty reduction and the worst performance (after South Asia) in employment indicators. What an urban analysis allows one to establish is that, far from having a contradiction between these two results, these outcomes ratify that social exclusion is rampant. They point out that what is at stake is that rights' violations have a spatial configuration and that intra-urban inequality has a direct effect on productivity.

Irrelevance of the Habitat agenda

The countries under study in this book show considerable variation in the member states' attitudes toward the Habitat II Conference and its Habitat Agenda. It has already been mentioned that the issuance of the City Statute and the creation of the Ministry of Cities of Brazil was seen as proof that the Brazilian government followed closely Habitat II guidelines. In fact, these institutional arrangements were put on display by UN Habitat as an example that it was possible to take concrete actions towards the objectives of the Istanbul Declaration. Indeed, it can be said that countries like Mexico and Colombia seemed to take the agenda seriously, whereas in Argentina, Chile, and Ecuador, the Habitat II agenda had little effect. In the latter, it cannot be said that it served as a guide to local governance, nor even that it was known – let alone used – by national or local authorities. For example, Mexico openly acknowledges that the 1996 conference transformed existing public policy. New instruments were designed in response to the specific components by which the Habitat II Agenda intended to influence urban territories. "However, this normative framework acts in a pragmatic and little articulated way," argues Ziccardi in this volume. Meanwhile, Chile did not even have any national urban development policy during most of these twenty years, and when it was finally issued, it turned out to be a "National Urban Development Policy with no binding character . . . that does not consider budgets nor fulfillment indicators," explain Rodríguez and Rodríguez in their chapter. In general, despite evident efforts and institutional innovations, countries show a very weak urban institutional structure at the national level. When it exists, it is usually outranked by other national institutions and lacks the capacity to steer housing policy, much less to establish a fruitful dialogue with national economic policy.

In the run-up to Habitat III, many analysts rightly wondered what the meaning of international commitments on a national urban agenda was when local governments are not invited to the table. However, fewer thinkers dare to ask, as Fernandes does in this volume, why is it that national governments have yet to understand the meaning of cities in the contemporary world, especially in a context of post-industrialization? Furthermore, we ask: What does it mean that most of the world's gross domestic product comes from cities? And how would economic policy and social policy change if state leaders truly understood the nature and behavior of cities? "Cities are no longer only the place where industrial economic development takes place (i.e. urbanization providing support to capitalist accumulation), but they have also become the very object of post-industrial, financial and services capitalism" (Fernandes, this volume). What this line of thought points out is that cities are not only the place and object of economic development but that they must also be understood as common goods, as the prime instruments of social promotion and redistribution opportunities. Disconcertingly, the urban dimension is so structural that most often it goes unnoticed.

Horacio Verbitsky put it in these terms during a public conference titled "Latin American Urban Dialogues": "Other problems that receive much more attention in the media and with higher relevance to the public opinion have their roots in habitat problems" (Verbitski, 2016). Judged in light of the difficulty of the urban agenda to reveal its true potential in the realm of the national political economy, Habitat III's global lobbying is weak. Part of the problem with Habitat's statements is that its principles are irrefutable, but there is very little clarity about *how* they are to be fulfilled so as not to betray its very purposes. "The latest draft of the New Urban Agenda reads as if reducing poverty and inequality and securing opportunities for all could be ensured by simply writing it down in a UN statement" (Cohen, 2016). It is in this sense that Cohen recently affirmed that the structure of Habitat III resembles a building on stilts, which rises above the ground on thin foundations that barely touch the surface.

A need for a new urban practice

In a regional environment like the one discussed in this book, the challenge for the next two decades after Habitat III is to identify how local practice can be truly strengthened and transformed. This implies defining the values and contents with which professionals and communities are prepared to face the issues of an urban agenda where all the objectives are interdependent, where problems cannot be solved one by one, but rather as a whole, in a network. For example, a neighborhood daycare program should be seen as a crucial component of a poverty reduction policy and as directly contributing to increase formal employment. Likewise, a waste management project can simultaneously have elements of public space, climate change, business formalization, and preventive health. The question is, then, what kind of professional is prepared to deal effectively with such chained effects?

The New Urban Agenda must undertake a series of institutional arrangements and redesigns with a local and community emphasis to ensure that it will not replicate sectorial structures and that it embraces complexity, coordinated actions, and the harmonization of nested – and often conflicting – governmental levels. This has not been the way urban practice has behaved so far. Rather, it is more frequent to find "obsolete institutional designs that reproduce the sectorial and vertical structure of central and state governments, without instances of institutional coordination" (Ziccardi, this volume). Another frequent problem is that urban designs and urban plans exist on paper, but on the ground, they turn out to be ineffective. Among the most discussed causes for this is that processes lack genuine community participation and thus they are disconnected from local realities. However, another less discussed cause is that plans are often ineffective simply because they use obscure legal jargon or technically imprecise language. But even more alarming still is the frequency with which urban planners believe they are devising urban inclusion opportunities, when in reality the projects they herald are trapped in speculative land markets. In urban development, says Fernandes, urban planners and administrators have been unaware of the exclusionary dynamics of the real estate market that they themselves help create.

It is important to reflect on this risk precisely now, when the region seems to be experiencing an ideological turn to the right. At this moment, the role of universities, organized communities, and organizations that defend the right to the city is to put certain issues on the table of public debate and to monitor urban practices, remembering that instruments are never neutral (Gutman, 2016). In general, it can be said that traditional professional practice is not aware of how it is pervaded by the market, nor does it recognize the need to work openly on conflicts of power, assuming beforehand that every urban action or inaction has interested stakeholders. These shortcomings must be tackled with a constant critical eye on urban practice, which can readily feed curricular structures that teach how to work on the city in a way that is professionally more self-aware.

Twenty years ago, it seemed unthinkable that a government could meet the quantitative housing deficit. Today we know that it is possible. But more importantly, today we know that this is not enough. Building large numbers of substandard housing, disconnected from urban services and far away from employment opportunities, is not enough. Building houses that people cannot afford to live in and that immediately swell the qualitative deficit the government is bound to deal with is not a solution. This is not a success to emulate. It is important to stop pursuing the chimera of "successful cases" that are decontextualized and that mistake what is desired with what is possible. It is important to stop repeating principles with which everyone agrees in the abstract but no one can claim off the paper. It is important to monitor the messianic projects that so often reproduce exclusionary real estate markets pushed forward by well-intended but unaware managers.

The inventory of Habitat II's "outstanding assignments" (Catenazzi and Reese, this volume) is clear, thanks to the critical analysis and synthesis done by researchers such as those who contributed to this book. Before abandoning optimism, the invitation made by the cross-sectional account of this chapter is to fully embrace new urban practices. Practices that weave functional networks of actors. Practices that sow roots in its place. Practices where solutions are enmeshed in symbiotic systems across different administrative and disciplinary sectors. Practices that invite us to put the collective intelligence to the service of fair and sustainable urban development.

Note

1 It should be highlighted that the Social Production of Habitat concept, promoted by Enrique Ortiz Flórez from the International Housing Coalition (HIC-AL), is an openly acknowledged term utilized by all authors. This is, in and of itself, a remarkable theoretical contribution from the Latin American region to the global urban knowledge that should not be overlooked.

Bibliography

Barbero, J. M., (2007), "Una mirada implicada y una lectura transversal", Revista Signo y Pensamiento, No. 50, Bogotá, June 2007.

Cohen, M., (2016), "The Brexit: An Alert Call for the New Urban Agenda", Citiscope en Español, July 24, 2016.

Gutman, M., (2016), "Latin American Urban Dialogues: From Habitat II to Habitat III", Conclusions of the Internal Workshop, Observatory on Latin America and Corporación Andina de Fomento, Buenos Aires, July 4.

Lemaitre, J., (2007), *Fetichismo legal: derecho, violencia y movimientos sociales en Colombia*, Derecho y Pobreza, Editores del Puerto, Puerto Rico, pp. 83–96.

López, R., Figueroa, E., and Gutiérrez, P., (2013), "La 'parte del león': Nuevas estimaciones de la participación de los súper ricos en el ingreso de Chile", Working Papers Series, SDT 379, Universidad de Chile, Economics Department, Santiago de Chile.

Moloch H., and Logan J., (1987), "The City as a Growth Machine", In *Urban Fortunes: The Political Economy of Place*, University of California Press, Berkeley.

Pírez, P., (2002), "Buenos Aires: Fragmentation and Privatization of the Metropolitan City", *Environment and Urbanization*, 14(1), 145–158. Available at: https://doi.org/10.1177/095624780201400112

Verbitski, H., (2016), "Latin American Urban Dialogues: From Habitat II to Habitat III", Public Conference, Observatory on Latina America and Corporación Andina de Fomento, School of Design and Architecture, University of Buenos Aires, July 5.

12 Conclusion: habitat in debt and future assets

Towards a new inclusive urban practice

Michael Cohen and Margarita Gutman

This book has shown the great variety of experiences of six Latin American countries in managing the challenges of urban growth. As well illustrated both in the individual country chapters and in the previous transversal analysis of this experience, there are important conclusions with regard to common themes and contextual factors that have operated to frustrate sustained progress in urban policy reform and in creating the material conditions for productive and equitable cities in these countries. The chapters are rich in their content, but they also need to be considered from a broader perspective that relates their findings to comparative global experience and to various urban analytic frameworks. This concluding chapter seeks to provide this analytic contextualization in the hope that recent Latin American urban experience can also enrich comparative global knowledge by demonstrating that some of the dilemmas facing these countries are not just *sui generis* to Latin America, but are part of a wider global urban experience. In this sense, these experiences are also significant in considering the likelihood that they will contribute to the implementation of the 2015–2030 Sustainable Development Goals and the New Urban Agenda. The country chapters and the discussion of the Habitat Commitment Index suggest that this likelihood is low.

Seeking to apply a broader perspective to Latin American urban policy experience from 1996 to 2016 cannot presume to be exhaustive; indeed, it would be another book. But three issues appear particularly important in a historical assessment of the past two decades and are relevant in thinking ahead.

First, the impact of exogenous forces, whether at the global or regional level, that have affected the outcomes of urban policy and programs in Latin American cities. How important have global economic changes and globalization been in affecting urban outcomes? Which kinds of urban outcomes are in fact more susceptible to exogenous forces and thus less controllable by national and local authorities?

Second, the significance of Habitat II and Habitat III in determining urban policy objectives and the design of public programs, investments, and institutions. Despite the intensity of activity and debates around these global conferences, do the country cases demonstrate that national and urban-level experiences have been significantly affected by these events and the processes they generate? These issues raise further questions about the nature of commitments that are made in these international processes, as illustrated in the two chapters on the Habitat Commitment Index.

Third, the analytic problem of distinguishing cause and effect in urban policy processes over this twenty-year period and how this relates to a broader understanding of what is "urban practice". How are we to more clearly understand the role of policy, planning, private investment, regulation, and civil society in these processes? Despite the high expectations about the effects of decentralization and subsidiarity, the processes of decentralization have not proven to be uniformly democratic, participatory, or effective in producing improved material conditions for urban residents. Decentralization may be a necessary but not sufficient condition to provoke meaningful urban policy reform. The same observation applies to urban planning, a subject that has received increased attention at the national and urban levels in various Latin American countries but which has not yet demonstrated widespread, sustainable benefits and results. In simple terms, we need more assessment of how public policies and institutional reforms are actually implemented.

These questions suggest the need for formal hypotheses and testing of theory. Indeed, what we are considering is actually the political economy of urban reform in general and how it has operated in six countries in Latin America over two decades. We argue, therefore, that this book cannot make a comprehensive assessment of these questions, but rather should propose a provocative set of questions: for research, for policy, and certainly for public debate. The country chapters themselves suggest many questions, but in this concluding chapter we wish to step back from the country examples to ask a broader set of questions. The three areas identified earlier are only three of many more.

The impact of exogenous factors on urban reform

There is now a large and growing literature about the impacts of exogenous factors on cities. Debates over two decades have focused attention on the role of global cities ((Sassen, 1991) and (Sassen, 1994)); on the tensions between local and global in their effects on urban institutions, political processes, and patterns of inequality (Borja and Castells, 1997); and the specific impacts of global economic crises on Latin American countries ((Borja et al., 2012) and (Cohen, 2012a)). This literature has demonstrated that exogenous forces – including conditions in the global economy such as the global demand for specific goods, services, and commodities; the price of money as expressed in global interest rates; exchange rates; oil prices; and the demand for specific kinds of labor and technology – have all had specific impacts on Latin American cities. A decline in the growth rate of the Chinese economy is immediately noted and felt in cities such as Buenos Aires or Sao Paulo.

What was first understood as a global financial crisis, as in 2008–2011, was quickly transformed into a credit shortage, a disruption of trade, reduced demand for goods and services produced in Latin American countries, reduced employment, and shortly thereafter in reduced public revenue, both in income taxes and production-related taxes such as value-added. All of these changes affect the behavior of local markets for labor, housing, land, and other valued assets. These cascading effects dramatically demonstrate the interdependence of the global, national, and local economies. It can therefore be expected that such events and processes will appear in the future. Indeed, some economists argue that these events are cyclical and are built into the process of economic expansion and contraction. They also appear to contribute to the persistence of short-term thinking at both the national and local levels.

This short-term thinking is reflected in the behavior of global and national financial players who look for profitable opportunities and have clearly identified urban real estate as a prime sector for quick returns (Buckley et al., 2015). As shown in the chapter on Mexico, this availability of global funds has fueled heavy public and private investment in housing, with the result that there are 5 million vacant housing units in the Mexico City region too distant from employment and other urban amenities. Similar patterns appear in Argentina and Brazil, demonstrating that global financial conditions can have determinant consequences for local housing markets, urban form, and public investment in infrastructure. The conclusion in several country chapters that housing policy has replaced urban policy reflects this power of global capital when it lands in local contexts.

One particularly clear impact of exogenous forces is the global pressure from the multilateral institutions for national governments to adopt economic austerity plans in response to global volatility, thereby curtailing local public expenditures, including needed subsidies for vulnerable groups or increasing tariffs for public utilities such as water, gas, or electricity. These impacts were dramatically shown in a study in the 1990s by Caroline Moser of Guayaquil, Ecuador, where poor communities felt the combined impacts of macroeconomic adjustment through higher prices, cuts in public expenditures, and reduced opportunities in labor markets (Moser, 1996). These impacts have also been demonstrated through their direct effects on municipal finance in Brazil and Mexico (Cook, 2012). And they are quite visible in Argentina in 2018.

The significance of Habitat II and Habitat III

One example of an exogenous factor, albeit much less determinant, is the pressure resulting from the international discourse arising from the preparatory processes for Habitat II and III, as well as the outcome documents that are approved by the United Nations conferences. For some countries, the content and language of the global declarations are officially perceived to have a moral and substantive content that, although not legally binding, has almost a juridical character. As noted in the previous chapters, there appears to have been little impact of the urban policies of the countries that signed the commitments present in the 1996 Habitat Agenda document. The notion of "commitment" is ambiguous, because neither governments, at any level, nor civil society organizations are "committed" or required in a legal sense to do anything. It remains largely ahistorical in the absence of specific deadlines or target time periods in which "commitments" are to be met.

Rather, there is some sense of global understanding, promoted by the United Nations, that governments should promote a set of values and objectives, such as reducing poverty, improving housing and infrastructure conditions, or promoting employment. This understanding, however, is not really rooted in local contexts, in the sense that it does not consider the legacy of contextual conditions, present circumstances, or the structural obstacles to these objectives. A good example of how present pressures affect national and local policies and resource allocation and can undermine the fulfillment of international commitments is the 2018 pressure coming from the emigration of Venezuelans to Brazil, Colombia, Ecuador, and Peru, and further south to Argentina and Chile.

There are some exceptions to this assessment – with perhaps Mexico and Colombia being exceptions by virtue of their close alignment with the Habitat II Agenda document. Nonetheless, as the country chapters show, this alignment turns out to be largely rhetorical rather than real in terms of improvements in specific indicators of urban progress.

This mediocre or even disappointing performance, however, raises the issue of what the mediating or intervening factors are that have limited the achievement of these objectives and goals. This question is at the core of this problem. If the rhetorical objectives are sensible and are supported by a global consensus, how should we understand the disappointing performance of governments at all levels in achieving the objectives? The editors of this book believe that the answer lies in part in *how* urban policy and urban plans are formulated. If there is agreement on the *what*, there is little attention to the *how*.

This observation is reinforced by the quantitative findings[1] of analytic work embodied in the Habitat Commitment Index that demonstrates that some countries outperform richer countries in specific areas, such as infrastructure provision or education. Indeed, analyses of the countries that are outliers in the quantitative study clearly show that resources are not strong factors in assuring performance.[2] This suggests that absolute levels of resources may be less important than the nature of policies adopted and how they are actually implemented. This takes us to the issue of urban practice.

Urban practice and the prospects for reform

In posing the question of urban practice, it is important to acknowledge that there has been a reappraisal of effective forms of urban policy, programs, and projects going on for many years. As noted in Chapter 2, the focus on urban master plans gave way in the 1960s and 1970s to community planning and participation, later on to projects, to so-called strategic urban plans, public investment programs, and public–private partnerships. Most, but not all, of these approaches for framing urban interventions included a heavy top-down, supply-side bias, in which sectors and institutions generally were perceived of and acted in disciplinary and sector silos. They tended to ignore local knowledge, actors, and priorities. Their legacy has been increasing exclusion and intraurban inequality in most cities, whether in industrialized or developing countries.

In many cities, urban planning was often neglected during the 1990s by the adoption of market-driven development policies and the high expectations that the private sector and private investment could be the major engine of economic growth. That view was not adopted everywhere, as shown by the successful active planning in Barcelona or Curitiba and many East Asian cities in the early 1990s. This negative view of planning has been somewhat rebalanced by the experience of the first decade of the 21st century when the exaggerated expectations for private-sector investment and management have proven to be disappointing. Instead, national and local governments in Argentina, Brazil, Chile, and Colombia, as well as in East Asia, have had notable periodic, but not sustained, successes in accelerating growth and reducing poverty and inequality through public action at national and local levels (Moreno, 2014). Efforts across Latin America have clearly demonstrated that "urban planning is back" as local governments seek to manage continuing urban spatial and demographic growth, even though there are many places where plans were formulated but not adopted or, worse still, not implemented.

Nevertheless, the city examples of Medellin, Bogota, Rosario, and Guadalajara, among others, have demonstrated to some observers that strategic city planning could provide a sound foundation for policies and investments that could dramatically improve urban conditions. The story of Medellin has become emblematic, not only in Latin America but in the world at large, despite the fact that many communities within the city have significant critiques, noting, for example, that they want jobs and security rather than cable cars. It has replaced Curitiba as the example of balanced, sustainable urban development. These well-known examples in large cities have also been accompanied by dozens of individual planning efforts at different scales in many countries. Some have led to policy reform and urban progress, whereas others have not been translated into action by local authorities, and yet others have been ignored at either the local or national level.

Some examples from earlier academic studies, however, illustrate the problem with this positive evaluation. A 2006 study of governance in Bogota by Alan Gilbert of University College, London, sang the praises of Colombia's efforts to manage its capital city, and particularly its urban transport system, but surprisingly ignored inequality and exclusion (Gilbert, 2006). Another study, a comparative analysis of strategic planning in nine Latin American cities in 2005 by Florian Steinberg of the Institute of Housing Studies in the Netherlands, showed the range of experience in strategic plans across these cities, but while praising the more democratic and participatory character of these efforts, also did not directly address the issue of inequality, which was a major problem in all of the cities studied (Steinberg, 2005). This work also did not report on the outcomes of strategic plans.

This leads to some simple but challenging questions: To achieve better urban outcomes, do Latin American countries and cities need to adopt different processes of urban planning and urban policy reform? What are the necessary conditions to ensure that planning positively affects policy and action? What is the current state of urban practice in specific cities? And most importantly, how does urban practice contribute to the persistence of social exclusion?

These concerns to reconsider urban planning were well articulated in the 2009 Global Report on Human Settlements, *Planning Sustainable Cities*, prepared by UN Habitat, which argued that current approaches to planning do not sufficiently take into account five major challenges: climate change, continued demographic growth, economic imperatives, sociospatial challenges including exclusion, and the need for democratization of urban planning and decision-making processes (UN Habitat, 2009).

The report identified key factors in relation to urban planning in developing countries where more than half of employment in the region is informal, where large shares of the total urban population live in informal settlements, and where governmental institutions are unable to respond to the breadth and depth of needs and demands from the growing urban population. This perspective was well expressed by Vanessa Watson from South Africa who has argued that urban planning models come from the developed countries and need to recognize the conditions found in cities in developing countries (Watson, 2009).

Ananya Roy deepened this critique of urban planning by arguing that urban theories of the North distort what researchers see in the South. She wrote of "the geographies of regional and urban theory", demonstrating that theoretical concepts such as urban regions and linkages to the global economy fit within what she called a "Darwinian ecology of cities: the survival of the fittest in the keen competition of network capitalism" (Roy, 2009). She referred to "process geographies", a term developed by Arjun Appadurai (Appadurai, 2000), which focuses on movement, encounter, and exchange. Area knowledge of these processes suggests a new set of questions about the internal dynamics of actual places as opposed to theoretical places.

These observations become even more significant after even a quick reading of the 2015 Sustainable Development Goals (SDGs) as listed here:

Goal 1. End poverty in all its forms everywhere

Goal 2. End hunger, achieve food security and improved nutrition, and promote sustainable agriculture

Goal 3. Ensure healthy lives and promote well-being for all at all ages

Goal 4. Ensure inclusive and equitable quality education and promote lifelong learning opportunities for all

Goal 5. Achieve gender equality and empower all women and girls

Goal 6. Ensure availability and sustainable management of water and sanitation for all

Goal 7. Ensure access to affordable, reliable, sustainable, and modern energy for all

Goal 8. Promote sustained, inclusive, and sustainable economic growth; full and productive employment; and decent work for all

Goal 9. Build resilient infrastructure, promote inclusive and sustainable industrialization, and foster innovation

Goal 10. Reduce inequality within and among countries

Goal 11. Make cities and human settlements inclusive, safe, resilient, and sustainable

Goal 12. Ensure sustainable consumption and production patterns

Goal 13. Take urgent action to combat climate change and its impacts

Goal 14. Conserve and sustainably use the oceans, seas, and marine resources for sustainable development

Goal 15. Protect, restore, and promote sustainable use of terrestrial ecosystems; sustainably manage forests; combat desertification; and halt and reverse land degradation and halt biodiversity loss

Goal 16. Promote peaceful and inclusive societies for sustainable development; provide access to justice for all; and build effective, accountable, and inclusive institutions at all levels

Goal 17. Strengthen the means of implementation and revitalize the Global Partnership for Sustainable Development

The most important feature of these goals is their interdependence and indeed, their interdependence in specific places, ecologies, economies, and societies. The obvious linkages between health and water, infrastructure and employment, or spatial planning and energy use in any given place raise the question of what the most effective strategies and entry points are to address these issues.

The outbreak in Latin America of Zika as a mosquito-induced epidemic was a good current example of this interdependence. Although clearly a public health problem, the Zika virus breeds in the thousands of miles of open drainage ditches in Latin American cities and thus can also be considered an infrastructure problem. Its crippling impact on newborn children will significantly reduce urban household incomes as a consequence of the births of many disabled children requiring daily childcare. Urban incomes will drop, increasing urban poverty. The gains of a decade of economic growth in the region could be lost. Acknowledging this level of interdependence and complexity in urban areas is a first all-important step towards finding meaningful solutions.

Within the list of SDGs, it is apparent that one goal – achieving social inclusion – captures many of the dimensions of all of the goals by focusing on differences between residents of cities in their incomes, opportunities, public services, quality of life, and vulnerability to the consequences of both economic change and climate change. Intraurban inequality has proven to be particularly difficult to address, as demonstrated by a 2014 CAF-UN Habitat research study that concluded that, even when inequality at the national level had been reduced, intraurban inequality had increased in a sample of 350 Latin American cities and towns (Moreno, 2014). Inclusion is now understood to be more than just income inequality, but rather a whole set of characteristics that exclude men, women, and children of certain ages, ethnicities, races, and other defining identities from enjoying the full range of opportunities within urban areas.

The need for a new urban practice for inclusion

One of the frequent critiques heard in the UN Habitat meetings leading to Habitat III, in the Preparatory Committee meetings in Surabaya, Indonesia, and New York of the various drafts of the New Urban Agenda was that it presented an old list of problems and sounded similar to the litany of challenges identified in the 1996 Habitat Agenda document. This is generally true, but two aspects of this list differ from the previous agenda: *first*, the looming dangers of climate change and *second*, growing global and national concerns about inclusion and inequality. Both of these additions should encourage urgent attention to their *causes*: What policies and behaviors in cities are contributing to climate change and exclusion? Although the causes of climate change are now quite well understood, the multiple causes of exclusion are perhaps even more complicated to address because they come from many dimension of urban life. The answers to the question of exclusion are to be found at many levels of institutional responsibility, urban scale, and practical knowledge. If we know why we have these problems, in other words, if we have a reliable, sensible, albeit complicated diagnosis, we should be able to see how these causal factors need to be addressed.

The call for a new urban practice, and particularly one that focuses on the challenge of inclusion in the context of the SDGs and the New Urban Agenda, results in part from the *cyclical swings in how urban issues have been addressed historically*. A telling example has been the spread of real estate investment in the form of planned communities and now-vacant housing stock on the distant edges of metropolitan areas in Mexico, Brazil, China, and other places, as mentioned in earlier chapters. This situation has resulted from the lack of urban regulations on private housing developers and the resulting waste of public investment in unused infrastructure. The resulting form of these cities is a major contributor to exclusion.

Although there is now a large literature on exclusion in cities, it is important to distinguish the multiple forms of differentiation and separation that occur in cities. These include spatial fragmentation, economic stratification and gentrification, social stratification, and cultural and identity segregation. Each one of these processes has their own logic, causes, and outcomes (Lacarriou, 2016). Although some diversity in urban areas should be welcomed, it is also true that exclusion can result from each of these individually and together in a cumulative manner.

Fragmentation: Most cities in the 21st century are highly fragmented in spatial terms. They extend over large areas and are frequently divided by infrastructure and/or ecological features such as waterways. Indeed, the physical distance between parts of urban areas may be less important than the nature or feature of fragmentation such as a highway. This "splintering" process has been well analyzed by Graham and Marvin in their now-classic book, *Splintering Urbanism* (Graham and Marvin, 2001). The logics of fragmentation include differentiation of the functions of specific urban places, the implications of infrastructure planning, economic incentives for specific land uses at specific locations, and the sheer spatial area and demographic magnitude of a given urban area. They are further institutionalized by processes of decentralization of urban institutions and thus the establishment of new jurisdictions for urban service delivery, public policy, and political representation. Fragmentation can lead to diverse physical forms such as mosaics, islands, or archipelagos.

Segregation: The logics of segregation vary from city to city, but usually reflect logics of separation between peoples of different cultural, economic, racial, or religious identities. These logics are usually very intense and generate similarly intense forms of separation across these different identities. Segregation tends to imply that individuals and groups live in a certain place and that they are not expected to leave that place. This varies importantly with the process of gentrification that assumes that people will leave certain neighborhoods because they cannot afford the rents or other costs associated with living there.

Gentrification: As noted earlier, the logic of gentrification, a term coined by Ruth Glass (Glass, 1989), is economic and is driven by a change in the value of housing and land in a specific neighborhood. Individuals and families are forced to leave neighborhoods because they can no longer afford to live there.

Each of these processes generates further differentiation among urban residents and establishes different forms of "distance" between specific individuals, households, and groups from the "city at large". It should also be noted that this "distance" and "difference" also translate into different economic, political, social, spatial, and cultural conditions that can be understood as "inequality" in terms of material conditions, in opportunities, and in human rights. The notion of exclusion, therefore, itself needs to be highly differentiated. Exclusion in urban South Africa is different from exclusion in Buenos Aires or New York.

The role of practices

Although social exclusion takes many forms and has specific causes and origins, it is, above all, an outcome of a range of public and private decisions and behaviors within urban areas that have individual and collective consequences for individuals, households, and communities. These consequences themselves result from patterns of cumulative causation (Galster, 1999). One thing leads to another.

In order to understand the causes of exclusion, these decisions and behaviors can be classified according to a basic typology of practices as suggested next.

Typology of practices affecting exclusion

Definitional causes include definitions that exclude specific individuals, groups, and/or communities. These might include:

- The definition of urban that might be high, say 10,000 people in a given settlement, and thus exclude people living in smaller places.
- The definition of an urban area as a city, town, or metropolitan area in which the definition is geographical or spatial, so "living outside" the boundaries or jurisdictions would exclude people.
- The definition of resident that might require an amount of time that an individual has lived in the place, thus excluding recently arrived peoples.
- The definition of resident that might require a street address, thus excluding people who live in places that have no addresses or for whom having an address would conflict with some other legal process.
- The definition of citizen that involves other requirements that an individual cannot meet.

Structural causes are causes that result in exclusion as a consequence of institutional arrangements and possible eligibilities to be included. It may have to do with organizational structures such as jurisdictions.

Regulatory causes are causes of exclusion resulting from specific rules, such as a prohibition on the water company to connect households to the water distribution network if they do not have legal occupancy rights. Other regulations could include building codes or zoning regulations. They may also interact with definitional causes.

Distributive or allocative causes are causes resulting from the pattern of distribution of some government service, payment, or opportunity. There may be cases where some service is in short supply or rationed, or simply that there is not enough budgetary resources to cover the entire population.

As demonstrated in this typology, some of these practices can be understood as "structural" in the sense that they are inherent in institutional processes of decision making, political representation, and the lack of public accountability in many urban areas. Other practices are "definitional" in the sense that they involve definitions of the boundary of the city itself: Which areas fall within legal boundaries and jurisdictions? Which buildings are defined as "legal" in terms of building codes and regulations? And which communities are considered "legitimate" and thereby qualified to receive public services or investments of public funds? Neighborhoods that are not considered to exist within city boundaries but which nevertheless are inhabited by households working and living within specific urban areas can be excluded, but with terrible consequences such as the lack of water supply or public transport.

This typology also suggests that some of the causes of urban exclusion can exist at the national level through public policies about the national census, eligibility for identity cards, eligibility to attend public schools or access to public health facilities, or tax laws. These national causes may not be directly "behavioral", yet their results can be exclusionary and contribute to intraurban inequality.

The fact that many excluded households inhabit Latin American cities and towns is accentuated by the reality that their presence is frequently not acknowledged in the disciplinary study of urban-related disciplines such as architecture or urban planning. Some, but not all, university schools of architecture and urban planning teach about the "informal city", but most do not. Part of the problem, therefore, is "visibility" – who is counted, who is included in definitions, and who is therefore entitled to make claims for public resources. It is not uncommon for students committed to design to be unaware of the actual conditions found in slums and squatter settlements. This suggests that part of the problem is how the "urban disciplines" are actually taught to students, what is included, and what subjects themselves are "legitimate" fields to be considered in higher education. In this sense, it may be that "urban education" is itself "exclusionary" by not including all of the groups in the urban population. This reality may help explain in part the persistence of social exclusion as an outcome.

It should be added that responsibility for this definition of legitimacy in the study and analysis of cities is not solely at the national or local levels, but also is a result of one version of the global discourse and media about the place of cities in global economic, social, and cultural progress. Global images of Shanghai show spectacular skyscrapers or ultramodern transport infrastructure. They do not show the poor neighborhoods of the city or the overcrowding faced by many Chinese urban residents. New York is an icon, but one that does not mention its crisis of affordability which led Mayor Bill di Blasio to declare that the city was in danger of becoming a "gated community". Only a small share of the many tourists attending the World Cup or the Olympics in Brazil visited the favelas where many Brazilians live.

The persistence of exclusion, therefore, is itself a result of multiple cumulative perceptions, definitions, decisions, and actions that have occurred through the history of individual cities and towns. Designing interventions that can "disrupt" these patterns requires some understanding of the chains of causation that produce them. A first step in this understanding is some form of "assessment" of the urban practices. That assessment should use the explicit criterion of how specific practices, as suggested earlier, actually contribute to the reduction of exclusion.

A concluding call

This book therefore ends with a call for new attention to the multiple causes of social exclusion in cities in Latin America. If this call is perceived as being a narrowing of the broad agenda of urban policy in the region, this need not be a fatal flaw in the argument. Rather, the editors wish to suggest that addressing the issue of social exclusion is in fact central to the political, economic, and social futures of Latin American urban areas. In the past, social exclusion was often acknowledged as significant but not central to the future. This is no longer the case. How differences are addressed is a central question of human rights and social justice.

Notes

1 Here it is important to add that a critical challenge in evaluating the performance of the urban sector in a global comparative perspective is the difficulty of accessing comparable data sources that present data disaggregated at the city level. Not only are there contrasting definitions for what different countries define as urban (to such an extent that different criteria often yield to incomparable results), but what is more, local governments – especially small and medium sized – have serious limitations producing, collecting, and analyzing statistical information. Big data and community-generated data are promising complements to public sources, but these are still unevenly gathered, prepared, and made available to researchers.
2 The editors are grateful to Gulelat Kebede for his insights regarding outliers.

Bibliography

Appadurai, A., (2000), "Grassroots Globalization and Research Imagination", *Public Culture*, 12.
Borja, J. and Castells, M., (1997), *Local y Global: La gestión de las ciudades en la era de la información*, Taurus, Madrid.
Borja, J., Belil, M., and Corti, M., (2012), "Ciudades: una ecuación imposible", In Borja, J., and Corti, M. (eds.), *La Ciudad: ¿Una ecuación imposible?*, Icaria, Fundació Fondo Universal des les Cultures, Barcelona.
Buckley, R., Kallergis, A., and Wainer, L., (2015), "The Housing Challenge: Avoiding the Ozymandias Syndrome", Conference proceedings, Rockefeller Foundation and the New School, New York.
Cohen, M. A. (ed.), (2012a), *The Global Crisis in Latin America: Impacts and Response*, Routledge, London and New York.
Cohen, M. A., (2012b), "La ciudad en el contexto de la crisis mundial: entender los efectos y reforzar la eficacia de los paquetes de estímulo", In Borja, J., Belil, M., and Corti, M. (eds.), *La Ciudad: ¿Una ecuación imposible?*, Icaria, Fundació Fondo Universal des les Cultures, Barcelona.
Cook, M., (2012), "Municipal Finance and Local Performance in the Crisis: The Experience of Brazil and Mexico", In Cohen, M. (ed.), *The Global Crisis in Latin America: Impacts and Response*, Routledge, London and New York.
Galster, G., (1999), *Econometric Model of the Urban Opportunity Structure: Cumulative Causation among City Markets, Social Problems, and Undeserved Areas*, Diane Publishing Company, Chicago.
Gilbert, A., (2006), "Good Urban Governance: Evidence from a Model City?", *Bulletin of Latin American Research*, 25:3.
Glass, R., (1989), *Clichés of Urban Doom*, Blackwell, London.
Graham, S. and Marvin, S., (2001), *Splintering Urbanism: Networked Infrastructures, Technological Mobilities, and the Urban Condition*, Routledge, London.
Lacarriou, M., (2016), "UBACYT Project Seminar: 'Diseño y Desarrollo'", conference presentation, Universidad de Buenos Aires, June.
Moreno, E., (2014), *Construction of More Equitable Cities: Public Policies for Inclusion in Latin America*, Corporación Andina de Fomento and UN Habitat, Nairobi.

Moser, C., (1996), *Confronting Crisis: A Comparative Study of Household Responses to Poverty and Vulnerability in Four Poor Urban Communities*, The World Bank, Washington.

Roy, A., (2009), "The 21st Century Metropolis: New Geographies of Theory", *Regional Studies*, 43:6.

Sassen, S., (1991), *The Global City: New York, London, and Tokyo*, Princeton University Press, Princeton, NJ.

Sassen, S., (1994), *Cities in the World Economy*, Pine Forge Press, Thousand Oaks, CA.

Steinberg, F., (2005), "Strategic Urban Planning in Latin America: Experiences of Building and Managing the Future", *Habitat International*, 29.

UN Habitat, (2009), *Planning Sustainable Cities*, Global Report on Human Settlements, Earthscan, London and Sterling.

Watson, V., (2009), "Seeing from the South: Refocusing Urban Planning on the Globe's Central Urban Issues", *Urban Studies*, 46:11.

Index